AF600360

Civil Society and Politics in Central Asia

Civil Society and Politics in CENTRAL ASIA

Edited by
CHARLES E. ZIEGLER

Scholarly publisher for the Commonwealth,
serving Bellarmine University, Berea College, Centre College of Kentucky, Eastern Kentucky University, The Filson Historical Society, Georgetown College, Kentucky Historical Society, Kentucky State University, Morehead State University, Murray State University, Northern Kentucky University, Transylvania University, University of Kentucky, University of Louisville, and Western Kentucky University.

Editorial and Sales Offices: The University Press of Kentucky
663 South Limestone Street, Lexington, Kentucky 40508-4008
www.kentuckypress.com

Library of Congress Cataloging-in-Publication Data

Civil society and politics in Central Asia / edited by Charles E. Ziegler.
pages cm
Includes index.
ISBN 978-0-8131-5077-2 (hardcover : alk. paper) — ISBN 978-0-8131-5078-9 (pdf) — ISBN 978-0-8131-5079-6 (epub)
1. Civil society—Asia, Central. 2. Islam and civil society—Asia, Central. 3. Public administration—Asia, Central. 4. Asia, Central—Politics and government—1991- I. Ziegler, Charles E., editor of compilation.
JQ1086.C57 2015
300.958—dc23 2014039421

This book is printed on acid-free paper meeting the requirements of the American National Standard for Permanence in Paper for Printed Library Materials.

Manufactured in the United States of America.

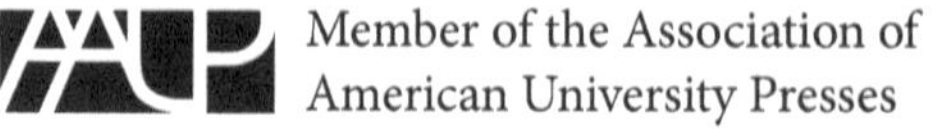
Member of the Association of
American University Presses

Contents

Introduction

Charles E. Ziegler

The five Central Asian states of Kazakhstan, Uzbekistan, Kyrgyzstan, Tajikistan, and Turkmenistan constitute a region of great importance in world politics. Historically, this remote area lay at the center of a struggle for influence and empire between Russia and Britain. Today's major powers—Russia, China, the United States, and the European Union—are not simply replaying the nineteenth-century Great Game. Geographic expansion and empire building may have become less relevant for the great powers, but security concerns remain, and in the twenty-first century these revolve around terrorism, narcotics, and hydrocarbons, all of which broader Central Asia has in abundance.

A quick glance at a map of the region confirms Central Asia's position at the center of Eurasia. Central Asia is the main transit route for heroin to Russia and was at one point the main transit route for American and NATO supplies and personnel into Afghanistan. Its Turkic Muslim peoples share ethnic and religious roots with China's restive Uighurs in neighboring Xinjiang province. Some Uighurs have connections to the Taliban in Afghanistan and Pakistan, fueling Beijing's acute fear of terrorism and separatism. The Caspian basin holds immense reserves of oil and natural gas. Those states rich in hydrocarbons—Kazakhstan, Turkmenistan, and Uzbekistan—can benefit immensely from this wealth, assuming they do not succumb to the resource curse, but they must rely on foreign companies (usually backed by foreign governments) to develop these resources.

Central Asia's stability, prosperity, and governance remain problematic. As the Arab Spring movements of 2011 attest, there are tensions between repressive and corrupt states and an educated and often dissatisfied population. Revolts in Kyrgyzstan (in 2005 and 2010) and Uzbekistan (in 2005), Tajikistan's civil war (in the 1990s), and continued terrorist incidents (in 2010–2011) and strikes and suicide bombings (in 2011) in normally quiet Kazakhstan do not bode well for the region. The manifold problems, threats, and potential of the region, and the uneasy relationship between these states and their societies, lead to the following broad research questions: What is the state of civil society in Central Asia today? How do diverse civil society groups relate to their respective governments? Are there autonomous spaces where social organizations can function free from state interference, and if so, what roles do they play in these societies? Could civil society in Central Asia become a force for democratization as it has in North Africa?

Central Asia and the Concept of Civil Society

There has been broad debate in the academic literature about the applicability of the concept of civil society to the authoritarian states of post-Soviet Central Asia. Some argue that, unlike the former communist states in Eastern Europe or the western part of the former Soviet Union, the Central Asian states of Kazakhstan, Kyrgyzstan, Uzbekistan, Turkmenistan, and Tajikistan do not have civil societies in the generally understood use of the term. Alternately, they may assert that an incipient civil society exists largely due to the financial support and educational efforts of foreign donors.[1] Others, including most of the authors of the chapters in this volume, find elements of civil society even within the repressive constraints of these authoritarian regimes, though they acknowledge that Central Asian activism may assume forms quite different from those in the West.[2] Since the Central Asian states are among the worst performers in terms of democratization following the Soviet collapse, it is worth considering whether such democratic deficits may be explained by the extremely weak and constrained civil societies in the region.

The authors in this volume agree that civil society is an important component of democracy at several levels. Civil society may play an active role in the eventual downfall of authoritarian regimes, as social pressures and political demands accompany modernization, though there are many examples of regime change in the absence of civil activism.[3] Civil society also plays a substantial role in deepening democracy once a transition has occurred, by broadening participation among various societal groups, strengthening citizens' rights to influence decisions affecting their lives, holding elites accountable to the public, increasing transparency, and in general providing for improved governance. Central Asian regimes have yet to begin the transition toward democracy, so our focus here is on the current relationships between state and civil society and the potential for political transformation in each of the five countries.

The question of the existence and extent of civil society in Central Asia is important for several reasons. First, the Arab Spring events of 2011 demonstrated the potential for civic activism even in the most repressive dictatorships. The success of the Arab Spring in contexts far removed from the American and Western European experience suggests that it is indeed legitimate to discuss civil society in non-Western and Islamic settings. Second, the potential for civil society activism to transform a region has particular relevance to American foreign policy goals. Democratization in the Middle East and North Africa may align these new regimes with Western democratic values; conversely, it may result in the rise of Islamic extremist parties hostile to U.S. interests. A similar process of political ferment in Central Asia could affect efforts to stabilize Afghanistan, rebuild Iraq, contain Iran, and develop the region's hydrocarbon resources, all U.S. priorities. For this reason, an analysis of the potential for civil society activism in Central Asia is valuable.

Third, for analysts of postcommunist societies one major challenge has been explaining large variations in these societies' political and economic performance following the collapse of communism. Since the Central Asian states are among the worst performers in terms of democratization following the Soviet collapse, it is worth considering whether such democratic deficits may be explained by the extremely weak and constrained civil societies in the region.

The comparative study of civil society raises difficult questions for researchers. Is civil society at least potentially a universal phenomenon, dependent on the level of modernization, or is it largely a Western construct that has little relevance to non-Western political systems? In discussing civil society do we count only associational activity independent of state and market? The boundaries between state, business, and voluntary organizations may be important to draw conceptually, but in practice these boundaries are blurred, whether in democracies or in authoritarian states. And how legitimate is it to claim that voluntary organizations in Western democracies are completely free from state influence? Nonprofit organizations in the United States receive tax-free status (in effect, a form of subsidy), while Protestant and Catholic churches in Germany receive funding directly from the state. Does that mean they have been "captured" by the state?

As Theda Skocpol has pointed out, the "classic" American civil society—that is, the type existing until the 1960s—was characterized by organizations that were heavily state supporting. These religious, veterans, and other popular fellowship organizations taught democracy and encouraged good citizenship, but they also recruited volunteers for military service, socialized Americans to understand and obey the law, and in general reinforced values supportive of the existing political system.[4] Moreover, many representatives of the new generation of civic organizations that emerged in the United States between 1960 and 1990 were formed as the result of the expansion of federal government programs. Jack Walker found that government agencies, together with corporations and other patrons, supported the formation and maintenance of a broad range of interest groups in the United States, including nonprofit voluntary organizations.[5] Obviously, it makes no sense to speak of civil society as only that part of associational life in opposition to the established state.

Much of Western, particularly Anglo-American, civil society scholarship is informed by a suspicion of strong states derived from liberalism's influence. But there is a clear difference between a strong state and a repressive state. Central Asian states are repressive but relatively weak in terms of their ability to provide security, education and health services, and a respectable standard of living.[6] At independence these states had weak state structures—the Soviet Union had been highly centralized and was federal only in form, so indigenous elites had little experience with genuine governing. The rulers of these states have emphasized the importance of building strong states in the volatile greater Central Asian neighborhood, both to ensure security and stability and, of course, to protect their positions of leadership.

In their efforts to maintain state and personal power, the region's authoritarian leaders have, like their Soviet predecessors, regarded virtually all social organizations as potential challengers to their political rule. Consequently, they tend not to differentiate between opposition groups like Hizb ut-Tahrir or the Islamic Movement of Uzbekistan and more moderate forms of political opposition that may well be loyal to the state. From the perspective of Tashkent or Ashgabat, groups not controlled by the state are seen as highly threatening. Only if they restrict their activities to "nonpolitical" service provision do they become tolerable to suspicious bureaucrats. Given this tenuous distinction between social and political activism, we have chosen to examine civil society in the context of Central Asian politics more broadly.

From the perspective of authoritarian regimes, civil society organizations may be divided into at least two categories defined by the level of threat they pose to regime legitimacy. The more threatening movements tend to be broader organizations that appeal to critical loci of identity and are therefore the more "political." These would include religious and ethno-national organizations, human rights groups, and labor unions. Less threatening movements include those often described as the "new social movements"—environmental and women's organizations, peace groups, and advocates for the disabled—which have highly specific, functional objectives. These movements do not challenge the legitimacy of the authoritarian state and indeed in many cases may enhance governance (and therefore legitimacy) by improving the provision of social services. Yet Central Asia's authoritarian states, much like the Soviet state that preceded them, tend to politicize society, so the distinctions between "political" and "nonpolitical" social organizations are tenuous at best. For that reason the following chapters analyze civil society within the broader context of Central Asian politics.

As with other studies of civil society, this volume focuses primarily on civil society as distinct from economic society and political society.[7] Economic associations in most of Central Asia are weak and either have been captured by the state, as in Uzbekistan, or confine their activities to resisting excessive state regulation and bureaucratic corruption that interfere with business, as in Kazakhstan.[8] Even in relatively pluralistic Kyrgyzstan there are virtually no entrepreneurial organizations aside from those promoted by international donor agencies or the state.[9]

In discussing civil society and the space allowed for nongovernmental groups, it is best to think of democracy and authoritarianism as points on a continuum rather than to dichotomize the concept. Totalitarian systems provide virtually no space for groups that are not tightly controlled by the state, but authoritarian systems vary widely in the degree of control exercised over society and the space in which civil society organizations can organize and operate. Although post-Soviet Central Asia consists of only five countries, and all are nondemocratic, these five exhibit a range of authoritarianism. Kyrgyzstan can be described as alternating between soft authoritarianism and anarchic democracy (anarchic regional oligarchy may be more accurate), Kazakhstan is an orderly soft authoritarian system, and Turkmenistan and Uzbekistan are extremely repressive dictatorships, while Tajikistan is moderately authoritarian with chaotic elements.[10]

While authoritarian states in general negatively impact civil society, the legacy of communist totalitarianism is even more pernicious, since these regimes atomized society and inculcated attitudes of deep mistrust among their populations. In addition, dictatorships of longer duration have a stronger negative impact on civil society than briefer periods of authoritarian rule.[11] Not only did the Central Asian states start from a relatively weak base in civil society terms, they experienced a much longer period of communist rule than did their Eastern European counterparts. Moreover, the dominance of clans in Central Asian societies tends to promote bonding rather than bridging social capital, impeding the formation of a national identity. But it would be wrong simply to dismiss clan and ethnic forms of organization as inimical to civil society.[12]

Central Asia's political systems are authoritarian, but they no longer exercise the absolute social control that was the hallmark of Soviet totalitarianism. Thus there are varying degrees of political space that have opened up for civil society organizations. In discussing civil society activities in authoritarian countries, we should count not only those that are critical of the status quo, but should also consider cooperative relations between nongovernmental organizations (NGOs) and the state. In democratic contexts social scientists generally consider both supports and demands from civil society, so it makes sense to use a similar approach in studying authoritarian systems. Of course, in an authoritarian context groups must tailor their actions in response to regime constraints, while in a democratic context groups generally are free to behave as they wish. But again, groups cannot function outside the state—the state provides basic legal and security conditions and sets the parameters for group activity, in the form of laws, regulations, and incentives that both enable and constrain civil society. As Juan Linz and Alfred Stepan have observed, without a state there is no chance for democracy—the state is a necessary precondition for civil society.[13] In other words, the amount of political space available to groups should not be dichotomized but rather evaluated on a continuum.

Autonomous groups are an important component of civil society, but the associational perspective can be accused of having a Western, more specifically American, bias. Perhaps more important, and often overlooked, are the activities of "uncivil" groups such as white supremacist organizations or criminal mafias, which may indeed generate bonding social capital within the group but whose norms are in conflict with the well-being of the larger society. A vibrant civil society in the absence of strong and responsive political institutions may lead to the collapse of liberal democracy.[14]

Moreover, it is important to recall that many Western countries have built respectable democracies even though they had anemic voluntary organizations. In Spain, civil society played virtually no role in that country's pacted transition, while group activity in France was weak or co-opted by the state throughout most of that country's democratic history.[15] Finally, as Michael Edwards observes, most political values and beliefs are fostered in families, schools, churches, and the workplace—not in voluntary organizations.[16]

Civil society may be described as a *kind* of society in which each set of institutions (political, economic, and social) has its separate role. While civil society plays an important part in ensuring the Aristotelian "good society," success in ensuring the good society can only come from the social contracts negotiated among government, business, and citizens. A better life is possible through development and modernization, which depend more on effective economic institutions and competent governance than a rich associational life.[17] Authoritarian states may provide improved levels of well-being to their people (think Singapore and China), but the record of dictatorial regimes is not on balance superior to that of democratic regimes in creating a better life. More often, unaccountable regimes are unresponsive to popular demands and may prove susceptible to challenge by broad-based opposition movements, as in the case of the color revolutions or the Arab Spring.

Finally, we can conceptualize civil society as the public sphere, where citizens argue and debate over the great questions of public life and through their discussions find a common interest. The emphasis here is on the "civil"—working together and recognizing shared interests while respecting deep differences and compromising. This derives from Jürgen Habermas and his idea that consensus is achieved through a process of reasoned argumentative speech, leading to the adoption of the "best" ideas, which is at the very heart of democracy. Consensus (truth) comes out of the "force of the better argument." However, civil society for Habermas operates in a sphere separate from the state and economy, avoiding the dominant influence of these two powerful sectors. Constitutional-legal protections guarantee political rights such as freedom of speech and assembly that allow individuals to shape public opinion.[18]

While Habermas perceived the fusion of political and economic spheres and the co-optation of mass media as inimical to democracy in twentieth-century Western bourgeois democracies, the parallels to some postcommunist states are obvious. Central Asian states, and authoritarian states more generally, tend sharply to constrain the ways in which civil society promotes the good society and the public sphere. In terms of the good society, and the respective roles of political institutions, the authoritarian state generally seeks to define institutional powers to its (that is, the executive's) advantage. Pluralism may be tolerated, but it is not welcomed, and in any case it is the responsibility of the state to define the good society. Similarly, authoritarian leaders are seldom willing to allow the free interplay of group interests, on the assumption that democratic deliberation among specific interests may contravene society's interests (or more accurately, the interests of the ruling elite). This is precisely Lenin's reasoning behind the 1921 proscription on party factions, and his logic continues to shape state-society relations in today's Central Asia.

Through his discussion of the views of Jürgen Habermas and Michel Foucault on civil society, Bent Flyvbjerg alerts us to the essential tension in modernity between consensus and conflict.[19] Habermas is the philosopher of consensus; Foucault focuses on power and conflict. The power side of the equation demonstrates that all societies are characterized by some degree of inequality, so some ideas have a greater chance of being heard than others. In capitalist democracies business and media interests skew public discourse in directions most responsive to the accumulation of profit. In many postcommunist systems the virtual merger of government and business interests creates a privileged class far removed from the average person and able to dictate the terms of public discourse to its advantage through its control of the media and other resources. Those outside the political-economic elite have few resources to make their viewpoints heard; they are not part of the Gramscian hegemonic order.[20] Only the elites can decide what forms of discourse are genuinely in the public interest. Serious debate on vital topics (for example, the venality of the ruling family) is deemed to be destabilizing and thus criminalized.

Cultures vary in the degree to which they accept conflict and dissent. Particularly in fragile new states, the prospect of political conflict can appear threatening. According to Foucault, power is the main threat to democracy, and though he does not advocate anarchy, the implication for civil society is that to promote democracy it should struggle against established authority. A Habermasian perspective, by contrast, suggests that civil society can accommodate itself to power by operating through legally established constitutions and institutions (procedural rationality). But to do this it must engage in a critical process of public communication through existing channels. Civil society activists, however, are no longer limited to commercial or state-monitored forms of mass communication, since they can access the Internet, engage in texting, and use blogs and other new forms of social media.[21]

Civil Society in Authoritarian Contexts

Civil society activity may involve speaking truth to power, as in Eastern Europe before the fall of communism. It may involve discretion and cooperation with those in power to avoid retribution, or with a resigned attitude that it is simply not realistic to expect to change the status quo. Or it may involve an acknowledgment that the state's goals, or at least some of them, are aligned with those of civic organizations and that cooperation with those in power is rational.

The broad variation in civil society development within the postcommunist world merits explanation, or at least consideration. All communist regimes sought to suppress civil society, since civil society challenged the Communist Parties' monopoly on political power. In some of these systems—most notably Poland, but also to a certain extent Hungary, Czechoslovakia, and Yugoslavia—there existed limited space for incipient civil society. These regimes simply could not exert the control needed to completely eliminate small, dedicated religious, human rights, and democracy-promotion groups. In fact, the reinvigoration of the term "civil society" in the late twentieth century is generally attributed to the East European opposition movements that challenged the existing regimes.[22]

Yet if we examine only the post-Soviet context, we find significant variation in levels of democratization and of civil society development. The Baltic States have been by far the best civil society performers, according to Freedom House and the U.S. Agency for International Development; Ukraine, Georgia, and Armenia are a bit weaker, followed by Russia and Moldova, with Belarus and Central Asia having the weakest civil societies.[23] Clearly the communist experience did not shape the fifteen successor republics into a homogeneous mass. Cultural differences traceable to the precommunist era may provide an explanation—the Baltics, after all, were historically European, while Central Asia was influenced more by Turkic, Persian, Mongolian, and Chinese cultures. Variations in economic development and market reforms may also provide a partial explanation.

State-society relations in Central Asia are in many ways comparable to those in present-day China, where the government faces a dilemma in how to deal with civil society. Civil society organizations can enhance governance by providing much-needed services and goods that the state fails to deliver, and so their contributions should logically be welcomed by officials. Yet to the extent that civil society groups challenge, either implicitly or overtly, the political monopoly and legitimacy of the ruling party and the authoritarian state their activities will likely be circumscribed by the government. Civil society in China, like that in Central Asia, tends to avoid confrontation with the state, and groups frequently claim that they are merely apolitical service providers with little interest in democracy promotion. Many civil society organizations are formed and funded by the government (government-organized nongovernmental organizations, or GONGOs); if they are genuinely private they tend to be supported by international donors and are closely monitored by the authorities. The result is neither a Habermasian civil society, with autonomous groups directly engaging the state in a contest of fundamental ideas, nor a state corporatist model of near-absolute government control, but rather something in between. There is some space for protodemocratic activity, and though it may be expanding gradually, it is still severely constrained.[24]

The Central Asian states could be said to exhibit elements of authoritarian deliberation on the Chinese governance model. In this system, limited public expression is tolerated by the authorities and utilized for guidance in forming public policy, while avoiding genuine political pluralism. Deliberative authoritarianism as observed in the Chinese model allows space for more forms of influential communication, although the power for setting the agenda and making decisions remains with elites. Power is concentrated, unlike in democracies, where it is dispersed, and the articulation of interests is confined within the narrow boundaries established by the state. Stability is preserved along with elite prerogatives.[25]

The color revolutions in Georgia, Ukraine, and Kyrgyzstan during 2003–2005, Kyrgyzstan's second uprising in 2010, the Arab Spring movements of 2011, and the massive protests in Russia in 2011–2012 were threatening to these regimes because the masses challenged elite prerogatives. For authoritarian leaders in China, Russia, and Central Asia these popular revolts are examples of civil society exceeding the boundaries of the permissible. Even more disturbing from the perspective of the ruling circles is the suspicion that organized opposition is a foreign import. Vladimir Putin's charges that foreign-supported NGOs constituted an unwarranted form of external interference in these countries' sovereign affairs struck a resonant chord in Beijing as well as the Central Asian capitals.[26] The Western tendency to "teach democracy" is especially galling when the liberal democratic model in the United States, Western Europe, and Japan has been plagued by economic crisis and an absence of effective governance.

The evidence from a wide range of countries confirms the contention that voluntary associations and civil society can emerge in authoritarian settings and may over time evolve toward autonomous political behavior, even if they started out as patriotic, nonpolitical organizations. Joseph Bradley's impressive history of nineteenth-century scientific associations in tsarist Russia provides evidence for the evolution of regime-approved groups, which were far more numerous than is generally realized. The tsarist government nurtured these associations and provided support for their scientific and educational endeavors but at the same time imposed restrictions on their activities. However, over time Russia's professional and civic organizations gradually broadened their scope, demonstrated greater initiative, and eventually acquired greater autonomy from the state.[27]

Perhaps these voluntary associations, the organizations that Alexis de Tocqueville identified as vital to American democracy and whose decline Robert Putnam lamented in his study of social capital in America, can grow and even flourish in Central Asia.[28] Such groups are critical, theorists argue, to build trust and generalized reciprocity, leading to more effective governance at the local if not national level. These civil society organizations may behave differently in Central Asia than in Europe or North America, and the relationship between state and society stands in marked contrast to that in liberal democracies, but the phenomena are comparable and deserve serious study. In the following chapters we detail the range of state-society relations in Central Asia, from the soft authoritarian regimes in Kyrgyzstan and Kazakhstan, to the poor, corrupt, and weak state of Tajikistan, to the highly repressive political environments in Uzbekistan and Turkmenistan.

Plan of the Book

The authors in this volume argue for a broader conceptualization of civil society, while recognizing that civil society tends to play a marginal role in Central Asia's governance. Andrey Kazantsev suggests that a path dependent perspective enhances our understanding of how civil society evolved in Central Asia. The Soviet totalitarian experience not only inhibited the development of genuine forms of democratic civil society, it paved the way for the emergence of a uniquely *uncivil* society in which nongovernmental organizations are under direct state control, or in which criminal gangs linked to the state are the most influential societal groups.

Opposition to authoritarian rulers in the Middle East and North Africa has been powerfully shaped by Islamic movements with deep roots in society, raising questions about the possibility of Islamic democracy and the potential for religious movements to topple regimes in Central Asia. Reuel Hanks directs our attention to the nation-building potential of Islam and its position in Central Asia's state-society relations. His analysis also stresses the important role of the state, as to a certain degree all Central Asian leaders have tried to harness Islam to achieve their goals of national unity and to avoid the politicization of Islam that might threaten their authoritarian governance. Central Asian Islam is quite different from that in the Middle East and North Africa, and it is doubtful whether religion could be a force for mobilization of the population against the regimes. Tajikistan and Uzbekistan are the more religious states, and here the *mahalla* (neighborhood associations) are key components of civil society. Yet the space for independent activity is constrained by states wary of the potential for opposition, as occurred in Andijan in 2005.

Dilshod Achilov asks how Islam shapes the formation of civil society in Central Asia. The country he chooses as a focus, Kazakhstan, is arguably the least religious society in the region, yet even here Achilov finds that emerging Islamic educational and financial institutions have great potential for mobilizing society and appear to be growing rapidly. The rise of a political Islamic movement modeled on those in Egypt or Tunisia cannot be excluded, though he suggests that if states chose a strategy of co-optation rather than repression, civil society will respond accordingly.

For Marlene Laruelle, the neoliberal model of civil society derived from Western experience overly simplifies our understanding of state-society relations in the Central Asian context. In dismissing government-organized nongovernmental organizations, neighborhood organizations (*mahallas*), and other non-Western practices as unrelated to genuine civil society, we lose sight of the "hybrid character of social reality." Minority associations in Kazakhstan, though "co-opted" by the state and seldom functioning as political groups in a Western sense, do occupy a niche between state and society, and between state and business, and so concern themselves with both the individual and collective good, the object of any civil society organization. The fact that their strategies tend to be integrative and conflict-averse does not negate their civil character.

Civil society organizations (CSOs) may play a particularly significant role in policy implementation and public administration, since the output side of governance is usually considered the least political, and hence least sensitive, aspect of the process. In such areas as environmental protection, health care provisioning, care for the elderly and for invalids, and women's interests, CSOs can and often do operate freely, and they may even receive assistance from the state. Authorities may be suspicious of such organizations and closely monitor their activities, but they also provide funding and facilitate service provision. New and relatively weak states may need to rely on civil society groups to perform certain vital social functions. Voluntary associations can provide services where the state is unwilling or unable, as Erica Johnson shows in her chapter on health care, and fill gaps where the official civil service proves inadequate, as demonstrated in the chapter on civil service reform by Ken Charman and Rakhymzhan Assangaziyev. These CSOs, though initially co-opted by the state, may seek a degree of independence over time.

For Kazakhstan, formation of a national identity within a context of ethnic, religious, and clan diversity has been a central goal of the country's political elite. Ruslan Kazkenov and Charles Ziegler argue that strengthening state authority has been key, with civil society playing a distinctly secondary role. As in the early American experience, the national interest is seen as distinct from, and not necessarily the simple aggregate of, specific interests or "factions" in society. Kazakhstan has also chosen a development path that has opened its society to the world, through exploitation of oil and natural gas resources and through Astana's leadership role in such forums as the Organization for Security and Cooperation in Europe and the Organization of Islamic Conferences.[29] Civil society is weak in part due to the Soviet legacy, but an impressive number of CSOs have emerged in the two decades since independence. Many of these organizations view their relationship with the state as collaborative rather than confrontational, partly in the interest of self-preservation but also partly out of a genuinely positive attitude toward a state that has "delivered the goods."

From the perspective of Western observers, Kyrgyzstan is often cited as the country in post-Soviet Central Asia that has made the greatest progress toward civil society. It is a matter of debate, though, whether Kyrgyzstan's tumultuous politics indicate a budding Western-style civil society or merely elite competition fueled by narcotics revenue and carried out by criminal gangs.[30] In his earlier work, Charles Buxton noted that civil society activism in Kyrgyzstan has been based on survival and "bread and butter" issues, rather than a deep commitment to social or political transformation.[31] Here, he traces the development of civil society in Kyrgyzstan from independence through the present, devoting considerable attention to the events of 2010. While Buxton finds that civil society organizations have had a limited role in building political society overall, they have provided critical assistance to people displaced by the ethnic violence of June 2010. He is modestly optimistic about the ability of civil society to improve service delivery and to support marginalized and vulnerable populations, particularly in the regions where NGOs have better access to local government.

Turkmenistan, as discussed by Charles Sullivan, is one of the most repressive countries on earth, regularly making Freedom House's "Worst of the Worst" list. In this harsh environment civil society faces many obstacles, and Sullivan suggests that the authoritarian state is likely to remain stable and durable. Economic modernization is not likely to facilitate civil society development, since Turkmenistan's political elite are attuned to the threat of potential opposition from society. Furthermore, as a rentier state heavily reliant on natural gas for revenues, Turkmenistan can mobilize the resources to both satisfy and repress popular aspirations, without opening political space for genuine participation. Under these conditions, only the support of influential external actors could empower civil society. Given Turkmenistan's highly controlled and isolated society, however, this scenario seems improbable.

Sabine Freizer argues that the neoliberal and communal forms of civil society, both of which are present in Tajikistan, have more in common than is generally acknowledged. Through contrasting case studies of a neoliberal NGO established by a Western international consultant and researcher (Ghamkhori) and communal village organizations funded by the Aga Khan Foundation, Freizer directs our attention to the service provision functions of these entities. Both types of organizations, she contends, have been more oriented toward engaging local communities and "filling gaps" than contesting the state over political issues. Both were financially dependent on foreign donors, and both contributed to social networking and trust building at the local level. Significant differences between the two derived from the neoliberal group's focus on universal values (including women's rights) and transformative approach, in contrast to the village organizations' acceptance of traditional, male-dominated power structures.

In the final chapter Graeme Herd and Maxim Ryabkov direct our attention toward the international context in which Central Asia's civil society operates. Given the strategic importance of Central Asia for the great powers, and the presence of U.S. and NATO forces in Afghanistan, the recent political upheavals in Kyrgyzstan threaten to further destabilize the situation in Western China, Uzbekistan, and Afghanistan. Neither the Collective Security Treaty Organization members nor those of the Shanghai Cooperation Organization appear to have seriously considered intervention during the 2010 events that resulted in Kurmanbek Bakiyev's ouster and the subsequent ethnic cleansing in the south. Other external actors, including the OSCE, World Bank, and European Union, are heavily vested in the humanitarian and economic dimensions of Kyrgyzstan's difficulties. Kyrgyzstan's weak and ineffective state has resulted in greater space for civil society organizations but has also made the country more susceptible to influence from the international community.

In recent years mass social movements have transformed the politics of authoritarian states as diverse as Ukraine, Tunisia, Georgia, Egypt, and Burma. If the color revolutions and Arab Spring events have taught us anything, it is that ideas of accountability, responsive government, and political activism are widespread and may be found in the most unlikely places and that opposition to corrupt authoritarian regimes may exist just below the surface. As the following chapters demonstrate, civil activism in Central Asia may take forms different from that in Western democracies, but it is comparable to those in other postcommunist or Islamic settings. Granted, political space for civil society is limited, nongovernmental organizations encounter many obstacles, and state co-optation and repression are routine. It would be a mistake, however, to dismiss the Central Asian states as incapable of transformation from below. In this volume we look beyond the surface of Central Asian politics to discover the forces for political change, and for continuity, in this critical region of the world.

Notes

1. For the skeptical view, see Kathleen Collins, *Clan Politics and Regime Transition in Central Asia* (Cambridge: Cambridge University Press, 2006); Edward

Schatz, *Modern Clan Politics: The Power of "Blood" in Kazakhstan and Beyond* (Seattle: University of Washington Press, 2004); Pauline Jones Luong and Erika Weinthal, "The NGO Paradox: Democratic Goals and Non-Democratic Outcomes in Kazakhstan," *Europe-Asia Studies* 51, no. 7 (1999): 1267–84. However, Western scholars who have adopted a liberal perspective on civil society have come under fire from anthropologists who view much of the civil society literature as hopelessly ethnocentric, preferring a more communal approach that recognizes the civic utility of traditional organizations and networks. See Chris Hann and Elizabeth Dunn, eds., *Civil Society: Challenging Western Models* (London: Routledge, 1996).

2. See, for example, M. Holt Ruffin and Daniel Waugh, eds. *Civil Society in Central Asia* (Seattle: University of Washington Press, 1999); John Anderson, "Creating a Framework for Civil Society in Kyrgyzstan," *Europe-Asia Studies* 52, no. 1 (2000): 77–93; Charles Buxton, *The Struggle for Civil Society in Central Asia: Crisis and Transformation* (Sterling, VA: Kumarian Press, 2011); Charles E. Ziegler, "Civil Society, Political Stability, and State Power in Central Asia: Cooperation and Contestation," *Democratization* 17, no. 5 (October 2010): 795–825; Alisher Ilkhamov, "The Thorny Path of Civil Society in Uzbekistan," *Central Asian Survey* 24, no. 3 (September 2005): 297–317; and Sabine Freizer, "Neo-liberal and Communal Civil Society in Tajikistan: Merging or Dividing in the Post War Period?" *Central Asian Survey* 24, no. 3 (September 2005): 225–43.

3. Ronald Inglehart and Christian Welzel, in *Modernization, Cultural Change, and Democracy: The Human Development Sequence* (New York: Cambridge University Press, 2005), make the revised modernization argument for political change. Spain is one prominent example where civil society did not play a role in democratic transformation. See Omar G. Encarnacion, "Civil Society and the Consolidation of Democracy in Spain," *Political Science Quarterly* 116, no. 1 (Spring 2001): 53–79.

4. Theda Skocpol, "Civil Society in the United States," in *The Oxford Handbook of Civil Society*, ed. Michael Edwards (Oxford: Oxford University Press, 2011), 109–21. Skocpol argues that the evolution of American civil society in recent decades has resulted in gains in public voice for the privileged, enhancing political inequality and diminishing democracy. See her *Diminished Democracy: From Membership to Management in American Civic Life* (Norman: University of Oklahoma Press, 2003).

5. Jack Walker, "The Origins and Maintenance of Interest Groups in America," *American Political Science Review* 77, no. 2 (June 1983): 390–406.

6. For example, Kyrgyzstan, Tajikistan, and Uzbekistan are in the top 40 in the 2011 Fund for Peace's Failed States Index (now the Fragile States Index), while Turkmenistan comes in at 75 and Kazakhstan fares much better at 107, though still falling in the "warning" category. Fragile States Index, Fund for Peace, http://ffp.statesindex.org, accessed September 23, 2011.

7. Jean L. Cohen and Andrew Arato, *Civil Society and Political Theory* (Cambridge: MIT Press, 1994).

8. Ilkhamov, "Thorny Path of Civil Society"; Dinissa S. Duvanova, "Interest Groups in Post-Communist Countries: A Comparative Analysis of Business and Employer Associations" (PhD diss., Ohio State University, 2007).

9. Gül Berna Özcan, "Djamila's Journey from Kholkhoz to Bazaar: Female Entrepreneurs in Kyrgyzstan," in *Enterprising Women in Transition Economies,* ed. Frederike Welter, David Smallbone, and Nina Isakova (London: Ashgate, 2006), 93–115.

10. In Freedom House's combined rankings (political rights and civil liberties) for 2013, Kyrgyzstan received a score of 5.0 (partly free), Kazakhstan a 5.5 (not free), Tajikistan 6.0 (not free), and Uzbekistan and Turkmenistan both scored 7.0, placing them among the world's most repressive states. Freedom House, *Freedom in the World 2013,* http://freedomhouse.org/report/freedom-world/freedom-world-2013.

11. Michael Bernhard and Ekrem Karakoç, "Civil Society and the Legacies of Dictatorship," *World Politics* 59, no. 4 (July 2007): 539–67.

12. Kathleen Collins, in *Clan Politics and Regime Transition in Central Asia,* holds that, on balance, Central Asia's clan structures inhibit democracy. Edward Schatz, in contrast, claims that kinship structures are not necessarily incompatible with modern politics. Schatz, *Modern Clan Politics.*

13. Juan J. Linz and Alfred Stepan, "Toward Consolidated Democracies," *Journal of Democracy* 7, no. 2 (April 1996): 14–33.

14. Sheri Berman, "Civil Society and the Collapse of the Weimar Republic," *World Politics* 49, no. 3 (April 1997): 401–29.

15. Encarnacion, "Civil Society and Consolidation of Democracy"; Pierre Rosanvallon, *The Demands of Liberty: Civil Society in France since the Revolution* (Cambridge, MA: Harvard University Press, 2007).

16. Michael Edwards, *Civil Society,* 2nd ed. (Cambridge: Polity Press, 2009), 58–59. The three types of civil society outlined in the following paragraphs are derived from this volume.

17. Edwards, *Civil Society,* 49.

18. Jürgen Habermas, *Structural Transformation of the Public Sphere* (Cambridge, MA: MIT Press, 1989).

19. Bent Flyvbjerg, "Habermas and Foucault: Thinkers for Civil Society?" *British Journal of Sociology* 49, no. 2 (June 1998): 210–33.

20. Tellingly, the title of a series of publications from civil society workshops conducted by the author and his collaborators in Kazakhstan in the period 2006–2008 was Dialogue of Power and Civil Society (Dialog vlasti i grazhdanskogo obshchestva). This suggests that a dialogue is indeed taking place between those in power and the country's civic associations, but it also implies that civil society is far removed from the seat of power.

21. On the variety of state approaches to the Internet in Central Asia, see Eric McGlinchey and Erica Johnson, "Aiding the Internet in Central Asia," *Democratization* 14, no. 2 (April 2007): 273–88.

22. Michael Bernhard's study of the transitional period found that while civil society displayed genuine opposition in the decade prior to the disintegration of the communist state, oppositional elements were much weaker in Hungary and severely constrained in East Germany and Czechoslovakia. Bernhard concludes that civil society can exist under milder forms of authoritarianism, though its existence is not a sufficient condition for democracy. Michael Bernhard, "Civil Society and Democratic Transition in East Central Europe," *Political Science Quarterly* 108, no. 2 (1993): 307–26.

23. Sylvana Habdank-Kołaczkowska, *Nations in Transit 2013: Authoritarian Aggression and the Pressures of Austerity* (Washington, D.C.: Freedom House, 2013), http://freedomhouse.org/report/nations-transit/nations-transit-2013; U.S. Agency for International Development, "The 2011 CSO Sustainability Index for Central and Eastern Europe and Eurasia," http://www.usaid.gov/europe-eurasia-civil-society/cso-sustainability-2011.

24. Denny Roy, "China's Dilemma over Civil Society Organizations," in *Engaging Civil Society: Emerging Trends in Democratic Governance,* ed. G. Shabbir and Vesselin Popovski (Tokyo: United Nations University Press, 2010), 174–92.

25. Baogang He and Mark E. Warren, "Authoritarian Deliberation: The Deliberative Turn in Chinese Political Development," *Perspectives on Politics* 9, no. 2 (June 2011): 269–89.

26. Jude Howell, "Civil Society in China," in Edwards, *Oxford Handbook of Civil Society,* 163.

27. Joseph Bradley, *Voluntary Associations in Tsarist Russia: Science, Patriotism, and Civil Society* (Cambridge, MA: Harvard University Press, 2009). I am indebted to Richard Sakwa for bringing this work to my attention.

28. Alexis de Tocqueville, *Democracy in America,* trans. Harvey C. Mansfield and Delba Winthrop (Chicago: University of Chicago Press, 2000); Robert D. Putnam, *Bowling Alone: The Collapse and Revival of American Community* (New York: Simon and Schuster, 2000).

29. Charles E. Ziegler, "Security, Sovereignty, and Democracy: The EU, the OSCE, and Central Asia," in *Competing for Influence: The EU and Russia in Post-Soviet Eurasia,* ed. Roger E. Kanet and Maria Raquel Freire (Dordrecht, Netherlands: Republic of Letters Publishing, 2012).

30. Kyrgyzstan is the only Central Asian nation regularly ranked by Freedom House as "partly free"; all the rest are classified as "not free." For a more critical perspective, see Scott Radnitz, *Weapons of the Wealthy: Predatory Regimes and Elite-Led Protests in Central Asia* (Ithaca, NY: Cornell University Press, 2010).

31. Buxton, *Struggle for Civil Society in Central Asia.*

Part 1

Civil Society in Context

1

Social Capital and Development of Civil Society in Central Asia

A Path Dependency Perspective

Andrey A. Kazantsev

The issue that I plan to analyze in this essay is that specific Central Asian political and social environments (including the legacy of Soviet totalitarianism and present-day clan-dominated societies) have significantly distorted the structure and function of nongovernmental organizations (NGOs) in Central Asia as compared to the liberal societies, where the theoretical concepts of NGOs and civil societies have been developed. Such type of argumentation is not new; theoretically, both totalitarian legacy and clan issues have been discussed already within the framework of Hannah Arendt's theory of totalitarianism (as connected to the atomization of society) and within the framework of the theoretical distinction between "positive" and "negative" social capital proposed by Robert Putnam.[1] Both issues are especially important for five post-Soviet states that constitute an international region of Central Asia: Kazakhstan, Kyrgyzstan, Tajikistan, Turkmenistan, and Uzbekistan. A path dependent theoretical approach, I argue, is particularly useful in the Central Asian case because it demonstrates the long-term influence of a nonliberal political and social environment on civil organizations.

Here I use the term "path dependency" in the sense that "history matters" and that the number of decisions that any actor can make is limited by the decisions made in the past. Analysis of the role of negative social capital within this chapter can be viewed as an illustration of the path dependent nature of the post-Soviet transition and institutions that have been formed in the post-Soviet states. Social capital can be also considered as a factor that can break or reinforce the path dependency of Central Asian societies. Positive social capital can serve as a remedy to the negative legacies of the past, while, as I argue below, negative social capital reinforces path dependency.

Analysis of the inner structure and external social role of NGOs demands development of a typology of such organizations adapted to specific regional cases. Otherwise one risks putting into the same category conventional civil organizations, quasi-NGOs established by the state (de facto state organizations), and criminal, terrorist, or extremist organizations using the label of civil organizations. Very often it is difficult to distinguish among these three types of organizations, especially in specific Central Asian circumstances defined by the heritage of Soviet totalitarianism, by weakly modernized social life, and by post-Soviet authoritarian politics. There are, for example, divergent opinions on whether religious revivalist groups should be designated extremist and terrorist groups (the position of many authoritarian Central Asian governments) or whether they are conventional civil organizations (the position of many opponents of these governments, both inside and outside Central Asia). And if these governments are authoritarian, does it automatically mean that they are wrong in this concrete case?

Correct application to the Central Asian case of a typology based not on current political considerations but on comparative social analysis can be useful for studying structural conditions and historical path dependencies in which emerging civil organizations and civil society in contemporary Central Asia exist. Moreover, such analysis can help us to discern conventional civil society, respective forms of NGOs, and different distorted models of NGOs that create "uncivil societies." I will use the term "uncivil society" both for the forms of self-organization characteristic of the communist establishment and for the malicious forms of society's self-organization in postcommunist countries that are conducive to the decline of civil society, democracy, and economic freedoms.[2] In this capacity such analysis can serve as a useful instrument for assessing the perspectives of modernization of political and economic systems of the five Central Asian states.

Therefore, below I will first describe modern theories of civil society in their connection with the issues of democratization and economic modernization. Then I will analyze the first model of "uncivil" society based on the "totalitarian" type of NGOs supported by highly authoritarian regimes still existing in the region. This model exists as a result of specific path dependency (that includes different societal structures and values) established by Soviet totalitarianism. After that I will turn to analysis of the second model of "uncivil" society, based on NGOs creating, according to Robert Putnam's typology, "negative social capital." Paradoxically, this model of NGOs becomes most dangerous in situations when the distorting influence of political authoritarianism becomes not so important, but some negative path dependencies based on premodern, Soviet, and marginal transitional structures still affect the societies. Finally, in the conclusion I will summarize all discussed issues and underline the importance of the dramatic fight between the elements of civil society and the elements of "uncivil" societies that can be observed in Central Asia today.

Theorizing Civil Society

How can the link between civil society, democracy, and development in contemporary social theory be applied to Central Asia today? As Leo Tolstoy wrote in *Anna Karenina,* all happy families are similar, all unhappy families have their specific stories. I would apply the same approach to civil society and NGOs. All civil societies, irrespective of their belonging to a specific civilization, culture, level of economic and technological development, or climate, are characterized by specific structures. Also, all civil societies perform a specific set of functions important for democratization and economic development.

Civil societies have become the subject of analysis of social theory on the basis of the experience of Western societies that are characterized by relatively liberal social structures, as compared, for example, to Central Asia or Russia. It is very important that these liberal structures include both political elements (democracy, freedom of association, human rights guarantees) and social elements (rule of law, individualism, modernized social structures). Elements of civil societies have been discovered in many societies that do not belong to the Western world. So this phenomenon is usually considered within political theory as universal and not belonging to a specific civilizational, historical, or cultural environment. However, many interpretations of civil society, especially within modernization theory, take the shape of linear "progressive" forms. Although in current social sciences there are many studies that oppose the idea of linear modernization (there is even the idea of "multiple modernities"), still, some elements of this linear modernization theory also feed the expectations of quick development of civil organizations and civil society, even in the most hostile political and social environment.[3] The aim of my essay is to demonstrate the unrealistic character of these expectations in the case of Central Asia and to propose a more cautious approach to civil organizations in the region.

My perspective on the development of civil society is that in the process of its development there can be many distortions based on specific political or social circumstances of societies with nonliberal environments (I call them "negative path dependencies"). These distortions in the structure and functions of NGOs deprive civil society of some of its characteristics, creating specific types of "uncivil societies." Here I define "uncivil society" as a system that includes civil organizations characterized by a set of specific *systemic* distortions created by long-term tendencies in the political and social environment. Quasi-civil organization is a basic unit of "uncivil society." Of course, this does not mean that there are no real civil organizations even within "uncivil society"; they do not define the general environment of the society, but they can be the agents of future positive evolution. My perspective should not be confused with different approaches according to which some societies cannot develop conventional civil society at all (such an approach would contain the elements of crypto-racism). I believe that the respective societies can in time overcome these distortions and develop real civil society; however, taking into account the systemic character of "uncivil society," this is not a quick or easy process. So my perspective can be reconciled with modernization theory, although it challenges some of its oversimplifications.

The key problem for my analysis is that in concrete cases it is sometimes very hard to discern between "civil" and "uncivil" organizations; one risks becoming involved in situational political discussions and being accused of specific politically motivated bias. Therefore, the typology of "uncivil societies" should be based on comparative and long-term historical considerations and should necessarily be divorced from situational political argumentation. That is, it cannot be used, for example, as a guiding principle for making political decisions about which organizations should or which should not be financially assisted by specific international donors. This is a separate issue based on specific values and interests of donors. Or it should not become a basis of argumentation that, for example, the international community should not defend the rights of activists of organizations that, according to this typology, belong to "uncivil" society (for example, dissident religious groups promoting radical visions of Islam). This type of argumentation is used by some Central Asian regimes (especially Uzbekistan), and it contains a basic misunderstanding of what human rights are. Human rights by definition should be defended irrespective of the religious or political background of human beings. The typology that I propose should be used only in order to explain some specific problems that appear before civil organizations in Central Asia and to understand the perspectives of development of civil society in the region in its organic connection with development of political and economic systems.

At present, there is a well-developed theory explaining the link between voluntary organizations of citizens, democracy, and development. It explains what the structure and function of civil organizations and civil society should look like. In general, this theory explains why the development of voluntary organizations and other elements of civil society is very important for democratization and economic development. This theory is familiar to specialists, and therefore I will give only a general outline of this theory, not concentrating on the details. I mention this theory because in order to show systemic distortions of structure and function within quasi-civil organizations of "uncivil society" one should define what the basic elements of nondistorted structures look like. I will also demonstrate some theoretical perspectives on the most typical distortions of civil society, focusing on Hannah Arendt's idea of the atomization of society within a totalitarian system and the respective replacement of civil organizations with state organizations as well as Robert Putnam's idea of "negative social capital," especially within clan-based societies.

The theory of dependence of effective democracy on civil society goes back to the writings of Alexis de Tocqueville, and it was supported by Gabriel Almond and Sidney Verba's book on civic culture.[4] Almond and Verba underlined the link between voluntary organizations and better awareness of citizens that permits them to more effectively participate in politics. In a famous work on totalitarianism, Hannah Arendt demonstrated a reverse link between development of nondemocratic totalitarian regimes and atomization of the societies.[5] This book is especially important for analysis of the fate of voluntary organizations within the Soviet Union and some successor states that retained the elements of Soviet-style totalitarianism (especially Turkmenistan under Saparmurat Niyazov).

The works of Robert Putnam, who introduced into the study of civil society the concept of "social capital," have opened a new era within this literature.[6] Social capital is the capacity of a person or group to utilize social relationships to mobilize resources embedded in a network structure, and it is directly connected to trust.[7] According to Putnam, voluntary organizations, even those of a nonpolitical nature, are important for the survival and development of democracy. Voluntary organizations such as NGOs build social capital and generalized trust in society. In the political sphere social capital and trust integrate the society, and therefore they facilitate mutual understanding and interconnectedness of interests between different political forces. In their famous book comparing northern and southern Italy, Robert Putnam, Robert Leonardi, and Raffaella Nanetti demonstrated that development of social capital in northern Italy was due to a well-developed system of voluntary organizations that promoted democratic participation and effective governance, which was not the case in southern Italy. In his later book on American politics Putnam argued that the decline of American democracy is directly linked with the decline of social capital, and therefore development of social capital can make American democracy more efficient.[8] The concept of social capital in connection with generalized trust in society is also important for contemporary theories of economic growth, development, and modernization.[9]

Another theoretical achievement of Putnam's was the introduction of the concept of "negative social capital."[10] This concept is specifically designed to analyze situations when social capital is invested not toward positive ends but in support of antidemocratic political or corrupt economic practices. Negative social capital has a negative, distorting influence on the development of civil society, and therefore it negatively affects the functioning of democracy and the market economy. Some analysts of former Soviet Union countries would even argue that negative social capital would create specific "uncivil societies."[11]

Negative social capital appears as a result of the contradiction between bridging and bonding functions of networks.[12] Network bonding can help to consolidate a homogeneous group by opposing it to all other groups, but a deficit of bridging can create negative social capital. In terms of formal network analysis, a structural hole in network configurations will appear. Some tightly integrated groups will not have enough bridging links between them. In this case a consolidated group characterized by strong trust between those who belong to it is opposed to the society in general. Moreover, society in general can become a virtual reality if the nation consists of strongly integrated groups without equally strong connections between them. Below I will use the theory of "fragmented societies," which describes such a situation, in order to demonstrate this role of negative social capital.[13] The idea of negative social capital is especially important for my analysis because of the clan-based nature of Central Asian societies, which are characterized by the prevalence of bonding over bridging functions.

It is well known from the theoretical literature that strong network links of clan-based societies, in the absence of effective institutions such as democracy or rule of law, can also lead to negative social capital. From a political point of view this "dark side" of networks was studied in the example of the collapse of the Weimar Republic in Germany.[14] From an economic viewpoint it has been analyzed as the problem of unproductive use of networks in the absence of strong institutional structures.[15] This aspect of negative social capital can be also easily applied to Central Asia, where there are strong clan connections based on tradition in the absence of strong institutions of democracy and a market economy.

So, from the point of view of contemporary theories of civil society, voluntary organizations are very important as a bridging form of social capital for supporting generalized trust in the society. Generalized trust, on the other hand, is key for the functioning of democracy and for economic development. However, atomization, which is characteristic of totalitarian systems, or negative social capital that can develop even within more pluralist clan-based systems can negatively affect generalized trust in society. Therefore, atomization and negative social capital are not conducive to democratization and economic development. Moreover, I would argue that atomization and the development of negative social capital caused by negative path dependencies have created in Central Asia two types of "uncivil society" with specific structures of NGOs that sometimes oppress the elements of real voluntary organizations.

In accordance with the reviewed literature I would define these two types of "uncivil society" existing in Central Asia as: (1) totalitarian "uncivil society" and (2) nonmodernized, transitional, or marginalized "uncivil society." Specific Central Asian empirical features of these "uncivil societies" are analyzed below, so this analysis can be considered only preliminary. However, here I can give some basic characteristics of Central Asian "uncivil societies" as they are defined by the theoretical literature. Totalitarian "uncivil society" is characterized by atomization (destruction of social capital). The prevalent structure of NGOs within this system is represented by de facto state organizations serving the totalitarian state. The most important function of such quasi-NGOs within society is representing the interests of the state. The premodern, transitional, or marginalized model of "uncivil society" is based on negative social capital, where bonding prevails over bridging. The prevalent structure of NGOs within this system is represented by quasi-civil organizations based on premodern forms of human association, first of all on clans. The social function of this type of "uncivil society" includes promoting authoritarianism and corruption, restraining economic development, and supporting intergroup conflicts and societal fragmentation due to prevalence of bonding over bridging and representation of the interests of isolated groups within society.

My perspective emphasizes the underlying *systemic character* of "uncivil society" based on negative path dependency (especially on the experience of Soviet totalitarianism and post-Soviet authoritarianism) as a critical challenge to expectations of rapid positive change advocated by earlier modernization theories. This, however, does not mean that positive changes are impossible over the longer term.

The Soviet Totalitarian Model of "Uncivil Society": Contemporary Central Asia and Government-Controlled Quasi-NGOs

The heritage of Soviet totalitarianism, by affecting the structure and functions of voluntary organizations, has created the first model of "uncivil society," which I would call a totalitarian one and which still has a hugely destructive and distorting influence on Central Asian civil organizations.

The heritage of Soviet totalitarianism in Central Asia has two different dimensions. First, some Central Asian countries (especially Turkmenistan and, to a lesser extent, Uzbekistan) still have some forms of NGOs (or more accurately, "quasi-NGOs") that are characteristic of the Soviet period due to their specific political systems. Second, Soviet totalitarianism, by affecting generalized trust in society, has predetermined some forms of evolution of civil society in Central Asia, even in countries where the political systems are not so oppressive (Kazakhstan, Kyrgyzstan, Tajikistan).

First I will analyze specific forms of totalitarian NGOs that still exist in Central Asia. There is a well-developed body of theory on totalitarianism that I can use in analyzing distortions of civil society under totalitarian dictatorship, going back to the works of Hannah Arendt.[16]

According to Arendt, totalitarianism is always characterized by a combination of an omnipresent ideological state developed on the basis of mobilized political movements and a highly atomized society. A totalitarian political movement, even before coming to power, is based on the atomization of its members; the central principle is that loyalty to the movement should prevail over personal connections. Later, personal connections should completely disappear in order to confirm the position of the member within the structure of the movement. After the establishment of totalitarian dictatorship, atomization is spread among society as a whole through the use of propaganda and enforcement agencies such as secret police. A system of denunciations is especially destructive for society because all close personal contacts between people outside of officially assigned tasks can be dangerous. The principle of atomization was always the basic element of communist propaganda and was a central feature of the culture that Soviet totalitarianism established.

Contemporary Russian researcher Vadim Damie writes about the "first wave" of societal atomization that covered the Soviet Union, especially as a result of the destruction of the village communes and their replacement by the kolkhoz system. At the same time, industrialization demanded concentration of people in the cities.[17] As a result of all these processes old social connections often disappeared. The wave of atomization connected with collectivization also affected the territory of contemporary Central Asia. First, collectivization in some of the regions of Central Asia was especially severe. For example, in Kazakhstan after collectivization the number of Kazakh households diminished twofold over a brief period. Second, Kazakhstan was a place where many repressed Russian and Ukrainian peasants were sent into exile. All these processes undermined generalized trust in the society.

On the other hand, the Soviet system preserved many traditional, premodern forms of human integration. For example, the kolkhoz system, especially in Central Asia, preserved traditional tribal and communal structures in the rural areas and, as a result, saved traditional forms of self-organization (the consequences of this for civil organizations will be considered below).

The Soviet ruling class that controlled a totalitarian state according to the tradition established by Milovan Djilas and Michael Voslensky is usually called the *nomenklatura.*[18] The system of *nomenklatura* was essentially a list of all individuals acceptable for appointment to the major political, economic, and cultural positions controlled by the Communist Party. It is very important to understand that membership in *nomenklatura* was always based on complete political loyalty to the Communist Party as a totalitarian movement. All Soviet social organizations lacked independence—their leadership was generally incorporated into the *nomenklatura,* and the status of an organization directly corresponded to the official weight of its leadership within the ranks of the *nomenklatura.*

NGOs didn't disappear completely within the Soviet system; rather, a specific system of NGOs was developed within the Soviet Union. This system was based on Marx's idea of the proletariat as a revolutionary "avant-garde" of society and on Lenin's idea of the Communist Party as a "leading and governing" force (*rukovodyashaya i napravlyaushaya sila*) embodying the revolutionary proletariat. So all other layers, structures, and organizations in society should obey Communist Party directives. As a result, a theory of NGOs as "driving belts" (sometimes referred to as "transmission belts") for the state machine appeared. According to this theory, trade unions, women's organizations, organizations for veterans or children, associations of atheists, professional associations, and sports associations were considered the mechanisms through which the state could impose its policy and ideology on society.

Another key element of the Soviet theory of NGOs was the idea of the *aktiv.* This was also based on Marx's theory of the proletariat and Lenin's theory of the party. This time there was an idea of opposition between, on the one hand, "active" layers of society that were highly indoctrinated by communist ideology (or "conscious") and actively fulfilled the policies proclaimed by the state and, on the other hand, "passive" layers of society. These "passive" layers were considered not as "the enemies" but simply as not actively supporting state policies and not so "conscious." The main sign of being a part of the *aktiv* was an active membership in the officially established NGOs.

Nomenklatura, aktiv, and other parts of population were considered as a social pyramid, with *nomenklatura* on the top, *aktiv* in the middle, and all others at the bottom. This model was realized even in the distribution of resources, because all the upper levels of the pyramid had privileges distinct from those available to the lower level. For example, the members of *nomenklatura* had very special privileges, such as specific food rations, separate shops, a separate health care system, and so forth. The *aktiv* also had an opportunity to receive some benefits, such as accelerated acquisition of flats or occasional additional food rations.

The efforts of the totalitarian state created a specific model of NGOs, or rather, quasi-NGOs that could be called "totalitarian organizations." Since such a model still exists in some countries of Central Asia, I will summarize the main characteristics of this model.

First, such NGOs are state-controlled, designed for the realization of governmental policy within specific social groups. They are, in fact, only quasi-independent and can be considered as state organizations. The ideological dimension of their activity is very strong. They serve as an instrument of political mobilization.

Second, officially established and supported NGOs monopolize certain sectors of public life due to de facto obligatory membership in specific organizations (for youth, veterans, etc.). As a result, they not only control specific sectors of public life but also suppress public activity. So, paradoxically, they not only promote contact between people but also promote atomization outside of officially supported spheres of activity. Third, there is a system of material incentives for the *aktiv* (people actively involved in these organizations). NGOs are led by the *nomenklatura,* since holding the top positions in them guarantees inclusion in the new ruling class.

All these characteristics are specific to a totalitarian model of NGOs. However, NGOs under a totalitarian system also perform some functions that are similar to those of "normal" NGOs. These include the representation of interests of specific social groups, lobbying and promotion of specific interests, development of informal norms within specific groups, and socialization of individuals within specific groups.

It is important to note that all these "normal" functions, according to Putnam's theory of "negative social capital," are mostly bonding (i.e., they connect people inside a specific group) but not bridging (i.e., they do not "bridge" different groups within the society). So even outside of atomization, the function of these NGOs is not positive; Putnam called such types of human connection, when bonding prevails over bridging, "negative social capital."[19] This prevailing of bonding over bridging is natural for totalitarian systems, because if Soviet NGOs performed the function of bridging it would mean that they would be able to coordinate their position outside of state and Communist Party mechanisms, which would undermine the basis of Soviet totalitarianism. The function of bridging was performed by the state and Communist Party apparat. This, as well as conservation of some traditional forms of social integration within Soviet totalitarianism, affects specific types of development of civil society, even in contemporary Central Asia, and creates the second type of "uncivil" society that I will analyze below.

The model of totalitarian "uncivil" society is still important for Central Asia. For example, the assessment of Freedom House can be used for verifying the negative influence of political systems on NGOs in Central Asia. According to Freedom House's report *Freedom in the World 2010* all five Central Asian nations have been included in the list of forty-seven countries considered "Not Free." Turkmenistan and Uzbekistan received the survey's lowest possible rating for both political rights and civil liberties and can be compared with seven other countries (Burma, Equatorial Guinea, Eritrea, Libya, North Korea, Somalia, Sudan) and one territory (Tibet) that have also been assessed as "worst of the worst." Of course, the fact of earning the lowest score by itself cannot prove the prevalence of the totalitarian form of NGOs (for example, Somalia has the lowest score, but its political system is characterized by anarchy, not by totalitarianism). However, these scores can be used as an indirect indicator, especially when combined with other data about Central Asian countries.

Most important for my topic is the subscore on associational and organizational rights in Freedom House's survey. The lowest assessment in this category indicates that the political system in each country is especially oppressive toward independent NGOs and so the respective country is

Table 1.1. Political Rights and Civil Liberties in Central Asian Countries According to Freedom House's Assessment, 2010

Country/category	Political rights	Civil liberties
Kazakhstan	6	5
Kyrgyzstan	6	5
Tajikistan	6	5
Turkmenistan	7	7
Uzbekistan	7	7

Source: Freedom House, *Freedom in the World 2010,* http://freedomhouse.org/report/freedom-world/freedom-world-2010.

Table 1.2. Associational and Organizational Rights in Central Asian Countries According to Freedom House's Assessment, 2009

Country/category	Associational and organizational rights
Kyrgyzstan	5
Kazakhstan	4
Tajikistan	4
Turkmenistan	0
Uzbekistan	0

Source: Freedom House, *Freedom in the World 2009,* http://freedomhouse.org/report/freedom-world/freedom-world-2009.

most inclined toward the totalitarian form of NGOs (once again, this is not a direct proof, only an indirect indicator).

This assessment by Freedom House correlates with the results of my personal observations, according to which two groups of countries can be distinguished in Central Asia. In the first group, Turkmenistan and Uzbekistan are totalitarian countries with zero associational and organizational rights and respective patterns of development of state-controlled quasi-civil organizations. According to my typology, these countries are characterized by the prevalence of totalitarian types of NGOs. The second group includes Kazakhstan, Tajikistan, and Kyrgyzstan. These countries are not free from the point of view of civil liberties. They do not give to their citizens substantial associational and organizational rights. However, civil liberties in these countries are not nonexistent. Some civil organizations still can exist. In principle, this difference is reflected in the Freedom House's assessment because scores in the range of 5–4 are drastically different from zero. According to my typology, these three countries are not characterized by the prevalence of totalitarian forms of NGOs.

It is also important to underline the specificity of Kyrgyzstan in the second group of countries. I used Freedom House's assessment of associational and organizational rights for 2009, just before the anti-Bakiyev revolution, with the purpose of outlining just this specificity. In 2010, after the anti-Bakiyev revolution and the mass violence directed against the Uzbeks in the south, Kyrgyzstan's scores both in terms of political rights and civil liberties were lower. However, since I am assessing long-term path dependencies, it is important to underline that traditionally Kyrgyzstan's scores, especially in terms of associational and organizational rights, were the highest in Central Asia. This corresponds to my own assessment that the mountainous Kyrgyz republic is characterized by much less influence from the totalitarian model of NGOs and "uncivil" societies than its neighbors.

NGOs in Turkmenistan under Saparmurat Niyazov (the self-styled "Turkmenbashi," or leader of Turkmen) were especially close to the Soviet totalitarian type. All NGOs were under direct state control and were considered as useful mechanisms for implementing state policy. The ideology that the state promoted through them was formulated in Turkmenbashi's book *Ruhnama,* characterized by Turkmen nationalism and the president's personality cult.[20] It is no wonder that this regime was quite frequently called the "Stalinist Disneyland."[21]

NGOs such as youth organizations, veteran's organizations, and women's organizations were considered as mechanisms for spreading Ruhnama ideology throughout society. Many of these organizations were carried over from the Soviet period totally unchanged or were reformed only superficially. Membership in these organizations was still considered as almost obligatory for specific groups, especially for youth. These organizations monopolized certain sectors of society—one organization for veterans, one for women, and so forth, with no competing groups allowed.

The Soviet concept of *aktiv* was also used as a guiding principle in the distribution of resources. Membership in certain organizations was, as in the Soviet period, considered as a way of promotion (for example, a key to receiving high education, or a key to membership in different prestigious representative organizations, such as Halk Maslahaty, or the Supreme People's Council). The Soviet principle of cooperation between *nomenklatura* and *aktiv* was also realized in cooperation between the Democratic Party of Turkmenistan (the only party of that period) and certain NGOs. However, according to Eastern tradition, a balance inside the *aktiv* (for example, within Halk Maslahaty) was changed to offer a higher role for elderly people (*aksakals*) as representatives of veterans' organization. Many *aksakals*—members of the *aktiv*—according to Soviet tradition also received food rations or "presents" from the state. Sometimes such presents were from Turkmenbashi himself. Once, for example, the president was annoyed that during his meetings with the veterans one *aksakal,* who was a veteran of World War II and a former Soviet-era minister of communications of Turkmenistan, reacted to his speeches inadequately. When the president asked why this person behaved so disrespectfully to the highest authority, it was explained to him that this person was deaf. So at the next meeting Turkmenbashi personally presented an earphone to this *aksakal.* After that this veteran became a strong partisan of Ruhnama ideology. This story of personal presents guaranteeing loyalty was typical also of Stalin's period.

In Islamic states—Karimov's Uzbekistan and Turkmenistan under current president Gurbanguly Berdymuhammedov—this model of NGOs still exists, but it is not realized in a "Stalinist Disneyland" form. For example, the state may actively support some NGOs that are considered most loyal to the authorities through the provision of resources (including finances, offices, access to state-controlled mass media, and schools and universities). The state can also guarantee monopolistic control of these loyal NGOs over certain sectors of the society, suppress alternative organizations, and so forth. Young people also know that membership in certain NGOs can be conducive to better future careers due to state support for these organizations. The parties in power in Turkmenistan and Uzbekistan, such as the Democratic Party in Turkmenistan, actively cooperate with certain NGOs, so participation in these organizations is a way to establish a political career.

The second group of countries of Central Asia (Kazakhstan, Kyrgyzstan, Tajikistan) is not characterized by the prevalence of totalitarian forms of NGOs, but the same phenomenon of privileged, politically loyal, and largely monopolistic NGOs (or quasi-NGOs) sometimes appears in these countries, although not to the same degree as happens in Turkmenistan and Uzbekistan. Some NGOs are politically close to the authorities and, as a result, it is easier to register them; they receive indirect state funding, enjoy access to state-controlled mass media, and receive other benefits. Very often this can be explained not only by political loyalty but also by the clan connections of the heads of certain NGOs, especially in Tajikistan and Kazakhstan (but clan connections also guarantee political loyalty, so the difference between the motives is not so great). In both Tajikistan and Kazakhstan the most important connections are with presidential families (including the presidents' wives, children, and children's spouses). For example, the wife of Kazakhstan's president is head of the charitable children's foundation Bobek. State support for specific NGOs can be also a result of electoral considerations (especially in the cases of trade unions and veterans and women's organizations) and attempts to "bribe" specific social groups, especially in Kyrgyzstan. This can be considered as a transitional model between a totalitarian form of "uncivil" society and the form of "uncivil society" based on negative social capital that will be considered in the following section of this chapter. As I have already mentioned, Kyrgyzstan is less inclined toward the totalitarian form of "uncivil" societies.

In sum, many de jure existing NGOs in all Central Asian countries are de facto organizations affiliated with the state. This is a result of the negative influence of authoritarian political systems on society. As a result, these quasi-NGOs do not promote trust in the society but rather atomize individuals and undermine trust.

My previous analysis concentrated on the negative influence of highly authoritarian political systems on NGOs. However, the negative influence of the Soviet past is not limited to this. There is also a specific structure of societies created by Soviet modernization that negatively affects Central Asian civil organizations. This second aspect of the negative influence of the totalitarian Soviet past on Central Asian nations is atomization of the societies.

Negative path dependency created by the processes of Soviet modernization is best illustrated by the example of contemporary Russia. Present-day Russian society is highly atomized and is characterized by very low social capital. For example, V. Babintsev and E. Reutov show that atomization prevails over self-organization among Russian youth.[22] Russian youth are highly individualistic, and their social networks are very weakly developed. NGOs in this social environment exist mostly formally and do not conduct any essential activity. My own previous research has shown that atomization and low social capital have been very important to the present-day dynamic of Russia's political system.[23] Development of NGOs as the centers of attraction in social networks can be conducive to "color" revolution in Russia, and therefore the government tries to suppress civil liberties. Vladislav Inozemtsev, the well-known expert in economics and politics and director of the Center for Postindustrial Society, has often expressed the point of view that low social capital (i.e., the inability to organize) offers the best explanation for the low resistance of Russian society to authoritarianism, irrespective of Russia's level of economic development (which, according to some theories, should be conducive to democratization) and high cultural capital. Low social capital among Russians also can explain why, in general, there are so few small-scale enterprises in Russia, while in Islamic regions of

Russia that are culturally close to Central Asian countries the number of small-scale enterprises is higher. Moreover, Muslim ethnic groups are overrepresented among the owners of small-scale enterprises in predominantly Russian regions of Russia.

According to the assessment of Vadim Damie, there was a wave of public activity at the grassroots level during Gorbachev's perestroika.[24] This pattern of behavior was officially encouraged by the state leadership and was promoted by the mass media. However, a "second wave" of atomization of society affected Russia after the collapse of the Soviet Union. Damie gives two explanations for this "second wave" of atomization. First of all, the population was dissatisfied with civil movements that became highly politicized and departed from their basic issues (in the spheres of ecology, culture, etc.). General public mistrust of politicians that developed in Russia in the early 1990s also affected the population's attitudes toward the leadership of civil movements. Second, in the situation of economic crisis everyone had to concentrate on his or her own survival. Besides, the transition to a market economy encouraged individualism. Successful businessmen, not activists of civil organizations, became the heroes of that period.

However, the explanation for a high degree of atomization among the Russians is not so simple. In order to explain this phenomenon one should go back to Soviet totalitarianism and even beyond that. The Russian state always tried to undercut horizontal self-organization and therefore destroyed social capital.[25] On the contrary, the historically weak development of horizontal ties among the Russian population always demanded the existence of a strong state. This was the argument constantly expressed by famous Russian historians, the Westernizers of the nineteenth century such as Sergey Soloviev.[26]

It is no wonder that atomization in Central Asia has mostly affected the areas that were exposed to Soviet modernization (cities) and those groups of the population that are most closely connected to Russian culture (Russian speakers). So the paradox is that in Central Asia a higher level of Soviet modernization promoted atomization, and therefore social capital and potential of self-organization remain higher among less modernized groups of society. This, as well as other factors, has predetermined the prevalence of premodern and negative forms of social capital functioning independently of the state. These types of Central Asian NGOs will be analyzed in the following section.

"Uncivil Society" and Negative Social Capital in Central Asia

The emergence of independent states could, in principle, manifest a radical breakthrough with the Soviet past and could lead to the development of new civil societies and democratic systems based on the rule of law, as happened in Eastern Europe. However, this has not happened in Central Asia. There are many reasons for the evolution from a totalitarian variant of "uncivil society" toward "uncivil society" based on negative social capital in Central Asia. Some of these can be discovered in the new political patterns of Central Asian authoritarianism, others in the societal path dependencies established during the late Soviet period. And, of course, there was an absolute absence of international factors leading to the decline of late Soviet-era structures of uncivil society (like Europeanization in Eastern Europe). Moreover, the threat of radical Islamism and the huge influence of Russia and China pushed the situation in Central Asia in directions different from those in Eastern Europe.

Russian and Soviet modernization in Central Asia followed the tradition of societal fragmentation that had existed in this region earlier as a difference between the highly developed cities on the Silk Road and their nomadic and seminomadic periphery. A division between modernized cities and rural areas even increased in some respects, due to the specific model of industrialization and of agricultural development. On the one hand, industrialization and urbanization were based on transfer from the European part of Russia and the Caucasus of masses of Russians, Ukrainians, Tatars, Armenians, and other ethnic groups. Unlike other parts of the Russian empire and Soviet Union, there was no tendency toward cultural exchange or intermarriages between these "Russian speakers" and local ethnic Muslim groups. As a result, the new industrial areas resembled "besieged fortresses" surrounded by culturally alien local populations, and they were culturally more linked to faraway Russia than to local traditions.[27] On the other hand, collectivization in the rural areas preserved to some degree traditional "solidarity groups" of the indigenous people based on primordial characteristics (such as tribe, neighborhood, and clan). Based on manual labor, cotton monoculture in all Central Asian countries (with the exception of Kazakhstan) also preserved the traditional patriarchal family and neighborhood structures under a superficial layer of communist ideology. This created a tendency toward archaization of rural areas compared to the late nineteenth and early twentieth century, when elements of a market economy penetrated into Central Asian rural areas. This shielded rural areas of Central Asia and even the majority of the local non-Russian urban population (still connected to their relatives in the villages) from Soviet atomization. But it also preserved the dominance of traditional social links among the rural population.

Soviet *korenization* policy (staffing the local bureaucracy with the representatives of local ethnos or "titular nation"), in combination with the repression of educated local city dwellers from the local intelligentsia (the Jadids, the Young Bukharans, and so forth), established the tendency to recruit political elites from the rural areas. As a result, local "solidarity groups" from rural areas turned into political bases for different clans fighting for power within late Soviet or contemporary post-Soviet neopatrimonial systems. Association with the solidarity groups from rural areas is still the power basis for dominant clans in the independent states of Central Asia. Dominance of clans and networks of power connected to primary solidarity groups in economic and political life still offer a basis for integration in which bonding connections prevail over bridging connections.[28]

This is one of the main societal reasons for the preservation of "uncivil society" even after the collapse of the Soviet Union and the emergence of the new independent states of Central Asia. This derives from the social structure and therefore cannot be overcome by attempts at formal introduction of democratic rules, as in the case of Kyrgyzstan, where the clan structure remained, irrespective of superficially democratic rules of the game.[29]

As mentioned earlier, given the extent to which totalitarian "uncivil society" still reproduced some elements of social capital (and it mostly destroyed it), the bonding function within Soviet NGOs prevailed over bridging functions. Bridging was reserved exclusively for the Communist Party and the state machinery. In the specific Central Asian environment where rural primary solidarity groups and clans based on them still played a key role, different Soviet NGOs fell under the control of these clans. So they became the embodiment of specific interests, and this enormously increased the bonding function of these NGOs, although it also weakened the negative totalitarian tendency toward atomization.

Corruption in the late Soviet period among the *nomenklatura* was widespread. In some respects, the late Soviet system could be considered as a huge administrative market.[30] Since this administrative market was based on close *nomenklatura* connections, it could be considered as a type of negative social capital. In Central Asia, especially in its rural part due to cotton monoculture, corruption and practices of an administrative market were especially widespread.[31] In Central Asia the administrative market was also closely intertwined with the clan system, so there was a system of exchange of administrative services not only between individual bureaucrats but also between clans. The system included not only exchange but also a power balance, or balance of conflicts between the clans. Finally, the system of solidarity within the clans and their connections with rural "solidarity groups" helped to promote the representatives of the clan within the Soviet hierarchy. Total corruption in Soviet Central Asia combined with the clan system was publicly revealed during an anticorruption campaign in Uzbekistan (partially; it also affected all other cotton-producing regions) initiated by Yury Andropov and then supported by Mikhail Gorbachev.

All these tendencies continued after the collapse of the Soviet Union and the appearance of the Newly Independent States. Specific ways of development chosen by Central Asian societies increased the elements of "uncivil society" based on negative social capital, the foundations of which had already been established by the late Soviet period. As a result of the late Soviet heritage, there were not only a set of specific social structures (for example, a specific structure of social capital) but also a set of negative social values connected to these structures, such as nepotism, high valuation of clan and relative connections, anti-individualism, and anti-meritocratic approaches. All these values inherited from the Soviet past continued to exist, distorting the functioning of society and preserving "uncivil societies," albeit sometimes in changed forms.

I would specifically mention three main reasons why the elements of "uncivil society" (and the respective social values) were preserved based on negative social capital in post-Soviet Central Asia.

First, Central Asian states are new. This territory has an ancient history, but the states were first established as Soviet republics in the 1920s and 1930s. Until the collapse of the Soviet Union they had not experienced independence. Their borders are somewhat artificial, and their national identities are in the process of evolution. This makes the issue of national integration and formation of positive social capital playing a bridging function on the national level quite problematic. People in Central Asia rarely perceive themselves as part of a single nation due to the prevalence of subethnic and regional identities even among the main ethnic group (or "titular nation"). Russian speakers and other national minorities also quite rarely identify themselves with these new nations. Only in Kazakhstan have there been some attempts (not always successful) to create a civil national identity not based on one ethnic group. Russian speakers and other minorities are considered as "Kazakhstanzy," citizens of Kazakhstan rather than ethnic Kazakhs; in all other cases national identity is based on one ethnic group.

Second, the absence of a single national identity makes even the notion of "bridging" quite problematic for the specific Central Asian case. This becomes clear if one compares the Central Asian cases with European ones. For example, Graham Pollock has argued that because the concept of civil society is essentially connected to democracy, it should also be linked with ideas of nationality and nationalist ideologies.[32] In the absence of a single national identity this connection between civil society, democracy, and democratic nation does not work.

Third, it is also well known on the basis of comparative studies that high societal fragmentation creates many problems for collective action and democratization.[33] Such fragmentation makes it difficult to develop a set of general moral and legal norms that would be acceptable for all groups. Within such a system promotion of the interests of the representatives of one's own solidarity group or clan prevails over the collective interests of the nation as a whole.

These tendencies toward disintegration into ethnic, subethnic, and regional groups are increased by a general moral crisis affecting all post-Soviet nations, manifested, for example, in high levels of crime and lawlessness. The endemic corruption that was a characteristic feature of the late Soviet system in Central Asia has also affected the Newly Independent States of the region. High levels of corruption are a logical continuation of the "administrative market" of the late Soviet period based on the dominance of power clans.

Table 1.3 shows measures of corruption in Central Asian countries based on Transparency International's Corruption Perceptions Index. First, it is important to notice that all Central Asian countries have a transparency score below 3 (10 is the highest score on Transparency International's scale). Central Asian systems are very corrupt compared to the world as a whole. Second, this level of corruption is comparable to that in other post-Soviet countries. For example, Russia has the same score as Tajikistan and is assessed as much more corrupt than Kazakhstan. Third, Kazakh-

Table 1.3. Corruption in Five Central Asian Countries

World ranking	Country	Transparency score
105	Kazakhstan	2.9
154	Tajikistan	2.1
164	Kyrgyzstan	2.0
172	Turkmenistan	1.6
172	Uzbekistan	1.6

Source: Transparency International, "Corruption Perceptions Index 2010," http://www.transparency.org/policy_research/surveys_indices/cpi/2010/results.

stan's system can be assessed as quite transparent compared to other Central Asian nations.

According to Victor Sergeyev's original analysis, there is also the specificity of the post-Soviet transition toward more pluralist political and economic systems.[34] This transition was accompanied by significant contradictions between official laws, traditions, and administrative practices. As a result, a huge "gray zone" covering nearly all aspects of economic and political life appeared. One result of this was "virtualization" of nearly every official, public aspect of economic and political life in post-Soviet nations.[35] The other result was the transfer of all real activity into corrupt networks, such as "blat" networks.[36] These close networks, which in specific Central Asian situations took the shape of power clans affiliated with rural solidarity groups, have become responsible for the prevalence of negative social capital.

The second set of values preserving certain types of "uncivil societies" comes directly from the political sphere. All Central Asian states are authoritarian, and as a result the relationships between the state and NGOs remain authoritarian. Turkmenistan and Uzbekistan may exercise control directly; other states do this through indirect influence shaped by a specific set of sociopolitical values inherited from the late Soviet Union. A set of authoritarian values continues to support the unquestionable authority of those at the top of the power hierarchy, facilitating corruption, the illegal exchange of resources on the shadowy "administrative market," the prevalence of networks of power in various forms, and mutually beneficial connections between networks of power and local solidarity groups. All these factors have significantly distorted NGO functioning and preserved "uncivil societies." The prevalence of these values in society has removed any incentives for the ruling elite to change the rules of the game.

Finally, if one considers Central Asian nations not simply within the context of other former Soviet Union states but within the context of political processes in the developing world as a whole, the theory of *neopatrimonialism* can be useful. The theory of patrimonialism was first formulated by Max Weber in his famous work *Economy and Society.*[37] Within this system ruling groups consider the state and all public functions as an analogue of their private property. Although this theory was first formulated on the basis of analysis of ancient Eastern societies, later studies discovered that many developing countries of Asia, Africa, and Latin America have elements of patrimonial systems.[38]

On the basis of this comparative research, S. Eisenstadt introduced the concept of "neopatrimonialism."[39] This is a type of modern society, yet it has some characteristics of ancient patrimonial societies. All political, economic, and symbolic resources are concentrated in a single center controlled by a ruling elite, and access to these resources is closed to all other social groups. The ruling elite still consider public functions and institutes as their private property. As a result, there is no differentiation between economic and political life, since the same patronage networks are the main players in both spheres. In politics formal institutions and ideologies become "virtual" cover for real network interactions.[40] Political regimes in this situation evolve in the direction of Weberian sultanistic regimes.[41] It is in the sphere of economics that corrupt rent-seeking behavior becomes the most widespread.

From the point of view of civil society in Central Asia the most interesting aspect of neopatrimonialism is that it preserves and even promotes the most archaic forms of social organization, such as clans and tribes. As Eisenstadt has shown, a tendency toward societal fragmentation was a characteristic feature of the patrimonialist system.[42] It was also a general characteristic of many Islamic societies and produced a tendency toward segregated change in different spheres of social life (and therefore it hinders progress in both economic and political life). This tendency toward fragmentation within patrimonial and neopatrimonial societies is a direct analogue of Robert Putnam's negative social capital, since within fragmented societies bonding by definition prevails over bridging. Therefore it serves as the major obstacle to political and economic modernization of Central Asia, creating the basis for the prevalence of clan-based economic and political structures.[43] This type of structure is characteristic of all contemporary Central Asian countries, irrespective of their level of political pluralism and economic and social development.[44] Of course, this specific structure of social capital has predetermined the character of development of "uncivil society" in Central Asia.

My previous discussion of the characteristics of "uncivil society" in Central Asia illuminates various institutional characteristics of agents, their roles, and their relations with the state; this focus is systemic, rather than individual. However, one should notice that such a system influences the characteristics of concrete individuals over decades if not centuries, as discussed within the framework of "political culture" theory or stable "traits of national character." As a result, mass corruption and nepotism develop, paternalistic relations between elite groups and ordinary members of respective regional or tribal "clans" predominate, and the general population views politics with apathy and mistrust. There is constant interaction between those individual-level characteristics and the institutional features of "uncivil society" in Central Asia. Individuals who have grown up within specific authoritarian or even totalitarian environments, with their specific sets of incentives, have a natural inclination to reproduce negative social capital in their personal behavior. Under these conditions, even rapid evolution of formal institutions would continue to reproduce negative behavioral stereotypes in the absence of a new set of incentives.

Types of NGOs Based on Negative Social Capital in Contemporary Central Asia

The historically defined path dependencies, specific social structures, values, and behavioral stereotypes described above have predetermined the specific forms of development of post-Soviet "uncivil" societies in Central Asia. Of course, this does not mean that Central Asian societies still have the Brezhnev-era structures of "uncivil society." They have different ideologies, usually based on some form of nationalism; their authoritarian systems are somehow different from Soviet totalitarianism; and they have the elements of the free market. So, of course, there are some changes, but the radical breakthrough, that is, the move from "uncivil" to "civil" societies, still has not happened.

Most important in terms of the change of economic structures is the experience of Kazakhstan, which has huge energy resources. The Kazakh government has formed relatively liberal rules of the game in the economic sphere and has attracted enormous foreign investments by regional standards. But this oil wealth has two diametrically opposing types of influence on the development of civil society. On the one hand, Kazakh society in the 2000s is much better educated (the Bolashak program, for example, has made foreign education available even for ordinary Kazakh youth), people have good access to the Internet and global mass media, and there are many opportunities to travel to democratic countries with well-functioning civil societies. Relative wealth also creates additional stimuli for the development of civil society, since people have more resources. On the other hand, there is also the effect of the "resource curse." Nazarbayev's government has acquired huge revenues from the oil boom since the beginning of the 2000s and, as a result, has become more independent from the people and from pressures toward democratization from abroad. In some respects, the policy of Kazakhstan during the relatively rich 2000s toward the development of civil society has become even less favorable than during the poor, crisis-prone period of the 1990s. The pernicious influence of a "resource curse" is even more visible in Turkmenistan, where the state has huge resources from the export of natural gas.

According to my observations, in Central Asia there are four different types of distortions of free public self-organization, as a result of which the bonding function starts to prevail over a bridging one: those based on religious extremist groups, those based on criminal groups, those based on clan groups, and those based on corrupt networks. Of course, the boundaries between these four groups can be very flexible; however, in all four types something like an "ideal type" of specific registered or unregistered organization can be discovered.

Organizations based on religious extremist groups are part of an Islamic renaissance in Central Asia. The situation with them is not so simple as official propaganda in the Central Asian states describes it.[45] Official propaganda, especially in Uzbekistan, uses the term "religious extremist" and *vahhabit* (a follower of a partisan or nonlocal, "Arab" version of Islam), very often as a synonym for one who follows an officially uncontrolled religious movement.[46] So there is a high hidden potential for real public self-organization and a great potential for political change of the sort that has been demonstrated during the Arab Spring. The United Tajik Opposition (UTO), which was integrated into the political life of Tajikistan, demonstrates this potential.[47] However, in specific circumstances in post-Soviet

Central Asia unofficial religious groups have become radicalized and have started to elevate their adherents as "true" Muslims, characterizing all other Muslims as "nonbelievers." They often advocate and use violence against their opponents. Moreover, since they are integrated with grassroots-level economic activities (especially with small businesses in bazaars), in the specific situation of post-Soviet Central Asia it also means extensive connections with the "gray" sector of the economy.[48] The movement Akramia in Uzbekistan that organized rebellion in Andijan in May 2005 demonstrates tendencies both to oppose society as a whole and to benefit from the "gray" sector of the economy. Quite often such organizations are connected to international terrorists (the Islamic Movement of Uzbekistan [IMU] affiliated with Al-Qaeda and the Taliban) and with Afghan drug traders (IMU's invasions into the Batken region of Kyrgyzstan in 1999 were usually explained by the local experts within the context of developing drug-smuggling routes). As a result, there is a tendency for unofficial religious groups (especially in Uzbekistan) to radicalize and to develop bonding rather than bridging social ties. The same situation is characteristic, to a smaller degree, of all other Central Asian countries, especially some parts of Tajikistan, southern Kyrgyzstan, southern Kazakhstan, and northern parts of Turkmenistan populated by Uzbeks.

Organizations based on criminal groups (or simply mafia, as they are called in Russian, after the Italian mafia) are widespread in Central Asia. This is a result of pervasive terrible poverty, the drug trade, crime, corruption, and general moral degradation in countries of the former Soviet Union. Drug smuggling is the most lucrative business of such groups. This tendency existed already in the late Soviet period; however, it intensified after Afghanistan took a global leadership position in poppy production.[49] The problem is a very high degree of interconnectedness between official and unofficial sectors of the economy in Central Asia. For example, Russian police very often find in Russia packages of heroin with official seals of Tajikistan's Interior Ministry, meaning officers of Tajik law enforcement agencies illegally resell drugs that they confiscate.[50] Another example of such integration between the authorities and criminal groups are reports from some reliable sources that Turkmenistan's secret police are also highly involved in the international heroin trade.

Many Central Asian clans have some interests in not only illegal but also legal types of economic activity. Moreover, in many cases it is impossible to distinguish between mafia and power clans because key transactions (including international ones, especially with Russia and other post-Soviet countries) are conducted with a substantial illegal component.[51]

Mafia-type organizations not only penetrate all levels of Central Asian societies, but they also have different types of connections with NGOs. For example, some types of illegal NGO activities are realized through mafia connections, and the mafia conducts some of its interests through NGOs. The last type of activity is best known by the example of Russia (especially in the Urals and Siberia), where some illegal criminal funds (*obshaki*) are quite often affiliated with officially registered NGOs and businesses. Russian police during the two Chechen wars frequently declared that some Chechen ethnic organizations had the same type of connections in Kazakhstan. In the cases of organized criminal groups, loyalty to the group is supposed to prevail over loyalty to the interests of the society as a whole, and therefore they can be described as a classical type of negative social capital.

Organizations based on clan groups have developed in post-Soviet Central Asia as part of the rise of a political and economic system based on clan connections, discussed earlier. Many successful NGOs in all Central Asian countries are included in the same networks of clan connections. These connections guarantee a flow of state resources to certain NGOs in return for personal loyalty. This loyalty (especially outside of the specific political systems of Turkmenistan and Uzbekistan) may not necessarily take the form of direct and openly proclaimed political loyalty to the regime. In Kazakhstan, Tajikistan, and especially Kyrgyzstan, these ties tend to be more indirect and personalized. These types of organizations are part of the transition from the totalitarian model of "uncivil" society to more free forms of social organization, although they, of course, are based on negative social capital.

Organizations based on corrupt networks are specific forms of quasi-business entrepreneurship. They are less connected to the power clans than the previous group. However, due to their good communicative and organizational skills their managers effectively exploit for their private purposes structural holes left by the clan system of Central Asian societies. In this case, quasi-civil projects (usually virtual or directly falsified) are used to attract finance from local or foreign sources. Corrupt connections are used both for obtaining funds (especially from local and Russian sources) and for falsifying the results of activities of such organizations. Falsified activity of such organizations can be understood only within the context of the total "virtualization" of political and economic life in former Soviet Union countries.[52]

The main problem is that Western governments and foundations supporting the development of civil society in Central Asia sometimes have no real instruments for discerning the virtual activity of corrupt networks from the work of real civil groups, and of course there are many real civil groups headed by the persons who are truly devoted to their mission. Moreover, corrupt networks create a continuum of organizations, ranging from totally corrupt NGOs, in which virtual activity prevails, to organizations that use such tricks only occasionally because they want to survive in the post-Soviet social environment. So this is the transitional type most closely related to real civil society. During the 1990s, for example, there was a substantial flow of Western assistance in the form of grants into Kyrgyzstan; these corrupt networks benefited from the quasi-democratic image of the country.

It is important to note that cooperation between Western donors and different social grassroots movements does have great positive potential for the development of genuine civil society in Central Asia. However, this potential needs time to develop.

One other problem is that such organizations can benefit from the "new great game" in Central Asia; that is, from the geopolitical competition between the West, Russia, China, and certain Islamic countries.[53] The competition for "soft power" is one of the most important aspects of this geopolitical competition.[54] Some corrupt NGOs, in order to receive financing from abroad, claim that they promote a specific model of development that a certain global player is proposing to Central Asia (although, of course, there are many honest NGO managers).[55] In cooperating with the West, corrupt NGOs pretend to promote democratization and civil society. In the 1990s there were many corrupt networks that were effectively parasites dependent on Western assistance, especially in Kyrgyzstan, and some corrupt networks that benefited from Islamic foundations throughout Central Asia.

The inflow of oil and gas money into Putin's Russia was accompanied by Moscow's efforts to reestablish influence in what Russian political discourse generally refers to as the "near abroad." One example in the form of soft power is the Russkiy Mir project, the Putin-inspired foundation to spread Russian language and culture and to reconnect Russians abroad with the homeland. As a result of the project, many opportunities for Russian financial assistance for "politically friendly" Central Asian NGOs appeared. The specific structure of Russian political and business life has made corruption and falsified activities a prevailing mode of cooperation within the framework of respective projects for some organizations.[56] Moreover, I have observed delegates from Central Asian NGOs who earlier pretended to promote a Western model of development for the region at Russkiy Mir conferences in Moscow. The growth of Chinese influence in Central Asia and increasing emphasis on "soft power" in Beijing's foreign policy indicates that an additional source of finance for Central Asian NGOs may now be available. Corrupt networks can also benefit from this money because the Chinese are famous for their "flexible" business practices in the developing world.[57]

The global economic crisis, unfortunately, also has negatively influenced the development of civil society in Central Asia, and therefore it also preserves uncivil society in the region. This influence develops in two key dimensions.

Domestically, the crisis has further increased the disparity between the state and society in Central Asia. There is an increased level of state control over the economy because there is a necessity to implement anticrisis measures. The society affected by the crisis becomes poorer, and this lack of resources available for the people also does not promote the development of civil society.

Internationally, the global crisis has caused the decline of Western influence on Central Asia. Europe and the United States are obsessed with domestic economic problems. The United States is also very busy addressing security problems associated with Afghanistan, so developing civil society is not a key priority. For the European Union, Central Asia has never been a priority (it is not even included in the Eastern Partnership program), since it is not considered part of the potential "Europeanization" sphere. The lack of resources available during the crisis simply underlines this European approach. Finally, there has been a significant growth of Chinese economic and political influence due to its booming economic development. Russia, with its formidable energy reserves also still has sufficient economic resources for an active Central Asian policy, for example, within the framework of developing a new generation of Eurasian integration structures. These influences are often not conducive to democratization and the development of civil society.

The analysis in this chapter gives us an opportunity to appreciate the dramatic character of the contest between civil society and different forms of

Table 1.4. Civil Society, Two Forms of "Uncivil Society," and Social Capital in Central Asia

Type of society	Civil society	Totalitarian "uncivil society"	Nonmodernized, transition, or marginalized "uncivil society"
Social capital	Positive social capital, both bridging and bonding	Atomization (destruction of social capital) with some elements of bonding (negative social capital)	Negative social capital, bonding prevails over bridging
Prevalent structure of NGOs	Conventional modern civil organizations created by voluntary association of the citizens, not based on clan or other premodern forms of associations	Quasi-civil, de facto state organizations serving the totalitarian state	Quasi-civil organizations based on premodern forms of human association, first of all on clans
Prevalent functions of NGOs within the society	Representation of the interests of the citizens, often acting independently of the political system; promotion of democracy, integration of society (due to prevalence of bridging), economic development, and rule of law	Most often, representation of the interests of the state within the social group, and, rarely, representation of the interests of respective social groups within the political system	Promotion of authoritarianism, corruption, intergroup conflicts, and fragmentation of society (due to prevalence of bonding), slowing down economic development; representation of the interests of an isolated group within the society

"uncivil societies" that are developing in contemporary Central Asia. Table 1.4 summarizes the role of social capital within civil society as compared to two different types of distortions within "uncivil societies." It also compares the role of social capital within the respective structures of NGOs and their functions within the society.

Both types of "uncivil societies" are the result of different negative path dependencies defined by the Soviet and post-Soviet history of Central Asia. Totalitarian Soviet modernization created a specific form of quasi-NGOs totally controlled by the state leadership and realizing the political agenda of the ruling party. This model, with some minor modifications, still exists in such Central Asian states as Turkmenistan and Uzbekistan. The post-Soviet Central Asian states of Tajikistan, Kyrgyzstan, and, to some degree, Kazakhstan, due to low levels of modernization, high levels of crime and corruption, and the dominance of different clans in political and economic life, have developed another type of "uncivil society" based on negative social capital, in which bonding prevails over bridging.

The functions and structure of NGOs in a specific environment of "uncivil societies" become distorted. For example, totalitarian NGOs, the first variant of Central Asian uncivil societies created in the Soviet period, were not NGOs by their structure at all because they were controlled by the government. Their function was also paradoxical: for the most part they did not create social capital and trust in the society, but destroyed it by atomizing society. Even when they reproduced some elements of social capital, this capital was negative. So the post-Soviet evolution of most Central Asian states toward the second variant of "uncivil society" (based on negative social capital) has been quite logical within this pattern of path dependency. I have distinguished four types of the distortions within the second variant of "uncivil society": those based on religious extremist groups, criminal organizations, clan affinities, and corrupt networks.

All these forms (especially the last one) have some transitional features of genuine civil society. This potential can develop if Central Asian societies evolve in the right direction, although, of course, this process would take a long time. For example, if the process of Islamic renaissance becomes more enlightened and liberal and is not repressed by suspicious governments, extremist religious groups could become pious civil communities based on traditional values. With economic reforms and increasing transparency the system of mutually contradictory institutions defining the dominance of the "gray zone" in the Central Asian economy can be corrected. If this is accompanied by an attack on corruption at the national level and international campaigns against such transborder evils as drug trafficking, then Central Asian economies could be decriminalized at the grassroots level. As a result, the dominance of criminal groups over some forms of social self-organization would disappear. Even former criminal capitals (Las Vegas could be cited) can, under certain favorable conditions, become productively invested. If Central Asian ruling elites develop a feeling of solidarity with society as a whole and a sense of responsibility toward their respective nations, clan connections can also be transformed into a form of bridging capital, as happened with the European aristocracy when the European states first became centralized monarchies and then gradually democratized. Finally, the talents of leaders of some independent NGOs, assuming economic and political systems send them correct signals, can shift from operating virtual projects and seeking corrupt schemes of financing through networking toward creating real civil projects. The possibility of all these developments toward civil society still exists only in the long-term perspective, and the probability of such positive unfolding of events is not high. But the fate of democratization and the development of effective market economies in Central Asia depends on such development.

Regrettably, the main thesis of this chapter seems to be negative. Many forms of civil organization that exist in Central Asia today do not represent genuine civil society, and this is a situation that cannot change overnight. However, there is also an element of a positive policy agenda: in the cooperation between Western donors and different social grassroots movements there is great positive potential for the development of genuine civil society in Central Asia over the long term. In all likelihood this assistance is crucial for the development of positive social capital in the region and for overcoming the negative heritage of the totalitarian past.

Notes

1. Hannah Arendt, *The Origins of Totalitarianism,* rev. ed. (New York: Schocken, 2004); Robert D. Putnam, Robert Leonardi, and Raffaella Y. Nanetti, *Making Democracy Work: Civic Traditions in Modern Italy* (Princeton: Princeton University Press, 1994); Robert D. Putnam, *Bowling Alone: The Collapse and Revival of American Community* (New York: Simon and Schuster, 2000).

2. Stephen Kotkin, *Uncivil Society: 1989 and the Implosion of the Communist Establishment* (New York: Random House, 2009); Andreas Umland, "Toward an Uncivil Society? Contextualizing the Recent Decline of Extremely Right-Wing

Parties in Russia," working paper 02-03, Weatherhead Center for International Affairs, Harvard University, 2002.

3. S. N. Eisenstadt, "Multiple Modernities," *Daedalus* 129 (2000): 1–29.

4. G. Almond and S. Verba, *The Civic Culture: Political Attitudes and Democracy in Five Nations* (London: Sage, 1989).

5. Arendt, *Origins of Totalitarianism.*

6. Putnam, Leonardi, and Nanetti, *Making Democracy Work.*

7. Nan Lin, Karen Cook, and Ronald Burt, *Social Capital: Theory and Research* (New York: Aldine de Gruyter, 2001).

8. Putnam, *Bowling Alone.*

9. Francis Fukuyama, *Trust: The Social Virtues and the Creation of Prosperity* (New York: Free Press, 1995).

10. Putnam, *Bowling Alone.*

11. See especially the works of Andreas Umland on radical nationalist "uncivil" organizations in Russia. Umland, "Toward an Uncivil Society?"

12. B. Bolin, E. J. Hackett, S. L. Harlan, A. Kirby, L. Larsen, A. Nelson, T. R. Rex, and S. Wolf, "Bonding and Bridging: Understanding the Relationship between Social Capital and Civic Action," *Journal of Planning Education and Research* 24 (2004): 64–77.

13. C. Winslow, *Lebanon: War and Politics in a Fragmented Society* (New York: Routledge, 1996).

14. Sheri E. Berman, "Civil Society and the Collapse of the Weimar Republic," *World Politics* 49, no. 3 (April 1997): 401–29.

15. Carlo Trigilia, "Social Capital and Local Development," *European Journal of Social Theory* 4, no. 4 (2001): 427–42.

16. Arendt, *Origins of Totalitarianism.*

17. Vadim Damie, "Atomization of Society and Social Self-Organization: The Russian Context" (in Russian), http://www.ikd.ru/node/87, accessed October 25, 2010.

18. Milovan Djilas, *The New Class: An Analysis of the Communist System* (New York: Praeger, 1957); Michael Voslensky, *Nomenklatura: Anatomy of the Soviet Ruling Class* (London: Bodley Head, 1984).

19. Putnam, *Bowling Alone.*

20. Saparmurat Turkmenbashi (Niyazov), *Ruhnama* (Ashgabat, Turkmenistan: Turkmenskaya gosudarstvennaya izdatelskaya sluzhba, 2002).

21. See "Stalin's Disneyland," in Lutz Kleveman, *The New Great Game: Blood and Oil in Central Asia* (New York: Grove Press, 2004), 144–64.

22. V. P. Babintsev and E. V. Reutov, "Self-Organization and 'Atomization' of the Youth as Actual Forms of Socio-cultural Reflection," *Sociologicheskie issledovania*, no. 1 (January 2010): 109–15 (in Russian).

23. Andrey Kazantsev, "Three Scenarios of 'Color' Revolution in Russia from the Point of View of Social Networks' Dynamics of Russian Polity," *Polis (Politicheskye issledovania)*, no. 1 (2006): 45–67 (in Russian).

24. Damie, "Atomization of Society."

25. Richard Pipes, *Russia under the Old Regime* (New York: Scribner, 1974).

26. S. M. Soloviev, *The History of Russia from the Ancient Times*, 2 vols. (Moscow: Golos, 1993) (in Russian).

27. S. Lurje, "Geopolitical Forms of Organization of the Space of Expansion and Their Influence on People's Character," 54–76, http://svlourie.narod.ru/imperium/expansion.htm, accessed July 2, 2014 (in Russian).

28. K. Collins, *Clan Politics and Regime Transition in Central Asia* (New York: Cambridge University Press, 2006); Olivier Roy, *The New Central Asia: Geopolitics and the Birth of Nations* (London: I. B. Tauris, 2007), 1–25, 98–100.

29. Collins, *Clan Politics and Regime Transition.*

30. S. Kordonsky, *Administrative Market of Soviet Union and Russia* (Moscow: OGI, 2006) (in Russian).

31. Only Kazakhstan avoided this tendency.

32. Graham Pollock, "Civil Society Theory and Euro-Nationalism," *Studies in Social and Political Thought*, no. 4 (March 2001): 31–56.

33. Winslow, *Lebanon.*

34. V. Sergeyev, *The Wild East: Crime and Lawlessness in Post-communist Russia* (Armonk, NY: M. E. Sharpe, 1998).

35. Clifford G. Gaddy and Barry W. Ickes, *Russia's Virtual Economy* (Washington, D.C.: Brookings Institution Press, 2002); A. Wilson, *Virtual Politics: Faking Democracy in the Post-Soviet World* (New Haven, CT: Yale University Press, 2005); Roy Allison, "Virtual Regionalism, Regional Structures and Regime Security in Central Asia," *Central Asian Survey* 27, no. 2 (2008): 185–202.

36. A. Ledeneva, *Russia's Economy of Favors* (Cambridge: Cambridge University Press, 1998).

37. M. Weber, *Economy and Society: An Outline of Interpretive Sociology*, 2 vols. (Berkeley: University of California Press, 1978).

38. G. Roth, "Personal Rulership, Patrimonialism, and Empire-Building in the New States," *World Politics* 20, no. 2 (1968): 194–206; R. Theobald, "Patrimonialism," *World Politics* 34, no. 4 (1982): 548–59; J. F. Medard, "The Underdeveloped State in Tropical Africa: Political Clientelism or Neo-patrimonialism," in *Private Patronage and Public Power: Political Clientelism in the Modern State*, ed. Christopher Clapham (New York: Palgrave Macmillan, 1982), 162–92; V. Murvar, "Patrimonialism, Modern and Traditionalist: A Paradigm for Interdisciplinary Research on Rulership and Legitimacy," in *Theory of Liberty, Legitimacy, and Power: New Directions in the Intellectual and Scientific Legacy of Max Weber*, ed. V. Murvar (London: Routledge, 1985), 40–85.

39. Shmuel N. Eisenstadt, *Traditional Patrimonialism and Modern Neopatrimonialism* (Beverly Hills, CA: Sage, 1973); Gero Erdmann and Ulf Engel, "Neopatrimonialism Revisited: Beyond a Catch-All Concept," GIGA Working Papers no. 16, German Institute of Global and Area Studies, February 2006; Ilkhamov, "Neopat-

rimonialism, Interest Groups and Patronage Networks: The Impasses of the Governance System in Uzbekistan," *Central Asian Survey* 26, no. 1 (2007): 65–84.

40. Wilson, *Virtual Politics;* Allison, "Virtual Regionalism"; Gaddy and Ickes, *Russia's Virtual Economy.*

41. H. E. Chehabi and J. J. Linz, eds., *Sultanistic Regimes* (Baltimore: Johns Hopkins University Press, 1998).

42. S. N. Eisenstadt, *Revolution and the Transformation of Societies: A Comparative Study of Civilizations* (London: Collier Macmillan, 1978), 75–80, 90–94, 134–39.

43. Collins, *Clan Politics and Regime Transition.*

44. E. Schatz, *Modern Clan Politics: The Power of "Blood" in Kazakhstan and Beyond* (Seattle: University of Washington Press, 2004), 3–21, 72–95; Dosym Satpaev, "An Analysis of the Internal Structure of Kazakhstan Political Elite and an Assessment of Political Risk Level," in *Empire, Islam, and Politics in Central Eurasia,* ed. Tomohiko Uyama (Hokkaido: Slavic Research Center, 2007), 283–300; Jonathan Murphy, "Illusory Transition? Elite Reconstruction in Kazakhstan, 1989–2002," *Europe-Asia Studies* 58, no. 4 (June 2006): 523–54; V. Khanin, "Political Clans and Political Conflicts in Contemporary Kyrgyzstan," in *Democracy and Pluralism in Muslim Eurasia,* ed. Y. Ro'i (London: Frank Cass, 2004), 215–32; E. Massicard and T. Trevisani, "The Uzbek Mahalla: Between State and Society," in *Central Asia: Aspects of Transition,* ed. T. Everet-Heath (London: Routledge, 2003), 205–19; L. P. Markowitz, "Local Elites, Prokurators, and Extraction in Rural Uzbekistan," *Central Asian Survey* 27, no. 1 (2008): 1–14; A. Taksanov, *Shadowy Economy and Corruption in Uzbekistan: Clans and Law-Enforcing Agencies in Illegal and Political Activities* (St. Petersburg: Komilfo, 2008) (in Russian); S. Kadyrov, "Turkmenistan: The Political Elite in an Ethnic Society," in *Oil, Transition and Stability in Central Asia,* ed. S. N. Cummings (London: Routledge, 2004), 108–18; K. Nourzhanov, "Saviours of the Nation or Robber Barons? Warlord Politics in Tajikistan," *Central Asian Survey* 24, no. 2 (2005): 109–30.

45. This is one of the reasons why I analyze these seemingly "new" groups within the context of negative "path dependency." One can consider these groups as completely "new" only if one completely believes in the official point of view that describes everything not authorized by current state authorities as "foreign" and "new." Some experts believe that the elements of *vahhabism* (as one of a number of traditional Islamic schools of thought, which should be differentiated from "*vahhabism*" as an element of the image of the enemy within state propaganda) have already appeared in the Ferghana Valley in the twenty-first century. Even the religious renaissance in Central Asia in its present form started in the 1970s, about thirty-five to forty years ago, long before the dissolution of the Soviet Union, making it not "new" after all.

46. For more detail, see my analysis of *vahhabism* as an element of political discourse in Russia and Central Asia in A. Kazantsev, "'Wahhabism': Institutions in

the Situation of Social and Cultural Crisis," *Polis (Politicheskye issledovania),* no. 5 (2002): 96–110.

47. Information from Uzbek secret services indicates that this process was not smooth, however; some Tajik authorities, through the UTO, were integrated with some terrorist groups like Islamic Movement of Uzbekistan and with drug traders from Afghanistan.

48. On the inevitable character of grassroots economic activity moving into a "gray zone" in post-Soviet countries, see Sergeyev, *Wild East.*

49. See, for example, European Monitoring Centre for Drugs and Drug Addiction and Europol, *Cocaine: A European Union Perspective in the Global Context* (Lisbon, April 2010), http://www.emcdda.europa.eu/publications/joint-publications/cocaine.

50. Russian law enforcement agencies typically do the same with confiscated goods, although usually not in the sphere of drugs.

51. See, for example, Global Witness, *It's a Gas: Funny Business in the Turkmen-Ukraine Gas Trade* (London, April 2006), http://www.globalwitness.org/library/its-gas-funny-business-turkmen-ukraine-gas-trade, accessed November 15, 2012.

52. Wilson, *Virtual Politics;* Allison, "Virtual Regionalism"; Gaddy and Ickes, *Russia's Virtual Economy.*

53. M. E. Ahrari, *The New Great Game in Muslim Central Asia* (Washington, D.C.: Institute for National Strategic Studies, National Defense University, 1996); S. Blank, "Energy, Economics and Security in Central Asia: Russia and Its Rivals," *Central Asian Survey* 14, no. 3 (1995): 373–406.

54. N. Popescu and A. Wilson, *The Limits of Enlargement-Lite: European and Russian Power in the Troubled Neighbourhood,* policy report (European Council on Foreign Relations, June 2009).

55. See in more details in my book, A. Kazantsev, *A "Great Game" with Unknown Rules: World Politics and Central Asia,* 2nd ed. (Moscow: Eurasian Home Publishing House, 2008) (in Russian).

56. Sergeyev, *Wild East;* A. Ledeneva, *How Russia Really Works* (Ithaca, NY: Cornell University Press, 2006); Ledeneva, *Russia's Economy of Favors;* F. Varese, *The Russian Mafia: Private Protection in a New Market Economy* (Oxford: Oxford University Press, 2001); V. Volkov, *Violent Entrepreneurs: The Use of Force in the Making of Russian Capitalism* (Ithaca, NY: Cornell University Press, 2002).

57. A. E. Goldstein, N. Pinaud, H. Reisen, and Chen Xiaobao, *The Rise of China and India: What's in It for Africa?* (Paris: Development Centre of the Organisation for Economic Co-operation and Development, 2006), 84.

Part 2

Religion and National Minorities

2

Islamization and Civil Society in Central Asia

Religion as Substrate in Conflict Management and Social Stability

Reuel R. Hanks

Landscapes of Identity

More than twenty years ago, the Turkish scholar Ozay Mehmet wrote of "a global identity crisis" sweeping the developing world, a crisis that in particular affected what he termed the "Islamic periphery."[1] He noted that "in Africa as elsewhere in the Third World, the central question at the dawn of a new century is still: Who am I? Is my identity national or religious?"[2] At the time Mehmet's book was published, most of Central Asia remained part of the Soviet Union, but within a year, five new states would appear in the region. Mehmet did not aim his penetrating analysis at this region, but many of the questions posed in his work continue to strongly resonate there. His observation that "the contemporary Islamic dilemma is . . . how to modernize Islam so that the Muslim world can come to terms with nationalism and its manifestation, the nation state" is also a dilemma faced by Central Asian societies and their governments, as identity landscapes evolve there.[3]

The notion of "landscape" is increasingly applied as a conceptual framework by cultural geographers, ethnographers, and other scholars. Indeed, the approach of articulating "culturescapes" and "ethnoscapes" has gained broad currency among cultural anthropologists and geographers seeking to identify the spatial parameters of identity.[4] Construction of "national" identities in Central Asia was initially stimulated in the early Soviet period via the development of national literary languages and the territorialization of the ethnic landscape, the latter process officially promoted as *razmezhevanie.*[5] This effort was later stultified in preference for the formation of a "Soviet identity" and the advancement of the *novoi sovetskii chelovek,* or "New Soviet Person." The ethnicities created would be "nationalist in form, but socialist in content" and ultimately, in theory, would meld into an overarching Soviet identity with primary loyalties to the state. The failure of Soviet identity policy and the emergence of sovereign, national states in the region has transformed the "identity landscape" in Central Asia, but this dynamic process has proven to be challenging, just as the related imperative of constructing a "civil society" has in most of the Central Asian countries been elusive.

Islam's role in crafting the identity landscape in Central Asia is multifaceted, as the political and social dimensions of the faith have historically varied between ethnic groups and continue to do so today between sovereign states. Uzbekistan and Tajikistan are considered the bastions of a "more Islamic" population, while Kazakhstan, Kyrgyzstan, and to a lesser degree Turkmenistan are viewed as "less Islamic" due to the "weaker" historical connections and lower level of devotion among the titular peoples in those states. This spatial variation provides the very fundament of the Islamic component of the identity landscape in Central Asia, a "topography" that became more defined as centralized authority from Moscow crumbled. There is no question that Islamic religiosity was becoming stronger, or at least more apparent, in the wake of Mikhail Gorbachev's social reform policy of glasnost.[6]

Civil Society and the Contours of Islamization

A clear understanding of what is meant by "civil society" is vital to conceptualizing its place in the social and political life of Central Asia. Peter Berger has recently argued that the term carries a certain duality, what he identifies as the "structural" elements of civil society, on the one hand, its "cultural" foundations, on the other. According to Berger, the latter are "institutions that are indeed *civil*—that is, institutions that mitigate conflict and foster social peace" (emphasis in the original).[7] He acknowledges that one of these "intermediate institutions," as he calls them, is potentially organized religion, although certainly not in all instances.[8] Moreover, in an age in which the social and political roles of Islam are frequently encapsulated in the discourse of conflict, articulated in terms such as "jihad," "Islamic militancy," and so on, there is evidence that the faith in some societies clearly contributes to the development of stable institutions and social harmony. Robert Hefner's work on Islam in Southeast Asia is compelling testimony on this point.[9]

Therefore, there is nothing "exceptional" or "contradictory" about the norms and functions of Islamic society that proscribe the emergence of relationships and social structures that would be recognized as belonging to civil society. Aziz Esmail submits that "what is true of the Muslim context is equally true of the religio-cultural and intellectual context of other societies, including those of the West, East and South Asia. The tendency to see Islam as a special case . . . is one of the ruling mystifications of today. If one opts to talk especially of the fate of civil society in Muslim states, it is for reasons of historical particularity. But particularity is not idiosyncrasy."[10]

The development of a territorialized identity conflated with the concept of the "nation" is closely associated with the structures of civil society. Edward Shils declared that, indeed, one is predicated on the other, holding that "nationality is a necessary ingredient, perhaps even precondition for civil society."[11] I have argued elsewhere that Islam serves as a cultural foundation for corporate identity in Central Asia, standing as the "framework for national identity."[12] This point, of course, is a reiteration of what Michael Rywkin described just prior to the Soviet collapse as the "national-religious symbiosis" in the region, and it remains a crucial precept for comprehending political and social evolution there.[13]

Yet Islam's status as a social component of identity in Central Asia remains poorly defined and inchoate. Since the emergence of the former Soviet states of the region (Kazakhstan, Uzbekistan, Kyrgyzstan, Tajikistan, and Turkmenistan), there has been a renewed interest within all five states in Islam and in their historical connection to the faith, to varying degrees. This can easily be measured in a physical sense by enumerating the number of structures and institutions constructed by either the indigenous governments or by external sponsors such as Saudi Arabia, Turkey, and Kuwait. Although concretely measurable, these tangible manifestations provide only a superficial and partial view of the emerging role of Islam in these societies and represent only the most obvious aspects of the Islamization of Central Asia. The social and political characteristics of Central Asian "Islam," and the process of inserting these into the corporate identity of Central Asian societies, both overtly and subliminally, carry great significance for the region's stability and integration into the greater global community. Islam has the potential to significantly affect trends in political stability, social development, and economic advancement across the region—indeed, it already has done so.

Religion's role in the formation of social and ethnic identity, and thereby obliquely of national identity, has been examined by scholars for some time. Some of the most influential social commentators of the nineteenth and early twentieth centuries, including Émile Durkheim, Sigmund Freud, Max Weber, and of course, Karl Marx, offered perspectives on religion's role in the formation of both individual and collective identity.

Durkheim argued in his seminal work on religion, *The Elementary Forms of the Religious Life,* that the basic epistemological structure of a society is rooted in its religious constructs.[14] That is to say, fundamental notions of space and time are crafted from a society's religious perspective. Identity is further defined and constrained by "rituals" and "totems" that invest the individual in a broader social context. Thus, for Durkheim, a society's religious characteristics are the very essence of its corporate functionality, a functionality that operates at a variety of levels, from the individual to the national. In an earlier work, Durkheim had proposed the existence of a "conscience collective" that contributes to order and civility in society, and this notion in regard to religion is rearticulated when he claims that "there can be no society which does not feel the need of upholding . . . the collective sentiments and the collective ideas which make its unity and personality; . . . hence come ceremonies which do not differ from regular religious ceremonies.[15]

Contemporary scholars will find in Durkheim's proposal on the social functionality of religion the nucleus of what is today identified as "social capital." Robert Wuthnow has made the case that religious institutions play an important role in the construction of social capital, an operative relationship that directly leads to the promotion of relationships and behavior conducive to a civil society.[16] Wuthnow's analysis of the role of religion is trained on the "revitalization" of Western structures of civil society, but it has broad application to Central Asia as well. In the aftermath of Soviet ideology, social structures there also require a form of "revitalization," since the imposition of Marxist-Leninist mores and social values disrupted the established order, but they in turn were jettisoned, leaving an ideological void that now represents a major obstacle to the formation of a civil society.

Weber, Freud, and Marx viewed religious sentiment as a kind of coping mechanism, which enabled the individual, and in aggregate, society as a whole, to philosophically deal with the injustices of life (Weber), construct a system to address "privation" and impose an order on one's existence (Freud), or rationalize economic exploitation (Marx). Marx drew little if any connection between group identity and religion, suggesting that religion's primary function was suppression of the proletariat, while Weber suggested that the place and influence of religion in society varied markedly as a function of social status, implying a diminished role for religious sentiment in the overall construction of national identity. Freud saw religious belief as a key to social order but also as the "universal obsessional neurosis of humanity."[17]

Many scholars writing in the second half of the twentieth century saw a closer linkage between religious identity, national identity, and at least indirectly, civil society. The late Clifford Geertz, for example, argued that the "sacred symbols" common to all faiths essentially generate an "ethos" that shapes a people's perception of their environment and intersocial relationships in terms of values, character, and order.[18] Geertz himself did not address the notion of corporate identity directly in his writings on religion, but his concept of "ethos" strikes very close to a definition of a collective worldview on which society is based—in other words, ethnic, and by extension, national identity and the constructs of civil society. Geertz was a leading proponent of the so-called primordialist school and in his later writings developed the notion of "assumed givens," a set of cultural characteristics that individuals are born into and that shape their conception of their surroundings—one of the primary "givens," according to Geertz, is religion.[19] Geertz in effect adopted the functionalist approach of Durkheim, albeit with considerable qualification.

A contemporary of Geertz, the sociologist Thomas O'Dea, offered that religious devotion in a society may well generate dysfunctional social forces but nevertheless noted that religion, "by showing the norms and rules of society to be part of a larger supraempirical ethical order, ordained and sanctified by religious belief, . . . contributes to their enforcement. . . . It sanctifies the norms of the established social order at . . . the 'breaking points.'"[20] O'Dea makes a trenchant point concerning the role of culture in defining "normative expectations" in society and the part religion has in shaping and directing the dimensions of culture. He revisits Durkheim's functionalism, contending that the approach conceives of "society as an ongoing equilibrium of social institutions which pattern human activity in terms of shared norms."[21] The "supraempirical ethical order" O'Dea describes is in fact a descriptor for the framework of a civil society.

A sizable body of work has emerged in recent years examining the nexus of identity and religion.[22] Anthony Smith in particular has been influential on this topic, arguing that "nationalists often found it necessary to appeal to the religious sentiments of the masses, . . . [and] identify the nation with the religious community."[23] Writing specifically about Islam, Ernest Gellner has suggested that Arab nationalism and reformist movements in modern Islam "can hardly be separated from each other," drawing a direct line between religion and identity at the national level, although Gellner's fundamental thesis is that modern nationalism is an outgrowth of industrialization and the Enlightenment, events that had only a marginal influence in the Muslim world.[24] Applied specifically to the case of Central Asia, the insights of Geertz, O'Dea, Gellner, and Wuthnow collectively suggest that the suppression of all unofficial Islamic activity as "fundamentalist" or "extremist" impairs the effort to forge a distinct identity. By creating the same totalitarian atmosphere toward Islam as held sway under the Soviet government, such an approach ensures that only the regime possesses the authority and expertise to differentiate between "good" and "bad" variants of the faith. Those who seek to include Islam as a crucial component of their identity run the risk of vilification and arrest under conditions where preservation of the "cultural heritage" is the constitutional duty of every citizen.[25]

Islamization, Identity, and Civil Society in Central Asia

The term "Islamization" is used here to connote the recovery of Central Asia's Islamic heritage, damaged but not eliminated under Soviet aegis. It does not imply a politicization of the faith, although this may be a component of the broader process.

Yet this should not be interpreted to mean that Islam in some respect universalizes identity in the region. Almost thirty years after Alexandre Bennigsen's famous formulation of a "supranational" level of identity, there appears to be little evidence that such identity functions any more effectively among Central Asian Muslims than it does among Muslims in the

Middle East or in other regions.[26] The failure of Islam to function as an element of a broader identity transcending national boundaries has not meant that the faith, at some level, has failed to be employed by every Central Asian regime in the process of national identity construction. Invoking the symbols and lexicon of Islam has frequently been a tactic of national leaders in the five Central Asian states, although of course, this has been undertaken selectively.

Before his death in December 2006, Saparmurat Niyazov, president of Turkmenistan, better known as Turkmenbashi, openly utilized the Islamic heritage of the Turkmen to solidify an incipient identity. In the introductory pages of his rambling tome *Ruhnama,* Niyazov consistently adjures the Turkmen nation to reclaim its heritage, a heritage in which the prophet Noah plays an oddly central part, along with other elements of Islamic iconography.[27] Indeed, Niyazov goes so far as to link the emergence of Turkmen independence directly to the will of God: "By the order of Allah the Most Exalted . . . in 1991, Turkmenistan became an independent state."[28] So that his readers do not miss the point, he restates the connection two pages later and credits the Almighty with providing not only Turkmenistan's physical abundance but also the mental acuity of the Turkmen people: "Allah the Almighty gave us limitless land and water. He gave us underground resources. He created our nation intelligent and able to judge their [*sic*] own conduct. In addition, *he gave us an independent Turkmen state*" (emphasis added).[29]

Nursultan Nazarbayev, the president of Kazakhstan, while forced to be more subtle and circumspect than Turkmenbashi due to the large non-Muslim population in his country, nevertheless has, at select times and places, engaged in the same identity-building tactics. Typically cautious in his public pronouncements and writings, Nazarbayev nevertheless on occasion has strongly endorsed the Islamic heritage of the Kazakh people. A prominent example of such endorsement may be encountered at the shrine of Ahmed Yasavi, in the city of Turkistan in southern Kazakhstan. Built by Amir Timur, the shrine is a place of pilgrimage not only for Kazakhs but for many devout Muslims from Uzbekistan and Tajikistan. Inside the entryway of a museum adjoining the shrine, a plaque prominently displays the following quotation from Kazakhstan's president: "We are a Muslim state, with the spirit of Islam; and we must not forget our holy book, the Koran." This passage appears only in Kazakh—no translation in Russian accompanies it.[30] This is a rare overt endorsement of Kazakhstan's

Islamic heritage by Nazarbayev, but the emphatic tone of the sentiment and its display at the most popular Islamic shrine in Kazakhstan run counter to the portrayal of the country as a completely "secular" state.[31]

Uzbekistan and Tajikistan are frequently considered the "most Islamic" countries in Central Asia, implying a greater depth of Islamic religiosity, and by extension Islamic identity, than among the traditionally nomadic Kazakhs, Turkmen, and Kyrgyz. Events in the region since 1991 appear to confirm this view, as do comparative statistics gathered in the early years of independence. For example, between January 1987 and January 1993, the number of Muslim religious organizations in Uzbekistan grew from ninety-four to more than one thousand, and those in Tajikistan from twenty-seven to three hundred.[32] These figures are far higher than those for the remaining three Central Asian states, indicating a stronger motivation to form new Islamic groups on the part of the Uzbeks and Tajiks, and most likely a higher level of devotion among them than among others in Central Asia.

Writing just before the collapse of Soviet administration, Muriel Atkin suggested that Islamic belief in Tajikistan was highly "localized" and that "many Tajiks have little interest in or knowledge of their own history."[33] Yet in the aftermath of Soviet collapse, Tajikistan was the only new state in Central Asia that witnessed the successful incorporation of an Islamic party into the country's national politics, albeit only after a bloody civil war. In addition, the alleged success of Soviet policy in eradicating Islamic identity may have been overestimated by Western scholars—a Soviet research team found in the late 1980s that in some regions of Tajikistan "the number of functioning underground mosques is roughly equal to the number that existed at the time of the Kokand khanate."[34]

Moreover, low public support for the Islamic Renaissance Party (IRP) in Tajikistan, indicated by polling that has shown in some instances that only around 5 percent of the public backs the party, should not be interpreted as a direct reflection of the depth of religiosity and identification with Islam in Tajik society.[35] While the IRP appears to have lost support in recent years, in the early years of Tajik independence the organization was seen as a viable and, for many Tajiks, a preferable alternative to former communist leaders: "The IRP also benefited from a politically inspired upsurge of religious ethno-nationalism. President Rakhmonov, though he enjoyed support from his native Kulyab region in the south, was perceived elsewhere in Tajikistan as a communist holdover and a puppet of Moscow.

Rakhmonov, in short, was the opposite of what many imagined national identity should encompass in post-Soviet Tajikistan. For many, supporting the IRP represented both a rejection of Rakhmonov and his Moscow handlers and an act of defining what it meant to be Tajik."[36]

Surveys appear to indicate that levels of religiosity in Tajikistan clearly are a function of age, with religious devotion increasing substantially with age. According to one study, more than two-thirds of people over the age of sixty-five pray five times a day in Tajik society, whereas 78 percent of youth between the ages of eighteen and twenty-four do not pray at all.[37] If it is true that historically in Tajikistan "religious identity was the main component of people's self-identity," then there is good reason to assume that in an independent Tajikistan, where identity at multiple levels in society is currently surfacing, Islam is a platform for such expression.[38] Observance of some Islamic rituals, such as Ramadan and Friday mosque attendance, is reportedly increasing.[39]

In fact, more recent survey data indicate that the Tajiks evince the highest level of Islamic religiosity in the post-Soviet space, with 97 percent self-identifying as Muslim: 87 percent consider themselves Sunni, 3 percent fall within the Shia community, and 7 percent prefer to self-identify as "just a Muslim." This stands in stark contrast to results obtained in other Central Asian countries. In Kazakhstan, Kyrgyzstan, and Uzbekistan a majority of respondents chose the "just a Muslim" category (74 percent, 64 percent, and 54 percent, respectively), although in Uzbekistan more than a quarter of those surveyed declined to respond (no data were reported for Turkmenistan).[40]

In Uzbekistan, President Islam Karimov, after independence, immediately attempted to bolster his Islamic credentials by making the hajj and publicly suggesting that he adhered to Islamic dietary requirements.[41] As some Western scholars have observed, Karimov recognized early on that Uzbek identity and Islam were "inextricably linked" and attempted to co-opt the Islamic heritage of his new state by using indirect references to that heritage.[42] Thus terminology such as "oltin meros" (golden heritage) and "manaviyet" (spirituality) were widely employed to craft an identity landscape that paid homage to Islam's role in Uzbekistan's past, but Karimov simultaneously attempted to avoid any politicization of the faith. An early encounter with the radicals of the group Adolat in the city of Namangan forced Karimov to recognize the potential of Islam as a political alternative to his autocratic rule, and since that time Karimov has tried to have it both ways: touting the Islamic underpinnings of *ozbekchilik* (Uzbekness) while maneuvering to secularize and monopolize the discourse concerning political dimensions of Uzbek Islam.[43]

The result of this approach has been to coin an exclusive, officially sanctioned lexicon when articulating Islam's place in guiding the civic and social identity relationships that continue to coalesce in Uzbekistan. President Karimov and his subordinates frequently speak of *musulmonchilik* (Muslimness) when discussing Uzbek spirituality, rather than referring to Islam per se. The preference for *musulmonchilik* as a religious identifier over Islam in public discourse is a central component of a strategy to deemphasize the external connections of Uzbek Islam with the remainder of the Islamic realm and its universal characteristics and instead portray the faith as holding specific "Uzbek" qualities. *Musulmonchilik*, therefore, functions "to give expression to the view that Uzbek 'Muslimness' is not Islam as such; rather it is inextricably bound up with national customs, norms and values."[44] Moreover, this theme of "Uzbek exceptionalism," as it were, seems to be embedded in the cultural identity of many in the Uzbek elite, who compartmentalize various qualities of their identity into the "particular," on the one hand, and the "universal," on the other.[45]

One of the effects of this strategy apparently has been to maintain an unparalleled ignorance among the Uzbek population about the basic characteristics of Islam, more than twenty years after independence from the Soviet Union. In response to the question "Are Sunnis Muslims?" an astounding 72 percent of those surveyed in Uzbekistan had not heard of Sunnis or did not know.[46] When asked if Sufis qualify as Muslims, 79 percent were either unfamiliar with the term "Sufi" or did not know.[47] This is an astonishing figure, given that the *mazar* (tomb) of Baha al-din Naqshband, founder of one of the largest Sufi orders in the Islamic world, is located near Bukhara, and during the Soviet era many Muslims in Uzbekistan made pilgrimage there, when making the hajj was prohibited for all but a select few.

The strategy to promote a concept of exclusive Uzbek "Muslimness" stands in sharp contrast to the regime's efforts to marginalize any unsanctioned manifestation of Islamic identity that has emerged in the post-Soviet era. For the past twenty years, any organized expression of Islam falling outside the strict control of the state has been swiftly crushed.[48] Moderate Islamic organizations like the IRP have been disrupted and decapitated, effectively removing them from the political arena.[49] Repression has radicalized a small percentage of the population, but a more pernicious effect may be the erosion of public perception of the benefits of investment in Western social norms, that is, civil society, for Uzbekistan.[50]

The *Mahalla*: An Islamic Civic Institution

In Uzbekistan and Tajikistan in particular, the institution of the *mahalla* (neighborhood association) has historically played a vital part in melding civic functions and duty with Islamic identity. As Johan Rasanayagam has recently noted, the *mahalla* serves as an "institution of social organization" as well as the foundation for a "moral community."[51] The *mahalla* functions as a social safety net and inculcates a moral code, rooted in Islamic principles, into young people who live in the neighborhood. A youth who has trouble with the law is typically called before the *aksakalar*, or elders, and advised or admonished to mend his ways. Frequently the elders will intercede with the authorities on behalf of the transgressor, with the understanding that he will be closely monitored and expected to avoid trouble in the future. The *mahalla* committee will also collect money to assist widows and orphans in the community, help poorer families pay for funerals and other rituals, and distribute food to those who are in need.

Linkages between the *mahalla* as a socializing institution and Islamic values and practices have existed in the urban areas of Central Asia for centuries. Prior to the Soviet era, the status of *aksakal* (literally, "white beard"), the civic leader of the *mahalla*, was often conferred via the good offices of the local mullah, and the *aksakal* was expected to oversee the performance of religious rituals and life ceremonies in coordination with the mullah.[52] Moreover, social norms governing public and private behavior, rooted in the precepts of Islamic scripture and tradition, were inculcated through both formal and informal structures operating within the broader organization of the *mahalla*.[53] In the context of society in pre-Soviet Central Asia, therefore, the *mahalla* served to channel and maintain standard Islamic values and conduct among its residents, resulting in a civic platform for local conflict resolution, counseling and guidance of youth, financial and moral support for those in need, and other services and functions associated with more current notions of civil society.

The geographical and social proximity offered by the *mahalla* plays a key part in reinforcing traditional familial and clan ties, which are frequently maintained and expanded through the structure of the *mahalla* itself. The *mahalla,* as a social institution, then emerges as a component of personal identity for many. For example, arranged marriages, still the norm among Uzbeks, may occur between young people living in the same *mahalla,* resulting in extended family structures and social networks. Donald Carlisle, writing about the function of the *mahalla* under Soviet control, has observed that such connections were the "keystones of identity" and the loyalties an individual developed through the local framework of the *mahalla* superseded those offered to the higher authority of the state, although other scholars have argued that the *mahalla* system was co-opted under Soviet authority and in fact became an instrument to circulate and enforce social and political policies.[54]

Since the late 1990s, Uzbekistani authorities have utilized the *mahalla* system to monitor the activities of society on the local level, a practice that may be undermining its role as an informal civic institution. In 1999 the Uzbek government enacted the so-called Mahalla Law, which assigned extensive duties of social monitoring to the *mahalla* committees. An ancillary to this statute was the establishment of the *posbon* system, designed to increase the powers of the state to penetrate and police activities occurring within the *mahallas.* The *posbons* are minders assigned to the *mahalla* who gather intelligence on the residents from the *mahalla* committee and other sources and report any "suspicious" individuals to the local police.[55] The *mahalla* committees appear to be directly controlled by the local *hakimiyat,* or city government, and thus have become co-opted as extensions of the state security system.

The establishment of state control over the *mahallas* and their conversion into extensions of the pervasive security structure in Uzbekistan have likely undermined the role of the *mahalla* in civil society. Traditionally the *mahalla* functioned outside of official power structures—miscreants and the wayward were brought to heel via the admonitions of the elders and peer pressure from other residents, since any member of the group who deviated from the accepted norms of civil behavior reflected badly on the *mahalla* as a whole. As the *mahalla* committee has become an arm of the NSB, the Uzbek security agency, this role has been removed and the implicit trust between the elders and the members of the *mahalla* has eroded. The *mahalla* is a traditional expression of civil society among urbanized Central Asians, but its absorption into the state apparatus weakens its potential as an instrument for the advancement of civil society, as the distinction between formal state structures and informal societal institutions becomes increasingly blurred.

The Role of Islam

The widespread failure in Central Asia to construct the necessary framework for civil society, promote pluralistic political systems, and build stable, expanding economies has indeed allowed for the establishment of Islamic extremism among some disaffected elements of society. Yet radical Islamic ideologies, after more than fifteen years of incubation, remain the refuge of a minute percentage of the region's population, and no serious observer of the political and social environment there would support the proposition that a mass movement rooted in radical Islam is an imminent development in any of the Central Asian states or that such a political shift is likely in the foreseeable future.

Moreover, in some instances it appears Islam may serve to build civic bridges between various ethnic groups, especially in regions that have witnessed an increase in ethnic tensions since the collapse of the USSR. Some Central Asian scholars have recently noted that in the Fergana Valley Islam provides a common basis of identity in the absence of a unified ethno-national identity. They hold that the ethnic animosities that erupted in southern Kyrgyzstan in 1990 and 2010, and that occasionally burst to the surface in other corners of the Fergana Valley, may be ameliorated by emphasizing the common Islamic values of these groups. Thus Islamic religiosity projects a sense of shared identity that may reduce social cleavages induced by ethnic, regional, or clan distinctions: "By affirming a religious identity these Uzbeks in Kyrgyzstan can find common ground with the Kyrgyz on a more universal level. In both cases the ethnic minority embraces religion rather than ethnicity or nationality as the core of its identity. The same can be observed among Tajik ethnics in the Uzbek part of the Fergana Valley, where the Tajiks identify themselves in terms of religion rather than ethnicity or nationality."[56]

It should be stressed that the discussion here is directed at Central Asian Islam's *potential* for promoting cross-ethnic bonds and increasing social stability and civility. To date, the faith has fulfilled this role to only a quite limited extent, possibly due to a dearth of qualified Islamic leaders who stand outside the state-sponsored and controlled hierarchy.[57] The repression of moderate, independent Islamic groups since independence by some of the local regimes has also eviscerated the broader impact of a common Islamic culture, even if that culture is seen differently to some degree by the region's various peoples. Yet even in the wake of the horrific violence between Kyrgyz and Uzbeks in southern Kyrgyzstan in the spring of 2010, Islamic organizations have rapidly emerged that seek to tighten social bonds by harnessing the common Muslim heritage of the combatants. Adep Bashati is a charitable society in Kyrgyzstan that promotes Islamic values and education, sponsors a small group for the hajj, and derives its funding entirely from local donations. The group has a presence in all of Kyrgyzstan's oblasts, welcomes students from all ethnic groups to its madrassas, and promotes interethnic harmony and cooperation.[58]

Central Asian society is unlike any other in the Islamic realm. Seventy years of repressive secularization under the Soviet regime, a century and a half of social integration and sustained close contact with non-Islamic populations, and relatively high levels of education and literacy among the population have seriously undermined the attractiveness of the antimodern, anti-Western rhetoric that lies at the heart of radical Islamic philosophy. Large swaths of the indigenous Central Asian population not only tolerate the behaviors of "infidels," many of whom still live among them, but in many cases they have adopted such behaviors themselves. This is most apparent in Kazakhstan, but even in Tajikistan, arguably the most "Islamic" and traditional of the post-Soviet states in Central Asia and the one with the smallest Russian population, the urbanized elite and their children continue to be heavily influenced by cultural values and mores firmly anchored in Western civilization.

Not only does the cultural influence of Russian/Soviet colonization of Central Asia inhibit the rise of Islamic extremism, but the historical character of Islam and society in the region also presents a barrier. A deeply embedded tradition of tolerance of other faiths and variants of Islam is the result of the centuries-old influence of Sufism. Some *tariqa*, or Sufi orders, actually were founded in Central Asia itself, such as the Naqshbandi, a sect established in the 1300s. Sufism continues to exert a strong influence on Muslims in the region and serves as a counterweight to the rigid doctrines of Wahabism, Salafism, and other fundamentalist movements founded outside the region. Indeed, the doctrines of Sufism have enjoyed a significant revival among many Uzbeks in recent years, a development the Karimov regime has encouraged. The increased interest in moderate Islam has been largely ignored by policy makers and pundits in the West, who tend to focus on the "rise of fundamentalism" and associated acts of insurgency perpetrated by small, but violent, fringe groups.

Moreover, many of the Kazakhs and Kyrgyz were not converted to Islam until the eighteenth century, and "fundamentalist" movements have never gained traction among those peoples. Chokhan Valikhanov, one of Kazakhstan's literati and a national hero, wrote in the 1860s that Islam had failed to "enter the flesh and blood" of his people, an observation still accurate today. Central Asia's urban centers along the old Silk Road have represented a strong cosmopolitan environment for two thousand years, and communities of Jews, Hindus, and other religious groups have lived peacefully among Muslims there for centuries. In contemporary Kazakhstan, the more tolerant and inclusive policies of the Nazarbayev government have allowed independent organizations such as Ak orda (the White Horde) to incorporate elements of Islam into a broader context of Kazakh identity, a policy that appears to have been fruitful in establishing the parameters of a nascent civil society.[59]

Islamization and Civil Society

Policy regarding Islam in Central Asia must be framed in the context of the region's recent history. This history is unique in regard to Islam. Central Asia is the only Islamic region where the colonial policy was to forcefully *eradicate* Islam as a cultural influence. Colonial powers at times attempted to limit or control the political reach of the Islamic faith, but only the Soviets sought to, at least in theory, completely degrade the religious landscape and replace it with a countervailing ideology. This effort at cultural reengineering obviously failed in its larger goal, but it was successful at splitting Central Asian Muslims away from the larger Islamic realm. With the collapse of that barrier in the early 1990s, many in the region looked to recapture the Islamic elements of their identity.

Therefore, the "rise of Islamization" in Central Asia over the last decade and a half stems from completely different historical circumstances than those of the Middle East, South Asia, and elsewhere in the Muslim world. For the vast majority of Muslims in Central Asia, rediscovering their religious heritage does not equate to a jihad against the West; due to cultural imperialism and the replacement of traditional Islamic values, many Central Asians are unclear about what those values actually are. Rather, the larger process that has been occurring in Central Asia since 1991 is the reconstruction, both figuratively and literally, of the Islamic landscape.

The political environment of the region must be assessed accurately in order to shape consistent and viable policy. Some commentators on social policy in Central Asia have suggested that the repressive character of some of the governments in the region is a response to the destabilizing effect of Islamic radicalism. In fact, it has been the brutality of regimes themselves, especially in Uzbekistan and Turkmenistan, that has raised the level of violence. The Karimov administration violently broke up meetings of both religious and secular opposition movements in the early 1990s, driving some potential rivals into exile as well as arresting and imprisoning Islamic leaders who strayed from the official line on Islam's role in Uzbek society. The political violence that has periodically swept Uzbekistan since the late 1990s is the outgrowth of President Karimov's refusal to build a pluralistic, civil society.[60]

In geopolitical terms, the Karimov regime has successfully utilized the acts of terrorism and insurgency it engendered to magnify the potential for a "fundamentalist" takeover and subsequent destabilization of the entire region. This in turn drew financial and military support from both Washington and Moscow, while at the same time muting criticism of the regime's internal policies and tactics. Uzbekistan's close relationship with the United States as an ally in the "war on terror" crumbled only in the wake of the brutal massacre of civilians in the city of Andijan in 2005.[61]

Yet the Uzbek regime's response in the face of global condemnation in the months following the so-called Andijan events was to label the demonstrators its troops had cut down as "extremists" and the members of Akromiya they had rallied behind as "terrorists." In a defiant monograph published in the summer of 2005, President Karimov implied that Hizb ut-Tahrir and other radical groups were behind the demonstrations in Andijan and had in fact initiated the violence there. The development of a democratic society, he held, could not tolerate such "extremist religious trends," but paradoxically he suggested as well that democracy represented the cure to the "drug" of Islamic extremism.[62] What the regime has consistently failed to comprehend and accept since independence is that an Islamic identity landscape cannot be partially constructed; the recovery of that landscape will necessarily encompass its share of political features. For Uzbekistan's government, all such features represent potential challenges and therefore are the work of "extremists," leading to an institutional "urge to control," as noted by one seasoned observer of religious policy in the region.[63] Recent limited signs of accommodation and moderation in the regime's policy toward Islamic believers can be taken as meaningful only if they are followed by sweeping reforms in the legal code and by lifting of the legal strictures enacted since 1991.[64]

The implementation of civil society in the new states of Central Asia cannot proceed without the incorporation of Islam, which has operated as a socializing substrate in the region for centuries. To a significant degree, the faith is already serving in this capacity. A recent survey conducted in Tajikistan discovered that *85 percent* of those questioned stated that Islam is "an important part of their lives," a manifestation of O'Dea's "supraempirical ethical order."[65] In addition to foundations like Adep Bashati in Kyrgyzstan, there are other groups that welcome Muslims from all ethnic groups, eschew a political agenda, and perform humanitarian, educational, and philanthropic services. The Fethullah Gulen Movement, a Turkish Sufi organization emphasizing humanitarian and ecumenical cooperation in the Islamic world, also has a presence in the region but its activities have been curtailed in Uzbekistan and Turkmenistan, while Tablighi Jamaat has been repressed in those states as well as in Tajikistan.[66] In order for civil society to flourish in Central Asia, moderate Islamic groups must be allowed to build the very social structures that provide the foundation for interaction, peaceful coexistence, toleration, and pluralism. Policy makers seeking to bolster this effort must develop and promote strategies that recognize that the reintegration of Islamic standards into the behavioral fabric of Central Asian societies is not necessarily anti-Western and indeed may be crucial to the processes of conflict management and stability in the region's multiethnic social environment.

Notes

1. Ozay Mehmet, *Islamic Identity and Development: Studies of the Islamic Periphery* (London: Routledge, 1990), 9. For Mehmet, the "Islamic periphery" is mostly Turkey and Malaysia.

2. Ibid.

3. Ibid, 10.

4. Some recent examples include Daniel Trudeau, "Politics of Belonging in the Construction of Landscapes: Place-Making, Boundary-Drawing and Exclusion," *Cultural Geographies* 13 (2006): 421–43; Amy Mills, "Boundaries of the Nation in the Space of the Urban: Landscape and Social Memory in Istanbul,"

Cultural Geographies 13 (2006): 367–94; Conrad Schetter, "Ethnoscapes, National Territorialization, and the Afghan War," *Geopolitics* 10 (2005): 50–75.

5. There are other variables in the formation of identity, of course, and I am not suggesting that the elements identified are the exclusive components of that process, only that these were, and in some cases still are, major influences. Issues such as linguistic identity were dealt with in all the Central Asian countries very early on and have now been accepted and incorporated to a large degree, thereby reducing their role in shaping the new identity "landscape."

6. By the late 1980s, the Central Asian media were offering almost daily reports on the growing influence of Islam in Central Asian society. For one example, see M. Alimov, "Otkuda Onï, Pokornye?—Pochemu tak ustoichivo vliyanie islama v zhizni mnogikh molodykh lyudei" [Where do they come from, the disciples? Why the influence of Islam is so strong in the lives of many young people], *Komsomolskaia Pravda,* March 20, 1988.

7. Peter Berger, "Religion and Global Society," in *Religion in Global Society,* ed. Mark Juergensmeyer (New York: Oxford University Press, 2005), 12.

8. Ibid., 13.

9. See Robert Hefner, *Civil Islam: Muslims and Democratization in Indonesia* (Princeton, NJ: Princeton University Press, 2000).

10. Aziz Esmail, "Self, Society, Civility and Islam," in *Civil Society in the Muslim World: Contemporary Perspectives,* ed. Amyn B. Sajoo (London: I. B. Tauris, 2004), 70.

11. Edward Shils, "Nation, Nationality, Nationalism and Civil Society," *Nations and Nationalism* 1, no. 1 (1995): 116.

12. Reuel Hanks, "Civil Society and Identity in Uzbekistan: The Emergent Role of Islam," in *Civil Society in Central Asia,* ed. M. Holt Ruffin and Daniel Waugh (Seattle: University of Washington Press, 1999), 160.

13. Michael Rywkin, *Moscow's Muslim Challenge,* rev. ed. (Armonk, NY: M. E. Sharpe, 1990), 87.

14. Émile Durkheim, *The Elementary Forms of the Religious Life* (London: Allen and Unwin, 1915).

15. Émile Durkheim, *The Division of Labour in Society* (New York: Free Press, 1964), 291; Durkheim, *Elementary Forms of the Religious Life,* 475.

16. Robert Wuthnow, "Can Religion Revitalize Civil Society? An Institutional Perspective," in *Religion as Social Capital: Producing the Common Good,* ed. Corwin Smidt (Waco, TX: Baylor University Press, 2003).

17. Sigmund Freud, *The Future of an Illusion* (London: Hogarth Press, 1928).

18. Clifford Geertz, "Religion as a Cultural System," in *Anthropological Approaches to the Study of Religion,* ed. M. Banton (London: Tavistock, 1966).

19. Clifford Geertz, "Primordial Ties," in *Ethnicity,* ed. Anthony D. Smith (New York: Oxford University Press, 1996).

20. Thomas O'Dea, *The Sociology of Religion* (Englewood Cliffs, NJ: Prentice Hall, 1966), 6–7.

21. Ibid., 2.

22. See, for example, Harold R. Isaacs, *Idols of the Tribe: Group Identity and Political Change* (Cambridge, MA: Harvard University Press, 1989); Ernest Gellner, *Nations and Nationalism* (Ithaca, NY: Cornell University Press, 1983); Ernest Gellner, *Culture, Identity and Politics* (Cambridge: Cambridge University Press, 1987); Anthony D. Smith, *The Ethnic Origins of Nations* (New York: Basil and Blackwell, 1987); Anthony D. Smith, *National Identity* (Reno: University of Nevada Press, 1993); Mark Juergensmeyer, *The New Cold War? Religious Nationalism Confronts the Secular State* (Berkeley: University of California Press, 1993); Tamara Sonn, "Phases of Political Islam," in *Religious Fundamentalism in the Contemporary World: Critical Social and Political Issues,* ed. Santosh C. Saha (Lanham, MD: Lexington Books, 2004).

23. Smith, *National Identity.*

24. Gellner, *Nations and Nationalism,* 41.

25. This civic requirement may be found in the constitution of Uzbekistan.

26. Alexandre Bennigsen, "Several Nations or One People? Ethnic Consciousness among Soviet Central Asian Muslims," *Survey,* no. 108 (1979): 51–64.

27. Saparmurat Turkmenbashi, *Ruhnama* (Ashgabat, Turkmenistan, 2005).

28. Ibid, 14.

29. Ibid, 16.

30. The author possesses a photograph of the plaque, taken in April 2005.

31. Kazakhstan's constitution carefully excludes any mention of Islam or an Islamic heritage.

32. See the table in Igor Ermakov and Dmitrii Mikul'skii, *Islam v Rossii i srednei azii* (Moscow: Lotos, 1993), 31.

33. Muriel Atkin, "Religious, National and Other Identities in Central Asia," in *Muslim in Central Asia: Expressions of Identity and Change,* ed. Jo-Ann Gross (Durham, NC: Duke University Press, 1992), 62.

34. Sergei Poliakov, *Everyday Islam: Religion and Tradition in Rural Central Asia,* ed. Martha Brill Olcott (Armonk, NY: M. E. Sharpe, 1992), 96.

35. M. Olimov and S. Olimov, "Dannie oprosa po politicheskoy siseme, provedennogo informatsionno analiticheskim tsentrom 'Shark' v yanvare," *Vestnik blagotvorritelnosti,* no. 7 (1999).

36. Eric McGlinchey, "Autocrats, Islamists, and the Rise of Radicalism in Central Asia," *Current History,* October 2005, 338.

37. Steven Wagner, *Public Opinion in Tajikistan, 1996* (Washington, D.C.: International Foundation for Electoral Systems, 1997).

38. Saodat Olimova, "Political Islam and Conflict in Tajikistan," Deutsche Gesellschaft fur Auswartige Politik, www.weltpolitik.net.

39. Colette Harris, *Muslim Youth: Tensions and Transitions in Tajikistan* (Boulder, CO: Westview Press, 2006), 16.

40. James Bell et al., *The World's Muslims: Unity and Diversity* (Washington, D.C.: Pew Research Center, August 9, 2012), 30, http://www.pewforum.org/2012/08/09/the-worlds-muslims-unity-and-diversity-executive-summary/.

41. Meryem Kirimli, "Uzbekistan and the New World Order," *Central Asian Survey* 16, no. 1 (1997): 58.

42. Tom Everett-Heath, "Instability and Identity in a Post-Soviet World: Kazakhstan and Uzbekistan," in *Central Asia: Aspects of Transition,* ed. Tom Everett-Heath (London: RoutledgeCurzon, 2003), 193.

43. Adolat ("justice" in Uzbek) had established, by some accounts, a kind of shadow government in Namangan. Two of the leaders of the organization were Tahir Yuldash and Juma Namangani, both of whom would eventually become terrorists with the Islamic Movement of Uzbekistan, linked to Al Qaida and the Taliban.

44. Krisztina Kehl-Bodrogi, *"Religion Is Not So Strong Here": Muslim Religious Life in Khorezm after Socialism,* Halle Studies in the Anthropology of Eurasia (Piscataway, NJ: Transaction, 2008), 85.

45. Laura Adams, *The Spectacular State: Culture and National Identity in Uzbekistan* (Durham, NC: Duke University Press, 2010), 66.

46. Bell et al., *World's Muslims,* 87.

47. Ibid, 91.

48. The repression of Islam by the Karimov regime has been well documented by several international organizations and led the Commission on Security and Cooperation in Europe to state that "Uzbekistan had declared war on its own citizenry." See Commission on Security and Cooperation in Europe, *Human Rights and Democratization in Uzbekistan and Turkmenistan* (Washington, D.C.: March 2000), 3; *Central Asia: Islamist Mobilization and Regional Security,* ICG Asia Report no. 14 (March 1, 2001); and Bureau of Democracy, Human Rights, and Labor, U.S. Department of State, *Uzbekistan Country Report on Human Rights Practices for 1998* (Washington, D.C.: February 26, 1999).

49. Abdullah Utaev and Abduwali Mirzaev, the founders of the IRP in Uzbekistan, have gone underground or disappeared after arrest by the Uzbek authorities. Utaev was arrested in 1992, well before any violence connected to Islamic radicals occurred in Uzbekistan, and subsequently vanished while in detention. A number of other Islamic leaders fled the country or were arrested during the late 1990s.

50. John R. Pottenger, "Civil Society, Religious Freedom, and Islam Karimov: Uzbekistan's Struggle for a Decent Society," *Central Asian Survey* 23, no. 1 (2004): 72.

51. Johan Rasanayagam, *Islam in Post-Soviet Uzbekistan: The Morality of Experience* (New York: Cambridge University Press, 2011), 49.

52. Paul Georg Geiss, "Mahallah and Kinship Relations: A Study on Residential Communal Commitment Structures in Central Asia of the 19th Century," *Central Asian Survey* 20, no. 1 (2001): 98–99.

53. Sabine Freizer, "Central Asian Fragmented Society: Communal and Neoliberal Forms in Tajikistan and Uzbekistan," in *Exploring Civil Society: Political and Cultural Contexts,* ed. Marlies Glasius, David Lewis, and Hakan Seckinelgin (London: Routledge, 2004), 116–17.

54. Donald Carlisle, "Uzbekistan and the Uzbeks," *Problems of Communism* 40, no. 5 (1991): 30. See John Schoeberlein-Engel, "Identity in Central Asia: Construction and Contention in the Conceptions of 'Uzbek,' 'Tajik,' 'Muslim,' 'Samarqandi,' and Other Groups" (PhD diss., Harvard University, 1994).

55. "From House to House: Abuses by Mahalla Committees," *Human Rights Watch* 15, no. 7(D) (September 2003): 7–11.

56. Pulat Shozimov, Joomart Sulaimanov, and Shamshad Abdullaev, "Culture in the Ferghana Valley since 1991: The Issue of Identity," in *Ferghana Valley: The Heart of Central Asia,* ed. S. Frederick Starr (Armonk, NY: M. E. Sharpe, 2011), 287.

57. Shirin Akiner, "Prospects for Civil Society in Tajikistan," in Sajoo, *Civil Society in the Muslim World,* 167.

58. Bruno De Cordier, "Kyrgyzstan: Fledgling Islamic Charity Reflects Growing Role for Religion," December 8, 2010, EurasiaNet.org.

59. Charles E. Ziegler, "Civil Society, Political Stability and State Power in Central Asia: Cooperation and Contestation," *Democratization* 17, no. 5 (2010): 814.

60. See B. Babadzhanov, "Islam in Uzbekistan: From the Struggle for 'Religious Purity' to Political Activism," in *Central Asia: A Gathering Storm?,* ed. Boris Rumer (Armonk, NY: M. E. Sharpe, 2002); Petra Steinberger, "Fundamentalism in Central Asia: Reasons, Reality and Prospects," in Everett-Heath, *Central Asia.*

61. Several international agencies issued reports on the so-called Andijan events. The OCSE produced one of the first accounts on the shootings just over a month afterward, based on interviews with refugees who had fled to Kyrgyzstan. Human Rights Watch, Amnesty International and the International Crisis Group also released findings. The OCSE document is "Preliminary Findings on the Events in Andijan, Uzbekistan, 13 May 2005," June 20, 2005, http://www.osce.org/odihr/15653.

62. Islam Karimov, *Uzbekskii narod nikogda i ni ot kogo ne budet zaviset'* (Tashkent: "Uzbekiston," 2005), 40, 63.

63. John Anderson, "Social, Political, and Institutional Constraints on Religious Pluralism in Central Asia," *Journal of Contemporary Religion* 17, no. 2 (2002): 188.

64. The Uzbek government, according to some reports, in 2011 relaxed restrictions on believers during the observance of Ramadan. See "Uzbekistan: Warily, Muslims Welcome Softer State Stance on Ramadan," EurasiaNet, August 31, 2011, http://www.eurasianet.org/node/64109.

65. Kayumars Ato, "Tajiks Increasingly Turning to Sharia to Resolve Disputes, Family Affairs," September 12, 2010, EurasiaNet.org.

66. Because of its origins in the Deobandist movement, some claim Tablighi Jamaat is "radical," but there is little evidence that it promotes violence or seeks to politicize its activities. The followers of Fethullah Gulen are sometimes called the Nurcu movement in the Western media and in Central Asia.

3

Islamic Revival and Civil Society in Kazakhstan

Dilshod Achilov

Whereas studies of compatibility between Islam and democracy have received wide scholarly attention, little research addresses the issue of rising effects of Islamic revival on civil society. Average public opinion in the Muslim world seems to support the increased role of religion in political life.[1] As civic involvement, social capital, and elite-challenging collective actions establish the core pillars of civil society, which is an important social force to foster and sustain democratization, the Islamic revival continues to play a central role in transforming the dynamics of sociopolitical landscapes in the Islamic world. Academic scholars and political pundits often link the development, maturity, and sustainability of a strong civil society to a democratization process.[2] How, if at all, does Islam help shape the formation of civil society? This chapter examines the role of Islamic revival in shaping the state of civil society in post-Soviet Kazakhstan. In the context of the present case study, I define Islamic revival as the systematically increasing resurgence of and return to Islamic values, practices, and orientations.

With its vast oil and gas reserves, rich natural resources, and rising geopolitical and economic influence, the Republic of Kazakhstan has emerged as a major regional power in Central Asia since its independence in 1991. Strategically located in the heart of Eurasia, it is one of the wealthiest and fastest-growing republics in the post-Soviet space. Kazakhstan is a highly secular society with a multiethnic population. Although Islam is not the only determinant of Kazakh national identity owing to the republic's long-held secular traditions, Islamic teachings have historically shaped Kazakh social values and national customary laws (i.e., Adat).

Although ethnic Kazakhs embraced Islam as a primary distinction of national identity after independence from the USSR, the return to Islamic values by the average ethnic Kazakh citizen was not realized in the form of a sudden and rapid return to a devout Islamic way of life. Rather, Islam's influence on Kazakh identity politics was gradual and complex in nature. One prevailing explanation is that the surge in Islamic orientations is linked to an increased sense of Kazakh nationalism as a titular ethnic group within a multiethnic society.[3] According to Sébastien Peyrouse, the new Central Asian states have seized their "religious identity in order to turn it into an element of national assertion as well as social bases of political power."[4] On the premise that Islam offered a national sense of being Muslim by attaching a religious *distinction* that separates Kazakhs from ethnic Russians, Islamic revival has also been linked to the rise of nationalistic identities mainly emphasized by Central Asian elites.[5] Analyzing Muslim attitudes in Kyrgyzstan, Eric McGlinchey found that Islamic revivalism shaped citizens' identity as a reaction to the autocratic rule and failed policies of central governments.[6] Drawing on extensive field research, Azade-Ayse Rorlich writes that what "we are witnessing in Kazakhstan is the unfolding of the process of 're-Islamization' of its eponymous population as one of the answers to the quest for the empowerment and reconstitution of Kazakh society in the post Soviet era."[7] Overall, the underlying scholarly consensus seems to confirm the increasing levels of Islamic revival, with important political implications in Central Asia. With this in mind, it is imperative not to exclude the impact of Islamic revivalism on the analysis of the determinants of emerging Kazakh civil society.

This chapter examines the interaction between Islam and emerging civil society in the Republic of Kazakhstan through institutional analysis of Islam in practice. More precisely, to scrutinize the role of Islam (and Islamic revival), I systematically analyze Islamic *educational, financial,* and *political* institutions to investigate the extent to which Islamic institutions contribute to the formation of civil society in Kazakhstan. The evidence suggests that the inclusionist policies of the incumbent regime with respect to emerging Islamic educational and financial institutions seem to encourage the development and representation of moderate Islam's voice, and Islamic social capital, within emerging Kazakh civil society.

Generally, various social and political Islamic groups operating in the

Muslim (and non-Muslim) world can be categorized as either *moderates* or *radicals*. In defining these two types, I rely on Mohammed Hafez's conceptualization of *moderates* as "individuals and groups that shun violence and insurgency as a strategy to effect social change and, instead, seek to work through state institutions, civic associations, or nonviolent organizations" and, by contrast, *radicals* as actors who "reject accommodation with the state regime, refuse to participate in its institutions, and insist on the necessity of violent revolution or mass mobilization to Islamize society and politics."[8] The representation of moderate Islam, I find, will be an essential institutional component of Kazakh civil society in terms of advancing transparency and social bridging and alleviating barriers to self-expression of Islam in society by allowing citizens to freely participate in various voluntary social, financial, and political associations.

My analysis is organized in four parts. First, I will explore the patterns of Islamic revival in the post-Soviet era. Second, I will review the theoretical explanations of Islamic revivalism and civil society. Next, I will explore the variation of Islam in practice in the context of emerging Islamic educational, financial, and political institutions. Finally, I will discuss the emerging patterns that link Islamic revival and rapidly evolving civil society dynamics in Kazakhstan.

Islamic Heritage

Ethnic Kazakh is the largest titular ethnic group in a diverse, multiethnic society. Islam is the primary religion, followed by Orthodox Christianity, which is practiced mainly by Russians. Although ethnic Kazakhs represent 60 percent of the population and ethnic Russians 24 percent, there is a rich array of other ethnic groups, including Uzbeks, Tatars, Bashkirs, Uighurs, and Ukrainians.[9] Having a diverse, multiethnic population makes Kazakhstan unique among Central Asian states, and the republic offers an important opportunity for examining the parallel development between Islamic institutions and civil society. Moreover, Kazakhstan is a revealing case because of its unique context in the Islamic world: a newly independent, transitional state with a distinct secular background and one that is experiencing Islamic resurgence.

Islam reached western Central Asia in the late ninth century. The roots of Islam as the main religion, along with early Islamic institutions, were strengthened by the Karakhanid rule in Central Asia during the eleventh and twelfth centuries. Distinct from other Central Asian peoples, Kazakhs embraced Islam significantly later. It was not until the late nineteenth century that Islam reached the vast Kazakh territory. Islam developed deeper historical roots in non-nomadic Tajik and Uzbek populations in comparison to nomadic Kyrgyz, Turkmen, and Kazakh tribes.[10] These differences remain today. Since the Kazakh, Kyrgyz, and Turkmen tribes maintained their nomadic way of life significantly longer than other ethnic groups in Central Asia, Islam did not spread among them in an institutional (mosque-centered) manner.[11]

During the Soviet period, the communist regime actively sought to restrict Islam by cracking down on the practicing Muslim population because of their potential for organized opposition against Soviet ideology, given that the first anti-Soviet struggles came from the local militia insurgent fighters (for independence) in the early 1920s.[12] At the core, the ideology of Islam was in direct conflict with Soviet Marxist-Leninist teachings. As a result, most of Central Asia's mosques and traditional Islamic schools (e.g., madrassas) were uprooted in the 1940s by the repressive policies of Joseph Stalin.

In 1943 the Soviet regime established the Spiritual Board of Central Asian Muslims (SADUM) in Tashkent, Uzbekistan, in order to maintain its tight control over religious affairs in the region. SADUM cadres were appointed by the Soviet regime as the board became the official state-approved governing agency of the Islamic faith for all of Central Asia. This Soviet government–sponsored agency would later be known as "official Islam" or "government-sponsored Islam."[13] As planned, SADUM worked in full collaboration with Moscow and did not challenge the Soviet ideology. Almost the entire staff of SADUM was composed of Uzbek clergy, who dominated the religious affairs of Kazakhstan and other Central Asian countries. This in turn impeded the emergence of ethnic Kazakh Islamic scholars for years to come.[14]

As Islam was repressed and numerous Islamic social institutions (e.g., mosques) were uprooted under the auspices of promoting secular communist ideology in Central Asia, a spiritual vacuum was opened for subsequent Kazakh generations.[15] In the post–World War II era, approximately thirty local mosques represented "official Islam" in the whole of Kazakhstan.[16] Even though religious affairs were under strict control by the Soviets, the communist regime failed to erase Islam from the Kazakh identity, attitudes, and traditions completely; Islamic norms and traditions distinctively separated Kazakhs from Russian-speaking immigrants, who would constitute more than half of the republic's population by 1980. In 1981 the first secretary of the Communist Party of Kazakhstan, Dinmukhammed Kunaev, indicated that the emergence of religious orientations among the population was remarkable and was steadily increasing in the south.[17] The years after 1988 saw an "unprecedented interest in rediscovery of the past" and the Islamic heritage in Central Asia.[18] With Gorbachev's perestroika initiative, the Soviet authorities partly accepted and tolerated the reality of the increasing resurgence of Islam in Kazakhstan, as was the case throughout Muslim Central Asia and the northern Caucasus.

The Post-Soviet Islamic Revival

Analyzing the initial phases of Islamic revival in the aftermath of the Soviet Union's collapse is essential for understanding the *current* state of Islamic affairs in Kazakhstan. In other words, the post-Soviet patterns of Islamic revival offer important clues about Islam's *evolving* role in Kazakh civil society.

Kazakh Muslims adhere to Sunni Islam. Since 1991, both the number of Islamic mosques and the number of people attending these institutions have increased. There were only 40 to 60 mosques open for prayer from 1975 to 1989 in the Soviet Republic of Kazakhstan. By 1993 this number had increased to 269.[19] By 2005 the estimated number of mosques in Kazakhstan exceeded 1,400.

Even though Kazakhstan is the most secular republic in Central Asia, in 2000 approximately 80 percent of Kazakhs indicated that they believed in God.[20] Among them, 48 percent stated that they "believe in God, but do not practice Islam," while approximately 38 percent responded that they "believe in God, but partly practice Islam" in daily life.[21] According to the Spiritual Association of Muslims of Kazakhstan (SAMK), approximately 10 percent of Kazakhs are reported to "follow the Koran, pray five times a day and wear *hijab* (Islamic veil)."[22] However, according to the Pew Research Center's recent survey findings, only 18 percent of Kazakhs said religion is "very important" in their lives, which is the second-lowest percentage after Albania (15 percent) within the post-Soviet Muslim-majority space.[23] Moreover, the Pew Research Center found that approximately 10 percent of the population in Kazakhstan attends mosque at least once a week (compared to an average of 17 percent in Central Asia), 36 percent gives annual alms (*zakat*) (69 percent in Central Asia), and 30 percent fasts during Ramadan (52 percent in Central Asia).[24]

After independence from Moscow, Kazakh president Nursultan Nazarbayev emphasized the centrality of Islamic identity for the Kazakh people.[25] Although he is predominantly secular, Nazarbayev performed the hajj (pilgrimage to Mecca) and made numerous public appearances at religious ceremonies. He personally sponsored the construction of many mosques and founded the Nurmubarak Islamic University in Almaty in cooperation with the Egyptian Al-Azhar Islamic University—the largest and most prominent Islamic educational institution in the world. These actions by the national leader further bolstered Islamic values and the Islamic identity of the Kazakh majority, which also served Nazarbayev's strategic interests: minimizing the influence of the sizable Russian minority in the republic in the early years of independence.

As the Islamic revival increasingly permeates Kazakh society, the number of youths attending local mosques and *masjids* (small mosques) is growing considerably. According to Kazakhstan Academy of Sciences fellow Dimash Surayev, "the growth in Islam's popularity in Kazakhstan is clear, and this is normal."[26] In 2006 the Ministry of Industry and Trade of Kazakhstan established the Halal Standards Committee to issue certificates for halal (a diet compatible with Islamic law) products. Within a short period of time, many dietary products produced in Kazakhstan started to carry halal labels to appeal to a wider population. Though it would be premature to conclude that the large majority of Kazakhs have become overly sensitive about buying halal products or that they have become highly religious, which is not the case, these developments help substantiate the extent of Islamic revival in Kazakhstan.

Moreover, there is strong empirical support for Kathleen Collins's and Eric McGlinchey's formulations in explaining the variations in Islamic identity in Kazakhstan.[27] McGlinchey observes that the combination of the following factors in a chain reaction helps explain the dynamics of Islamic revivalism in Kyrgyzstan: (1) increased Islamic values and traditions promote interpersonal trust in local communities, (2) deepening trust stimulates social capital, (3) accumulating social capital yields Islamic institutions in the form of charities, businesses, and social services, and (4) these effective Islamic institutions win local admiration and help disseminate Islamic identities. This formulation also largely applies to Kazakhstan. More precisely, the increasing effectiveness of Islamic institutions in winning local admiration is aiding the process of dissemination and expansion of Islamic norms and values in the republic.

Islam and Civil Society: Competing Theoretical Explanations

Drawing on Robert Putnam's and Jean Cohen and Andrew Arato's conceptualizations, I frame civil society broadly as an aggregate social space for uncoerced collective action by public associations, social organizations, social movements, and civic institutions based on voluntary cooperation of citizens.[28] Civil society is distinct from mainstream society "in general in that it involves citizens acting collectively in a public sphere to express their interests, passions, and ideas, exchange information, achieve mutual goals."[29]

Gabriel Almond and Sidney Verba identify the role of civil society as vital for democracy and argue that it is virtually impossible to imagine a democratic state without a robust, uncoerced civil society that facilitates better public awareness of the need to make better voting choices, participate in politics, and produce alternatives by holding the government more accountable.[30] Larry Diamond claims that in order to "comprehend democratic change around the world, one must study civil society" and defines "extensive mobilization of civil society" as a "crucial source of pressure" for democratic change in countries such as South Korea, Taiwan, Chile, Poland, China, Czechoslovakia, South Africa, Nigeria, and Benin.[31] Furthermore, Ronald Inglehart asserts that vibrant civil society is important not only for the development but also for the *maintenance* of democracy.[32]

In the wake of the Arab Spring of 2011 and given the current pace of Islamic revivalism, studying Islamic civil society remains central to further understanding of prospects for democratization in Muslim societies. To what extent is religious revival related to the formation of civil society? A structural incompatibility of religion with liberalization and democratic civil society has been a long-standing assumption in the social sciences.[33] On the grounds of European experience, some Western observers exclude religion (especially Islam) as a potential source for building strong civil societies.[34] By advancing this assumption, some scholars have proposed a neo-Orientalist argument that Islam is exceptional, suggesting that Muslim societies are uniquely resistant to secularism and thus to liberal democracy. By framing it as "Islamic exceptionalism," they voice skepticism regarding Islam's potential compatibility with modern, liberal democratic norms.[35] Put differently, the main argument of neo-Orientalism is that a separation of church from state is not compatible with Islamic teaching, and thus Islam is an obstacle to democratization.

In contrast, some studies have emphasized the role of churches as vital social organizations in promoting social capital and have highlighted that they are inseparable components of civil society.[36] For instance, Alfred Stepan's *twin tolerations* thesis draws lessons from the historical relationship between Western Christianity and democracy, arguing that only through the context of the twin tolerations can the concept of separation of church and state in Western Europe be properly understood: "Virtually no Western European democracy now has a rigid or hostile separation of church and state. Most have arrived at a democratically negotiated freedom of religion from state interference, and all of them allow religious groups freedom not only to worship privately but to organize groups in *civil society* and political society."[37]

By "twin tolerations," Stepan refers to "the *minimum* boundaries of freedom of action" that both religious organizations and the state must mutually recognize in order to coexist. In line with Stepan, Amy Freedman examines the patterns of coexistence between Islamic political forces and democracy building and asserts that "Islam and democracy can coexist and that Islamic actors can, under certain conditions, be a force for democracy."[38]

A timely analysis of the theoretical relationship between Islam and liberal democracy by Nader Hashemi helps further explain this church-state relation paradox. He maintains that "religious traditions are not born with inherent liberal, democratic or secular orientations" but that these ideas can and must be socially constructed. Thus democratization and liberalization do not necessarily require a rejection (or *privatization,* as he puts it) of religion, but what they do require is a "reinterpretation of religious ideas" in accordance with "legitimate political authority and individual rights." He argues that through a process of *reinterpretation,* religious groups can play a central role in not only accommodating and developing but also consolidating democracy.[39] Furthermore, according to Abdullahi An-Na'im, secularism is not a prerequisite for liberalism and tolerance; rather, religion (Islam) and civil society are highly interdependent, which mutually supports the democratization process.[40] Raising the issue of compatibility between religious institutions in communities that exhibit high degrees of social capital and civil society dynamics, Frank Adloff challenges the conventional wisdom of secularist dichotomization of religion and civil society and defends the relevance of religion, in general terms, as a resource for civic action, social capital, and civil society.[41]

Even though there are remarkable procedural similarities in transitions toward democracy as experienced in Europe, Latin America, and some Asian states, individual paths to democratization have never been identical. As institutional theories assert, for a stable democracy to emerge, it must be anchored in *democratic institutions* that promote human rights, the rule of law, tolerance, good governance, and justice.[42] Citizens participate in politics via institutions that represent citizens' social, political, and economic interests by channeling their preferences and ideological orientations into politics. If Islam is to play a constructive role in shaping the social landscape of Kazakh civil society, then the function of Islamic institutions will be central to systematic representation of Islam in society. In this context, the relevance and importance of Islamic institutions stem from the notion that institutions can be considered stable and effective only when they grow and flourish in an *indigenous* setting. That is, social, cultural, and historical experiences provide essential contexts, making institutions more suitable for an indigenous social and political environment.

As I examine the empirical nexus between Islamic educational, financial, and political institutions and emerging Kazakh civil society, I conceptualize an "institution" as a set of formal and informal structures, an organization or a mechanism represented by a collective body of individuals that generates a specific set of rules and procedures to reach common (social, political, economic) goals. By highlighting the importance of civil society as an *institutional mechanism* (central to democratization), Diamond maintains that "citizens pressed their challenge to autocracy not merely as individuals, but as members of student movements, *churches,* professional associations, women's groups, trade unions, human rights organizations, producer groups, the press, civic associations, and the like."[43]

Yet how does the *civil society* argument apply in the context of the Islamic world? In this respect, Francesco Cavatorta cites three reasons for Islamist associations being a potential force for, not an obstacle to, democratization: (1) Islamic civil society movements are capable of political learning; (2) they generate secular civil society activism as a response to their activities, increasing the number of actors in the political and social system; and finally (3), they can cooperate with *other* civil society groups on a variety of issues, provided that they are all subject to the same autocratic rule.[44]

Examining the centrality of civil society in the democratization process, Charles Ziegler shows that Kazakh civil society is unique in post-Soviet space, in which civil society actors are less willing to confront the state and tend to work in cooperation with the authoritarian system.[45] This is largely due to "authoritative structures and cultural traditions" that make it "difficult to develop strong, independent civic organizations."[46] These structures are pressuring civil society organizations and movements into co-opting and cooperating rather than confronting or challenging the state. Ziegler's study is essential for understanding the structural and cultural variables that help explain the state, trends, and volatility of civil society in modern Kazakhstan. He concludes that for the members of civil society to survive, they must work in cooperation (not in contestation) with the state, as the incumbent regime will not tolerate any uncontrolled collective movement(s), which may pose threats to the present authoritarian status quo.

From this perspective, the *inclusionist* policies of government with respect to emerging Islamic institutions may significantly integrate Islamic revival into civil society in the context of representation of moderate Islam's voice in Kazakh civil society, though at the initial transitional stage, the relationship between Islam and civil society may carry a cooperative and restrained character between state and Islamic institutions.

Drawing from this literature, this chapter argues that a government's *inclusionist* policies that allow social space for Islamic institutionalization may help promote more open and vibrant civil society. However, at present, Kazakh Islamic actors have no choice but to work *in cooperation* with the state, which limits the "uncoerced" aspect of civil society. Yet little or limited representation may be better than nonrepresentation. In the long run, Islamic institutions may become important players within an *uncoerced social space* in which (1) the moderate voice of Islam, not the voice of radicals and extremists, may arise as a result of adequate Islamic educational training (and Islamic social capital); (2) political participation is tolerated for future Islamic political organizations; and (3) faith-sensitive business opportunities (Islamic finance) will emerge as civic social organizations in evolving civil society. Conversely, the *exclusionist* policies of government with respect to Islamic institutions may impede the development of moderate Islam's voice and representation in Kazakh civil society.

Government Regulation of Religion

Many authoritarian regimes in Muslim-majority countries today, including Kazakhstan, often employ restrictive and *exclusionist* policies with regard to Islamic revival in the political arena in order to maintain the status quo of their authoritarian regimes. In the case of Kazakhstan, President Nazarbayev holds de facto control over all state, social, economic, and political institutions. It is important to note, however, that although the Nazarbayev regime is highly authoritarian, his leadership enjoys wide legitimacy and political support from the public. The president enjoys wide public approval and is seen as a "guarantor" of the republic's continued economic and political stability.[47] While Islamic revival is generally accepted as a positive development within the framework of returning to the traditional cultural heritage, the fear of Islamic resurgence appears to emanate from Islam's potential to mobilize a political movement (e.g., an Islamic political party).

The Nazarbayev regime has firmly banned any potential Islamic institution from participating in the political system.[48] Islam's role has largely been restricted to individual social life. Table 3.1 summarizes for five Central Asian states the key indicators of B. J. Grim and R. Finke's and Jonathon Fox's index for state regulation of religion. Grim and Finke define government regulation as "restrictions placed on the practice, profession, or selection of religion by the official laws, policies, or administrative actions of the state."[49] On this index of government regulation of religion, low meaning less regulation, Kazakhstan scores 7.2 out of a possible 10, whereas Tajikistan has the lowest score in the region for government regu-

Table 3.1. Government Regulation of Religion in Central Asia

Religion and state indexes	Kazakhstan	Kyrgyzstan	Tajikistan	Turkmenistan	Uzbekistan	Central Asia	World
Government regulation of religion index[a]	7.22	7.78	5.56	10.00	9.17	7.95	3.10
Social regulation of religion index[a]	8.00	8.00	7.30	6.67	5.33	7.06	2.90
Censorship of religious texts	Low	Low	Low	Moderate	High	—	—
Censorship of religious clerics	Moderate	Moderate	High	High	High	—	—
Institutionalization of and access to Islamic education at higher educational institutions	Emerging	Emerging	Low	Low	Low	—	—

Source: ARDA (Association of Religion Data Archives), 2010, http://www.thearda.com.
[a]0–10, low is less regulation

lation. Although Kazakhstan has the second-lowest score in the region, the level of state regulation of Islamic affairs is still high overall in the republic.

Next, for social regulation of religion, low meaning less regulation, the country scores 8.0 out of a possible 10. Overall, that level of governmental regulation is barely different from that of the rest of the Central Asian countries (average 7.1), suggesting that the government is systematically keeping religious affairs under strict surveillance.

Why Is the Regime So Fearful?

The killing of seven people by a radical militant in 2011, the deadliest event since Kazakhstan's independence, renewed public discourse on religious extremism. Although the threat of radical extremism is often exaggerated by the incumbent authoritarian regimes in Central Asia, the underlying danger of religious extremism is real and has risen significantly in recent years. According to a public opinion survey conducted in 2010, approximately 62 percent of Kazakh citizens indicated that they were "very or somewhat concerned" about the rise of Islamic extremism. While only 11 percent of respondents were "not too concerned," nearly 12 percent indicated that they were "not at all concerned" about the rise of religious extremism in the republic (see figure 3.1).

In his 2010 public announcement, the governor of Atyrau province, Bergei Ruskaliyev, indicated that the frequency of religious extremism among young people is growing and therefore closer monitoring is necessary.[50] According to Emmanuel Karagiannis, twelve Pakistani Islamic preachers were expelled from southern Kazakhstan and the city of Almaty by Kazakh authorities in 2003.[51] In 2004 Kazakhstan's Ministry of Education closed down the South Kazakhstan Humanitarian Academy on the grounds that its curriculum was promoting radical teachings. The academy was founded by Jamaat al-Islah al-Ijtimai (the Social Reform Society), a Kuwait-based charitable organization that was listed at the time as a terrorist organization by Russia.[52]

In November 2011 a radical militant killed seven people in the city of Taraz.[53] A thirty-four-year-old "follower of jihadism," as he was described by the prosecutor general's office, blew himself up after a long gun battle with the police. This was the worst and deadliest attack by religious radicals in the country. While this assault was highly unusual for Kazakhstan, it came after a few bomb attacks in the preceding months. In fact, earlier

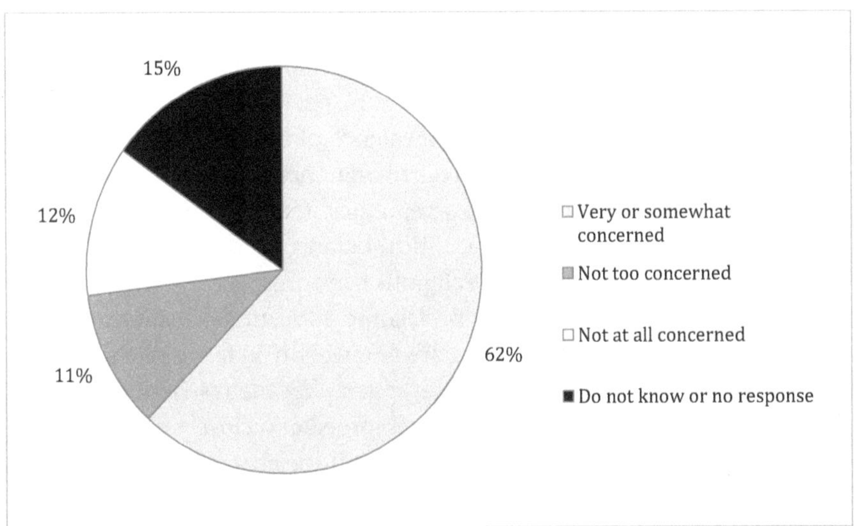

Figure 3.1. Public concern about the rise of Islamic extremism in Kazakhstan
Source: International Republican Institute, Baltic Surveys Ltd., and the Gallup Organization. *N* = 1,527. The national representative survey (face-to-face interviews) was carried out April 3–13, 2010.

that year at least eighteen people had been arrested on the basis of religious extremism.[54] According to the *New York Times,* the members of Jund al-Khilafah (Army of the Caliphate) had vowed to launch attacks against the Nazarbayev regime to avenge the government's recent restrictions on religion.[55] These recent terrorist attacks committed by militant religious radicals were mainly in response to previous state-sponsored repressive policies.[56] Religious radical networks often use state repression as a pretext to promulgate their ideology and attract new members. As such, harsh state crackdown on emerging Islamic actors is one of the leading factors that contribute to the radicalization of Central Asian youth.[57] Applying Gartner and Regan's study of government and opposition, Jessica Trisko finds that Islamist political groups in Central Asia are violently repressed more often or to a greater degree than other, non-Islamist opposition groups, irrespective of whether they pose a threat to regime survival.[58]

When compared with the rest of the Central Asian republics, Kazakhstan is less repressive politically and more liberal economically by many metrics.[59] President Nazarbayev seems to realize that maintaining a delicate balance between fighting against religious extremism and protecting wider religious freedoms advocated by moderate and nonviolent conservative Muslims will be a key issue. In this respect, the long-term solution to radicalism seems to rest on the prevalence of moderate Islamic actors. Arguably, Nazarbayev seems to realize that heavy-handed policies, as implemented in neighboring fellow republics, may in fact jeopardize the emergence of moderate Islam if a critical balance is lost between government crackdown on religion and religious freedoms.

Nazarbayev's decisions allowing Islamic educational institutions and the development of Islamic banking are noteworthy in terms of channeling the rising Islamic revival in the public sphere. Yet the restrictions on religious *political* mobilization are strictly enforced and closely monitored. In general, any contestational disposition by civil society activists is not tolerated by the regime.

Islamic Financial Institutions (IFI)

Why do Islamic financial institutions matter in a Muslim-majority civil society? The public's participation in the development process is central in achieving sustainable economic development and social progress. The financial system can facilitate such civic participation by making its services both acceptable and accessible to the public. Furthermore, the public's trust and confidence in local institutions that are compatible with indigenous beliefs, values, and orientations are important determinants of economic and political stability. In this regard, the presence of Islamic financial institutions not only indicates the level of Islam in practice in a given society but becomes an important element of civil society dynamics. As a viable alternative, the availability of Islamic financial institutions may significantly increase the level of activity and effectiveness of Muslim participation, not only in the economic sector but also in social and political arenas.[60]

Islamic finance has a potential market of 1.5 billion Muslims, which continues to strengthen its global appeal.[61] Today, Islamic banks are offering a wide range of services in the financial sector consistent with Islamic principles of monetary lending. Increasing numbers of Muslims around the world, regardless of religiosity status, are attracted by financial services free of *ri'ba* (forbidden interest). Assuming that the assets of Islamic banks worldwide were worth $700 billion in 2005 and had an annual growth rate of 15 percent until 2010, they could potentially grow beyond $3 trillion by 2015.[62]

In post-Soviet Central Asia, Kazakhstan has emerged as a leading economic powerhouse. Fueled largely by energy exports, the Kazakh economy gained a steady momentum of high economic growth starting in the late 1990s. High oil and gas prices in world markets significantly boosted the share of foreign revenue. While this energy-driven revenue played a key role in enduring the aftershocks of Russia's 1998 financial meltdown, the global financial crisis of 2008 severely interrupted the momentum of Kazakh economic growth.[63]

Notably, Kazakhstan is the first post-Soviet republic to establish an Islamic banking sector. Islamic finance is applied in accordance with Islamic law (Shari'a) and guided by Islamic economics. Islamic law prohibits usury and the collection and payment of interest. The first Kazakh Islamic financial sector was established in early 2007. More Kazakh local banks are showing increasing interest in offering Islamic Shari'a-compatible financial services as a result of legislative support by the government. Although Islamic financial institutions are new, this early stage of institutionalization is another indication of Islamic revival, which is slowly and systematically evolving in the country.

In January 2009 the Darahim Sukuk Basket was introduced by Encore Fund Management Co. Ltd., a holding company that was established to manage Islamic funds.[64] This historic event was organized by Kausar Consulting, a Kazakhstan-based Islamic finance consultancy firm.[65] John N. Sandwick, speaking for Encore Fund Management, said, "We are the first-ever investment company to offer high-quality Sharia-compliant structured investments to Kazakhstani pension funds, corporate treasuries, commercial banks and national government agencies."[66] On similar grounds, Dhafer S. Alqahtani, the CEO of Encore Fund Management and managing director of Darahim Capital, affirmed, "[Islamic finance] is the beginning of the remaking of the modern Silk Road by creating an important two-way flow of capital. Kazakhstan is similar to the Gulf region in many aspects, as they are richly endowed with oil, gas and mineral resources, and an up-and-coming emerging market with a rich history and deep roots in Islam."[67]

Islamic banks are particularly interested in tapping into rising demand from the world's 1.3 billion Muslims for investments that comply with tenets of their religious faith. Given the global financial crisis that erupted in 2008, the need for liquid funds has never before been as high. This situation puts oil-rich Gulf States that sit on large cash reserves generated by oil wealth at an advantage. In this respect, Kazakhstan is a safe investment from all aspects: being a Muslim-majority country, having a skilled workforce, having relatively favorable investment laws and regulations compared with neighboring Central Asian states, and, perhaps most importantly, holding vast oil and gas reserves. In May 2008 the Qatar Islamic Bank and Bahrain's Ithmaar Bank announced moves into Kazakhstan, an increasingly popular destination for Gulf Islamic lenders eyeing deals outside their crowded home markets. In its public statement, Ithmaar Bank emphasized that "Kazakhstan's political and social stability, skilled workforce and bright economic outlook enhance the country's favorable investment climate."[68]

Al Hilal group, a subsidiary of the United Arab Emirates state bank (assets worth over $41 billion), opened its first branches in 2009. A regional director of Al Hilal, Timur Alim, expressed high optimism about future growth of Islamic banking in Kazakhstan. By the end of 2011, after only two years of operation, the number of loans extended by the Al Hilal group was expected to double (reaching a value of approximately $60 million).[69]

The state of Islamic financial institutions in Kazakhstan can be described as "emerging." With a green light granted by the incumbent government to savvy international investors (mainly Muslim, wealthy oil-rich states) to develop the Islamic banking sector further, the Islamic-based financial sector is rapidly developing. While it is premature to discuss the far-reaching impact of Islamic financial institutions on civil society, as they are still in a transitional stage, it is important to emphasize that the pace of development of Islamic financial institutions is not insignificant.

In sum, the government's *inclusionist* support seems to allow Islamic revival from the economic (financial) perspective in terms of allowing relatively free access to Islamic representation in Kazakh civil society. Allowing Islamic financial services in the country suggests that the Kazakh government is responsive, to a certain degree, to the local needs and preferences of devout Muslims in the country.

Islamic Educational Institutions (IEI)

Education is widely believed to be a critical social prerequisite for mankind's intellectual progress. From a political perspective, many scholars have demonstrated the existence of an empirical link between higher levels of education and democratization.[70] Given the rising influence of Islam, providing access to teaching and learning the mainstream (nonradical or nonextremist) interpretations of Islamic jurisprudence is as important as mainstream secular education. More precisely, Islamic educational institutions can play an essential role in providing (1) a source for the mainstream teachings of Islam, (2) an opportunity to study both aspects of Shari'a (Islamic law)—Ibadat (worship, prayers, and technical rituals) and Mu'amalat (social relations and social applications)— (3) an effective antidote to religious radicalism, and (4) the promotion of Islamic social capital within newly emerging Kazakh civil society.[71]

Although the majority of Muslims are knowledgeable about the Ibadat (technical aspects of worship and prayer rituals) part of Shari'a, very few fully understand Mu'amalat (the way Islam affects everyday life and its social implications). However, what is more challenging, and consequently more important, is to *contextualize* Islamic teachings in the modern social, political, and economic realities of the twenty-first century. Islam, like other world religions, needs to be interpreted in the light of contemporary social, political, and economic contexts. Since interpreting Islamic teachings in accordance with the modern age and the contemporary global social context is necessary in order to deter and perhaps preempt the spread of radical literal interpretations of Islam, educational opportunities for teaching and learning mainstream (nonradical) Islamic teachings must come from legitimate, reliable institutions that employ qualified educators (e.g., imams).[72]

Many young Muslims who do not have any prior knowledge of Islam are more prone to accept radical teachings as "genuine" Islamic teachings, as they hear them for the very *first time* from radical preachers.[73] Therefore, Islamic educational institutions can play an imperative role in deterring the spread of radicalism in newly independent Central Asia. In fact, one of the main reasons why religious extremists target teenagers is because "[the youth] do not yet have fully formed ideals and they are easier to manage."[74] Without any context (i.e., Islamic knowledge) for evaluating claims about Islam promoted by radicals, those exposed to radicalism often develop sympathy for those views and potentially accept those views as genuine messages of Islam.[75]

Finally, Islamic educational institutions are instrumental in facilitating social trust among moderate Muslims as a counterweight to radical social (trust) networks. Social capital can be defined as a "culture of trust and tolerance, in which extensive networks of voluntary associations emerge."[76] IEIs can bring an Islamic aspect to this traditional (social capital) conceptualization and consequently help construct *Islamic social capital,* which may play a key role in raising, and thereby representing, the moderate voice of Islam by promoting tolerance and the ability of people to work together for the common good and for collective purposes in rapidly emerging Kazakh civil society.[77] To this end, Islamic social networks may act as a vehicle for self-expression and thereby reduce the growing threats of radicalism and extremism in the region. As a result, increasing access to Islamic education may be imperative not only for fostering stronger civil society and (general and Islamic) social capital but also for diminishing the spread of religious radicalism.

Kazakhstan does not have a history of indigenous Islamic educational institutions (e.g., madrassas).[78] Nearly all mosque imams in Muslim Central Asian states were trained and sent from Uzbekistan during Soviet rule. Since Kazakhstan's independence, Islam has emerged as a major social force to shape Kazakh identity and has gained increased momentum in filling the gap left by communist ideology. Motivated by the surge and revival of Islamic traditions across the country, numbers of mosques, madrassas, and Islamic departments of higher education have started to emerge. A central administrative body, the Spiritual Association of Muslims of Kazakhstan, also known as Muftiyat of Kazakhstan, was established in 1991 to oversee and coordinate the newly established and growing number of Islamic social institutions.

In the early years of independence, new venues for Islamic education became necessary in order to address the public's aspiration to learn Islam. The Kazakh government was not prepared to meet that challenge due to the suddenness and rapidity of Islamic resurgence and the limited governmental resources available. Yet Nursultan Nazarbayev allowed multiple religious groups to register and operate with equal rights during the early years of independence. As a result, two types of Islamic education institutions were established: traditional Islamic madrassas and secular, public institutions of higher education offering Islamic studies.

The development of Islamic educational institutions was uneven and inadequate. This inadequacy was largely due to the lack of funding, which continues to date, for SAMK effectively to coordinate all religious affairs in the republic. The constitution states that Kazakhstan is a secular republic with no established religion; thus the government chooses to allocate very limited funds to SAMK. As a result, SAMK has become dependent on private funds and donations from the public and foreign donors.

Teaching religion in public schools is not permitted. There are approximately forty to fifty after-school, Islamic-based private gymnasiums, which are operated by trained scholars, mostly educated in Egypt and Turkey, who teach the basic principles of Islam and the Qur'an. These gymnasiums were established by foreign volunteers to help educate Kazakh youth on the main pillars of Islam. One of these gymnasium-like institutions is operated by volunteers who represent the Sulaymaniye Jamaat, a group dedicated to teaching the recitation of the Qur'an and basic tenets of Islam in an after-school or summer-school setting.[79] It is one of very few institutions that offer Islamic education to the youngest in the population (elementary and secondary levels) in a structured, transparent, and systematic fashion. The Sulaymaniye volunteers do not appear to hold any political ambitions and seem devoutly committed to promoting the basics of Islamic faith. The government is supportive of these institutions, as they provide open and transparent education to Kazakh youth.

There is one Islamic university—Nur-Mubarak Islamic University—and sixteen madrassas. Most of the graduates from the Islamic university and madrassas are placed in imam positions in mosques throughout the country. Yet not all mosques are run by adequately trained imams; many imams today lack basic educational training.

Although the threat of radicalism has largely been prevalent in Tajikistan, Uzbekistan, and southern Kyrgyzstan, Kazakhstan's sizable Russian Orthodox minority seemed to dilute the influence of religious extremism to a certain degree. Still, there are some who argue that radical Islam is inevitable in Kazakhstan and that "the real Islamization of the Kazakhs is beginning only now."[80] As Kazakhs increasingly reclaim their religious identity after the collapse of the USSR, some Kazakh pundits warn that representatives of various radical groups are also actively seeking ways to take advantage of Kazakhs' lack of religious education in order promote their own agendas.[81]

The government seems to employ *inclusionist* policies with regard to Islamic educational institutions. Consequently, their development in Kazakhstan seems to benefit from relative transparency and political support from the state as long as they have no political ambitions. Compared with his heavy-handed Central Asian counterparts, Nazarbayev has been very supportive of IEIs. It is possible that efforts in the early years of independence (1990s) to build Islamic educational institutions make the reality today relatively stable and might have reduced the early influence of foreign-supported radical preachers. However, emerging IEIs have not been completely free from governmental pressure. There is limited to no financial support extended by the government, which seems to threaten the stability and the long-term sustainability of Islamic education in the country. This issue remains a grave concern for the Republic of Kazakhstan, particularly for the substantial population under the age of twenty. Inadequate funding of Islamic education may undermine national security by attracting foreign-supported radical groups to recruit uninformed or ill-informed Kazakh youth.

Nevertheless, in the twenty years since independence, the state of Islamic education has improved. However, it is still far from sufficient to meet the basic demand for highly qualified imams to accommodate a rapidly growing number of mosques across the republic.

Islamic Political Institutions

Politics in Kazakhstan is strictly monitored by the authoritarian structures controlled by the president. There are no officially registered political parties with any religious affiliation. They are illegal. The government backs this policy by claiming that religious affiliation is unconstitutional since Kazakhstan is a secular republic.[82] After independence from the USSR, Muslim intellectuals made moderate attempts to form a party to represent the views and preferences of the devout Muslims in the country. They wanted a voice through which they could argue their political views from an Islamic perspective in the formation of the new Kazakh state. I define an Islamic political party or Islamic political institution as an organized political structure or movement whose political ideology is inspired by Islam and thereby envisions a space for Islam in politics.[83] The only party in Kazakhstan with roots in Islamic ideals, the Alash party, was established with a vision of achieving the "real status of an independent ethnic state, the integration and propagation of the ideas of Turkic unity and Moslem solidarity, and the national rebirth of Kazakhstan as the historical nucleus of the future unified Islamic Turkic state."[84]

In the early years of independence, Alash sought (1) to establish Islam as an official religion (not to establish an Islamic state) and (2) to found the new and independent Kazakh Muftiyat (the central institution for overseeing religious affairs) separate from Uzbek clergy. Supporting the need for such an institution, Nazarbayev quickly established SAMK. In part intended to address the growing Islamic revival, SAMK was also meant to minimize Uzbek domination in educating the new religious cadres. Disagreements between the government and the Alash party about "who should run SAMK" arose, however, over Nazarbayev's appointment of Ratbek Nasynbay to the top SAMK post. Because of this disagreement, Alash clashed with the Kazakh authorities, resulting in the arrest of the leading members of the Alash party. The founder of the party was forced into exile, making him the first political exile in the history of independent Kazakhstan. In 1994 the Alash party was formally disestablished.

Even though the constitution states that the "Republic of Kazakhstan shall recognize ideological and political diversity," the reality on the ground is the opposite.[85] No legitimate Islamic political movement is allowed to articulate its preference in Kazakh politics. Any attempts by any Islamic political activists to mobilize support in order to establish a political party are currently blocked by the legislative ban on political parties having any religious affiliation. Reacting to the issue of inclusion of Islamic political institutions, under the theme of "war on radical-extremist groups" such as Hizb ut-Tahrir and neo-Wahhabism, the government has sponsored a series of crackdowns. Especially in southern Kazakhstan, the radicalization of Muslim youth has been on the rise.[86] Recent government-sponsored crackdowns are geared to preempt any possible future political opposition, particularly groups with potential religious (Islamic) roots. This could yield unanticipated results. Specifically, exclusionist policies could block the emergence of moderate, peaceful Islamic political organizations and voluntary political associations in the near future. While Nazarbayev has pragmatically adopted a milder approach in order to maintain the critical balance between fighting against radicalism and suppressing the rise of moderate Islamic actors, on the whole, the level of religious freedom remains inadequate.

The findings suggest that the government is employing *exclusionist* policies by curtailing political freedoms. Even though there are no emerging Islamist parties in Kazakh politics today and the rise of Islamist parties is not imminent, the exclusionist policies may still repress the development of free and voluntary Islamic political movements within emerging Kazakh civil society.[87]

Discussion

This chapter empirically examined the rising role of Islam and its role in shaping the civil society dynamics in Kazakhstan, operationalizing Islam via Islamic institutions. I find that even though Islamic educational and financial institutions are at an "emerging" level, they are rapidly growing in size and influence in terms of representing the voice of moderate Islam in emerging Kazakh civil society. The government of Kazakhstan maintains a strict ban on Islamic *political* activities. Although these exclusionist policies are not widely contested by the public, possible support for future Islamic political organization cannot be excluded when the foundations for free and vibrant civil society in Kazakhstan are constructed.

The rise of Islamist political opposition is not imminent in Kazakhstan. Though unlikely in the foreseeable future, the prospect that the rise of political Islam in the Middle East (in the wake of the Tunisian, Egyptian, and Libyan revolutions) could spread into Muslim Central Asia through a domino effect should not be ignored.

Figure 3.2 illustrates the interaction between emerging Islamic institutions (as a proxy measure for Islam) and their role in emerging Kazakh civil society. The government's *inclusionist* policies with respect to emerging Islamic *financial* and *educational* institutions seem to facilitate the integration of Islamic revival in the context of developing moderate Islam's voice and representation in Kazakh civil society. This governmental inclusion stems from *cooperative* behavior of Islamic financial and educational institutions with state elites. The government, however, remains determined to maintain its exclusionist policies with regard to Islamic political institutions, which carry a *contestant* behavior against the regime. This finding is consistent with Ziegler's classification of cooperative civil society dynamics in Kazakhstan.

Islamic financial institutions are too new and relatively nascent to analyze their substantive impacts on Kazakh society overall. Islamic educational institutions, however, are playing a central role in developing Islamic leaders (e.g., imams) and indigenous scholars of Islamic jurisprudence (Shari'a) who are not only versed in technical Islamic knowledge (e.g., Fiqh) but also literate in the social and scientific innovations of the twenty-first century. Islamic educational institutions are emerging as instrumental entities capable of teaching Islam's social dimensions in accord with contemporary social, economic, and political discourses. Moreover, Islamic

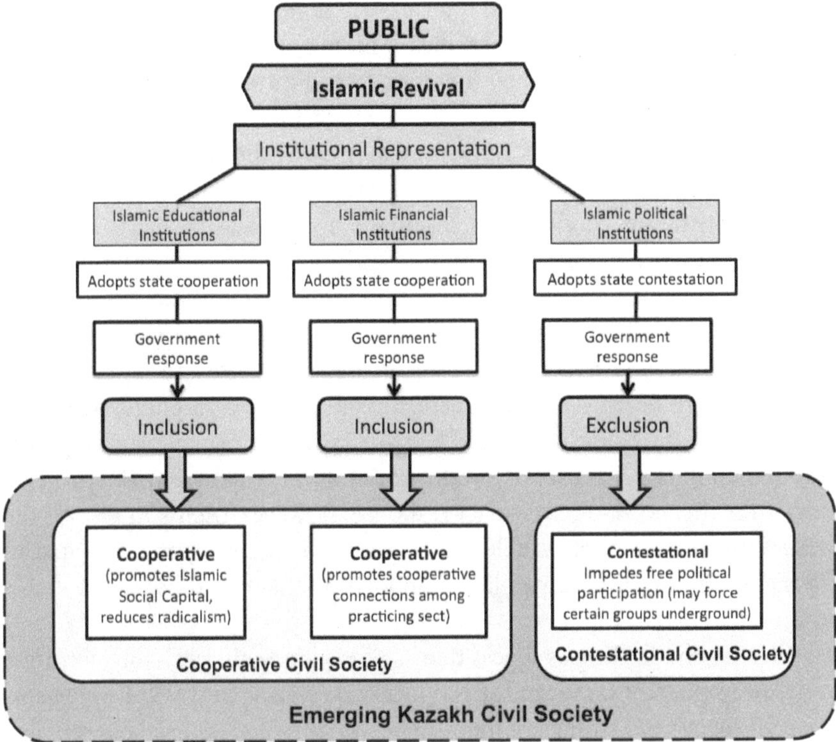

Figure 3.2. Emerging patterns between Islamic institutions and civil society in Kazakhstan

educational institutions may be an effective tool in impeding the growth of foreign-supported religious radicalism. According to the deputy mufti (grand imam) of SAMK, understanding and teaching the authentic message of Islam is an important prerequisite for Kazakhstan and youth should have adequate knowledge about Islam in order to properly channel their social development.[88]

Since 1995, a significant amount of literature on the mainstream and modern teachings of Islam has been published. An increasing number of university departments are collaborating with Islamic madrassas by organizing joint panels on democratization, exchanging guest speakers, engaging in debates, and organizing various workshops and conferences to increase awareness of what Islam has to say about modernity, including concepts such as "civil society," "jihad," "terrorism," and "women's rights."

There is minimal governmental interference in terms of restricting or limiting the curriculum of Islamic studies at higher educational levels (university and college). Nonetheless, there are very limited venues for primary and secondary students to study Islam, which increases the likelihood of youth being influenced by a radical ideology. On the whole, Islamic educational institutions appear to be of importance in educating the public on Islam's mainstream (nonradical) teachings and norms in order to minimize the influence of radical recruiters and foreign ideological meddling. Consequently, these institutions may provide a strong social basis, albeit indirectly, for facilitating Islamic social capital in Kazakh society.

In contrast, the government's exclusionist policies are blocking any possible future Islamic *political* institutionalization. Compared with current trends in the Middle East and North Africa, the rise of Islamist political opposition is not presently on the horizon in Kazakhstan. The primary motive for the government's strict response, however, seems to rest on the preservation of the comfortable status quo of the incumbent authoritarian regime, which opposes any political opposition that could become a viable political force.

In sum, the findings suggest that Islam is, and will probably continue to be, an important factor in forming Kazakh civil society. While *cooperative civil society* is gaining momentum, *contestational civil society* remains extremely weak and under close government watch. Thus the state of emerging Kazakh civil society can be described as more "coerced" than "uncoerced" space for collective action by public associations, social organizations, social movements, and civic institutions based on voluntary cooperation of citizens. However, the ongoing development of cooperative civil society may still be better than having an oppressive civil society. In this vein, the inclusionist policies of incumbent regimes with regard to Islamic institutions that adopt cooperation with the state, rather than contestation, appear to be instrumental in developing a moderate voice of Islam that can notably contribute to the formation of a stronger and more vibrant civil society.

Notes

1. John Esposito and Dalia Mogahed, *Who Speaks for Islam? What a Billion Muslims Really Think* (New York: Gallop Press, 2008).

2. Gabriel A. Almond and Sidney Verba, *The Civic Culture: Political Attitudes and Democracy in Five Nations* (Newbury Park, CA: Sage, 1989); Robert D. Put-

nam, *Bowling Alone: The Collapse and Revival of American Community* (New York: Simon and Schuster, 2000); and Robert D. Putnam, Robert Leonardi, and Raffaella Nanetti, *Making Democracy Work: Civic Traditions in Modern Italy* (Princeton, NJ: Princeton University Press, 1993).

3. Adeeb Khalid, *Islam after Communism: Religion and Politics in Central Asia* (Berkeley: University of California Press, 2007).

4. Sébastien Peyrouse, "Islam in Central Asia: National Specificities and Post-Soviet Globalisation," *Religion, State and Society* 35, no. 3 (2007): 245–60.

5. See, for example, Adeeb Khalid, "A Secular Islam: Nation, State, and Religion in Uzbekistan," *International Journal of Middle East Studies* 35 (2003): 573–98.

6. Eric McGlinchey, "Islamic Revivalism and State Failure in Kyrgyzstan," *Problems of Post-Communism* 56, no. 3 (2009): 16–28.

7. Azade-Ayse Rorlich, "Islam, Identity and Politics: Kazakhstan, 1990–2000," *Nationalities Papers* 31, no. 2 (2003): 157.

8. *See* Mohammed M. Hafez, *Why Muslims Rebel: Repression and Resistance in the Islamic World* (Boulder, CO: Lynne Rienner, 2003); Akbar S. Ahmed, *Journey into Islam: The Crisis of Globalization* (Washington, D.C.: Brookings Institution Press, 2007). Akbar Ahmed categorizes Islam into three broad categories: mystic, modernist, and literalist. He refers to literalists as "radicals" who believe that Muslims must mirror the Islamic way of life as practiced in seventh-century Arabia. The literalists hold that they are under attack from the West and thus adopt a defensive posture. While not all literalists advocate violence, many do pursue extremist ideology that justifies violence. According to Tawfik Hamid, an Islamic reformer and a senior fellow at the Potomac Institute for Policy Studies (who was a former member of the Islamic radical group Jamma Islamiya), "Moderate Islam should be defined as a form of Islam that rejects [radical] violent and discriminatory edicts. . . . This violent concept fuels jihadists, who take the teaching literally and accept responsibility for applying it to the modern world." See "A Symposium: What Is Moderate Islam?," *Wall Street Journal,* September 1, 2010, http://online.wsj.com/article/SB10001424052748703369704575461503431290986.html.

9. *Kazakhstan's News Bulletin,* April 20, 2007, http://prosites-kazakhembus.homestead.com/042007.html. The majority of minority groups were deported from their homelands for political reasons during Stalin's repressive years.

10. Ahmed Rashid, *Jihad: The Rise of Militant Islam in Central Asia* (New Haven, CT: Yale University Press, 2002), 33.

11. Shirin Akiner, *The Formation of Kazakh Identity: From Tribe to Nation-State* (London: Royal Institute of International Affairs, 1995).

12. Also known as the Basmachi national movement in Central Asia, which fought a guerrilla war against the occupying Soviet Red Army from 1916 to 1931.

13. See Akiner, *Formation of Kazakh Identity.*

14. Martha Brill Olcott, "Islamic Consciousness and Nationalist Ideology in Central Asia: What Role for Foreign Actors?," in *From the Gulf to Central Asia:*

Players in the New Great Game, ed. Anoushiravan Ehteshami (Exeter: University of Exeter Press, 1994).

15. See, for example, Zeyno Baran, S. F. Starr, and Svante E. Cornell, *Islamic Radicalism in Central Asia and the Caucasus: Implications for the EU* (Washington, D.C.: Central Asia–Caucasus Institute and Silk Road Studies Program, 2006).

16. Alexandre Bennigsen and S. E. Wimbush, *Muslims of the Soviet Empire* (London: C. Hurst, 1986).

17. Emmanuel Karagiannis, "The Rise of Political Islam in Kazakhstan: Hizb Ut-Tahrir Al Islami," *Nationalism and Ethnic Politics* 13, no. 2 (2007): 297–322.

18. See Khalid, *Islam after Communism,* 126.

19. See D. Trofimov, "Friday Mosques and Their Imams in the Former Soviet Union," *Religion, State and Society: The Keston Journal* 24, no. 2 (1996): 193–219.

20. Center for Public Opinion Research and Analysis (CPORA), Report on Research Results of Public Social Orientations in Kazakhstan (Almaty, 2000).

21. Ibid.

22. See, for example, Anar Kuanyshbekova, "Halal Markets Gain Popularity in Kazakhstan," *Central Asia Online,* September 4, 2010, http://centralasiaonline.com/cocoon/caii/xhtml/en_GB/features/caii/features/main/2010/09/04/feature-02.

23. *See* James Bell et al., *The World's Muslims: Unity and Diversity* (Washington, D.C.: Pew Research Center, August 9, 2012), http://www.pewforum.org/Muslim/the-worlds-muslims-unity-and-diversity-executive-summary.aspx.

24. Ibid.

25. The president, Nursultan Nazarbayev, is the head of state and the commander in chief of the armed forces. The prime minister chairs the Cabinet of Ministers and serves as Kazakhstan's head of government. De facto, the president holds the ultimate control over the Kazakh parliament, all legislative processes, and all state socioeconomic-political institutions.

26. See Yelena Sorokina, "Kazakhstan Concerned over Radical Movements Influencing Children," Internet Gazeta, October 15, 2010, http://engnews.gazeta.kz/art.asp?aid=323611.

27. See, for example, McGlinchey, "Islamic Revivalism and State Failure"; and Kathleen Collins, "Ideas, Networks, and Islamist Movements: Evidence from Central Asia and the Caucasus," *World Politics* 60, no. 1 (2007): 64–96.

28. Jean Cohen and Andrew Arato, *Civil Society and Political Theory* (Cambridge, MA: MIT Press, 1994).

29. Larry Diamond, "Toward Democratic Consolidation," *Journal of Democracy* 5, no. 3 (1994): 4–17.

30. See Almond and Verba, *Civic Culture;* and Putnam, Leonardi, and Nanetti, *Making Democracy Work.*

31. Diamond, "Toward Democratic Consolidation," 5.

32. Ronald Inglehart, *Culture and Social Change: Findings from the Value Surveys* (Leiden: Brill Academic, 2003); and Christian Welzel, Ronald Inglehart, and Franziska Deutsch, "Social Capital, Voluntary Associations and Collective Action:

Which Aspects of Social Capital Have the Greatest 'Civic' Payoff?," *Journal of Civil Society* 1, no. 2 (2005): 121–46.

33. For insightful coverage of the debate, see Pippa Norris and R. Inglehart, *Sacred and Secular: Religion and Politics Worldwide,* Comparative Sociology series (Cambridge: Cambridge University Press, 2004).

34. See Samuel P. Huntington, *The Clash of Civilizations and the Remaking of World Order* (New York: Simon and Schuster, 1996); Bernard Lewis, *What Went Wrong? The Clash between Islam and Modernity in the Middle East* (New York: Oxford University Press, 2002); and Bernard Lewis, "Islam and Liberal Democracy: A Historical Overview," *Journal of Democracy* 7, no. 2 (1996): 52–63.

35. M. Steven Fish, "Islam and Authoritarianism," *World Politics* 55, no. 1 (2002): 4–37.

36. See, for example, Putnam, *Bowling Alone.*

37. Alfred Stepan, "Religion, Democracy, and the 'Twin Tolerations,'" *Journal of Democracy* 11, no. 4 (2000): 37–57.

38. See Amy L. Freedman, "Civil Society, Moderate Islam, and Politics in Indonesia and Malaysia," *Journal of Civil Society* 5, no. 2 (2009): 107–27.

39. Nader Hashemi, *Secularism and Liberal Democracy: Toward a Democratic Theory for Muslim Society* (New York: Oxford University Press, 2009), 3, 172.

40. Abdullahi An-Na'im, "Religion and Global Civil Society: Inherent Incompatibility or Synergy and Interdependence," *Global Civil Society* (2002): 55–76.

41. Frank Adloff, "Dichotomizing Religion and Civil Society? Catholicism in Germany and the USA before the Second Vatican Council," *Journal of Civil Society* 6, no. 3 (2010): 193–203.

42. See, for example, Gretchen Helmke and Steven Levitsky, *Informal Institutions and Democracy: Lessons from Latin America* (Baltimore: Johns Hopkins University Press, 2006).

43. Diamond, "Toward Democratic Consolidation," 5.

44. Francesco Cavatorta, "Civil Society, Islamism and Democratisation: The Case of Morocco," *Journal of Modern African Studies* 44, no. 2 (2006): 203–22.

45. Charles E. Ziegler, "Civil Society, Political Stability, and State Power in Central Asia: Cooperation and Contestation," *Democratization* 17, no. 5 (2010): 795–825.

46. Ibid., 795.

47. Martha Brill Olcott, *Kazakhstan: Unfulfilled Promise* (Washington, DC: Carnegie Endowment for International Peace, 2002).

48. Jessica N. Trisko, "Coping with the Islamist Threat: Analysing Repression in Kazakhstan, Kyrgyzstan and Uzbekistan," *Central Asian Survey* 24, no. 4 (2005): 373–89.

49. B. J. Grim and R. Finke, "International Religion Indexes: Government Regulation, Government Favoritism, and Social Regulation of Religion," *Interdisciplinary Journal of Research on Religion* 2, no. 1 (2006): 1–40, quote on 7.

50. See Sorokina, "Kazakhstan Concerned over Radical Movements."

51. Emmanuel Karagiannis, *Political Islam in Central Asia* (New York: Routledge, 2011), 47.

52. Ibid., 302.

53. See Robin Paxton, "Islamist Militant Kills Seven in Attack in Kazakh City," Reuters, November 12, 2011, http://www.reuters.com/article/2011/11/12/us-kazakhstan-blast-idUSTRE7AB08220111112.

54. Ibid.

55. Jund al-Khilafah (Army of Caliphate) was reportedly established in the summer of 2011 inside Kazakhstan. Known as a terrorist organization, Jund al-Khilafah is believed to have links with the Taliban and Al Qaida. Also see Michael Schwirt, "Fatal Rampage by a Gunman in Kazakhstan," *New York Times*, November 12, 2011, http://www.nytimes.com/2011/11/13/world/asia/gunman-goes-on-fatal-rampage-in-kazakhstan.html.

56. Dilshod Achilov and Renat Shaykhutdinov, "Islamic Revival, Education and Radicalism in Central Asia," *Journal of Central Asian Studies* 20 (2011): 37–60.

57. Ibid.

58. See Trisko, "Coping with the Islamist Threat."

59. See, for example, Sally N. Cummings, "Islam in the Former Soviet Union," *Global Review of Ethnopolitics* 3, no. 2 (2004): 67–72.

60. Douglas Davis and Dilshod Achilov, "Configuration of Islamic Financial Institutions: A Fuzzy Set Analysis" (paper presented at the Midwest Political Science Association Conference, Chicago, IL, 2008).

61. Since 2000, Islamic finance has grown by 20 to 29 percent annually, with an estimated $700 billion in assets controlled by approximately four hundred Islamic banks in more than twenty-five countries.

62. Islamic Financial Service Board, *Islamic Financial Services Industry Development* (Kuala Lumpur, May 2007), http://www.ifsb.org.

63. See, for example, Martha B. Olcott, *Central Asia's Second Chance* (Washington, D.C.: Carnegie Endowment for International Peace, 2005).

64. The Darahim Sukuk Basket is a three-year note to be issued by BNP Paribas Bank.

65. Kausar Consulting is a leading Kazakhstan-based company specializing in Islamic finance consultancy. Kausar Consulting contributes to systematic development of Islamic finance in Kazakhstan and the Commonwealth of Independent States, working closely with major industry professionals in the Middle East, Europe, and Malaysia.

66. John N. Sandwick has long been a professional advocate of Islamic asset management and was recently listed by the Swiss Bank's magazine as one of the world pioneers of Islamic banking.

67. See CPI Financial News, "Islamic Finance: 'Darahim Sukuk Basket Evokes Silk Road,'" http://www.cpifinancial.netv2/news.aspx?v=1&aid=1675&sec=Islamic%20Finance, accessed February 2009.

68. "Qatar, Bahrain Islamic Banks Eye Kazakh Growth," Reuters, http://www.reuters.com/article/idUSL1925001520080519, accessed May 2008.

69. See A. Donskikh, "Al Hilal, Flagship of Islamic Banking in Kazakhstan, Has Ambitious Plans," *Astana Times*, 2011, http://www.astanatimes.kz/index.php?uin=1290951468&pg=1299137760.

70. See, for example, Robert J. Barro, "Determinants of Democracy," *Journal of Political Economy* 107, no. 6 (1999): 158–83; and Adam Przeworski, *Democracy and Development: Political Institutions and Material Well-Being in the World, 1950–1990* (Cambridge: Cambridge University Press, 2000).

71. See Achilov and Shaykhutdinov, "Islamic Revival, Education and Radicalism."

72. In legal, legitimate institutions, the educational backgrounds of highly qualified teachers are verifiable, transparent, and open to the public. With no such information available, it would be hard for students to question the teacher's credentials, making students vulnerable to biased (and possibly radical) teachings.

73. Rashid, *Jihad.*

74. Sorokina, "Kazakhstan Concerned over Radical Movements."

75. Dilshod Achilov, "Islamic Education in Central Asia: Evidence from Kazakhstan," *Asia Policy* 14, no. 1 (2012): 79–106.

76. Ronald Inglehart, *Modernization and Postmodernization: Cultural, Economic, and Political Change in 43 Societies* (Princeton, NJ: Princeton University Press, 1997), 188.

77. See Achilov, "Islamic Education in Central Asia."

78. A madrassa is a traditional Islamic or secular educational center or institution. Translated from the Arabic, it literally means "a place where learning and studying are done."

79. Sulaymaniye Jamaat (aka Sulaymancilar) is a peaceful, highly spiritual group that originated in Turkey and was founded by Suleyman Hoca Efendi (1888–1959). The movement's mission is to help people learn how to read, recite the Qur'an, and understand the core pillars of Islam in contemporary context.

80. See the discussion in Djanibek Suleev, "Pridet li radikalniy Islam v Kazakhstan?" [Will radical Islam come to Kazakhstan?], Zona KZ, 2000, http://www.zonakz.net/articles/12986.

81. According to Ashirbek Muminov, the head of Kazakhstan's Oriental Studies Institute. See Farangis Najibullah, "Is Kazakhstan under Threat of Radical Islamization?" Radio Free Europe, March 30, 2011, http://www.rferl.org/content/chaikhana_kazakhstan_islamization_-threat/3542185.html.

82. Constitution of Kazakhstan, 1995, Article 1.1.

83. It is important to distinguish moderate Islamic parties from militant, radical "Islamic" groups that pursue various radical ideologies (e.g., neo-Wahhabism, Al Qaida, and Hizb ut-Tahrir).

84. Ludmila Polonskaya and Alexei Malashenko, *Islam in Central Asia: National Specificities and Post-Soviet Globalisation* (Reading, UK: Ithaca Press, 1994), 136.

85. Constitution of Kazakhstan, 1995, Article 5.1.

86. Karagiannis, "Rise of Political Islam in Kazakhstan."

87. Except for Tajikistan, no Central Asian country has any registered Islamic political parties.

88. Mr. A. Davronbekov, deputy imam of SAMK, interview by the author, Almaty, Kazakhstan, July 2008.

4

Negotiating Social Activism

National Minority Associations in Kazakhstan, or the Other Face of "Civil Society"

Marlene Laruelle

In this chapter I seek to deconstruct the one-size-fits-all concept of civil society in several of its postulates, in particular those that assume a clear separation between society and state, between nongovernmental organizations (NGOs) and government-organized nongovernmental organizations (GONGOs), between the interests of individuals and those of the nation, and between charitable activities and private business. Based on interviews conducted with community associations of the Assembly of the People and in-depth fieldwork among the Russian, German, and Dungan communities, I aim to discuss the role of national minorities' associations in Kazakhstan as a way to articulate the issue of "civil society" with regard to social activism and citizen belonging. Through this prism, this chapter highlights the multiple elements involved in formulating informal social activism and dissociates the latter from more institutionalized forms of civil society involvement. It demonstrates the autonomy of these associations, the importance of informal links and networks, the strategies of integration and affiliation of individuals, and the interactive role these associations play in the different facets of the everyday social fabric.

Theoretical Weaknesses of the "Civil Society" Concept

The term "civil society," often defined in a consensual manner as "the arena of uncoerced collective action around shared interests, purposes and values," has long been subject to debate within the scientific community.[1] The meanings of this term are in fact multiple, especially as it covers different realities: philanthropic associations, advocacy groups for human rights or free media, women's groups, veterans groups, youth or elderly groups defending specific rights, ecological associations, ethnic- or faith-based groups, and so on.[2] The simplistic model of the triad with the state, commercial, and noncommercial sectors separated from one another is no longer considered germane. It has been replaced by more complex models, hierarchizing regime system, market, and citizens with greater or lesser areas of overlap between them.[3]

Applied to Central Asia, probably the most widespread use of the term "civil society" employs the neoliberal and Western-centered definition, even if some works provide a more complex reading.[4] Civil society is held to be a free grouping of volitional individuals, all of whom seek to advance their progressive political and social aims (not economic ones, since in this case they would enter into the definition of lobbies).[5] This definition widely dominates the field of studies on civil society in the postsocialist world.[6] It seems the Soviet-period focus on dissidence as societal combat for more autonomy and an increased right to participation in authoritarian states has been transferred to the postsocialist situations of the 1990s and 2000s. The dominant postulate is that exiting from authoritarianism necessitates state influence being reduced as civil society exerts pressure for more political and economic freedoms.[7] Civil society is thus held to be a key element of the processes of "transition"—another postulate—a reading that is often validated by the so-called color revolutions in Serbia, Georgia, the Ukraine, and Kyrgyzstan, in which the established political authorities were overthrown. Civil society and democratic and/or pro-Western revolution are therefore broadly associated.[8] In Central Asia, Kyrgyzstan is the republic to have been most studied from this angle, since there the life of associations is the most developed and the overthrow of the established powers in 2005 and 2010 gives off the image of a livelier "democracy."[9]

The postulates implied by the standard definition of civil society must, however, be largely put into question at multiple levels, which I will mention here only briefly. The link between civil society and democratization is probably the least pertinent. Works on the "illiberal" or "uncivil" society have grown in number over recent years. Studies on pre-Nazi Germany, for example, constitute classics of an "uncivil" society that has succeeded in influencing state policies.[10] Closer to us, analyses conducted on nationalist or extreme right-wing movements in Russia or in the former communist Eastern Europe, as well as those on Islamist associations, work to confirm that the dynamism of civil society can very often go against a Western vision of democracy.[11] Scholars studying this "negative" civil society often presume that the "positive" character of civil society is self-evident, based on the values of parliamentary representation, human rights, and the market economy. The movements that fight against these values or appeal to different legitimacies (ethnic, religious) would therefore constitute sorts of "errors" or "deviations" in the necessarily progressive logic of civil society.[12] However, this implies confounding a personal political and philosophical opinion with a theoretical framework of analysis. In Central Asia, the Hizb ut-Tahrir is just as legitimate in its representation of civil society as a human rights NGO, whatever the personal opinion of the researcher.[13]

In this framework, it is worth discussing rapidly the postulates of Western policies for supporting civil society, policies that were put in place by the international community in the countries of the former Socialist Bloc.[14] These policies tended to avoid state reform, instead anticipating that changes would come from the so-called civil society: if elections cannot be free and just, then bypassing them through the daily activism of NGOs will compensate for it. However, liberal theories of the Bretton Woods institutions, endorsing a limitation of the state as a key element for "emerging" democratic societies, have failed, as it is "state policy rather than civil society [that] will determine the shape and direction of national development in Eurasia."[15] In fact, the Central Asian populations would like more state, not less state. The state is seen as the embodiment of a pacified national identity and of international recognition of the nation, as a guarantee of economic prosperity, and as a potential symbol of good governance. The delegitimization of the state apparatus, as occurred during the Tajik civil war and as can more and more clearly be seen to be happening in Kyrgyzstan, is not only dangerous for the future of Central Asian societies, but it is not desired by the populations. The liberalization of the individual from state tutelage is not always perceived by the most interested persons as a positive development: this is autonomy by default, a "no other choice solution" to cope with the collapse of the state. Many NGO activists working on poverty, ecological questions, or the status of women, children, the handicapped, the homeless, or aged persons do not promote any political agenda of democratization: they seek to respond to humanitarian emergencies only because of the absence of the welfare state.

If the state did "its work," then they would not be involved in the associative domain.[16]

In addition, the idea of a clear distinction between society and state is particularly simplistic. The state is an abstract, philosophical notion, the reality of which is implemented by individuals who belong to society just as much as the persons they administer.[17] They have their own analytical biases, their personal, familial, and regional interests to defend, and their own political choices and priorities. Here, too, this phenomenon is not a "deviation" of the post-Soviet states or of developing countries but is also to be found in the old European democracies. Here there is no difference in principle (perfect versus imperfect state) but only one of degree, and thwarting this phenomenon depends on extant mechanisms, which, while developed in the old democracies, are more fragile elsewhere.

Another example of clear nonseparation between state and society is the phenomenon of GONGOs, often presented as a usurpation of civil society's "authenticity."[18] Studies conducted on the GONGOs in China reveal that they cannot be reduced to simple façades of democracy, or instruments of the state in its "manipulation" of democracy: even in authoritarian states, the legitimating of the regime and its governance is founded in large part on cooperative mechanisms. The Chinese government, for example, co-opted the leaders of associative movements in the environmental domain to give them positions in the GONGOs it had created.[19] The force of the grassroots phenomenon thus enabled people to have their voices heard in the state institutions and then to make a bridge between "society" and "state." Quite clearly, co-optation signifies the imposition of certain limits to the commitments, since the regime accepts the improvement of some elements of governance but refuses to engage in discussions on a scale that it deems contests the political order. Here, too, many civil society activists do not have as their objective to change society or the regime but solely to make governance more efficient in the domain that is dear to them. In this case, the line of division between NGO and GONGO can lose its legitimacy, since it is the result that counts.

Another absence of separation between state and civil society concerns the internal dynamics of their functioning. Analyses of the degree of corruption and nepotism in Central Asian state institutions are well known by researchers and considered as legitimate topics, but civil society is often spared similar analyses. There is a tendency to consider civil society only as the victim of corrupt state practices. However, many NGOs in Central Asia have also had to manage multiple cases of corruption, nepotism, or ethnic preference, which go against their proclaimed universal and egalitarian goals. The subject remains in part taboo, as civil society is held to be free of particularistic bias and to embody the ideal of the common good.[20] Recognizing the divergence of agendas between international donors and local receiving associations is another topic that is difficult to address, as civil society aims by definition to be transparent and well governed.[21] The idea that local actors use the money distributed to them for ends other than those anticipated by the donor and have their own agendas is not easily recognized. Similarly, to assert that civil society is not a commercial institution of the market assumes a simplistic view of the market as being about material goods and not cultural and social capital. For many activists, a position in an NGO is a sign of social promotion, and indeed a means of making money. In Central Asia as elsewhere in the developing world, civil society may offer an envied professional niche, a guarantee of good salaries and opportunities to travel and to study, and a springboard for emigration or toward a political career.[22]

Finally, there often exists an excessive focus on the institutional character of civil society, which is deemed to materialize through institutions with a legal status or that are battling to obtain one. This institutional view of NGOs in Central Asia, however, is not very pertinent: an NGO can gather a small number of persons, and individuals can belong to many of them or conduct a single activity under several institutional umbrellas; NGOs may appear and disappear very quickly, without any real institutional monitoring, unless by those who lead them.[23] Quantified civil society seems to validate intuitions: there are statistically more NGOs in Kyrgyzstan than in Turkmenistan, and the greater democratization of the former compared with the latter is not in doubt. However, the cause-effect relation remains to be demonstrated and should even be inverted: it is because there is more democracy in Kyrgyzstan than in Turkmenistan that NGOs prosper there. This institutional focus tends also to ignore issues of social mobilization. However, the mechanisms of social mobilization make it possible to grasp more accurately the multiplicity of identities of individuals.[24] They have to hierarchize their family, community-based, and regional identities and to have commitments as citizens, multiple informal networks, and material interests; but they also make their decisions in accordance with their perceptions and moods, rumors, hopes and disillusions, and so on.

One of the most well-known examples to come from Central Asia, and the one that seems to plead clearly in favor of leaving these quite naïve readings of civil society behind, is that of the *mahalla* in Uzbekistan. Uzbek society grants importance to social networks such as the extended family and the neighborhood community, or *mahalla*. The *mahalla* comprises the *aksakals* ("white beards"), that is, the elderly to whom decision making and mediation are reserved. During the Soviet period, in particular the Brezhnev decades, the authorities sought to revalorize the neighborhood association by giving it a socialist aspect: the idea of collective decision making in popular committees corresponded well to socialist ideology and enabled the state to penetrate the social fabric, right into the everyday life of citizens. In 1993 the independent Uzbek government reinforced this logic by officializing the system of *mahallas,* which today forms links across the whole national territory, in rural areas as well as in urban zones.[25] Each *mahalla* has one or several state-salaried employees and is directly dependent on the *hakimiyat,* or local government. The *mahallas* have been granted increased rights, ranging from the distribution of social aid to the mediation of neighborhood conflicts and of conflicts within families (adultery, divorce, polygamy, vanished husband, etc.). They have offices that manage marriages, births, and deaths, as well as population censuses and the land register, and they coach for military conscription. They are in charge of all the functions of population control: control of minors, of behavior considered deviant (drugs, prostitution, sexually transmissible diseases such as HIV), political surveillance of dissidents or prohibited religious groupings, and so on.[26]

The *mahalla* is therefore at once a form of self-administrative unit and a mode of vertical control of the state over society. The official discourse on the "return to tradition" and the emergence of civil society in national colors enables paternalist regimes to present a democratic façade while also reinforcing their modes of control over citizens. It is, however, too simple to denigrate the *mahalla* as a simple GONGO, organized by the bureaucrats and without impact on daily life; precisely because the *mahalla* interferes with social mechanisms that grant importance to the individual's integration into the collectivity, whether it be familial, clannish, or regional, it contributes to modeling the social fabric.[27] While some reticent persons may see in the *mahalla* the "hand of the state," the majority of individuals project the informal *mahalla*—the community links—onto the administrative cell and have extensive recourse to the services offered by the latter. We thus see that the distinction of NGO and GONGO is artificial and that citizens appropriate for themselves the control structure put into place by the authorities—cognizant of how to use it, though sometimes wanting to bypass it.

Civil Society *à la Kazakh*: The Assembly of the People

How does this discussion on the concept of civil society apply to the case study of interest to us here, namely that of the ethnic associations in Kazakhstan? More than in any other of the former Soviet states, the Kazakhstani authorities have kept the Soviet cult of multinationality alive.[28] Official discourse vaunts the harmony in which Kazakhstan's more than 130 "nationalities" live, thanks to the "hospitality" of the native Kazakh people on its own soil. The official narrative hones in on the idea of being the crossroads of the Old World. It exults the median character of Kazakhstan, in a geographical but also a cultural sense, and presents it as the axis of universal history, where peoples and world religions have been generously received for more than two millennia. Such a discourse is reinforced by Nursultan Nazarbayev's interest in so-called Eurasianist ideology of the early 1990s, in a version of which Kazakhstan is the synthesis of the West and the East, of European and Asian cultures, of Christianity and Islam.[29]

This mythical Eurasia offers the Kazakhstani authorities the possibility to present themselves as an indispensable ally of all their international partners: Russia, China, the European Union, Turkey, Iran, India, Japan, South Korea, and so on. It cannot, however, be interpreted uniquely as a foreign policy strategy and as an economic pragmatism favorable to the maintenance of privileged links between former Soviet republics, especially links with Russia. The Eurasianist narrative also constitutes a modernized version of the former internationalist Soviet discourse and has a domestic aspect that concerns the ethnic balance within the country. If in the first years of independence Nazarbayev expressed an overtly nostalgic discourse of the USSR and negated any national expression that was too strictly Kazakh, in the second half of the 1990s he was forced to tone down his statements on the country's civic identity and the importance of the Russian language: to avoid losing political clout, he had to present himself as both the president of all Kazakhstanis *and* that of the Kazakhs only. This inherent paradox is reflected in the country's constitution, which defines it as both the state of the Kazakhstanis and that of the Kazakhs, as well as in its policy of repatriation of ethnic Kazakhs living abroad.[30] The preamble of the Constitution of 1995 indeed claims, "We, the people of Kazakhstan, united by common historical destiny, creating statehood on the ancient Kazakh land . . ." (na iskonnoi kazakhskoi zemle).[31] Since that time, many legislative texts have continued this ambiguity by insisting as much on the fundamentally civic character of national identity, without ethnic distinction, as on the specific rights of the Kazakhs, who have become "the first among equals."

However, the stance of the state is ambiguous: while official discourse speaks about integration and multinationalism, in practice non-Kazakh components are excluded from decision-making processes. The Kazakhstani state does not actually pursue multicultural policy per se and has, for example, abolished the principle of positive discrimination through quotas. Although in compact residential areas some national minorities have schools teaching in their language, members of these communities are supposed to use both official languages, Kazakh and Russian, when communicating with the government. No national minorities have access to special rights like quotas for entry into university or the administration. The country uniquely recognizes the right to organize associations on an ethnic basis, but no political parties or demands for recognition of territorial autonomy will be accepted, since Kazakhstan, like all the neighboring post-Soviet states, with the exception of Russia, is a unitary and not a federal republic.[32] While cultural, religious, and linguistic diversity is promoted, it is thus strictly controlled and regulated by law, as was shown in the *Doctrine of National Unity of Kazakhstan* published in 2010.[33]

Expressing one's ethnic identity is considered a form of civil society that is both easily tractable and to be placed uniquely at the service of the political authorities' interests. To institutionalize this "nationalities' civic society," Nazarbayev founded the Assembly of the Peoples of Kazakhstan, which was later renamed the Assembly of the People of Kazakhstan. Created by decree on March 1, 1995, and not mentioned in the constitution, the assembly is directed by the president of the republic on the basis of a supposed "people's will." Although it is merely a consultative body, the assembly has initiated two referendums, one on extending the presidential term of office and the other on the new constitution. Its 350 members are not elected but appointed by the president. They are supposed to represent all the minority cultural centers, from the smallest (Assyrians) to the most numerous (Russians). In terminology that is still very Soviet, the assembly is presented as the "laboratory of the friendship of the peoples."[34] In reality, about half of its members come from the cultural centers; the others work in the administrative organs that manage the nationalities policy.

The assembly functions, therefore, on a co-optation principle, not on proportional representation; it gives priority to administrative staff specializing in the national question and to cultural centers faithful to official priorities.[35] Folkloric activities—like days of Slavic culture, Armenian music, Tatar chorale, and Korean cuisine—dominate the work of the assembly. It oversees and finances about 170 weekend schools where twenty-three native languages are taught, several minority-language newspapers, and the Kazakh, Russian, German, Korean, Uzbek, and Uighur national theaters. Debates on politicized issues, such as minority representation in the political life and the high echelons of the national economy, are totally absent from the preoccupations of the assembly.[36] All the nationalities' cultural centers with a status in the Assembly of the People or in small regional or municipal assemblies therefore fit the definition of GONGOs. They are elements of a would-be civil society that is largely organized and managed by the state.

Since its creation in the mid-1990s, the assembly has aimed to sidestep the so-called Russian problem by taking a much wider view of the nationalities question. The authorities' aim was to show that the country was not binational, Russian and Kazakh, but multinational and that the Russians therefore did not possess a privileged status in it. Thus the Assembly of the People includes about 26 percent Kazakhs, 15 percent Russians, 6.5 percent each for Koreans, Germans, and Tatars, and less for other, smaller groups.[37] The assembly has also strongly promoted the Ukrainians and the Byelorussians so as to detach them from Russian demands and undermine the idea of a great Slavic mass present in considerable proportions in the country. Although the "Russian question" has now disappeared from the Kazakhstani political scene (even during the Ukrainian crisis of 2014), the propaganda related to the nationalities policy remains characterized by a hierarchy of ethnic identities.[38]

The eponymous or titular nationality dominates in symbolic terms: Kazakhstan is legally recognized as a state created on the territory of the Kazakhs and they are "first among equals." The country's multinationality is celebrated not in the name of the universality of humanity beyond cultural differences but as a proof of Kazakh "hospitality" in receiving other peoples on its land.[39] The place of each nationality is therefore dependent on what it brings to the country's international branding and the historical memory of Kazakhstani society. The Russians are not considered titular, but their number makes them an ethnic group like no other and they are rarely presented as a "minority." They are the former colonizers and brothers-enemies of the Kazakhs, but also often the only people with whom reference and comparison is considered relevant. Astana has continued to keep up direct and friendly relations with Moscow and has prevented the Russians of Kazakhstan from becoming intermediaries in the relationship with Russia, a strategy that Moscow has validated without any difficulties.[40] The Kazakhstani authorities tend to celebrate national minorities who represent countries with which Kazakhstan has developed close economic ties—mostly Germany and South Korea. In this framework, the Germans and the Koreans are held up as well-integrated minorities for their active involvement in the development of Kazakhstan.[41] Poles, Armenians, and Greeks are also valorized, although the economic links with their kin states are fewer.

For other minorities, symbolic integration is more complicated. This is the case, for example, for the Uighurs and Chechens: the former were in symbolic competition with the Kazakhs in the 1970s, as the Uighur intelligentsia began to present themselves as autochthonous on the territory of the republic and demanded an autonomous status, raising the ire of the Kazakhs; the Chechens, for their part, bear a long-standing historical disapproval since the deportations in the Second World War. Moreover, both peoples are today considered to be hidden Islamists, or at least as troublemaking elements in the relations with, respectively, Moscow and Beijing, and no one in Astana desires to protect them. The case of the Uzbeks is also difficult. More than 90 percent of them live in South Kazakhstan, where they make up 17 percent of the population (but 60 percent in the Sairam district and 42 percent in the town of Turkestan).[42] They are hostages of difficult Uzbek-Kazakhstani relations, and Astana is becoming afraid of the growing "Uzbekization" of the country's south, where local economic rivalries between Uzbeks and Kazakhs around market produce and farming have increased.[43]

The Assembly of the People thus has several missions: it symbolizes a recognized national diversity to the international and the domestic community; it supports small and depoliticized minorities that are satisfied with the cultural rights they are given; and it marginalizes more political minorities like Russians, Uighurs, or Uzbeks. The Kazakhstani strategy is to show diversity of opinion via the national question, in order to avoid debating issues with real political stakes that could endanger the regime. It seeks to replace representative democracy with the expression of a civil society in which the structuring element is not social class or political orientation but national belonging.[44] The role of ethnic cultural associations is therefore highly instrumental. And yet, when one delves into the daily practices of these associations, a different picture emerges.

The Multiple Framing of Social Engagement

As one possible form of social mobilization, the issue of ethnic affiliation merits further investigation. It is not enough to be an active member of an NGO in order for one to feel a sense of citizenship in a country or to consider oneself represented by the political organs that symbolize a nation. To grasp the social contract between the state and citizens, which is frequently not formulated in an explicit manner, as well as to understand how citizenship is rooted in everyday practices and meanings, one needs to look at nation making not only as a citizenship challenge and a myth-making process but also as the performance of everyday activities.[45] Traditionally, academic studies on national identity have been chiefly concerned with the political and cultural construction that the elite perform from the top down. While there is a consensus that nationalism is a mass phenomenon, the masses have been curiously missing from much of the scholarship. However, there can be no statehood without nationhood and no citizenship without a somewhat elaborated symbolic formulation of it, or without multiform practices in everyday habits and routines.

It should first be noted that few people who are identified as non-Kazakhs in their passports (nationality is still mentioned in the fifth point of the Kazakhstani passport) are familiar with the associations that allegedly represent their national minority. Instead many individuals work within personal and professional networks that are absolutely unrelated to the so-called ethnic identity ascribed to them. Many people see themselves as Kazakhstani and harbor no desires to have another identity. The expression of this allegiance to the regime is often understood as a means of personal promotion in the context of a client relationship.[46] But it is not only opportunistic; most of them regard themselves as legitimate citizens. Even among those who attach importance to identity issues and feel themselves to belong to a minority in a state that is primarily Kazakh, the associations are not necessarily appreciated or valued.[47] They are often criticized as corrupt, disconnected from the community, advocates for the personal interests of their leaders, and subject to the political intrigues of the moment. It is therefore necessary to be wary of "the illusion of community," which leads to situations in which characteristics are ascribed to nationality. Individual behavior and strategies transcend singular affiliations.[48]

Nationalities' associations have no representativeness at all in sociological terms. However, they are an important part of the social fabric for their active members, allowing them to conduct social activism without having to get involved in "high politics." While the latter is denounced for its notorious corruption and hypocrisy and for the careerism of those within it, the charitable activities of social activists, or *obshchestvenniki,* are presented as generous, selfless, and having the sole aim of filling in the lack of state assistance and ensuring the autonomy of the community. One can thus schematically categorize the persons who work full-time for the national centers—and who are often remunerated by very small salaries out of the center's monies or those of the Assembly of the People—into two categories: the old *obshchestvenniki* of the Soviet era, who had functions either within the same type of institutions or else within the Komsomols or organs of the party, and who therefore pursue the previous logic of social activism; and businessmen who have built their fortunes on the basis of the post-Soviet liberalization and who now seek forms of notabilization by involving themselves in the social activities of the cultural center of their minority. This twin identity, culture based and business related, is central to the functioning of the immense majority of ethnic associations.[49]

Despite their GONGO characteristics, minority associations have some autonomy. Unable to speak on political issues and obliged to continually demonstrate their loyalty to the authorities, they are limited to cultural categories of activities: the preservation of the national language and religion, as well as feast days or historical commemorations, are obviously considered the foremost priorities. The major Soviet holidays (May 9 for veterans, March 8 for women, the day for retirees, etc.) are always given special attention. The Russian associations are all heavily oriented toward the Orthodox Church, even if some are formed by activists close to the communist movements.[50] For the ethnic groups of Muslim tradition, the aid in the hajj, the pilgrimage to Mecca, forms part of the seminal measures, but the associations often remain discreet on this sensitive question in order to avoid criticisms of rampant Islamicization.[51]

Associations also uphold a role as vector of sociability for the members of the community who frequent them. They try to push the young generations—bearers of the future of the ethnic group—to remain in the community framework by favoring their professional and familial integration within the group. The activists—often women—of the Tatar cultural centers recognize, for instance, the preference for marriages within the community in order to maintain the collective identity and avoid its "dissolution" through mixed marriages with Russians or Kazakhs. Cultural activities, such as the celebration of the traditional summer festival, Sabantuj, thus serve as moments for matchmaking.[52]

The role of social links between community members also signifies solidarity with the poorest. Almost all the minority cultural centers have a section for humanitarian aid, which is distributed to the poorest and elderly. The German center Vozrozhdenie, one of the most powerful thanks to the financing it receives from Germany, has, for example, several pharmacies and small medical sections that receive members of the community but are open to all.[53] The Jewish association Mitsva—which is reliant on the network of the Jewish Eurasian Congress, led by one of Kazakhstan's most powerful oligarchs, Aleksandr Mashkevich—also offers food and medical aid.[54] Even the smallest centers, such as the Hungarian or Kalmyk cultural centers, though without much financial capacity, play the card of social aid. These forms of social support within the community are considered particularly important since they give the association a raison d'être and materialize the unity of the community in everyday life.

National associations also develop forms of unionism and lobbying for their community, mostly in education. In particular, associations of Germans, Ukrainians, Byelorussians, Poles, Greeks, and Tatars organize the departure of "their own" to the kin state.[55] The associations therefore occupy an ambiguous position, since they use their official mission to promote minorities as an intervening means for personal career and activist goals and present themselves as essential intermediaries for the kin state. For some of their members, this form of "ethnic unionism" is considered more important than cultural activities: interviews conducted among young activists in German associations confirm that they interpret their involvement as a means of getting noticed so that they will be sent to study in Germany, or indeed can emigrate permanently.[56] The setting in place by some kin states of ethnic repatriation policies has underscored this utilitarian reading of involvement in associations.[57] In the 1990s the leaders of the most virulent Russian associations also played the political refugee card in order to be able to emigrate to Moscow and enter the lobby associations involved in the defense of "compatriots."[58]

Social activism is not always disinterested; it is also part of processes of notabilization for the most visible figures, that is, essentially for businessmen, who are often also the presidents of the cultural centers. In this way, the president of the Turkish cultural center Ahiska, Ziyatdin Kasanov, personally financed the construction of some houses for homeless members of the community and supplied the necessary capital to help members to open a first business.[59] The president of the Dungan center, Husei Daurov, also finances the modernization of some Dungan farms in the Korday district, near Dzhambul.[60] Some national associations have specialized in specific commercial activities, similar to the types of ethnic businesses that are common throughout the post-Soviet space. With the acceleration of migration flows to Russia, Russian associations have quickly specialized in helping their members to prepare for migration, providing, for example, services to obtain Russian passports, legal assistance, and departure organization.[61] Many of these associations thus occupy a complex niche. They present themselves as cultural associations but in reality are commercial organizations. They represent only themselves but often get official intermediary status (*posredniki*) from both the Kazakhstani authorities and the Russian consular services.[62] Some national German associations also tried to invest in this sector in the 1990s but were brought into line by the German authorities, which sought to stamp out any corrupt practices concerning emigration applications.[63]

Still other associations have managed to create specific economic niches. Here, too, everything depends on the state of relations between Kazakhstan and the kin state—whether or not it creates opportunities—and on the initiative taken by the director of the cultural center. In this way, the German, Korean, Polish, Greek, Armenian, and Turkish cultural centers seem to enjoy, at diverse levels, roles as intermediaries in the relations with kin states.[64] The president of the Turkish cultural center, for example, runs some small private companies that engage in trade with Turkey, and he has close contacts with some Turkish businessmen settled in the country.[65] Similarly for the Azeri cultural center, which Azerbaijan seems to support strongly and which benefits from the growing trade between the two countries to create niches for its members.[66] The Byelorussian center is also partially financed by its connections with Byelorussian companies settled in Kazakhstan.[67]

The case of the Dungans is particularly revealing of this logic. Today they play a role as cultural "shuttles" and economic mediators between Central Asia and the Chinese world. Since the late 1990s, the Dungan Association of Kazakhstan, led by the businessman Husei Daurov, has organized cultural exchanges between Kazakhstan and the Shaanxi and Gansu provinces for Dungans in search of their roots and for students. In 2003, anxious to respond to a request by the Assembly of the People, but also to avoid communitarian criticisms, the association launched a massive program to send Kazakhstani students to China without regard to their ethnic nationality. It currently manages all the Kazakhstani students (about six hundred) in Xi'an. Daurov has succeeded in transforming cultural exchanges into commercial partnerships and in moving from the nongovernmental sector into the governmental one. The association has played the hand of ethnic solidarity, re-creating from scratch the links between the Kazakhstani Dungan diaspora and its provinces of origin. But it has also managed to avoid getting stuck in a too-restrictive Dungan/Hui framework, by convincing the administrations of Gansu, Shaanxi, and Dzhambul, and also Kazakhstani authorities in Astana, to utilize it as a cog in state-level commercial relations. The association therefore uses its official status within the Assembly of the People to serve as an intermediary for Kazakhstani businessmen looking to do business in China and has opened offices in Xi'an, Shenzhen, Beijing, Shanghai, Lanzhou, Urumqi, and Yinchuan.

More and more Dungans are taking full advantage of their role as cultural mediators between the two worlds: the association has inked agreements with Chinese companies to build modest hotel infrastructures in two areas of compact Dugan settlement, near Dzhambul and around Shortiube. This tourism is expected to provide additional income to rural Dungans based on the folklorization of culture. The hotels will be built in a Qing-era Chinese style and offer "traditional" activities such as festivals in Dungan costume. Daurov's goal is to transform his home village, Shortiube, into a symbolic port of entry for Chinese culture in Kazakhstan by encouraging a sort of re-ethnicization of the Dungan community.[68] Thus, through private funding, either from their country of origin or from local patrons, some associations have been able put in place social promotion strategies for group members, and not only for their leaders.

The large range of activities covered by the national cultural centers proposes original material for reflecting on the meanings of so-called civil society in Kazakhstan. These associations can quite rightly be defined as

GONGOs, since they are clearly controlled by state structures and have to manifest their enthusiasm toward Nazarbayev's policies. However, these GONGOs do not necessarily "usurp" the role of NGOs: they make it possible to relay specific information from the grass roots to the top of the political power pyramid and also offer a new framework to organize the social fabric in an autonomous fashion. They have no general political message to deliver—the ethnic associations that undermined the global domestic order, mainly Russian and Uighur associations, were eliminated—and they rest content with militating for precise and pragmatic objectives, such as more schooling in the national language, public financing for their activities, more opportunities for small-scale business and collaboration with kin states, more social aid to distribute, and so on. They therefore play a role that is both bottom-up and top-down, and their status as state intermediary does not indicate that they are completely losing credibility through their actions.

Although GONGOs, they preserve their social autonomy to the extent that they seek to maintain the links between members of the community, to conserve the feeling of ethnic unity, and also to participate in the process of integrating into Kazakhstani society via strategies of ethnic business development, patronage, co-optation, and participation in national symbolism. They thus form a junction between "minority" and "majority" by showing that the preservation of the specificities of the "minority" is not contrary to the interests of the "majority." They therefore offer two forms of social integration: one into the ethnic community and the other into Kazakhstani society, since both are socially valued and often included within a common ideological framework shared by all citizens regardless of their ethnic identification. Neither are these associations exempt from the evils of the society in which they live—corruption, nepotism, patronage. On the contrary, their participation in these processes guarantees them both better integration and protection against potentially discriminatory measures thanks to networking and informal connections. Finally, they straddle the charitable activities of the Soviet tradition of *obshchestvennost'* and those of small businesses that emerged with the transition to the market economy. To claim that at issue are Machiavellian strategies designed to dissimulate commercial activities behind associations would be a simplistic reduction of the motivations of individuals' involvement, which are by definition multiple and interlocking.

The attempts to classify political regimes according to different degrees of authoritarianism and civil society organizations in accordance with their status, number, objectives, members, and so on are often reductive, since they lose sight of the fundamentally hybrid character of social reality. The concept of civil society thus tends to obscure the social fabric in Central Asia more than clarify it. In fact, the Kazakhstani state, somewhat similar to its neighbors, is a consultative authoritarianism; it seeks to co-opt citizens in order to improve its mechanisms of governance, lest discontent becomes politicized, to its detriment. Associations thus have a broad range of possibilities for engaging in cooperation with the Kazakhstani state, especially those that defend precise objectives (women's rights, and minority rights) and not political ideals (human rights). The co-optation runs in both directions, since the associations also succeed in acquiring an institutional status, which in return gives them legitimacy among those they consider as their members.

In Kazakhstan, minority identity is not necessarily an issue, but, on the contrary, can be valorized as positive cultural capital, which helps to promote the individual in society. It is in this niche that the ethnic associations work to foreground their relation with the kin state, their cultural heritage, their language, and their participation in the Kazakhstani civic consensus. Even in a multiethnic post-Soviet country dominated by a primordialist approach to the individual and the group, the sense of civic community is more complex than it may seem. Minority associations provide an interface between the "state" and "society," between "majority" and "minority," and between *obshchestvennost'* and business. The distribution of resources is carried out on the basis of ethnic belonging: it is therefore often more worthwhile to be linked to an ethnic group than it is not to lay claim to such an identity. Minority associations seek to make compatible the individual good, the community good, and the national collective good and to avoid patterns of conflictuality. They are situated among a wide range of strategies based on patterns of both ethnic and nonethnic sociability that allow for the creation of a "life together." This hybrid nature is interesting to analyze because it forces one to challenge the idea that there are well-defined borders that circumscribe so-called civil society, and to shift from institutional frameworks to informal ones. The involvement of the individual in his or her society and therefore his or her role as a civic partner of the state structure must be understood through a study of social networks, of the flexibility of affiliations, of hybridity, and of the informality of integration strategies.

This chapter sought to discuss the various ambivalences contained in the concept of "civil society" and the numerous niches of activity through which some individuals—here those identified as belonging to minority ethnic identities—can become involved in public life and forge their identities as citizens, even in a regime without large political liberties such as that in Kazakhstan. This study of "minorities" leaves open the question of knowing how the "majority" of ethnic Kazakhs manage to build themselves niches of autonomy away from the authorities, or niches of cooperation and negotiation with them. These niches depend to a large extent on the social and cultural dichotomy opposing city dwellers and country folk: among ethnic Kazakhs the urban/rural divide in living standards is huge, as is that in professional and personal prospects and in cultural orientations (Russian-speaking versus Kazakh-speaking, relations to traditional identities like genealogical filiations and to the neighborhood community, attitude toward Islam). This divide is being profoundly reshaped by the considerable migration of people from the country to the city, which is transforming the urban social fabric and creating new tensions between the "old" Russified city dwellers and the new and poorly integrated country folk. Paradoxically, there is probably less common consensus about social activism for ethnic Kazakhs than about what the "minorities" have succeeded in forming: the former challenge more overtly, or are called upon to challenge the established regime, including its authoritarian political foundations (contestation came, for example, through oil industry workers during the Zhanaozen riots in December 2011), its secular nature (Islamism is developing as a political alternative), and its "internationalism" (Kazakh ethno-nationalism has the wind in its sail among the youth).

Notes

1. This definition is the classic one, given by the London School of Economics Centre for Civil Society, "What is Civil Society?" 2006, archived at UK Web Archive, http://www.lse.ac.uk/collections/CCS/introduction/what_is_civil_society.htm.

2. M. Edwards, *Civil Society* (Cambridge: Polity Press, 2004).

3. A. Fowler, *Civic Driven Change: Citizen's Imagination in Action* (The Hague: Institute of Social Studies, October 2008).

4. C. Buxton, *The Struggle for Civil Society in Central Asia: Crisis and Transformation* (Sterling, UK: Kumarian Press, 2011); M. Holt Ruffin and D. Waugh, eds., *Civil Society in Central Asia* (Seattle: University of Washington Press, 1999); C. Buxton, "NGO Networks in Central Asia and Global Civil Society: Potentials and Limitations," *Central Asian Survey* 28, no. 1 (2009): 43–58.

5. P. Burnell, and P. Calvert, eds., *Civil Society in Democratization* (London: Routledge, 2004).

6. For Central Asia, see T. Atabaki, "The Impediments to the Development of Civil Societies in Central Asia," in *Post-Soviet Central Asia,* ed. T. Atabaki and J. O'Kane (London: I. B. Tauris, 1998), 35–43; S. Gretsky, "In Search of Civil Society in Central Asia," in *Oil, Transition and Security in Central Asia,* ed. S. N. Cummings (London: Routledge, 2003): 84–95.

7. See the discussion on this relation in D. J. Galbreath, "Putting the Colour into Revolutions? The OSCE and Civil Society in the Post-Soviet Region," *Journal of Communist Studies and Transition Politics* 25, no. 2–3 (2009): 161–80; L. Way, "The Real Causes of the Color Revolutions," *Journal of Democracy* 19, no. 3 (2008): 55–69.

8. See the debates on this issue in *After the Color Revolutions: Political Changes and Democracy Promotion in Eurasia* (Washington D.C.: PONARS, George Washington University, July 2010).

9. Discussed in S. Radnitz, "A Horse of a Different Color: Revolution and Regression in Kyrgyzstan," in *Democracy and Authoritarianism in the Post-Communist World,* ed. V. Bunce, M. A. McFaul, and K. Stoner-Weiss (New York: Cambridge University Press, 2009), 300–324.

10. R. S. Levy, *The Downfall of the Anti-Semitic Political Parties in Imperial Germany* (New Haven, CT: Yale University Press, 1975); D. J. Goldhagen, *Hitler's Willing Executioners: Ordinary Germans and the Holocaust* (New York: Vintage Books, 1997).

11. On Russia and the former communist East Europe, see S. E. Hanson and J. S. Kopstein, "The Weimar/Russia Comparison," *Post-Soviet Affairs* 13, no. 3 (1997): 252–83; S. E. Hanson and J. S. Kopstein, "Paths to Uncivil Societies and Anti-Liberal States: A Reply to Shenfield," *Post-Soviet Affairs* 14, no. 4 (1998): 369–75. On Islamist associations, see, for instance, N. Salam, *Civil Society in the Arab World: The Historical and Political Dimensions,* Occasional Publications 3 (Cambridge, MA: Islamic Legal Studies Program, Harvard Law School, October 2002); S. Berman, "Islamism, Revolution, and Civil Society," *Perspectives on Politics* 1, no. 2 (2003): 257–72.

12. See Andrey Kazantsev, "Social Capital and Development of Civil Society in Central Asia: A Path Dependency Perspective," chapter 1, this volume.

13. On the importance of social networks and the local agenda in the success of Islamist currents, see K. Collins, "Ideas, Networks, and Islamist Movements: Evidence from Central Asia and the Caucasus," *World Politics* 60, no. 1 (2007): 64–96.

14. For the case of environmental NGOs, see P. Jones Luong and E. Weinthal, "The NGO Paradox: Democratic Goals and Non-democratic Outcomes in Kazakhstan," *Europe-Asia Studies* 51, no. 7 (1999): 1267–84.

15. T. W. Simons Jr., *Eurasia's New Frontiers: Young States, Old Societies, Open Futures* (Ithaca, NY: Cornell University Press, 2008), 4.

16. Anonymous NGO activists working with children in difficulties, interviews by author, Tashkent, March 2008.

17. P. Rosanvallon and A. Goldhammer, *Counter-Democracy: Politics in an Age of Distrust* (Cambridge: Cambridge University Press, 2008).

18. On the complexity of the difference between NGOs and GONGOs, see, for instance, *Uzbekistan Third Sector Survey* (Eurasia Foundation, August 2007).

19. Fengshi Wu, "Environmental GONGO Autonomy: Unintended Consequences of State Strategies in China," *Good Society* 12, no. 1 (2003): 35–45; Seungho Lee, "Environmental Movements and Social Organizations in Shanghai," *China Information* 21, no. 2 (2007): 269–97; T. Salmenkari, "Searching for a Chinese Civil Society," *China Information* 22, no. 3 (2008): 397–421.

20. Anonymous people working in Soros and Central Asian branches of the Red Cross, interviews by author, Tashkent, June 2005, Dushanbe, June 2010.

21. J. Cooper, "The Real Work: Sustaining NGO Growth in Central Asia," in Holt Ruffin and Waugh, *Civil Society in Central Asia,* 214–34.

22. B. Hours, "Les ONG immobilisées," in *L'Ouzbékistan à l'heure de l'identité nationale: Travail, science, ONG,* ed. L. Bazin, M. Selim, and B. Hours (Paris: L'Harmattan, 2009), 277–360.

23. A. Garbutt and S. Heap, eds. *Growing Civil Society in Central Asia,* INTRAC Occasional Papers Series, no. 39 (Oxford: INTRAC, July 2003).

24. See, for instance, S. Radnitz, *Weapons of the Wealthy: Predatory Regimes and Elite-Led Protests in Central Asia* (Ithaca, NY: Cornell University Press, 2010); M. Fumagalli, "Framing Ethnic Minority Mobilization in Central Asia: The Cases of Uzbeks in Kyrgyzstan and Tajikistan," *Europe-Asia Studies* 59, no. 4 (2007): 565–88; E. McGlinchey, "Central Asian Protest Movements," in *The Politics of Transition in Central Asia and the Caucasus,* ed. A. Wooden and C. Stefes (London: Routledge, 2009).

25. E. W. Sievers, "Uzbekistan's Mahalla: From Soviet to Absolutist Residential Community Associations," *Journal of International and Comparative Law* 2 (2002): 91–158.

26. Suda Masaru, "The Politics of Civil Society, *Mahalla* and NGOs: Uzbekistan," in *Reconstruction and Interaction of Slavic Eurasia and Its Neighboring Worlds,* ed. Ieda Osamu and Uyama Tomohiko (Sapporo: Slavic Research Center, 2006), 335–70.

27. E. Massicard and T. Trevisani, "The Uzbek Mahalla: Between State and Society," in *Central Asia: Aspects of Transition,* ed. T. Everett-Health (London: Routledge-Curzon, 2003), 205–18.

28. On Kazakhstan's identity construction, see B. Dave, *Kazakhstan: Ethnicity, Language and Power* (London: Routledge, 2007).

29. On Eurasianism in Kazakhstan, see M. Laruelle, *Russian Eurasianism: An Ideology of Empire* (Washington, D.C.: Woodrow Wilson Press/Johns Hopkins University Press, 2008), 171–200.

30. G. Mendikulova, *Kazakhskaia diaspora i irredenta: Istoriia i sovremennost*

[The Kazakh diaspora and irredentism: History and actuality] (Almaty, 2005); S. Cummings, "The Kazakhs: Demographics, Diasporas, and 'Return,'" in *Nations Abroad: Diaspora Politics and International Relations in the Former Soviet Union*, ed. C. King and N. J. Melvin (Oxford: Westview Press, 1999), 133–52; A. Diener, *One Homeland or Two? The Nationalization and Transnationalization of Mongolia's Kazakhs* (Palo Alto, CA: Stanford University Press, 2009).

31. *Kazakhstan: Etapy gosudarstvennosti. Konstitutsionnye akty* (Almaty: Zheti Zhargy, 1997), 443.

32. See B. Dave, *Kazakhstan.*

33. "Doktrina natsional'nogo edinstva Kazakhstana," Assemby of the People of Kazakhstan, Astana, 2010, www.assembly.kz/?ft=2000&type=93.

34. O. Dymov, *Teplo kazakhstanskoi zemli* (Almaty: Arys, 1999), 39.

35. See the official publications during the first years of its creation; for example, *Istoricheskaya pamyat', natsional'noe soglasie i demokraticheskie reformy—grazhdanskii vybor naroda Kazakhstana* (Almaty: Zhazushi, 1997); *Natsional'noe soglasie—osnova stabil'nosti i razvitiya Kazakhstana* (Astana, 1999); *Dukhovno-kul'turnoe razvitie naroda—osnova ukrepleniya gosudarstvennoy nezavisimosti Kazakhstana* (Astana, 2001).

36. Interviews with different national cultural centers in Almaty, June 2009.

37. Meetings with the cultural center administrative heads at the Assembly of the People of Kazakhstan, Almaty, March 2000, May 2003, February 2005, June 2008, and June 2010.

38. M. Laruelle and S. Peyrouse, *Les Russes du Kazakhstan: Identités nationales et nouveaux; Etats dans l'espace post-soviétique* (Paris: Maisonneuve & Larose/IFEAC, 2004).

39. Yeraly Tugzhanov, vice chairman of the Assembly of the People of Kazakhstan, interview by author, Astana, September 29, 2010.

40. M. Laruelle, *Russian Policy on Central Asia and the Role of Russian Nationalism*, Silk Road Papers (Washington D.C.: Central Asia-Caucasus Institute, April 2008).

41. Natsuko Oka, "The 'Triadic Nexus' in Kazakhstan: A Comparative Study of Russians, Uighurs, and Koreans," in *Beyond Sovereignty: From Status Law to Transnational Citizenship?*, ed. Ieda Osamu (Sapporo: Slavic Research Center, Hokkaido University, 2006), 359–80. See also Natsuko Oka, "The Korean Diaspora in Nationalizing Kazakhstan: Strategies for Survival as an Ethnic Minority," in "Koryo Saram: Koreans in the Former USSR," ed. German N. Kim and Ross King, special issue, *Korean and Korean American Studies Bulletin* 12, no. 2/3 (2001): 89–113.

42. A. Alekseenko, "O nekotorykh itogakh perepisi naseleniia Kakhazstana," *Demoscope,* no. 57–58 (March 4–17, 2002), http://www.demoscope.ru/weekly/2002/057/analit04.php.

43. Natsuko Oka, "Neither Exit nor Voice: Loyalty as the Survival Strategy for the Uzbeks in Kazakhstan," IDE Discussion Paper no. 286, March 2011.

44. Natsuko Oka, "Ethnicity and Elections under Authoritarianism: The Case of Kazakhstan," IDE Discussion Paper no. 194, March 2009.

45. M. Billig, *Banal Nationalism* (London: Sage, 1995); T. Ederson, *National Identity, Popular Culture and Everyday Life* (Oxford: Berg, 2002).

46. Y.-M. Davenel, "'Sous le même toit': Affirmation culturelle et intégration citoyenne de la minorité tatare dans le Kazakhstan contemporain" (PhD diss., EHESS, Paris, 2009).

47. N. Kosmarskaia, *"Deti imperii" v postsovetskoi Tsentral'noi Azii: Adaptivnye praktiki i mental'nye sdvigi (russkie v Kirgizii)* (Moscow: Natalis, 2006).

48. On "ethnic identity as filter to reality," see A. M. Danzer, "Battlefields of Ethnic Symbols: Public Space and Post-Soviet Identity Formation from a Minority Perspective," *Europe-Asia Studies* 61, no. 9 (2009): 1557–77, esp. 1566.

49. Regular fieldwork in Kazakhstan and interviews with activists from the national cultural centers, 2002–2010.

50. Regular interviews in Russian associations in Almaty, Ust-Kamenogorsk, Pavlodar, Karaganda, Semei, Kokchetau, Petropavlovsk, and Astana, 2002–2010.

51. Discussions with anonymous people from Dungan, Uighur, Tatar national centers, Almaty, June 2009.

52. See Davenel, "Sous le même toit."

53. See the website of the Germans of Kazakhstan, http://wiedergeburt.kz/index.php?option=com_content&view=article&id=177&Itemid=56&lang=ru.

54. See Jewish Eurasian Congress, http://www.eajc.org/index_r.php; and Mitsva, http://www.mitsva.kz/heseds.shtml.

55. See Belarus Portal in Kazakhstan, http://www.belarus.kz/company/business. On the question of the different definitions of the nation and the homeland, see R. Brubaker, *Nationalism Reframed: Nationhood and the National Question in the New Europe* (Cambridge: Cambridge University Press, 2004).

56. Anonymous German young people working at the German cultural centers in Almaty, interviews by author, March 2003.

57. On the repatriation programs, see S. Peyrouse, "Former 'Colonialists' on the Move? The Migration of Russian-Speaking Populations," in *Migration and Social Upheaval as the Face of Globalization in Central Asia*, ed. M. Laruelle, forthcoming.

58. Former Russian leaders from Kazakhstan, now based in Moscow, at the Institute for Diaspora and the Compatriots, interviews by author, Moscow, May 2002, March 2003, September 2007.

59. See Ahiska, http://ahiska-gazeta.com/ru/pages/201.html.

60. Husei Daurov, interview by author, Almaty, June 6, 2008.

61. Regular interviews in Russian associations in Almaty, Ust-Kamenogorsk, Pavlodar, Karaganda, Semei, Kokchetau, Petropavlovsk and Astana, 2002–2010.

62. Fieldwork observations at the Russian consulates and the Russian compatriots associations in Almaty, Bishkek, Tashkent, 2002–2005.

63. German associations in charge of repatriation, German embassy in Almaty, interviews by author, April 2005.

64. Regular interviews in these associations in Almaty and Astana, June 2009.

65. See Ahiska, http://ahiska-gazeta.com/ru/pages/196.html.

66. See Vatan, http://www.vatanpress.com.

67. See Belarus Portal in Kazakhstan, http://www.belarus.kz/company/business.

68. For more details, see M. Laruelle and S. Peyrouse, "Cross-Border Minorities as Cultural and Economic Mediators between China and Central Asia," *China and Eurasia Forum Quarterly* 7, no. 1 (2009): 93–119.

Part 3

Policy and Administration

5

Nonstate Health Care Provision in Central Asia

Cooperative or Competitive?

Erica Johnson

Under what conditions does nonstate welfare provision become politicized? That is, when do nonstate actors not only challenge a government's welfare provision capacity but, perhaps as importantly, use welfare service provision as a tool for entering the political sphere to act as, or challenge, a state? I examine this question through an analysis of newly emerged health sector NGOs in post-Soviet Kazakhstan and Uzbekistan, where, increasingly, the central governments are wary of health provision NGOs and nonstate, private health care providers as potential threats to the state. For example, in May 2010 the government of Uzbekistan announced plans to ban private medical practice in the country.[1] In addition, the Central Asian regimes attempt to substitute government funding for foreign grants to co-opt the agendas of health care NGOs, lest nonstate health care provision begin to challenge state social services and regime legitimacy. Are the Central Asian leaders justified in their fears that nonstate social welfare provision might challenge current regime legitimacy?

Throughout the Middle East, South Asia, and other developing regions, civil society organizations use service provision as a means of building political support, especially when ethnic or religious cleavages are deep and/or states fail to provide basic public goods and social services.[2] Large infusions of external funding are often used to develop organizational capacity in welfare provision and political action. Two primary models of state-NGO interaction emerge: cooperative or competitive and politicized. The majority of these state-NGO arrangements can be termed cooperative. Governments and NGOs work together to avoid redundancy, promote efficiency, and exploit their unique comparative advantages. In rare cases, nonstate health care provision has become highly politicized and does aim to challenge state legitimacy or take on the roles of a state. Hezbollah in Lebanon, Hamas in Palestine, and the Zapatista movement in Chiapas, Mexico, are a few such examples. In these instances, the politicized nonstate actors arose under conditions of perceived persecution, military violence, and/or the absence of a functioning state that had already debilitated social welfare and/or governance capacity. Central Asia's authoritarian governments might justify their repression of domestic health-oriented NGOs in order to avoid the development of highly politicized nonstate service providers on their own soils, but evidence from interviews with Central Asian NGO activists indicate that these goals are far from the local NGO agendas.

Most studies of the dynamics of nonstate health care provision have focused on the "NGO-ization" of societies around the globe and the "ghettoization" of local NGOs to foreign donors' agendas, especially in the post-Soviet region.[3] Other studies have focused exclusively on understanding isolated cases of extremely politicized nonstate health care provision, such as with Hamas, Hezbollah, or the Zapatista social movement, without exploring cross-national lessons for how politicized nonstate actors employ health and social services to challenge or take on the role of states.[4] To understand what might trigger politicized nonstate social welfare provision in Central Asia, I draw lessons from the dynamics of state-NGO cooperation and competition in health care provision in other regions and cases around the world.

The purpose of this chapter is to explore the commonalities and differences that Central Asia's health service NGOs have with their cooperative and politicized counterparts in other regions. In the next sections, I outline how nonstate health care services emerged in other contexts, exploring both cooperative and competitive state-NGO relationships and the role of external donors. I then present data on state and NGO health care delivery in Central Asia, comparing Uzbekistan and Kazakhstan to emphasize the similarities and differences between these Central Asian cases and other countries. I conclude that Central Asia's NGO health care provision is not likely to become politicized and that international donor support has actually created "civic" nonstate health care providers that want to meet societal needs even if it means cooperating with authoritarian regimes.

Government-NGO Partnerships in Health Care Delivery

International development assistance for health reform rose fourfold between 1990 and 2007, and most of these initiatives require the participation of nonstate actors in health policy decisions and delivery.[5] In a range of political and geographic environments, international organizations such as USAID, the United Nations system (e.g., WHO, UNICEF, and UNFPA), the World Bank, the Gates Foundation, the Global Fund, and others promote health care NGOs as important partners to governments, as "gap fillers" for states or market entities that are withdrawing or failing to provide adequate health care, and as critical bridges between state agencies and local populations.[6] Many of these initiatives tap existing social or religious groups; others create new organizations from scratch.[7] In developing countries, most of these NGOs are small and work in communities where the capacity for government intervention is limited or nonexistent.[8] In extreme cases, nonstate health service delivery has led to the development of strongly politicized actors that challenge state legitimacy or seek to act as states themselves. More commonly, however, nonstate actors cooperate with state agencies and central governments to meet the population's health and social welfare needs.

State-NGO relationships are often fraught with tensions between the different sectors and actors.[9] Finding institutional mechanisms that ensure accountability and cooperation and mitigate agency conflicts is challenging for many nongovernmental organizations, and the significant power disparity between governments and NGOs exacerbates these problems.[10] NGO leaders often fear that interaction with the state will limit their organizations' autonomy—a problem in relatively democratic contexts that becomes much more acute in nondemocratic regions such as Central Asia.[11] Tensions increase in state-NGO partnerships when government officials are distrustful of NGOs and concerned that NGO health provision encroaches on the state's responsibilities or challenges state legitimacy.

Nevertheless, evidence from around the world demonstrates that nonstate actors add valuable services for communities. These efforts are most successful where there is no direct competition between state and NGO services or constituencies. For example, since 1995 state-NGO health care partnerships in Mexico have become vital in geographical areas where the population is underserved and NGOs offer services that the government does not provide.[12] Mexico's state-NGO partnerships have arisen in response to the politicization of health care provision by the Zapatista movement. In Pakistan, the Aga Khan Rural Support Program emerged as a substitute institution when the state's policies failed. Rather than challenging the government, the NGOs moved into a complementary role as the government adjusted national policies.[13]

In most cases, the rise of NGO health services does not challenge state capacity or legitimacy, nor do NGOs that provide health and social services aim to take on roles and responsibilities of governing states. Indeed, the state is often the primary actor in health service delivery or is seen as the primary actor responsible for health delivery decisions. NGOs develop services and partnerships with the government, but rarely with a goal of supplanting the government's responsibilities, challenging the legitimacy of the regime, or becoming the state. In this way, nonstate health provision furthers the state's promises to the population and helps garner political support and legitimacy for the government.

Politicized Social Welfare Provision

In most cases around the world, NGOs provide health care services that make government policies more effective. In extreme cases, however, health and social welfare NGOs have become antagonistic to the state or have emerged as powerful political forces that seek to become a governing entity. Hamas, Hezbollah, and the Zapatista movement are examples. These organizations have intentionally emphasized the primacy of health and social welfare provision from their founding moments. Their extensive provision of health and social services allowed these nonstate actors to establish popular support bases and accrue legitimacy as political actors. Each was also founded with an express goal of becoming a political, if not a governing, entity to represent its constituency. This section presents, in a highly stylized fashion, some of the key features that motivated these nonstate actors to engage in politicized service provision. In particular, I focus on the role of foreign financial support in the founding and sustainability of these organizations and their use of violence as a means of asserting their political goals to highlight similarities and differences between these organizations and the organizations in Uzbekistan and Kazakhstan discussed in the next section.

Organizational Foundations, Sustainability, and Foreign Financial Support

Unlike the Central Asian health service NGOs and most service-oriented nonstate actors around the world, these organizations were *founded* as politicized actors. They formed and became highly politicized around issues of perceived injustices against their constituencies committed by an outside force. Hamas and Hezbollah were formed to protect their constituents from a perceived external enemy, Israel.[14] Likewise, the Zapatista movement arose to protect its constituents from a negligent and corrupt Mexican state, which was also framed as an external other.[15] These organizations were all founded with political objectives. They all made provision of health and social services central to their organizational goals, and through their health and social service provision they became legitimate political actors.

In each case, international sponsorship has been critical to the founding of the organizations and their sustainability. In this respect, there are some important parallels with the foundational moments of health-oriented NGOs in Central Asia. Financial and technical support from Egypt was central to Hamas's early agenda and success, and support from Iranian and Saudi sources has also been central to Hamas's continued political strength and influence.[16] Hezbollah emerged in Lebanon during the 1982 Israeli invasion, with financial and technical support from Iran. Today the sources and sums of Hezbollah's financing are contested, but official and private funds from Iran and charitable contributions from supporters in Lebanon are critical.[17] Likewise, much of the Zapatistas' social and political work is supported by international NGOs, but the full nature of the movement's funding is unclear.[18] While foreign financial support is critical to these organizations' survival, domestic support is also crucial to their survival and effectiveness. These organizations are able to convince their constituencies to donate money and time, and they can mobilize cadres of individuals with specialized organizational and technical skills to address the social welfare needs of local communities.

Central Asia's NGOs similarly receive significant external funding, a feature that Central Asian government leaders identify as a negative. The financial support that Hamas and Hezbollah receive from sources in Egypt, Iran, and Saudi Arabia and from their domestic constituencies, however, is qualitatively and quantitatively different from the types of support that Central Asian nonstate health care and social welfare organizations have received. Beyond the fact that Central Asian NGOs are a much more diffuse group of actors that receive relatively small individual grants from international donors, Central Asia's NGOs have had very little luck in motivating the domestic populations to financially support their activities, and there is little public support for politicized activities among health-oriented organizations in the region.

Use of Violence and Elections to Forward Goals

Unlike most NGOs engaged in health and social service provision around the world, the politicized organizations examined here have all engaged in violence to forward their goals. Hamas and Hezbollah are more extreme in this respect. While the Zapatistas movement was founded to rise up in arms against the Mexican government, it emphatically moved away from violence, military action, and illegal activity in the face of an indomitable Mexican armed response.[19] Hamas and Hezbollah, in contrast, have increased their militarized actions even as they continue to build grassroots support through health and social welfare service provision. Indeed, military assaults "only increased Hamas's appeal with ordinary Palestinians."[20]

Moreover, as Hamas and Hezbollah gained popular support through provision of health and social services and the use of violence, they also developed strategies to enter candidates in political elections. As its popular appeal grew in the late 1990s and 2000s, Hamas competed with the PLO and the Palestinian Authority.[21] Since 2007, Hamas has served as the governing authority in Gaza and has achieved many of the functional roles of a sovereign state. Likewise, Hezbollah gradually entered Lebanese electoral politics in order to gain recognition as a political institution and shape political dialogue to its benefit, while maintaining its militia and social welfare services in the post–civil war period.[22] By the mid-2000s, Hezbollah topped its main rivals in local government seats and had strong national showings as well.[23]

Despite the intended goal, the move into politics may have undercut these organizations' traditional means of garnering support. As Hamas and Hezbollah candidates took office, vociferous accusations of unfair distribution of health and social benefits sounded. For example, members of the defeated Fatah Party burned tires in the streets to protest the new Hamas-led government's failure to pay medical benefits, and accusations have arisen that Hamas targets benefits only to its supporters.[24] In addition, international condemnation of the groups' terroristic actions blocks access to key financial assets, making delivery of social welfare promises difficult.

While by no means an exhaustive analysis, the examples above remind us that nonstate health and social service providers can, and do, adopt political and oppositional goals. Lest the suspicions of Central Asia's authoritarian leaders be allowed too much currency, we also must remember that, in the universe of nonstate actors that provide health and social services, these are very rare cases. While Central Asia's health service NGOs share some important features with these politicized cases in other regions, understanding the sources of support and violent activities of these organizations helps us understand why similar outcomes are not likely in Kazakhstan and Uzbekistan.

Similar to Central Asia's health-oriented NGOs, the three politicized nonstate actors examined here included health and social services as a central feature of their promises and appeal to their local constituencies. They each relied on external financing and support to emerge and sustain their activities. The similarities with Central Asian health NGOs end there. The discussion above highlights important distinctions from the cooperative nonstate social welfare provision under way in Central Asia. All three of the organizations examined above were created to be politicized actors. They all clearly identified an external enemy against which to mobilize their supporters, and the organizations moved into greater political roles as their social welfare services accrued legitimacy and support from the populations they serve. Moreover, they all emerged with a willingness to engage in violence as part of their repertoires for advancing their goals. These organizations expressed early goals of becoming legitimate governing actors or oppositional forces. As the following section demonstrates, the same cannot be said about Central Asia's health care–oriented NGOs.

Central Asia's Nonstate Health Care Provision

When the Soviet Union collapsed, the state-guaranteed "cradle to grave" social safety net unraveled in the newly independent Central Asian countries. The governments of Uzbekistan and Kazakhstan adopted widely different health care strategies in the independence era: Uzbekistan's government aimed to maintain as much of the state-run Soviet socialist system as possible and to retain state control of health care. The resulting system is highly centralized and has very little room for private, for-profit health care provision. In contrast, Kazakhstan's government adopted a strategy to withdraw state health care spending and services and to develop private health care provision, including nongovernmental organizations. While Kazakhstan moved further to incorporate private health care provision into its post-Soviet system, both countries continue to have a very strong role for public health care provision.

In the following discussion, I primarily explore the role of nonstate organizations (NGOs) in health care delivery and policy making in Kazakhstan and Uzbekistan. These are actors that either do not engage in for-profit health care provision or engage in for-profit activities only in order to reinvest in their not-for-profit health care provision. I distinguish these NGOs from private, for-profit organizations and institutions, which operate with a market orientation and distribute profits to owners and/or shareholders. While some private, market-oriented health care provision does exist in Kazakhstan, it is severely restricted in Uzbekistan. Despite the divergent focus on private actors, nonstate organizations emerged in both countries to provide health and other social welfare services in response to state failure and gaps in traditional state provision.

International donor organizations play an important role in developing Central Asia's NGO capacity and state-NGO international health care provision. Although international organizations arrived in Central Asia with an early focus on human rights and democratization and neglected local social issues, donors and foundations working in Central Asia gradually shifted their funding priorities to include health and social service activities.[25] USAID was one of the earliest international development agencies to incorporate NGOs in its health work in Central Asia. Today most international grants to support Central Asia's health care systems stipulate cooperation between state and nonstate health care agencies as a condition of donor support. International donors and local patients now credit Central Asia's private health care providers and NGOs with better quality and better priced health services than their state counterparts, and the international donor community believes the NGOs reach marginalized communities more effectively than state agencies do. Regional governments justify working with nonstate actors because they assist the state in fulfilling its duty to provide social welfare services to the population, a strong legacy of the Soviet social contract.

Since the mid-2000s, international donors have been closing down projects in Central Asia—either because government policies have pushed them out (as in Uzbekistan) or because they deem that the countries have reached levels of economic stability that no longer warrant donor support (most notably in Kazakhstan). As a result, local health care NGOs must seek government grants to support their operations. Even without international grants, NGO actors are committed to improving health and social welfare conditions in their countries and to working with their governments to fulfill such goals.

Despite their divergence in initial health care strategies, the governments of both Kazakhstan and Uzbekistan grew wary that nonstate health service providers would threaten state legitimacy, and both regimes have made moves to co-opt nonstate health care provision, either through direct control or through direct funding of their activities. Nevertheless, it is unlikely that Central Asian NGOs will follow a politicized path, as the actors involved see their roles as complementary to the state. As the case study evidence below demonstrates, nonstate health care providers do not view themselves as challengers to state authority, nor do they bristle at being co-opted by the state. Agreeing to government partnerships or even accepting co-optation ensures organizational survival, and it also ensures survival of an organization's mission to serve local populations and fill in gaps in state services. In addition, Central Asia's NGOs have a civic identity, serving the population and assisting government agencies as goals in and of themselves, not on the basis of religion, ethnicity, or other attributive characteristics that led to the politicization of nonstate health care in other contexts. My analysis below draws on fieldwork; primary source material from NGOs and government officials; sixty interviews in English and Russian with representatives of local NGOs, international donor organizations, ministries of health, and city-level public health offices in Tashkent, Samarqand, and Buxoro in Uzbekistan in summer 2006 and Almaty and Astana in Kazakhstan in winter 2008; and secondary research materials.[26]

Uzbekistan: Co-opted Nonstate Health Care Provision

For the first decade after independence, Uzbekistan's central leadership aimed to maintain as much of the Soviet social welfare system as possible.

The government tasked existing state agencies and primary care providers with carrying out health promotion and health educational campaigns or created new state agencies for these purposes. Most notably, President Islam Karimov co-opted the centuries-old system of neighborhood committees, *mahallas*, to administer health and social welfare services at the most local level and with close government supervision.[27] In addition, a 1998 presidential decree established a national Institute of Health to initiate and supervise the healthy lifestyles program, but NGOs were not involved and, several years later, the program had not reached the population.[28] Moreover, in 1998 the Karimov regime established the Republican HIV/AIDS Center as a vertical structure for HIV prevention, analysis of HIV/AIDS epidemiology, and treatment, but observers contend that the government is not as effective at reaching local and vulnerable communities as local NGOs might be.[29] As a USAID representative said, "The traditional [state] health care facilities don't have the abilities to do outreach to these communities. Our goal is to get the target communities to get care and maintain it. On this project we are working with local service providers in government or NGOs, especially for communication with sex workers and drug users, where government agencies don't exist."[30] Instead of creating space for local NGOs to emerge, Uzbekistan's government agencies undertake roles in health educational campaigns, outreach to vulnerable populations, and free testing and treatment for HIV/AIDS and other STDs.[31]

During a brief opening of the nation to international interaction from 1999 to 2004, foreign donors actively helped foster a more autonomous NGO community. International donors provided financial and technical assistance to a range of NGOs working in democratization, human rights, and health and social issues. Although the exact number of NGOs in Uzbekistan is uncertain, according to Uzbekistan's Ministry of Justice, twenty-three hundred NGOs were registered in Uzbekistan by 2000.[32] Even then, Uzbekistan's state limited the role of foreign donors and hindered the development of the full range of NGOs that arose in Kazakhstan and Kyrgyzstan. NGOs that received foreign grants relied on close connections with state structures, state funding, government-provided office spaces, and waived or subsidized fees for utilities, phone and Internet, and other operating expenses. In these ways, Uzbekistan's state leadership maintained control over the civil society sector and prevented the politicization of nonstate actors that might challenge the state's legitimacy.

Despite, or perhaps because of, the regime's repressive stance, Uzbekistan is the only Central Asian country in which a local domestic organization, the Akromiya Movement, is alleged to have engaged in both nonstate social welfare provision and violent mobilization with the goal of creating an Islamic state in Uzbekistan. Uzbekistan's state officials accused members of the Akromiya Movement of having links with the nonviolent Islamist Hizb ut-Tahrir and of causing a violent uprising in Andijan city in May 2005.[33]

Named after Akrom Yuldoshev, the Akromiya Movement emerged in 1992 and gathered a group of followers across the Ferghana Valley, and especially in the Andijan region of Uzbekistan.[34] The movement is credited with creating jobs, engaging in charity and public works, and improving the welfare of residents of the Andijan region and with promoting a return to Islamic values of peace and social kindness.[35] Long-term observers of Uzbekistan describe the organization as a "unique model of Islamic socialism in the town [of Andijan]" and "an Islamic equivalent of 'social democracy,' or even 'moral economy.'"[36] Perceiving a threat from this alternative authority, on June 23, 2004, the Karimov government ordered the arrest of twenty-three businessmen for their alleged connections with the Akromiya network and other banned Islamist movements.[37] Close observers suspect the true reason behind the arrests and sentences was that these men represented the accumulation of economic and social power outside of President Islam Karimov's inner circle, and they track the evidence against the organization to government propagandistic works and documents from the country's repressive courts.[38] The sentencing of the twenty-three businessmen on May 12, 2005, and a subsequent armed attempt to break them out of jail are cited as principle catalysts of the mass public protests in Andijan's central square on May 13.

Regardless of the validity of the accusations against the Akromiya Movement, the violence in Andijan had widespread repercussions for NGOs throughout Uzbekistan. The Karimov government intensified crackdowns on any potential opposition, and the prospects for NGO survival looked bleak. In 2005–2006, court decisions led to temporary or permanent closure of nearly all foreign-funded organizations in Uzbekistan.[39] In particular, fearing the spread of the color revolutions, the Karimov regime intensified efforts to stifle individuals and institutions that could encourage the spread of people's power.[40] Even in this repressive environment, however, the Karimov regime continued to allow health- and welfare-oriented NGOs to exist.[41] In mid-2006 international and local NGO representatives unanimously stated that five to six thousand NGOs remained active in the country. A proportion of those are engaged in helping the state fill gaps in health care and social services, but many remaining NGOs are government-organized NGOs (GONGOs) and have limited or no autonomy from the state.

Importantly, leaders of local health and social welfare NGOs do not see their organizations as antigovernment or opposition groups, nor do they identify with religious groups or have other such affiliations. To distance themselves from the perceived antigovernment position, some NGOs changed their legal status from "nongovernmental" organizations, which in Russian (*nepravitel'stvennaya*) carries the connotation of "antigovernmental," to "social organizations."[42] As the following statement summarizes, health-oriented NGOs, in particular, desire to act in cooperation with government programs, even as an extension of government bodies, and operate according to government directives: "We are always working with government, never against it. Without working with government, there is no point to our work. In other places it might not be that way. But here, if you say you are an NGO, the government is afraid. We try to have regular contact with government officials to keep them abreast of [our organization's] issues."[43] Of course, in Uzbekistan, taking an opposition stance is organizational suicide, but the desire to cooperate with government structures is more than a survival strategy.

NGO leaders and employees view close cooperation as fundamental to serving their various constituencies. One NGO leader recounted how the organization came to cooperate with the government to open a center for physically handicapped people in 2000:

> There was the idea, Why not join up with a government structure, government partnership, and the [state] budget.? In principle, the laws state that the government must protect society and it seemed to be a good match. With that idea I worked for three years, and we made a partnership with the city administration [*hakimiyat*] and we started a specialized center with four grades [for physically handicapped children]. We have the building for free [from the government]. [Cooperation with the government] was possible and necessary and we are getting results. There is a big difference

> between the type of school [we started] and the type of school the government might have started.[44]

Thus, even before the post-Andijan crackdowns, NGOs viewed cooperation with government agencies as an important way to achieve their health service goals.

While NGO development in Uzbekistan is closely associated with international donor agencies, some local civil society participants see this type of social organization as a natural part of life. The fact that NGOs have formed and continue in a very restricted political environment attests to the desire of groups of individuals to work together in an organizational structure to address social needs. As a representative of an NGO serving physically handicapped populations said, "People realized that without the third sector, without participation in the civil society, there will be no democratic progress. That's why NGOs appeared. If they hadn't been called NGOs, some other similar kind of organizations and efforts would have appeared."[45] While these developments are potentially positive for meeting the health and social welfare needs of the local population, the government's perception of threat from any social actors and its desire to co-opt social organizations are likely to outweigh any autonomy in the third sector in the short term. As an important corrective to Western interpretations of NGO activities, this respondent indicated that health-oriented NGOs, or NGOs more generally, should not be interpreted as democratizers. More important, in this respondent's view, is the role of NGOs in meeting societal needs, and most organizations are reasonably content to work cooperatively with the repressive Karimov government in order to fulfill that role.

In an attempt to supplant foreign funding and control the remaining NGOs, the Karimov government established an NGO umbrella organization, the National Association of Noncommercial, Nongovernmental Organizations of Uzbekistan (NANNOUZ), in June 2005. The association's mission is "uniting all NGOs in Uzbekistan because they are so weak and poor."[46] Although the NANNOUZ representative that I interviewed adamantly stated that NANNOUZ is not a governmental organization, all local and international NGO representatives were certain that it was created at the government's orders.

Nearly all of the NGO representatives and donors that I interviewed were skeptical of the association and its strong-arm tactics, but, with the ouster of international donors, NANNOUZ remained one of the only possible NGO funders. Of the thirty-five NGOs that I visited in Uzbekistan, all but a few had joined. Those that refused NANNOUZ membership acknowledged that the decision excluded them from applying for financial support from the association. The organizations that do receive NANNOUZ funding are bound to state conditions and oversight, and their activities are also limited to those that the government has identified as priority areas. As a result, there have been several cases of NGOs completely shifting their missions in order to be competitive for these grants. NANNOUZ gives only a handful of grants in each funding cycle, but the lack of alternative sponsors means that NGOs are not likely to survive without becoming co-opted by the government.

In pursuit of longer-term sustainability, local NGOs are attempting to find resources through fund-raising from the population and offering commercial goods and services to finance their free services. Local NGO actors were surprisingly optimistic about the prospects of sustainability, stating, "If an organization wants to, it will find ways to support itself. The situation now is more difficult, especially as international organizations are being closed. Without that support, NGOs are limited in what they can do. This is the reason many NGOs have recently closed. The ones that remain are the ones that figured out that they had to raise their own money and become self-sustaining."[47] A small number of organizations have also begun to engage in microfinance lending to individuals and organizations as a way to support their organizations' other activities. As the director of one such NGO said, "Now people are saying maybe you should become a commercial organization, but we won't. We want to help poor people who can't afford commercial services. If we were to open a commercial part, it would be to support our social work. The microfinance center is, in a way, a form of this type of fund-raising. The interest from the loans is used to support other center activities. We might also do research or trainings for profit."[48] Thus, organizations find ways to operate without government grants. Fund-raising from local communities is an important new direction, but all NGO leaders and international donors agree that neither individuals nor corporations in Uzbekistan are ready to step into a role of funding local NGOs.

Even in Uzbekistan, advocacy on health and social decision making is part of NGO work. In their policy work, however, local NGOs make no claims about challenging the legitimacy of the regime. As one NGO leader said, "These activities are mostly directed at the national-level government, but don't get the wrong impression. It isn't easy to criticize. It is hard and we also get pressured. We have agreements and disagreements and we try to make sure that our comments to the government stem directly from our activities and our experience."[49] In these small ways, then, NGOs in Uzbekistan find ways to help the state provide health and social welfare services and perhaps even make policy choices that better lives. Unlike those in other settings, Uzbekistan's NGO leaders do not wish to take on the "watchdog" role of political criticism, nor do they strive to be an alternative to the state. To a large degree, they are willing to work as co-opted organizations to ensure that their services reach the population.

The international donor community also adjusted to Uzbekistan's more restricted NGO environment. Several donors decided that GONGOs are "civil society-ish" and that working with them is better than not working to develop civil society activity in Uzbekistan.[50] Indeed, both international and local NGOs are often eager to work with *mahalla* committees and other GONGOs because they provide important access to local communities that can improve the effectiveness of health and social services. As one international donor representative said, "The *mahalla* committees have so many functions they are overwhelmed. I don't know if it will be easy to work with them, but it's a good opportunity to get to the population. Without the *mahalla,* no one can do anything at the grassroots level."[51] International donors pursue cooperation with the *mahalla* committees and other GONGOs to ensure their own organizational survival in Uzbekistan and to implement local-level health and social programs.[52] While the *mahalla* committees facilitate access to local communities, they are not likely to engage in confrontation with the government. Indeed, even with some access to external support, the *mahalla* committees are state agencies beholden to the government and will not challenge government authority.

The Karimov government actively prevents competition from nonstate actors that might develop alternative services to challenge state legitimacy. Nearly two decades after independence, the state continues to own, finance, and manage most health care facilities. To the extent that private medical practice was permitted, it was usually undertaken in state-owned hospitals and clinics and the government mandated that private practices provide at least 20 percent of their services in the state program.[53] In May 2010 the state further asserted control over the health care sphere when it announced a ban on private medical practice.[54] In all of these steps the Karimov regime pursued the strategy of retaining state ownership and control of health care as a mechanism for ensuring regime legitimacy and survival.

Uzbekistan's co-opted health service environment is not new, but it is now more pronounced with the absence of foreign donors. Many organizations, such as those providing services and assistance to disabled populations, enjoy close ties to the government that were forged during Soviet times. Some health and social organizations that were developed with international tutelage remain, but they now look to government for support or to other creative methods of fund-raising. Such organizations do not pursue Western-style civil society, nor are they attempting to build local power bases and legitimacy that might enable them to challenge state capacity. These nonstate health care organizations do not have goals of replacing the state, they do not claim religious or political affiliations, and their leaders do not see government co-optation as a limit on the organizations' rights or goals. The decision to work closely with government structures is certainly a matter of organizational survival, but NGO actors also see it as a commitment to meeting societal needs. Uzbekistan's health care and social welfare NGOs largely see their role as supporting government services and acting to ensure that the government fulfills its promises to the population.

Kazakhstan: Cooperative, Controlling, or Competitive State-NGO Health Care Delivery?

Nursultan Nazarbayev's government has pursued two distinct health care strategies in post-Soviet Kazakhstan. From 1991 to 1999 the Nazarbayev government adopted a strategy to shift responsibility for health care protection from the state and to create self-managing health care organizations. In the second phase, starting in 2000, Kazakhstan's government began to reassert centralized control over health care, increasing state spending and health care provision in hospitals and clinics. These two strategies demonstrate that, even in authoritarian regimes, state health care policies are dynamic and governments respond to changes in the political and economic climate in the country.[55]

Under Kazakhstan's initial health care strategy, state health care policies were made on an ad hoc basis, and the government's demotion of the Ministry of Health to a committee in 1997 and then to an agency in 1999 demonstrated the low priority of state health care provision. The Nazarbayev regime incorporated independent NGOs and other private actors in health care provision as a strategy to transition from the Soviet system and to develop an entrepreneurial spirit in the country. Kazakhstan's government worked to attract international donors and foreign investors to all sectors, and the international community viewed favorably the government's withdrawal from the economy, including health care provision.

International donors actively fostered the formation of NGOs in health care and other sectors. From 1995 to 2005, NGOs proliferated in Kazakhstan, growing from four hundred to five thousand, and the NGO sector continues to expand.[56] Approximately 5–10 percent of Kazakhstan's active NGOs work in the health sector, and the most active health-oriented NGOs are those working with patients and professional associations.[57] Health care NGOs now work in research on the spread of diseases and health impacts of potentially dangerous industrial projects, quality control of state and private health services, health information and education campaigns, and policy development. Both state and private health care providers and Ministry of Health officials look to health care NGOs to provide independent expertise and unbiased evaluations and research.[58]

In addition, NGOs are filling gaps in state health services, but they are not replacing government services. As a representative of an international agency said, "[NGOs] arise to address real needs or certain interests and lobbying, but they are not authoritative. They are filling gaps. For example, [the NGO] Healthy Asia focuses on breast cancer. There is no similar state system for referral or counseling, even though it is covered by insurance. The state oncology division and the state health sector are vertical. NGOs respond to needs of individual women, help with prostheses, and make doctor recommendations. They help [the women] return to life. There are millions of dollars for [NGOs]. This money is food for NGOs with such missions."[59] In these ways, NGOs supplement state and private medical services. In addition, international agencies view NGOs as more effective than state and private, for-profit health services at meeting the needs of diverse communities.[60]

Kazakhstan's NGOs must overcome substantial regulatory obstacles to offer medical services that might compete with state or for-profit services. Health service NGOs often employ medical personnel (doctors and nurses) and social workers, but because of difficult licensing procedures, most of these NGOs cannot offer medical treatments as part of their services.[61] As a Kazakh doctor who works part-time in an NGO and part-time as a physician in a private practice said, "I previously worked as a [state] pediatric neurologist, but I wasn't satisfied with my work and I was ready for a new challenge [at a health-oriented NGO]. [Our] center does not have a license to practice medicine. Getting such a license would be a long procedure. We are just licensed as a humanitarian organization."[62] In addition, the profit motivation that has been introduced to Kazakhstan's health care system prevents NGOs from providing medical treatment. As another local physician who now runs an NGO stated, "NGOs are not providing medical services because providing medical services means earning a profit and NGOs are nonprofit. All medicine is for profit."[63]

To address the challenge of financial sustainability, some of Kazakhstan's health service NGOs have converted into multiprofile organizations. In addition, some private, for-profit medical clinics have parallel NGO activities that offer medical services at low or no cost to the beneficiaries and thus get around the NGO licensing issues. Regulations and licensing procedures have prevented NGOs from directly competing with state medical providers. Private, for-profit clinics, hospitals, and other medical and social welfare facilities are in direct competition with state services, and their services are highly preferred by those citizens who can afford them.

Because of the higher bar to entrance for providing services, many of Kazakhstan's NGOs engage in advocacy and policy making. International donors have tried to foster advocacy activities among local NGOs, and they find that Kazakhstan's NGOs are improving in this effort, especially vis-à-vis NGOs in neighboring countries, including Kyrgyzstan.[64] International health advisors value the policy making capacity of NGOs more than many government officials do. An international agency representative said, "NGOs are new, but they have more [policy making] capacity than politicians because they employ health professionals."[65] Many international agencies thus positively evaluate the knowledge level and capacity of NGOs working in Kazakhstan's health sector. None of these international or domestic actors, however, see Kazakhstan's NGOs as using their health and social services to build a political base that will challenge the government. Nevertheless, government officials are not always receptive to NGO efforts to participate in policy debates, and upper-level elites view NGO policy activities as competitive and resist them.

Starting in 2000 and becoming more apparent in 2004–2005, Kazakhstan's leadership adopted a new health care strategy to reassert the state's role in health care provision as a response to political and social pressures on the regime's legitimacy.[66] In this second phase, the Nazarbayev regime bolstered government spending and provision of health care and social services and, in 2004, adopted, for the first time, a comprehensive national health care plan. In addition, the national government moved away from its stated commitment to rationalizing the hospital, primary care, and health care financing systems, and Nazarbayev's administration rejected international donors' intellectual contributions to health policy reform and training programs.[67] This shift marked a significant departure from the state's earlier strategy of self-managed, decentralized, and privatized health care, but it did not reverse those changes. Instead, the government increased state provision of health care benefits and services in parallel with private services. Responding to the population's expectations that government *should* provide health and social protection and to evolving political pressures, state services are increasingly remonopolizing the health and social sectors.[68]

Coupled with efforts to reassert government control of the health sector, President Nazarbayev also increased efforts to cooperate with health care and other NGOs. Formalizing this goal, the Nazarbayev administration adopted a law on nonprofit organizations in 2001, developed a law for state support of NGOs in 2002, and included contributions from regional and city-level administrations as part of state commitments to NGOs for 2003–2005.[69] Buoyed with energy wealth in this second period, the government began offering grants to local NGOs in order to limit influences from international donors and to control NGO activities. Although intolerant of political opposition and no more immune to the threat of a color revolution than its counterparts throughout the post-Soviet region, Kazakhstan's presidential regime decided to find ways to collaborate with and accommodate NGOs and other private actors to accomplish its health and social goals.

Indeed, the fear of color revolution contagion seems to have fueled Nazarbayev's commitment to funding NGO activities. Despite the earlier promises of support, it was only in 2005 that Nazarbayev's government really began to allocate public funds to NGOs working on health and social welfare issues, such as the rehabilitation of patients and prevention of drug use.[70] In July 2006 Nazarbayev issued a decree on civil society development and state-NGO cooperation for 2006–2011.[71] Furthermore, in 2007 all the ministries were required to create advisory committees with NGOs to discuss their agendas and policies. Following the government's orders, on

February 5, 2008, the minister of health in Astana issued a memorandum to the entire ministry staff that henceforth the Ministry of Health would prioritize cooperation with NGOs. When I met with Ministry of Health officials on February 7, 2008, however, no one was able to explain how this cooperation would take shape, what it would entail, or who among the ministry staff would actually be involved in working with NGOs. As a local representative of UNDP said, "The government does not want cooperation in [the social sphere]. Government officials say that they know everything. It is difficult to receive information about what government is doing in this sphere. The situation would change only if the government had to depend on the population through elections, and so on. Sure, there are formal demonstrations of cooperation (roundtables, debates, reports), but it is not real cooperation and mostly the NGOs say it is just words, no real commitment. The officials are not interested in society's cooperation or advice about policy from NGOs."[72] While policies on state-NGO cooperation have continued to develop, distrust on each side prevents real deepening of these relationships.

International observers directly link the government's increased interest in civil society with its fears for regime survival. As one individual said, "Since the Andijan events in Uzbekistan and the Kyrgyzstan revolution [in 2005], the president started discussing restrictions on NGOs but did not issue a *prikaz* [order]. In 2006 and 2007 President Nazarbayev gave an announcement that the government will work with NGOs. The existing law does restrict NGO freedom or, better to say, it creates obstacles. However, NGOs are operational and have some opportunities to take government grants and do good work."[73] While state-NGO cooperation and government funding for NGOs do improve NGOs' policy influence and capacity, these measures are also interpreted as the authoritarian government's effort to control civil society groups. Explaining the government's motivation to invest in NGOs, a representative of ZdravPlus, a USAID-funded project on health quality improvement, said, "Politically, the government cannot close its eyes on the maturity of NGOs. The international community helped to develop this sector and rather than banning NGOs or ignoring them the government is taking a creative approach to present government funding to NGOs in a way that they will take it to survive. NGOs are increasing and surviving but they don't need international funders as much, at least not the big ones."[74] International donors' demands for state-NGO collaboration created some of these unexpected patterns, but the ultimate result is greater service to the population's health needs.

So far, health NGOs welcome government grants and are not concerned that government financing will result in a loss of organizational autonomy or a reduction in access to other (foreign) sources of funding: "For now they are definitely not interpreting the government funding opportunities as a negative. They see it as an opportunity."[75] Nor does accepting government funding mean NGOs must curtail activities aimed at criticizing the government or gaining political legitimacy over the state. Such activities are not pursuits of Kazakhstan's health care NGOs.

Although local NGO representatives are wary about the government's commitment to NGO independence, they are also skeptical of international donors' support for NGO activities. They point out that international donor assistance in the formation of NGOs has not resulted in greater democratization among government officials. As one NGO representative said, "I do not want to minimize the importance of international grants, but at the same time they have not really affected the democratization of the government. And there are cases where NGOs have manipulated their missions, etc., to get grants."[76] In this respect, local NGO actors question the goals of international donors and realize that gaining funds for organizational survival may be more important than the source of the grant. International donors are no longer seen as more virtuous or legitimate than the government, especially when the government is promoting state funding and cooperation. Nevertheless, government funding for NGOs is causing foreign donors to reconsider their roles in the country. International agencies are now beginning to pull out of Kazakhstan because it has reached "middle-income status."[77] Absent international grants, government funding to NGOs could limit NGO activities and innovations and create a more co-opted environment like in Uzbekistan.

At the same time, Kazakhstan's NGOs recognize the importance of donor funding and argue that, regardless of donor or government policies, they will continue to write grants for international support. As a local public health NGO representative said,

> It is not possible that there would be no international donors. There is the Internet. Or the government would have to grow the funding for NGOs and we would have to have our own donors and foundations. The government recognizes that NGOs have goals and mis-

> sions to help the people and fill in the services that government just cannot provide. This is good and NGOs are doing good work. The arms of the government just are not enough. NGOs are working to support government. Health is good because the health of the people is always related to all other topics. Health influences the economy. We cannot do anything without health and so we should be able to find funding.[78]

Thus Kazakhstan's NGOs do not position their activities as challenging the government. Rather, they see a complementarity of goals and services. Furthermore, representatives of health-oriented NGOs believe their organizations will survive because they provide important services to both the government and society. While presently willing to accept government grants and cooperation, NGO leaders are cautious that the government might attempt to limit their independence.

Fortunately for NGO independence, Kazakhstan's economic prosperity also created other domestic sources of funding for local NGOs. Business and opposition groups are beginning to support NGOs working in health care and other sectors. A number of former government officials and opposition leaders have formed NGOs or social funds to support the development and work of civil society groups. As the leader of one such organization stated, some of these organizations still maintain relationships with government structures and have access to government funding: "We can get 30 percent of [our] support from the government. We want to get 70 percent of our funding from alternative sources so that we can be independent. The institute is not opposition. Of course, our boss left government because he wanted to make changes that were difficult, and he thought he could do things better without being dependent on the government."[79] Other former government officials have founded more oppositional organizations, and they have independent sources of funding. These funding sources are kept secret, lest they dry up or become targets of government repression. As an opposition-led social fund representative said, "We are getting help from businesses. You will forgive me, a fund should be open but we cannot say where our funding comes from. In general, business is helping NGOs but mostly in nonpolitical areas [of health care and social protection]."[80] These individuals argue that working as independent NGOs is more effective than trying to accomplish the same goals in the state sector, as this statement attests: "We are doctors and we have a lot of experience and work in the health sector and medicine. I was deputy to Aikan Akanov in the health ministry. I was and am a member of an opposition party working on social activity, but because of repression I left [government] to create an independent NGO."[81] Medical expertise and high-level government involvement make these individuals highly qualified and competent. Despite repression in and out of the government, they are accomplishing important health services for society.

While these NGOs and social funds are not currently aiming to build political bases through provision of social services, their activities might come to be perceived as competition to state health care services and challenges of regime legitimacy. Nevertheless, the motivations and organizational goals of these NGOs are very different from the politicized goals behind the health care services offered by Hamas and Hezbollah. To the extent that NGO leaders are interested in challenging Kazakhstan's government, it is with a goal toward democratization and transparency—very different motivations than those promoted by Hamas and Hezbollah. Opposition assistance to health NGOs is not, for now, aimed at creating a political support base. The situation might change if opposition business leaders and philanthropists begin to claim credit for financing health and other NGOs.

Thus opposition NGOs and social funds have alternative sources of financing that could help the NGO sector remain independent but should not be seen as politicized health care provision along the lines of Hamas or Hezbollah. If the government perceives these groups as growing too strong or too rich, however, the regime might intensively crack down on political opposition that provides alternative sources of NGO support and funding in health care and other sectors. Under this scenario, we would expect to see greater state control of health care, including a reversal of privatization, in order to further limit the influences of political competition in society more broadly.

For now, the Nazarbayev government wants to maintain domestic and international legitimacy and so will not completely crack down on political opposition or NGOs. Unlike in Uzbekistan, the Nazarbayev government is working to establish cooperative relationships with NGOs instead of attempting to eradicate these organizations from the political and social landscape. In addition, the Nazarbayev government has not restricted foreign donors' support of local NGOs. To date, the Nazarbayev government has promoted state-NGO cooperation to help fill in gaps in state provision and provide alternative health services to consumers. In sum, Kazakhstan's government-NGO relationship is characterized as cooperative although a more co-opted relationship might be expected if government funding becomes more extensive, international donors withdraw support, and the national government attempts to control NGO actors.

Implications

This discussion outlines two primary models of nonstate health care provision: cooperation and competition. Many international aid programs now promote state-NGO partnerships in health care programs. State-NGO cooperation is certainly one possible outcome, but NGO services can also been seen as competing with or challenging state services. In the extreme, nonstate actors have emerged as stronger and more legitimate social welfare providers *and* political actors than the state. Despite the alarmist claims of national government leaders, the cases of Uzbekistan and Kazakhstan demonstrate that nonstate health care provision in Central Asia is unlikely to become politicized for a number of reasons.

First, as a legacy of the Soviet social contract, Central Asia's nonstate actors are committed to helping the state meet the needs of the local population. The Central Asian governments use health care provision to demonstrate state capacity and legitimacy, local citizens expect such services from the state, and NGOs work to help the state meet citizens' needs. Even while recognizing problems in governance and policies—both in health care and more broadly—NGO actors see their role as supporting the state, not as replacing or challenging to the state. Markedly, these NGOs do not see their role as opposition to the government or as a challenge to government capacity and legitimacy. Of course, to declare opposition to the government would be tantamount to organizational suicide. Nevertheless, these Central Asian NGOs universally express a commitment to service for their constituents despite the repressive environments, strapped finances, and hard work required. Central Asia's local NGOs have some comparative advantages for meeting the needs of underserved populations and expanding the range of services available to the local population, but they do not aim to replace state services.

Second, the Central Asian states have, so far, been spared the types of external threats that helped mobilize politicized nonstate actors and their support bases in Palestine and Lebanon. Both Hamas and Hezbollah emerged to address threats from Israel, and the organizations' ability to stand up in the face of the external threat strengthened their legitimacy in society. In Uzbekistan and Kazakhstan, the absence of similar external threats has reduced the importance of alternatives to the state. The June 2010 ethnic violence on the border between Kyrgyzstan and Uzbekistan that killed three hundred people, left four hundred thousand homeless, and caused Uzbeks to flee Kyrgyzstan may have been such a challenge. The events demonstrated the critical role of health service provision in a time of perceived external threat, but they have not resulted in local NGOs claiming to delegitimize or replace the state on either side of the border. Instead, international NGOs, especially the international organization Doctors without Borders, are trying to serve as a bridge between the two countries and their populations.[82]

Third, the Central Asian regimes analyzed here are repressive and their control over and co-optation of NGOs run the risk of alienating some potential partners and leading to the development of politicized actors, but this scenario is not visible in the sphere of health service provision. Although the government of Uzbekistan identified a potential threat from the nonstate Akromiya Movement, evidence suggests that the allegations were based on government perceptions of threat rather than the actual development of a politicized nonstate movement with the aim of delegitimizing and unseating the government. By contrast, domestic opposition funding of NGOs in Kazakhstan has more potential to become a political force that calls for reform or regime change. Nevertheless, these demands are not likely to come from health service NGOs but from the business and former government leaders who support them. Central Asian NGOs are not organized around political goals, nor do they desire to delegitimize the government.

Finally, the funding structure that led to the development of Central Asia's nonstate health care provision is important in many respects. Support from Western development agencies has shaped the nature and agenda of Central Asia's nonstate health care providers. Most notably, foreign donors have instilled a cooperative, civic orientation in Central Asian NGO activists. NGO actors claim a civic identity based on serving the population and assisting government agencies rather than one based on religion, ethnicity, or other attributive characteristics that have led to politicized nonstate health care in other contexts. Many are, in fact, quite content to work cooperatively with government agencies and to be financed with government contracts. Moreover, most nonstate actors never gain access to the levels of resources available to even the poorest government agency.

The mix of resources that Central Asia's NGOs receive from foreign donors does not match the levels of funding available to the internationally politicized Hamas, Hezbollah, and Zapatista movements. In addition, because of the newness of the organizations and the relatively low level of income throughout the region, Central Asia's populations are reluctant to be financiers of the NGO sector. As discussed above, Kazakhstan is the one case in which business groups are starting to take interest in charitable giving for social welfare services, but this practice is still quite small and does not extend beyond Kazakhstan. Finally, grant opportunities have led to small-scale NGO activities with very local influence rather than organizations working to create a national political presence. Central Asia's health care NGOs may challenge the government through their capabilities as alternate service providers, but none is likely to try to act directly as a state or governing entity.

Central Asia's nonstate health care provision is unlikely to become politicized. While outside the scope of this project, small-scale faith-based health delivery does exist in Central Asia, but it does not occur within the NGO organizational format and neither is it focused on delegitimizing the regional governments. Instead, NGOs very willingly look for cooperation and partnership with state agencies. If the funding sources expand to include politicized and/or religious influences, the situation might change. Likewise, foreign military attack or internal turbulence could lead to greater politicization and military engagement of nonstate actors. But evidence from instances such as Tajikistan's civil war, the 2005 Andijan uprising, and even the 2010 Osh crisis suggests that politicized nonstate health care provision is an unlikely outcome in Central Asia.

Notes

1. "Uzbekistan: Chastnaya Meditsinskaya Praktika budet zapreshchena," Ferghana.ru, May 11, 2010, http://www.ferghana.ru/news.php?id=14692.

2. Nonstate charity and health care services also have their origins in religious groups in England, in the United States, and throughout Europe. See, for example, Gosta Esping-Andersen, *The Three Worlds of Welfare Capital* (Princeton, NJ: Princeton University Press, 1990); Theda Skocpol, Marshall Ganz, and Ziad Munson, "A Nation of Organizers: The Institutional Origins of Civic Voluntarism in the United States," *American Political Science Review* 94, no. 3 (2000): 527–46; John D.

Stephens, Evelyne Huber, and Leonard Ray, "The Welfare State in Hard Times," in *Continuity and Change in Contemporary Capitalism,* ed. Herbert Kitschelt, Peter Lange, Gary Marks, and John D. Stephens (New York: Cambridge University Press, 1999). Religious groups have, to date, played a minor role in health care provision in Central Asia, with the possible exception of the importance given to traditional faith healers and small-scale faith-based charities.

3. Julie Hearn, "The 'NGO-isation' of Kenyan Society: USAID and the Restructuring of Health Care," *Review of African Political Economy* 25, no. 75 (1998): 89–100; Sarah L. Henderson, "Selling Civil Society: Western Aid and the Nongovernmental Organization Sector in Russia," *Comparative Political Studies* 35, no. 2 (2002): 139–67; Sarah E. Mendelson and John K. Glenn, eds. *The Power and Limits of NGOs: A Critical Look at Building Democracy in Eastern Europe and Eurasia* (New York: Columbia University Press, 2002); Alexander Cooley and James Ron, "The NGO Scramble: Organizational Insecurity and the Political Economy of Transnational Action," *International Security* 27, no. 1 (2002): 5–39.

4. Peter E. Hilsenrath and Karan P. Singh, "Palestinian Health Institutions: Finding a Way Forward After the Second Intifada," *Peace Economics, Peace Science and Public Policy* 13, no. 1 (2007):1–15; Matthew Levitt and Dennis Ross, *Hamas: Politics, Charity, and Terrorism in the Service of Jihad* (New Haven, CT: Yale University Press, 2007); Kim Murphy, "Hamas Victory Is Built on Social Work," *Los Angeles Times,* March 2, 2006; Eitan Azani, *Hezbollah: The Story of the Party of God: From Revolution to Institutionalization* (New York: Palgrave Macmillan, 2009); Melani Cammett, "Habitat for Hezbollah," *Foreign Policy,* August 2006; Dahr Jamail, "Hezbollah's Transformation," *Asia Times,* July 20, 2006; Maria Inclan, "Zapatista and Counter-Zapatista Protests: A Test of Movement-Countermovement Dynamics," *Journal of Peace Research* 49, no. 3 (2012): 459–72; Richard Stahler-Sholk, "The Zapatista Social Movement: Innovation and Sustainability," *Alternatives* 35, no. 3 (2010): 269–90; Alicia C. S. Swords, "Neo-Zapatista Network Politics: Transforming Democracy and Development," *Latin American Perspectives* 34, no. 2 (2007): 78–93.

5. World Health Organization Maximizing Positive Synergies Collaborative Group, "An Assessment of Interactions between Global Health Initiatives and Country Health Systems," *Lancet* 373, no. 9681 (July 2009): 2137–69.

6. Hearn, "'NGO-isation' of Kenyan Society"; Nauro F. Campos, Feisal U. Khan, and Jennifer E. Tessendorf, "From Substitutional to Complementarity: Some Econometric Evidence on the Evolving NGO-State Relationship in Pakistan," *Journal of Developing Areas* 37, no. 2 (2004): 49–72; Lester M. Salamon, *Partners in Public Service: Government-Nonprofit Relations in the Modern Welfare State* (Baltimore: Johns Hopkins University Press, 1995); Jesica Gomez-Jauregui, "The Feasibility of Government Partnerships with NGOs in the Reproductive Health Field in Mexico," *Reproductive Health Matters* 12, no. 24 (2004): 42–55; Derick W. Brinkerhoff, "Government-Nonprofit Partners for Health Sector Reform in Central Asia: Family Group Practice Associations in Kazakhstan and Kyrgyz-

stan," *Public Administration and Development* 22, no. 1 (2002): 51–61; Erica Johnson, "Authoritarian Regimes and Nongovernmental Organizations: Transitions in Health Care Provision in Central Asia" (PhD diss., University of Washington, 2009).

7. Gerard Clarke and Michael Jennings, eds., *Development, Civil Society and Faith-Based Organizations: Bridging the Sacred and the Secular* (Basingstoke, UK: Palgrave Macmillan, 2008).

8. Gomez-Jauregui, "Feasibility of Government Partnerships."

9. Michael Reich, "Public-Private Partnerships for Public Health," in *Public-Private Partnership for Public Health*, ed. Michael Reich (Cambridge, MA: Harvard Center for Population and Development Studies, 2002); Gomez-Jauregui, "Feasibility of Government Partnerships"; Elinor Ostrom, "Crossing the Great Divide: Co-production, Synergy, and Development," *World Development* 24, no. 6 (1996): 1073–87.

10. Reich, "Public-Private Partnerships for Public Health"; Erica Johnson and Aseem Prakash, "NGO Research Program: A Collective Action Perspective," *Policy Sciences* 40, no. 3 (2007): 221–40.

11. Garth Nowland-Foreman, "Purchase-of-Service Contracting, Voluntary Organizations, and Civil Society," *American Behavior Scientist* 42, no. 1 (1998): 108–23; Gomez-Jauregui, "Feasibility of Government Partnerships."

12. Gomez-Jauregui, "Feasibility of Government Partnerships," 43.

13. Campos, Khan, and Tessendorf, "From Substitutional to Complementarity."

14. For a discussion, see Andrew Higgins, "How Israel Helped Spawn Hamas," *Wall Street Journal*, January 24, 2009, http://online.wsj.com/article/NA_WSJ_PUB:SB123275572295011847.html; Cammett, "Habitat for Hezbollah"; Melani Cammett and Sukriti Issar, "Bricks and Mortar Clientelism: Sectarianism and the Logic of Welfare Allocation in Lebanon," *World Politics* 62, no. 3 (2010): 381–421.

15. Alicia Ely Yamin, *Health Care Held Hostage: Human Rights Violations and Violations of Medical Neutrality in Chiapas, Mexico* (Boston: Physicians for Human Rights, 1999); Ginna Villarreal, "Health Care Organized from Below: The Zapatista Experience," *Narco News Bulletin*, January 11, 2007, http://www.narconews.com/Issue44/article2502.html.

16. Don Van Natta, "Flow of Saudis' Cash to Hamas," *New York Times*, September 17, 2003; Higgins, "How Israel Helped Spawn Hamas."

17. The amounts from Iran are estimated at $100 million a year. Augustus Richard Norton, *Hezbollah: A Short History* (Princeton, NJ: Princeton University Press, 2007), 110.

18. Geoffrey Ramsey, "How Mexico's Zapatista Guerrillas Stayed Clear of Organized Crime," *Christian Science Monitor*, January 10, 2012, http://www.csmonitor.com/World/Americas/Latin-America-Monitor/2012/0110/How-Mexico-s-Zapatista-guerrillas-stayed-clear-of-organized-crime.

19. Ibid.

20. Higgins, "How Israel Helped Spawn Hamas."

21. Levitt and Ross, *Hamas,* 8.

22. Norton, *Hezbollah,* 101.

23. Ibid., 98–107.

24. "Palestinian Territories: Inside Hamas, Story Synopsis," *PBS Frontline/World,* May 9, 2006, http://www.pbs.org/frontlineworld/stories/palestine503/; "Hamas Leader Condemns Islamist Charity Blacklist," Reuters, August 23, 2007, http://www.reuters.com/article/idUSL23611943._CH_.2400.

25. Eurasia Foundation representative, phone interview by author, May 20, 2006.

26. I also conducted parallel research in Kyrgyzstan in winter–spring 2008.

27. For a detailed discussion, see Marianne Kamp, "Between Women and the State: Mahalla Committees and Social Welfare in Uzbekistan," in *The Transformation of Central Asia: States and Societies from Soviet Rule to Independence,* ed. Pauline Jones Luong (Ithaca, NY: Cornell University Press, 2004).

28. Farkhad A. Ilkhamov and Elke Jakubowski, *Health Care Systems in Transition* (Copenhagen: European Observatory on Health Care Systems, 2001), 40.

29. Mohir Ahmedov, Ravshan Azimov, Vasila Alimova, and Bernd Rechel, *Uzbekistan: Health System Review* (Copenhagen: European Observatory on Health Care Systems, 2007), 117.

30. USAID representative, interview by author, Tashkent, June 23, 2006.

31. An important supplement to government service gaps was the creation of 230 "trust points" for anonymous HIV and STD testing and treatments. The program was created through the AIDS Center Initiative, which receives the Global Fund grants. In this way, a limited number of NGOs continue to exist, have connections with international donors, and supplement state health care services.

32. Gregory Gleason, *Nations in Transit Country Report: Uzbekistan* (Freedom House, 2003), http://www.freedohouse.org/template.cfm?page=47&nit=302&year=2003.

33. Official figures say the violence resulted in 187 deaths of armed, hostage-taking insurgents. All other eyewitness reports estimate that 800–1,000 or more individuals were killed, including women and children. International Crisis Group, "Uzbekistan: The Andijon Uprising," *Asia Briefing,* no. 38 (2005), http://www.crisisgroup.org/en/regions/asia/central-asia/uzbekistan/B038-uzbekistan-the-andijon-uprising.aspx; Freedom House, "Central and Eastern Europe/FSU," in *Freedom of the Press 2008,* http://www.freedomhouse.org/template.cfm?page=251&year=2008; Sarah Kendzior, "Inventing Akromiya: The Role of Uzbek Propagandists in the Andijon Massacre," *Demokratizatsiya* 14, no. 4 (2006): 545–62. President Karimov repeatedly rejected calls for international investigation of the events and banned representatives of international organizations from visiting the city for months. One foreign scholar did immediately gain access to the site of the uprising. Her controversial account supports the government's position. Shirin Akiner, *Violence in Andijan, 13 May 2005: An Independent Assessment* (Washington, D.C.: Johns Hopkins University-SAIS, 2005).

34. After a series of bombings in Tashkent in 1999, which the Karimov regime

blamed on Islamic extremists (for a detailed discussion, see Monica Whitlock, "The Glinka Street Plot," in *Land Beyond the River: The Untold Story of Central Asia* [New York: Thomas Dunne Books, 2003]), Akrom Yuldoshev was arrested and sentenced to seventeen years in prison.

35. Kendzior, "Inventing Akromiya"; Alisher Ilkhamov, "The Phenomenology of Akromiya: Separating Facts from Fiction," *China and Eurasia Forum Quarterly* 4, no. 2 (2006): 39–48.

36. Igor Rotar, "Uzbekistan: What Is Known about Akramia and the Uprising?," Forum 18 News Service, June 16, 2005, http://www.forum18.org/Archive.php?article_id=586; Ilkhamov, "Phenomenology of Akromiya," 42.

37. The arrests were not unprecedented. In 2002, Uzbekistan officials arrested twelve individuals for following a moderate Turkish movement, Nurchu, which engages in building a group of devout Muslims via charity and welfare activity, but with firm commitment to democratic governance and avoidance of an Islamic state. Ilkhamov, "Phenomenology of Akromiya," 41. In Fall 2010 a trial of twenty-five alleged members of the religious group Shoxidiillar was under way in Andijan. "Uzbekistan: B Andizhane osudili chlenov religioznoi gruppy 'Shoxidiilar,' osnovannoi mestnym prorokom Xamidullo," Ferghana.ru, September 12, 2010.

38. The organization itself released only one publication, *Yimonga Yul,* a pamphlet, which makes no mention of the government or its overthrow nor even uses the word "Uzbekistan." For a discussion, see Ilkhamov, "Phenomenology of Akromiya"; and Kendzior, "Inventing Akromiya."

39. Freedom House, "Central and Eastern Europe/FSU."

40. Ibragim Alibekov, "Central Asian Leaders React to Developments in Kyrgyzstan," *Eurasia Insight,* March 22, 2005.

41. U.S. embassy representative, interview by author, Tashkent, June 15, 2006; Samarqand Social Services NGO, interview by author, Samarqand, June 26, 2006.

42. Amnesty International representative, interview by author, Tashkent, June 22, 2006.

43. Samarqand Health Services NGO, interview by author, Samarqand, June 27, 2006.

44. Local representative of a health services NGO, interview by author, Tashkent, June 19, 2006.

45. Samarqand Health Services NGO, interview by author, Samarqand, June 27, 2006.

46. NANNOUZ representative, interview by author, Tashkent, June 14, 2006.

47. Samarqand Health Services NGO, interview by author, Samarqand, June 27, 2006.

48. Samarqand Social Services NGO, interview by author, Samarqand, June 26, 2006.

49. Ibid.

50. Eurasia Foundation representative, phone interview by author, May 20, 2006; Laura Adams, "Actually Existing Civil Society in Central Asia" (paper pre-

sented at the annual meeting of the Eastern Sociological Association, Washington, D.C., March 17–20, 2005); local Representative of a donor NGO, interview by author, Tashkent, July 6, 2006; USAID representative, interview by author, Tashkent, June 23, 2006.

51. Local representative of a donor NGO, interview by author, Tashkent, July 6, 2006.

52. Eurasia Foundation representative, phone interview by author, May 20, 2006; USAID representative, interview by author, Tashkent, June 23, 2006; international representative of an international NGO, interview by author, Tashkent, June 23, 2006.

53. Only pharmacies and some dentistry practices were truly privatized, but even then the state controlled the pricing structure for some key products and services. Ilkhamov and Jakubowski, *Health Care Systems in Transition,* 21.

54."Uzbekistan: Chastnaya Meditsinskaya Praktika Budet Zapreshchena," Ferghana.ru, May 11, 2010, http://www.ferghana.ru/news.php?id=14692.

55. Johnson, "Authoritarian Regimes and Nongovernmental Organizations."

56. Ariel Cohen, *Kazakhstan: The Road to Independence* (Washington, D.C.: Johns Hopkins University-SAIS, 2008), 39.

57. Maksut Kulzhanov and Bernd Rechel, "Kazakhstan: Health System Review," *Health Systems in Transition* 9, no. 7 (2007): 31.

58. Ibid.; local representative of a donor NGO, interview by author, Astana, February 7, 2008; deputy director of National Analytical Center (government funded), interview by author, Almaty, January 28, 2008.

59. Local representative of UN Population Fund, interview by author, Almaty, January 22, 2008.

60. Local representative of UNICEF, interview by author, Astana, February 7, 2008.

61. In Kyrgyzstan, health care NGOs do have legal status to administer a range of medical treatments, as long as the doctors and nurses providing such treatments are legally licensed.

62. Local representative of Astana social services NGO, interview by author, Astana, February 7, 2008.

63. Local representative of Columbia University Global Health Research Center, interview by author, Almaty, January 17, 2008. Without the legal status necessary to generate profits, long-term funding and organizational survival are concerns for NGOs.

64. Local representative of the National Democratic Institute, interview by author, Almaty, January 18, 2008.

65. Local representative of UN Population Fund, interview by author, Almaty, January 22, 2008.

66. Johnson, "Authoritarian Regimes and Nongovernmental Organizations."

67. World Bank, *Implementation Completion Report on a Loan in the Amount of US$42.40 Million to the Republic of Kazakhstan for a Health Project in Support*

of the First Phase of a Health Reform Program (Washington, D.C.: World Bank, 2002), 10.

68. Kelly M. McMann, "The Shrinking of the Welfare State: Central Asians' Assessments of Soviet and Post-Soviet Governance," in *Everyday Life in Central Asia: Past and Present,* ed. Jeff Sahadeo and Russell Zanca (Bloomington: Indiana University Press, 2007).

69. Nursultan Nazarbayev, *Ukaz Presidenta no. 154: Kontseptstiya razvitiya grazhdanskogo obshchestva v Respublike Kazakhstan na 2006–2011 gody* [Presidential decree no. 154: Concept of civil society development in the Republic of Kazakhstan for 2006–2011] (Astana: Government of the Republic of Kazakhstan, 2007), 38.

70. Kulzhanov and Rechel, "Kazakhstan: Health System Review," 32.

71. Nazarbayev, *Ukaz Presidenta no. 154.*

72. Local representative of UNDP HIV/AIDS, interview by author, Almaty, January 21, 2008.

73. Foreign representative of a donor NGO, interview by author, Almaty, February 4, 2008.

74. Ibid.

75. Ibid.

76. Representative of a social sector NGO, interview by author, Almaty, January 29, 2008.

77. Foreign representative of a donor NGO, interview by author, Almaty, February 4, 2008.

78. Representative of a health system reform NGO, interview by author, Almaty, January 29, 2008.

79. Ibid.

80. Representative of an opposition NGO, interview by author, Almaty, January 28, 2008.

81. Representative of a social sector NGO, interview by author, Almaty, January 29, 2008.

82. Medecins Sans Frontieres, "Kyrgyzstan: Ongoing Care for Victims of Violence in the South," August 9, 2010, http://www.doctorswithoutborders.org/news/article.cfm?id=4664&cat=field-news.

6

Civil Service and Public Satisfaction

From Functions to Services—the Case of Kazakhstan

Ken Charman and Rakhymzhan Assangaziyev

Among the former centrally planned economies, Kazakhstan has been one of the leading proponents of improvements in public service provision. Civil service reform has been at the top of the government's agenda in the two decades since independence, as an integral component of the republic's overall strategy to build a competitive socioeconomic environment that can efficiently exploit the republic's abundant natural resources. As a newly emerging nation with a strong cultural identity derived from its nomadic past, Kazakhstan is ambitious, exerting international influence as a secular republic and leading the emergence of the Central Asian region in the post-Soviet era. Improvement in public services delivery, a very visible sign of public sector reform, was one of several such reforms set out in the republic's governing strategy, "Kazakhstan 2030," published in 1997 and endorsed in the updated "Kazakhstan 2050" strategy announced by the president of Kazakhstan in December 2012.

Under the leadership of President Nursultan Nazarbayev, and within the overarching strategic framework of "Kazakhstan 2030," Kazakhstan has a stated aim of building an independent, liberalized, and secular economy, open to trade and attractive to foreign investment, and has long proclaimed a desire to be considered one of the top fifty competitive countries worldwide. Part of this desire derives from a wish to create a prosperous independent Central Asian state in the historic Kazakh territories. But Kazakhstan also needs to attract foreign direct investment to build the capacity to develop its industrial potential and more specifically to exploit its huge hydrocarbon and mineral reserves, which are mainly situated in the Caspian Sea region in the west of the republic. Quality of public service provision has always been an integral part of the drive to competitiveness that Kazakhstan has committed to undertake. In this chapter we assess the progress that has been made in improving public service provision in Kazakhstan since the mid-1990s, with special attention to the link between civil society and public services.

We first provide a background to developments in the public sector since independence and highlight problems in implementing public service reforms that arise in the context of a civil service emerging from a structure and culture based on principles developed during the central planning era. We then assess the framework under which the republic has set out its public service reform agenda, the initiatives that have been taken to build infrastructure for public service delivery, and changes to legislation that have enabled these reforms to take place. We then examine the results of the program, not only in introducing changes in delivery practices but in making an overall change from a functional to a service-based, customer-oriented public service culture, similar to that attempted by North American and European countries since the early 1990s. We find that while impressive in terms of infrastructure development, and with certain sectors of the civil service taking an enthusiastic lead, public service delivery in Kazakhstan has still not fully emerged from its centrally planned past, and the service culture that is so forcefully put forward by the lead ministries has not been shared across all ministries. This has restricted the republic's ability to get a new public service–oriented culture accepted throughout all services, republic-wide.

Finally, we look at the growth of civil society organizations (CSOs) in Kazakhstan and assess the role that CSOs are undertaking in the promotion of a public service culture in Kazakhstan. A strong and active civil society, by voicing public expectations, plays a significant role in ensuring that public expectations are at the forefront of public policy. This increases pressure on public service providers to deliver quality public services, and in order to do that the civil service must create an environment with well-organized, motivated, and appropriately rewarded civil servants. So a vision that expectations and the status of civil servants will increase is shared and maintained. In Kazakhstan, while expectations for public service delivery have increased and, to a very great extent, an infrastructure is in place to deliver quality public services, civil society does not play an active role in the process of managing public expectations, and pressures from public opinion play a lesser role. Consequently, the process of driving public service improvement is primarily "top down," the "vision" of maintaining high standards of public services to meet high public expectations is not wholly shared among ministries, and improvements in public service delivery are limited.[1] Greater participation by civil society in Kazakhstan would create greater incentives and a more conducive environment for reaching the levels of quality in public service delivery that the authorities have set out to achieve. We find that while the growth in CSOs has been impressive, they lack the participation, organization, and critical mass to effectively lobby at the policy level for further implementation of public sector reform initiatives. We conclude by looking at ways that CSOs can play a more significant role advocating for public service delivery reforms and improvements and highlight the need for CSOs to promote greater transparency and to adopt more transparent practices themselves in order to become a more effective lobby for the full implementation and effectiveness of public service delivery and, more widely, public sector reforms in Kazakhstan.

Challenges of Public Administration in the Post-Soviet Era

Since independence, Kazakhstan's public administration system has gone through substantial changes over a relatively short period of time. As in other post-Soviet countries, reform in Kazakhstan took place in parallel with wider transformation processes, but in the republic it faced specific challenges and implications. The country, first of all, had to transfer from a socialist and planned economy to a market- and competition-driven economy, which was a painful process, with thousands of people losing their jobs and hundreds of enterprises losing their business ties with partners in other former Soviet republics. Representatives of many ethnic minority groups, mainly those whose ancestors had been deported during the Stalin regime, started to leave the country for their historic motherlands. Over the course of six years, from 1991 to 1996, about 2 million people left

Kazakhstan, and insufficient immigration led to a fall in population from 16.4 million in 1991 to 14.9 million ten years later. The peak was in 1994, when more than 470,000 Kazakhstanis emigrated to states in the Commonwealth of Independent States and other, mainly neighboring, countries. The majority of emigrants were qualified skillful workers, and their departure resulted in distortions in the labor market. GDP per capita in the period between 1991 and 1996 steadily declined, and during the same period life expectancy fell from 67.6 years to 64.6 years.[2]

In the midst of such economic turmoil a political system had to be built to ensure adequate development. The period between 1991 and 1993 marked a shift to independent development, yet legislative provisions of the former Soviet republic remained in effect and the public administration system remained highly centralized. A closed bureaucratic system lacking open recruitment processes and transparency was inherited from the Soviet *nomenklatura* model. It became obvious that the inherited system of public administration was not able to cope with the constant and complex problems arising in the transitional society, especially in the economy. Members of the bureaucratic apparatus did not have an understanding of market concepts. President Nazarbayev recalled anecdotally that, after a long conversation on market reforms in 1992, one of the governors confessed to the president that "he had understood nothing of what had been said but would do whatever he would be asked to do."

The adoption of the first constitution in January 1993, which set provisions for the main branches of government and established a parliamentary-presidential form of governance, was a major factor influencing developments during the period 1993–1995. Difficulties in establishing a productive dialogue among Parliament, the prime minister and the Cabinet, and the ministries and departments that constitute the executive branches of the government led to dissolution of Parliament and adoption of a new constitution in August 1995. The new constitution vested the president with greater powers, creating in effect a centralized presidential republic in Kazakhstan. In the period between March and November 2005 the president signed 147 laws and decrees with the force of law regulating different aspects of the economy, including the budget system, banking, and the stock market.[3] The president was granted the right to appoint the prime minister (with Parliament's approval), members of government, and governors (*akims*) of oblasts (regions) and the power to establish and reorganize government institutions and nominate candidates for the position of senate speaker and prosecutor general. The president was also given the power to appoint a certain number of senators and members of the Constitution Council, Central Election Commission, and Accounting Committees.[4]

Some experts consider this step to have been a justified change to implement reforms. V. Chzhan states that "in terms of structural and functional perspectives, development of a Kazakhstani model with the Presidential form of government conditionally corresponded to the logics of 'top-down' modernization, where the transfer is carried out from the administrative commanding system of public administration to a new one, consistent with realities of a 'to-be built' market economy and civil society."[5]

At this point there was a need to develop a strategic document that would set development perspectives and priorities. The development strategy "Kazakhstan 2030," adopted in 1997, set a vision of the country's development for the following three decades. The document set forth strategies for economic and democratic reform in Kazakhstan and proclaimed that a professional state was one of the long-term priorities.[6] The program consisted of seven principles: a comprehensive and professionally trained government concentrated on fulfillment of certain key functions; work on action programs on the basis of the proposed strategies; efficient interinstitutional coordination; an increase in the authority and responsibilities of ministers, in their accountability, and in strategic control over their activity; decentralization within ministries, from the governing center to the region and from the state to the private sector; decisive and merciless combating of corruption; and improvement of the system of personnel hiring, training, and promotion.

The need to cope with a severe budget crisis forced the reorganization of central and local bodies with a focus on optimizing the bureaucratic apparatus, which was done in accordance with a presidential decree in October 1997. Several oblasts were merged, which resulted in a major cut in the number of staff in the civil service. Rapid economic growth, starting in 2000 and led by increases in world prices for Kazakhstan's major export commodities, oil and mineral resources, had given the authorities opportunities for wide-scale modernization of the civil service.

Laws on civil service and the "fight against corruption" were passed in 1999, and the Agency for Civil Service Affairs was established as an "authorized state body on the civil service affairs issues."[7] The introduction of competitive testing and interviews for entrance into the civil service was a major breakthrough in forming a modern civil service. Previously potential applicants had not had access to information on vacancies and qualification requirements for civil service; upon passage of these legislative acts, all state bodies had to announce in the central newspapers all open positions, with qualification requirements and remuneration. These measures were taken to curb a system based on patronage and personal relations. According to the chairman of the Civil Service Agency, Alikhan Baimenov, in 1999 changes in the political echelons (ministers and governors) on average resulted in a reshuffle of 60 percent of subordinate staff.[8] Twelve years later such turnover reportedly went down to 25 percent, but it remains high and is indicative of a system with nepotism and a "team-based" approach to recruitment. Further distinctions were made between administrative and political civil service positions. A register of civil servants' positions and pay grades was introduced accordingly. The Civil Service Agency was positioned as an entity responsible for civil service reform at large. Simultaneously, the Academy for Civil Service was established, with a focus on training and retraining of civil servants. Retraining institutions for regional civil servants were established in all oblasts. A parallel budget decentralization and transfer to midterm fiscal planning commenced during this period. Steps were taken to give more spending authority to regions and to make regional governance more transparent and accountable.

The transfer to a strategic planning system and performance-based budgeting in the ministries and local bodies was an effort to combine the strategic goals of the ministries with their operational plans and actual performance, including budgetary efficiency. Adoption of a presidential decree on performance assessment of ministries and local bodies in March 2010 was followed by a further cut in the number of staff in the civil service at the end of 2010 (15 percent, or twenty-six thousand people), including law enforcement bodies.[9]

As of the beginning of 2011, the structure of civil service personnel was represented by the following statistics. Out of more than 102,000 civil servants (excluding law enforcement and military), more than 99,000 were administrative civil servants and 3,000 were political appointees. Civil servants claim to represent sixty ethnic groups in Kazakhstan, with Kazakhs dominating (more than 50 percent).[10]

Though women constitute 57 percent of all civil service employees, the number of women at a decision-making level is limited—only 9.8 percent of women are political appointees. At the time of this writing only two members of government (out of seventeen) were women. The share of women is low at the legislative level as well. As of 2012 only 18 percent of deputies in Parliament were women, which is far fewer than in most of the EU countries. The average civil servant is thirty-nine years old with a university degree.[11]

A decision to move to a performance assessment system for state bodies was a step toward making authorities accountable before the public and more efficient in providing services. A presidential decree in March 2010 introducing performance assessment stipulated that there be annual assessments of all ministries and regional authorities. The evaluation covers six aspects of public management performance: implementation of presidential decrees, budget management, service delivery, strategic planning, human resources management, and information technology.

During the early 2000s attention was also given to the provision and delivery of public services, with ambitions to revise and renew the whole basis under which public services are delivered, shifting from a service provider model (usually organized by ministry) to a more customer friendly and efficient "one-stop shop" and e-government format.

The Framework for Public Service Provision and Delivery in Kazakhstan

The E-Government Program, launched in 2004, aimed at a reduction in administrative barriers in the civil service and represented a major turn toward customer-oriented service. Perhaps a more important milestone was the establishment of "one-stop shops," entities providing a variety of public services in one place. Implementation of this initiative across the country was very rapid and impressive. More than two hundred one-stop shops were established within three years (2005–2008), with shops in each district (*rayon*) of each of the oblasts of Kazakhstan.[12] The one-stop shops were staffed initially with civil servants delegated from other state bodies, such as the Tax Committee and Department of Justice, and subsequently had their own staff trained and qualified.

A number of projects funded by international donors assisted in removing the administrative barriers business had to overcome and contributed to the ease of doing business, which resulted in improvement of Kazakhstan's position in the World Bank's *Doing Business* report. While in 2006 the *Doing Business* report placed Kazakhstan in eighty-sixth place in the world in terms of business conditions, six years later the country was ranked forty-seventh.[13] Projects have included the USAID-funded Business Environment Improvement Project, which has provided support to build capacity within government and the private sector to engage in effective dialogue, strengthen the commercial law framework, and improve implementation of business-related legal reforms to reduce costs and barriers for small and medium-sized enterprises.

The government of Kazakhstan's initiatives to develop customer-oriented public services were based firmly on the notion that the satisfaction of customers, namely the public, plays a pivotal role in the evaluation of the performance of state bodies and civil servants. With this recognition that the interests of the public are at the heart of public service delivery, the initiatives to improve public services in Kazakhstan have incorporated the principles of New Public Management, a term described as "shorthand for a group of administrative doctrines" aimed at "providing responsive service."[14] The "reinventing government" model developed by David Osborne and Ted Gaebler proposes that "they (entrepreneurial governments) redefine their clients as *customers* and offer them choices."[15] This concept has, to an extent, been implemented in Kazakhstan through the "one-stop shop" model of service delivery.

As part of the overall civil and public service reform agenda, the government of Kazakhstan introduced performance standards for public services delivery. The two-and-a-half-year, EU-funded technical assistance project entitled "Support for the Development of Standards for Civil Service Provision" from 2005–2008 assisted the Agency for Civil Service Affairs in introducing performance standards in public services in four pilot ministries—the Ministry of Justice, the Ministry of Finance (Tax Committee), the Ministry of Health Care, and the Ministry of Labor and Social Protection. Following the concepts of New Public Management, the government of Kazakhstan proclaimed its focus on meeting clients' needs and introduced public service standards, a register of public services, and clients' charters. Under a law passed in 2007, designed in conjunction with the EU-funded technical assistance, all public service providers were obliged to develop and publish their performance standards under generally accepted criteria for measurement of quality in public services, namely politeness of the staff, quality of the services provided, accessibility of the service from the standpoints of both physical distance and availability of facilities, timeliness of service provided, and satisfaction with the procedures for dealing with complaints.

Some state entities, such as the Tax Committee, started providing customer charters (*reglaments*) to demonstrate their commitment to improving standards in public service delivery. The charters are based on those adopted by European countries and state the main mission of the body and list the rights of taxpayers, including the rights to receive information, to file official complaints, and to request timely and high-quality services. The high visibility of one-stop shops as single-point public service delivery sent a clear message to the public, the international community, and the public sector in Kazakhstan itself that a competitive public sector was an integral component of the "Kazakhstan 2030" (now "Kazakhstan 2050") strategy for overall competitiveness.

The Successes of the One-Stop Shop and E-Government Programs

The one-stop shop model for improving public service delivery in Kazakhstan has, on the face of it, been impressive. These accessible customer interface points (one-stop shops) have provided physical accessibility to public services and increased Internet accessibility. (Kazakhstan ranks high in terms of Internet access, according to the World Economic Forum Global Competitiveness Index.)[16] Kazakhstan also has provided accessibility to services through the E-Government Program. Both one-stop shops and e-government are now key to governmental service delivery strategies. Under these initiatives, members of the public are able to experience public sector accountability for the first time.

Ministers are held accountable for the quality of the services that their ministry delivers, whether it involves the issuing of a driving license or passport, the application for a social benefit, or a visit to the doctor. An amendment to the Law on Administrative Procedures of 2007, which was introduced as a result of the EuropeAid technical assistance program (2005–2008), requires all public service providers to publish performance standards for the services they provide, under the framework established under the "General Principles of Public Service Delivery" for measuring the quality of public services. To promote the idea of customer orientation, a consultation process has been introduced through surveys, interviews, and focus groups, which have been administered through the one-stop shops, and performance statistics for each public service provider have been published in the national press. Increased expectations for quality of public services from within the government have been matched by higher status and new reward systems for the public servants who provide such services.

The one-stop shops have an impressive array of measurement systems to assess the quality of public services and public satisfaction with these services. So quality in service provision is now measured and the results published, and the time customers spend in line at one-stop shops is closely monitored, as are processing times for passports, licenses, and registration documents. Detailed procedures are published so that legitimate complaints can be followed up, and staff are obliged to adhere to given levels of politeness and presentability. Customer charters hang on the walls of the one-stop shops and at other service centers of each of the ministries, detailing the levels of service that customers can expect and procedures to follow if they wish to raise a complaint. The introduction of the amendment to the Law on Administrative Procedures of 2007 resulted in a flurry of activity among public service providers in Kazakhstan, primarily in the form of ministries and *akimats* (regional authorities) publishing performance data on the public services they provide.

The result has been significant progress in some areas, primarily the development of infrastructure for provision of public services and the customer interface. But the adoption of public service principles has not received universal acceptance across the whole public sector, as the new principles of public management have been imposed on a civil service partly entrenched in the former Soviet administration system and partly influenced by transitional factors arising from twenty years of market reform and the associated transition of Kazakhstan's society.

The one-stop shops are a front office and provide only a customer interface for services that are still processed at the ministry that issues them. For example, members of the public apply for passports and registration documents at a one-stop shop, but these documents are still processed at the issuing ministry. Therefore, public service agreements exist between the one-stop shops and the ministries.

Behind the very efficient and impressive front office provided by the one-stop shops, something has been lacking. Initial enthusiasm for publishing performance data has waned, and while some ministries, such as the Ministry of Justice, provide annual data on performance in public service delivery, other ministries are reluctant to do so. Not all ministries use the well-equipped one-stop shops to deliver services; those that cannot establish their own one-stop shops or service delivery points due to budget constraints are still reluctant to relinquish control and transfer those services to functioning one-stop shops, which are now under the supervision of the Ministry of Transport and Communication. The key decisions on institutional responsibility for one-stop shops also serve as an example of a lack of prior consultations and negotiations. Initially one-stop shops were the domain of the Ministry of Justice, and responsibility for them was transferred to the jurisdiction of local authorities without proper budgetary and methodological preparation. As a result, a significant deterioration of the quality of services took place in 2010. As Sergey Pizikov, country director of the USAID Business Environment Project has stated, "the number of satisfied users [of government services] had fallen drastically."[17] Taking into account the ongoing efforts of the government to implement its E-Government Program, responsibility for the accountability of the one-stop shops was given to the Ministry of Information and Communication in March 2011.

As enthusiasm for publication of performance standards has waned, so has public consultation on development and monitoring of public service standards, which is not common to all ministries. Civil servants tend to refer to the guidelines of the civil service code rather than to customer surveys. As one civil servant responding to a European Commission survey observed when asked about politeness, "We are obliged by the civil service code to be polite, therefore we are, now go away please." Customer surveys, which indicated the contrary, were not referred to.[18]

Reward systems for civil servants, especially for those who work in regional offices, have not progressed in line with the expectations of them as service providers, and public sector pay rates lag well behind those of the private sector and state-owned enterprises. Therefore, the civil service system is still not capable of attracting talented staff and the majority of young graduates of Western universities prefer working in the private sector and for foreign companies. At the same time, as we discuss later in this chapter, civil society, while present and active in Kazakhstan, does not yet have a primary role in influencing policy and debate. NGOs, including many international NGOs, are consulted because ministries are obliged to consult them (according to Government Resolution no. 840, dated August 21, 2003), but they are not necessarily listened to.

This is indicative of a system that has made great strides to improve public services and the status of the civil servant but has been fundamentally "top-down" in its delivery. Public participation and the involvement of the public in determining the future of public services delivery are not at the levels they could be, thus restricting the ability to create a shared vision of what public services should offer. The lack of ability to demonstrate high performance in public service delivery also restricts the growth in status and rewards available to public servants and civil servants themselves. The authorities have, for the most part, addressed the issues of "architecture" of civil service and introduced appropriate legislation, but commitment and vision are not shared across all ministries and local governments (*akimats*), public involvement in decision making is limited, and the cultural shift in civil service culture from the "functional" premise inherited from central planning days to the "service" principle required of New Public Management has not been fully realized.

The initial enthusiasm for publication of public service performance standards under the amendment to the Law on Administrative Procedures of 2007 and subsequent lack of support for this law from several ministries indicates that a lack of shared values within the public sector still remains and a culture of entrenched "old-school" principles still exists in some sectors of the civil service. A lack of progress in improving reward systems in the public sector vis-à-vis the growing private sector and the continued culture of corruption have not allowed the status of the public service providers to improve in accordance with the increase in the quality of services that they are expected to provide. A number of issues need to be addressed to turn functions into public service. It has been more than twenty years since the fall of the Soviet Union, and the top-down approach has its limits. A wider platform for civil society would assist in bringing to the forefront the nature of public expectations and matching them to the limited resources that every public service provider has.

So, despite overall progress and improvement there are still areas and gaps requiring substantial attention and changes. Out of the six areas of assessment, service delivery is one of the most important and challenging since it reflects customers' expectations and perceptions. It can also be considered an external view of how the government works and whether it meets its obligations.

Though the term "customer" has now been introduced in legislation and is being widely used in the public administration of Kazakhstan, the recipient of civil services is not a customer in a full sense. A customer is by definition "a party that receives or consumes products (goods or services) and has the ability to choose between different products and suppliers."[19] In the current system a citizen does not have a full choice in getting a particular service—many of the services are provided by state institutions and where there are alternative private providers the services are either not affordable (as in the education sector) or of lower quality (as in the health care sector).

An EU-funded survey project implemented in 2007, Support to Development of Public Service Standards in Kazakhstan, found overall satisfaction among customers in the quality of services provided by several pilot entities in Almaty city and South Kazakhstan oblast was just 55 percent; that is, almost every other customer was not content with the quality of services rendered by state bodies. Focus groups were conducted with customers to identify the main obstacles to satisfaction with services rendered by civil servants. Among the main difficulties customers faced were limited accessibility of information on procedures for the service (39.6 percent responded that they had difficulty obtaining information of required quality and 45.6 percent failed to receive answers over the phone), delays in provision of services (50.6 percent were dissatisfied with the timeliness of service), impoliteness (40.5 percent responded that they had been dealt with impolitely), and low qualification of the staff (42.2 percent of customers reported insufficient qualification of a civil servant with whom they had interacted).[20] All these figures demonstrate that the quality of services was far from satisfactory.

To have a fuller picture, perspectives from different sides should be taken into account. As in many of the post-Soviet countries, civil servants in Kazakhstan inherited a bureaucratic mentality that they were above ordinary citizens. Most civil servants still tend to think of themselves as officials authorized to give orders and decide for others but not to serve in the sense that they are employees paid from taxpayers' money. This attitude represents one of the most difficult issues the government needs to address. According to a Civil Service Agency report for 2010, 3,673 complaints were received from citizens and legal entities about violations of anticorruption and civil service legislation and 3,138 inspections took place, as a result of which disciplinary measures were taken against 1,084 civil servants.[21] The challenge is that these problems cannot be overcome within a short period of time, and much depends on whether the long-term measures aimed at establishing a robust link between civil servants' performance assessments and customers' satisfaction will be put in place and properly implemented.

Understanding and broad discussion of the nature of the reforms is another stumbling block. Many of the new initiatives are the consequences of decisions made at the central level, and a top-down approach prevails in the process of reforms. A civil servant from South Kazakhstan oblast confessed during the focus group that usually all instructions came from the top and they did not particularly know why certain services had to be evaluated.

Such misunderstanding is due in part to the weaknesses of private or nongovernmental institutions and in part to the absence of traditional cooperation between the executive and other institutions. Provisions for prior discussions and consultations with main stakeholders are enshrined in the legislation but are far from being implemented in the decision-making process. Public dialogue to help resolve these administrative problems should be strongly encouraged, but there is no mechanism to ensure such dialogue is effective.

There is a lack of understanding of what administrative reform is about among the civil servants, especially those in the regions. Therefore it was quite common that civil servants, not knowing the purpose, driving forces, and implications of new regulations, had to implement something they did not support themselves. "Development of [performance] standards takes so much of our time and we had difficulties in understanding why it was needed," complained one of the focus group participants representing providers of services.[22]

A greater obstacle is deliberate resistance to reforms. When reforms are perceived to threaten the privileges of powerful groups, they are unlikely to be implemented. In many cases this resulted in resistance to changes, especially when it came to norms that limit civil servants' authority and functions, that transfer services from one institution to another, or that involve greater business process reengineering. For example, some institutions strongly resisted the transfer of services to the one-stop shops, partly due to fear of losing personnel vacancies, institutional influence, and so forth.

There is a misperception of the ultimate purpose of administrative reforms on both sides. Some officials understand the changes and innovations in public administration as tools for punishment and prosecution and not as means for improvement. Customers sometimes tend to think that the changes are needed for officials to justify the job they do, creating additional bureaucracy.

The fourteen oblasts of Kazakhstan have been obliged to manage the changes in public sector reform imposed from above. While the reforms were greeted with overall enthusiasm, some negative reaction emerged from the regions, mainly due to the changes not being well understood or well communicated. The significant distances between regions in Kazakhstan has played a part, but the bigger issue has been communication between the central government, the regional *akimats* and the territorial subdivisions of the ministries as to what the introduction of performance standards actually means.

In 2007 we conducted a survey on public service standards on behalf of the European Commission Project Assistance to the Development of Public Service Standards in Kazakhstan. We administered questionnaires and conducted interviews with over two thousand respondents in southern Kazakhstan and Almaty city regarding the quality of public service delivery in major urban and rural areas of Kazakhstan. Our data consisted of opinions and descriptions of experiences from members of the public who used public services in South Kazakhstan and Almaty city, where performance standards for the public sector were piloted. We found that communication between the central government and regional authorities occurred through simple fax or e-mail messages requiring the region to provide data on performance standards, without sufficient explanation as to the philosophical basis behind the request. Imposing standards on remote regions where there were well-established practices for public service delivery required significant communication from the central authorities, several visits, and cross-communication between regional *akimats*. Where such communication took place, the *akimats* became, in many cases, fully committed to the notion of interviewing members of the public who used their services and reporting performance data. Ensuring complete explanation of the top-down communications from central government to the regions was the biggest issue in rolling out the public service delivery agenda. However, having the one-stop shop model implemented across the republic provided a strong basis for reforms in service delivery to be effected.[23]

We found significant differences related both to the attitudes of those public servants charged with implementing the improvements in service delivery and to the availability of appropriate infrastructure for service delivery. The survey found that 63 percent of service providers had a positive attitude toward the implementation of standards and were ready to help with it and that there was a greater commitment to the implementation of standards in urban areas (66 percent) than in rural areas (48 percent). This was most likely due to the fact that in urban areas there is better infrastructure to improve the quality of services and a closer liaison between the central government and the service providers in the field.[24] This is clearly demonstrated in comments from the service providers. One provider in South Kazakhstan pointed out that institutions' technical equipment did not meet the standards of service for the procedure: "This is ahead of our technical base. Our workload has increased by 50%, and we work on Saturdays and Sundays. It is necessary to automate [our work]; we have a lot, of course. We do not have a copy machine, there are not enough comfortable places for customers to wait, we have a lack of furniture, and a lack of adequate room."[25]

The survey also provided evidence of the differences in time taken to process applications for social benefits between the city of Shymkent, the capital of South Kazakhstan, and the *rayons* of South Kazakhstan, which are primarily rural. Service provision was found to be quicker in Shymkent, where 40 percent of respondents had been required to wait from two to four weeks for their application for social benefits to be processed and 51 percent had been required to wait more than one month. In the rural *rayons*, only 12 percent had managed to complete the application process within two to four weeks, with 88 percent waiting for more than one month. This was explained, at least in part, by the fact that the procedures for application for social benefits are very different in Shymkent and the *rayons* of South Kazakhstan. In the urban areas of Shymkent, applications for social benefits are undertaken at the one-stop shops, which are located within reach of the majority of the population. In the *rayons* there is a far greater incidence of applications being undertaken informally through personal contact. In the more crowded urban areas, where procedures are more readily adhered to, informal application based on personal contact was much rarer. Lengthy delays, where they occurred, caused dissatisfaction in both urban and rural areas, but the lack of infrastructure for public service delivery in the *rayons* was the key criterion; it simply was not possible to replicate the procedural and scale economies of the one-stop shops in the sparsely populated rural areas.[26]

In assessing the reforms in public administration of Kazakhstan, an obvious conclusion is that reform was built on existing legislation. The legislative infrastructure is in place, but that is not enough. Customers are not knowledgeable about their rights and entitlements. Out of all respondents surveyed in the abovementioned study of the EC project, 30 percent stated that they had had cause for complaint while dealing with providers of services, but none of them had actually filed a written complaint. This is a troublesome figure. The attitude toward formal complaints comes from a mentality based on skepticism about the justice and efficiency of the complaints system. People filing complaints are perceived by civil servants as "pettifoggers complicating the work of officials and distracting from their main work."[27]

Civil Society Organizations and the Civil Service

In general there is little citizen involvement in civil society organizations. There are also very few active CSOs protecting the rights of customers. The low level of participation in civic networks is also reflected in the UNDP Regional Human Development Report for 2011. The "Social Exclusion Survey" found civic participation in Kazakhstan to be very low. Just 21 percent of those surveyed participated in any kind of association, club, or leisure group, which is just over half the rate of participation in southeast Europe, where almost 40 percent of respondents reported being active in some kind of civic activity.[28]

The absence of civil society organizations leaves the less powerful vulnerable to predatory government. A Business Environment Improvement Project survey implemented in 2010, for example, shows that 90 percent of respondents—small business representatives in Almaty city—claimed fines had been arbitrarily imposed on them by tax inspection and control authorities.[29] This percentage is very high, even allowing for exaggeration by respondents unwilling to disclose details of their personal income. The striking thing is that 91 percent of them reported that they would try to negotiate informally with a tax inspector and bribe an official.[30] Corruption is widespread and an acknowledged problem, but few victims think of organizing to combat the problem.

Civil servants in turn feel themselves unprotected and vulnerable to many risks in pursuing a career with the civil service. The staff in the civil service system lack motivation and confidence. The major issue in this regard is the remuneration scheme. Strong economic growth in recent years, driven mainly by the oil and gas industry, reduced the competitiveness of the public sector as an employer. The conservative policy on wage development in the civil service is negatively affecting the quality of the civil service, as the private sector is able to offer significantly better pay and benefit packages. When asked to assign scores on a five-point scale to different factors of motivation, civil servants who participated in our focus group rated remuneration items as the lowest motivators: "Our problem is a low salary but regardless of this we strive to improve the quality of service and we are happy if we do not hear rude words from customers," wrote one of the civil servants in response to the question about which problems concerned him most.

The government is trying to address the issue by essentially increasing the salary level almost every two years. However, the civil service is still not competitive with the private sector and big industrial enterprises, and the outflow of personnel from civil service agencies with a greater workload is impeding many initiatives and undermining personnel management reforms. The turnover ratio, according to data from the Civil Service Agency, is about 13 percent, while in the established civil service systems this ratio does not exceed 4 percent.[31] There are no separate pension benefits for civil servants, as there are in many other developed countries. Periodic changes in structure and staff cuts are also disincentives to a career with the civil service.

The civil service is still in need of greater efficiency and justice within the system. Deficiencies in the transparency of the promotion and performance appraisal system are one of the major concerns of civil service

Table 6.1. Satisfaction of Civil Servants by Factors of Motivation Parameters (on a Five-Point Scale)

Social stature and prestige of the job	3.5
Civil servants' moral motivation system	3.2
Material reward system of civil servants	2.3
Base salary level	2.2
Amount of bonuses	1.8

Source: Public Services: Experience of Measuring Quality and Introducing Standards, survey report implemented with the support of the European Commission Project Assistance to Development of Public Service Standards in Kazakhstan and DAI Europe Ltd. (Astana, 2007), 61.

Table 6.2. "Learning and Promotion" Parameter Components of Civil Servants (on a Five-Point Scale)	
Competence of civil servants in your unit	4.0
Skills upgrading opportunities	3.7
Career growth opportunities	3.3
Relation between reward and performance	2.9
Source: Public Services: Experience of Measuring Quality and Introducing Standards, survey report implemented with the support of the European Commission Project Assistance to Development of Public Service Standards in Kazakhstan and DAI Europe Ltd. (Astana, 2007), 61.	

staff. When asked to assign scores on a five-point scale to different factors of "learning and promotion," civil servants who participated in our focus group rated "relation between reward and performance" lowest, with value of 2.9, while "career growth opportunities" were rated just 3.3 (see table 6.2).

All these findings signal that there are many external and internal factors impeding the establishment of a link between civil servants' performance assessment and customers' satisfaction. The primary factor is the lack of progress in raising the status of the civil service to correspond with the new expectations attached to the public services it provides.

In the following section we provide an overview of the development of civil society in Kazakhstan and assess the capacity of civil society in Kazakhstan today to influence the development of a service culture in Kazakhstan's public services.

The Role of Civil Society in Kazakhstan

Civil society, "the arena, outside of the family, the state, and the market, which is created by individual and collective actions, organizations and institutions to advance shared interests" has grown from a low base in Kazakhstan.[32] Organizations "outside the state" are a relatively new concept in former centrally planned economies, as they did not exist before perestroika in the mid-1980s, when some civic participation was permitted. However, such freedoms for civil society organizations have been hard earned. In the early 1990s around four hundred NGOs were established in Kazakhstan, mainly to foster the protection of various human rights decreed under the law. Between 1994 and 2001 the number of NGOs increased significantly and the diversification of the services that they offered also increased, supported to a large extent by the establishment of a number of international NGOs in Kazakhstan. Since then the environment for NGOs has become much more supportive, with greater recognition from state bodies and active consultation between the state (particularly by the Nur Otan Party, which currently holds a majority of the seats in the Mazhilis) and the NGOs themselves.

There are currently around twenty thousand national and international NGOs registered in Kazakhstan, according to government figures, representing a diverse range of areas, including environmental organizations, business associations, chambers of commerce, mass media associations, religious and charity organizations, cultural centers, universities and educational organizations, think tanks, health and social service organizations, gender organizations, youth and children's organizations, and human rights and anticorruption bodies. However, not all registered NGOs are active, and few, if any, are politically strong enough to collectively harness public opinion. Although NGOs are numerous, it is hard to conclude that civil society is well developed. In practice, the freedom to develop organizations independent of the state is not well accepted. A 2010 Freedom House report argues that governmental organizations in Kazakhstan use NGOs to promote their own agenda and do not recognize those organizations that are developing their own views independently.[33] According to the Civil Society Index, the level of "civic engagement," the extent to which people engage in NGOs, is not high (46 percent), and although NGOs practice values of democratic decision making, nonviolence, and equal opportunity, they do not tend to promote anticorruption efforts as much, which is indicative of the high levels of corruption that are present in Kazakhstan.[34] Transparency International's 2012 Corruption Perception Index placed Kazakhstan at 133rd (out of 174 countries), with a score of 28.[35]

Most outside observers agree that the impact of CSOs on policy in Kazakhstan is limited, although CSOs are considered to play a role in encouraging change in some social areas, such as environment control and monitoring of execution of local budgets. This is understandable given the short time that CSOs and NGOs have had to establish themselves in the republic.

The strengths of CSOs in Kazakhstan appear to be their flexibility and ability to acquire and exchange information and their ability to promote certain causes, such as equal opportunity and local participation in the democratic process. However, their weaknesses include the absence of participatory democracy and low levels of participation—with so many people with low incomes and with CSOs having such a short history in Kazakhstan, large-scale participation in CSOs is something for the future rather than the present. We conclude from this that, while there is acknowledgment of the need for CSOs and lip service is paid to their activities, they do not have the profile, the status, or participation levels to effectively lobby at government-policy level. The work of CSOs (particularly NGOs) may be effective at the local level, and this is a good basis for future development, but for the present CSOs are too thinly spread and cannot provide a "bottom-up" influence on government initiatives to promote wider acceptance of customer focus in public services in Kazakhstan. The initiatives for public service improvements, while laudable, remain "top-down," and this limits their overall effectiveness.

Throughout the period of economic and public sector reform, the role of civil society appears to have been accepted, but it has been peripheral to policy making. Both Parliament and the Nur Otan Party make a point of consulting with NGOs and wider CSOs on issues before they are brought to parliamentary debate. But unlike the case in more established democracies, NGOs are not seen to be taking a lead in putting forward issues that they deal with (for example, equal rights); instead, they tend simply to respond to government-led consultation exercises. Nevertheless, the role of CSOs and in particular NGOs in consultation has been growing. Being active to the extent of shaping the agenda is the next step for NGO activity in Kazakhstan.

In the following section we examine the changes in public administration to assess how far the public sector itself has built the capacity to implement the necessary cultural changes to fulfill the government's public service initiatives.

Where a Strong Civil Society in Kazakhstan Could Play a Role

Civil society could play a lead role in promoting and maintaining pressure for reforms, once initiated, to be consolidated. Following the methodology set out in the Civil Society Index (CSI), civil society organizations can do this in a number of ways. First, in terms of "civic engagement," there is the degree to which members of the public take part in civil society. In Kazakhstan, engagement in community activities is relatively diversified and social engagement scores relatively highly on the CSI. However, civic engagement at the political level is quite low, scoring only 18.3 percent on the CSI, indicating that CSOs do not have a lead role in the political arena where policy is formed. One can picture children's groups and activities for the disabled being well serviced by NGOs in Kazakhstan, but direct involvement in the policy debate is limited to official bilateral communications between the ministries, the Nur Otan Party, and NGOs, whereas a higher profile in the political arena would assist CSOs in shaping the policy agenda, of which public services are one.

Second, the level of organization of NGOs itself is preventing this increase in profile. NGOs in Kazakhstan are seen by the CSI as having "limited financial opportunities and resources, as well as short term project-oriented activities."[36] The main sources of funding for NGOs are grants from international donors. Grants through the government's social contracts are distributed through a relatively small number of NGOs (only 206), and the procedures for state social funding lack transparency. Although we are seeing an increase in the level of activities of a number of NGOs, the sustainability of the NGOs themselves is not yet at the level where it can expect to influence policy debate.

Third, transparency among CSOs is also an issue. According to the CSI, the strongest values of Kazakhstan civil society are democratic decision making, nonviolence, equal opportunities for men and women, peace, and tolerance. But most CSOs in Kazakhstan do not have a code of conduct, and almost half do not make their financial information publicly available. Without such transparency there is little basis for trust in the NGOs themselves, and it is this fundamental degree of trust from within the community that can increase participation and affect policy-making areas as well as community activities that are already well served in the republic. Most CSO members and nonmembers agree that civil society has a more limited impact on policy than it does in a range of social fields, such as supporting poor and marginalized communities (disabled persons, for example), education, housing, health, social development, humanitarian relief, food, and employment.[37]

CSOs in Kazakhstan have to operate within an external environment where there remain, according to the CSI, high levels of corruption, limited political rights and personal freedoms, constraints on the rule of law, and limits on the state's effectiveness. All this adds to the need for CSOs to rise above this and to gain the trust of the population in order to begin to have a significant impact on policy making and in maintaining the voice of public expectations.

In Kazakhstan, real accountability before citizens still needs to be achieved and the civil service should be made more efficient and competitive, and to do this the status of civil service careers vis-à-vis those in state-owned enterprises and the private sector needs to be raised. In other countries, such as the United Kingdom, this has been done by progressive appointment of senior-level public servants who have salaries and career paths that compete very favorably with those in the private sector but come with genuine accountability for public service provision. Leaders in the private sector are often offered similar positions in leading public sector organizations, and the reward systems in each are comparable to reflect this. Career paths for all levels of civil servants and public service providers can be made increasingly attractive if they are set against measured accountability for performance. The quality of public services, as assessed by customers, should be reflected accordingly while building the measurement systems. Now that greater emphasis is being placed on the role of the private sector in economic growth and the development of society, public administration should transform itself and assist in transforming society so that opportunities are created for partnership between the public sector and its customers as well as the private sector and NGOs.

A civil society with a stronger voice and more influence in the policy-making debate would become a vehicle for challenging the government more widely in the performance of public services. At present there appears to be a lack of momentum in the push to achieve high standards for public services. Currently there is no pressure from groups outside the state, and while the state has done a considerable job in establishing the legislative and operational infrastructure to establish high performance in public services, the lack of an independent voice for public opinion has meant that there is no incentive to ensure that improvements in public services are followed through and made fully accountable to the general public.

Shared vision, both at the central level and in the regions, and public expectations, including active consultation with the public and being able to see the published performance of public services, are critical, and it is these aspects of a delivery culture that will have to be in place before public service functions can genuinely become services. The case of Kazakhstan, which has made very considerable progress in improving public services, illustrates these next steps required to complete the transition. The next stage for civil society in Kazakhstan is to become active in policy making, which will assist in establishing and developing a common vision for public services and in achieving the full transition from a functional to a service culture.

Notes

1. For a discussion of the complexities of public administration reform in developing countries, see United Nations, Division of Public Administration and Development Management, Department of Economic and Social Affairs, *Rethinking Public Administration: An Overview* (New York, 1998).

2. *Kazakhstan over the Years of Independence, 1991–2009* (Astana: Statistical Agency of the Republic of Kazakhstan, 2010).

3. Kamalidin Burkhanov, "Strengthening Statehood: At the Turn of the Ages," *Kazakhstanskaya Pravda,* July 13, 2010 (in Russian).

4. Constitution of the Republic of Kazakhstan, adopted on referendum, August 30, 1995.

5. Quoted in Askar Shomanov, *Reforming of Public Administration System: International Experience and Kazakhstan* (Almaty: Kazakhstan Institute of Strategic Research under the President of the Republic of Kazakhstan, 2005).

6. "Kazakhstan—2030:. Prosperity, Security and Well Being for all Kazakhstanis," development strategy, 1997.

7. Law no. 453, "On Civil Service in the Republic of Kazakhstan," July 23, 1999.

8. "Staff Turnover in State Bodies Caused by Changes of Political Appointees Decreased by Three Times," Zakon (the government's information portal), September 25, 2012, http://www.zakon.kz/4515378-smenjaemost-kadrovogo-sostava.html.

9. Decree of the President of Kazakhstan no. 954, "On the System of Annual Performance Appraisal of Central and Local Executive Bodies of Oblasts, Cities of Republican Significance, Capital," March 19, 2010.

10. "Civil Service in Figures," Civil Service Agency of the Republic of Kazakhstan, October 5, 2012, http://www.kyzmet.kz/?lang=ru&id_1=62&month=10.

11. "Deputies of Mazhilis," Parliament of the Republic of Kazakhstan, September 1, 2012, http://www.parlam.kz/ru/mazhilis/deputies.

12. World Bank, *Kazakhstan: Reforming the Public Sector Wage System,* policy note (Washington, D.C., April 14, 2005).

13. World Bank, *Doing Business in 2006: Creating Jobs* (Washington, D.C., 2006); World Bank, *Doing Business 2011: Making a Difference for Entrepreneurs* (Washington, D.C., 2011).

14. Romeo B. Ocampo, "Models of Public Administration Reform: 'New Public Management (NPM),'" *Asian Review of Public Administration* 10 (January–December 1996): 248–55.

15. David Osborne and Ted Gaebler, *Reinventing Government: How the Entrepreneurial Spirit Is Transforming the Public Sector* (Reading, MA: Addison Wesley, 1992).

16. World Economic Forum, Global Competitiveness Index 2012, http://www.weforum.org/issues/global-competitiveness.

17. "USAID Has Observed the Deterioration of the Quality of Public Services in One-Stop Shops as They Have Been Transferred to the Local Executive Bodies," Ministry of Justice, Republic of Kazakhstan, April 28, 2010, http://www.minjust.kz/node/16542.

18. *Public Services: Experience of Measuring Quality and Introducing Standards,* survey report implemented with the support of the European Commission Project Assistance to Development of Public Service Standards in Kazakhstan and DAI Europe Ltd. (Astana, 2007).

19. Burkhanov, "Strengthening Statehood."

20. *Public Services.*

21. Annual Report of the Civil Service Agency for 2010, http://www.kyzmet.kz/?lang=ru&id_1=3&id_2=251&month=10.

22. *Public Services.*

23. Ibid.

24. Ibid., section 2, main results, p. 13, and annex, tables, pp. 178–79.

25. Ibid., 19.

26. Ibid., section 5, "Social Service," subsection 5.1.3, timelines, pp. 28–29.

27. Ibid.

28. UNDP, *Beyond Transition: Towards Inclusive Societies,* Regional Human Development Report (Bratislava, 2011), 31.

29. USAID, Business Environment Improvement Project, http://www.bei-ca.net/eng/library.asp?DocCountryID=1&DocumentTypeID=13.

30. Survey of entrepreneurs on the shadow sector of the small business in Almaty city and Almaty oblast, funded by the USAID Business Environment Improvement Project, PowerPoint presentation, April 2010.

31. Civil Service in Figures, Civil Service Agency of the Republic of Kazakhstan, http://www.kyzmet.kz/?lang=ru&id_1=62&month=10; World Bank, *Kazakhstan: Reforming the Public Sector Wage System.*

32. Meruert Makhmutova and Aitzhan Akhmetova, *Civil Society Index in Kazakhstan: Strengthening Civil Society,* CIVICUS Civil Society Index 2008–2010, Analytical Country Report (Almaty, March 2011), 17.

33. Freedom House, "Country Report: Kazakhstan," in *Nations in Transit 2010,* www.freedomhouse.org.

34. Makhmutova and Akhmetova, *Civil Society Index in Kazakhstan,* 16.

35. Transparency International, Corruption Perceptions Index 2012, http://cpi.transparency.org/cpi2012/results/.

36. Makhmutova and Akhmetova, *Civil Society Index in Kazakhstan*, 29.

37. Ibid., 36.

Part 4

State Power and Social Turmoil

7

Civil Society in a Period of Transition

The Perspective from the State

Ruslan Kazkenov and Charles E. Ziegler

Kazakhstan is in many respects the Central Asian nation best situated to build a civil society, a market economy, and a functioning democracy. Education levels are high, economic growth rates have averaged over 10 percent per year since 2000, and the country has an abundance of natural resources. Most importantly, Kazakhstan has an abundance of human capital. Social organizations are stronger than those found in other Central Asian countries, with the possible exception of Kyrgyzstan, though they remain relatively weak and ineffective compared to those in Western democracies. There are many nongovernmental organizations (NGOs), although few of them have regular access to the country's decision makers. An additional problem is that many officials still display a Soviet-style mind-set contemptuous of public opinion.

In this chapter we discuss the development of civil society in the Republic of Kazakhstan since independence, focusing on the interplay between state and society; more precisely, we develop the Kazakh state's perspective on civil society, supplemented by the perceptions of civil society actors. Our research questions are the following: First, what role does the central government envision for civil society in Kazakhstan? Second, what have been the major obstacles to realizing this vision, according to officials and analysts? Third, what are the prospects for civil society development? To address these questions, we examine official government laws, programs, and statements related to civil society, together with insights from a series of civil society workshops we conducted in Kazakhstan.

Prior to 1991 Kazakhstan was a union republic in the USSR, before that part of the Russian Empire, and before that a series of khanates. Its existence as a modern, sovereign state dates from the collapse of the Soviet Union, and great effort has been expended simply in creating a viable, effective state. In this context a historically weak civil society has functioned more as a partner to, or even a creation of, the new state, rather than a dynamic force influencing government. Kazakhstan's government has officially promoted the idea of a vibrant civil society, but its preference is for one that seldom challenges state prerogatives.

Although civil society remains weak in Kazakhstan, in contrast to the rest of Central Asia, the Kazakh state has promoted civil society—albeit a docile, co-opted form of it—as a vital component of its national identity. The reason for this seeming anomaly, we argue, rests with Kazakhstan's aspirations to global prominence. Kazakhstan's government regularly declares its commitment to democratic norms, including political pluralism, religious tolerance, and respect for human rights and the rule of law, at least when speaking to Western audiences. In the context of Kazakhstan's multivector foreign policy, the goal is to retain and strengthen ties with the West without sacrificing relations with the country's influential authoritarian neighbors, China and Russia. Proclaiming a commitment to building a strong civil society, even if that society is carefully managed and controlled, preserves the Western dimension of Kazakhstan's foreign policy.

Civil Society and the State in Kazakhstan

In Kazakhstan, the growing role of the state in public life, acting as the major engine of development in a globalized world, logically reduces the space for civil society activity. For Kazakhstan, as well as for other countries of the former USSR, implementing radical social reforms is difficult because it is necessary simultaneously to pursue a major economic transformation while maintaining (or creating) a viable, strong state. The first order of business following independence was to ensure security of the population, to avoid chaos and instability, and to start the nation on the path to free-market economic development. Civil society had played virtually no role in political reform in Central Asia and clearly could not be expected to follow the pattern of opposition to authority observed in Eastern Europe. Civil society, such as it was in the early 1990s, was subordinate to the state and was expected to participate in building the new economic and political order envisioned by state authorities.

Shortly after its birth as an independent state, Kazakhstan appeared to be on the road toward some form of democratic political system. As in any democratic transition, this process includes the formation of a law-based state, the development of competitive political parties, the transformation of the mass media into a relatively independent source of information, the formation of nongovernmental and religious organizations, the creation of institutions of self-governance, and the growth of a solid middle class with a stake in representative government. Kazakhstan has made some progress in realizing these components of democracy but lags behind in others and is best characterized as a "soft authoritarian" political system. However, the government consistently promotes the image of an emerging democracy to enhance domestic legitimacy and international standing.

Vocal support for civil society demonstrates the government's commitment to democracy and, if properly controlled, may facilitate official goals. From the perspective of the Kazakh state, the social function of civil society is to consolidate and integrate society, a particularly important function during the transitional period. Civil society may assist the state in determining priorities, coordinating interests, achieving compromise and consensus, and solving problems that arise. The state provides the organizational and administrative mechanisms through which citizens' actions are channelled and directed toward purposeful activity. From the state's perspective, civic activism has the potential for violence and may threaten the entrenched regime and so must be carefully managed. Since civil society is at present quite weak, cooperation with the government tends to be the norm, supplemented by the occasional protest.[1]

The experience of many developed countries, and some developing states, shows that reliable guarantees of human rights and freedoms can be established only through the joint efforts of a lawful democratic state and developed civil society. While states may be instruments of repression, without a viable state there can be no democracy. Civil society involves the striving by citizens to achieve social or political goals through free associations, in which members observe the rule of law and respect human rights. Civil society may be considered an independent realm, occasionally standing against the state and yet inseparably linked with it through a great number of interactions. Civil society stands between the individual and the state, the organs of power and society, and carries out the function of integration (that is, promoting the cohesion) of public and private interests. Civil society encourages the state to be useful to its citizens and to serve their interests. The more educated and mature the civil society, the more successfully it solves this complex and challenging task.

Kazakhstan may have a long historical tradition, but it has existed as an independent, modern state only since 1991. From the state perspective, then, civil society has a role to play in partnership with the state in developing the national idea—the national identity—of Kazakhstan. President Nursultan Nazarbayev, in his address to participants of the Civil Forum, noted, "We face a serious challenge today. Unlike many countries where democracy was formed on the basis of a developed civil society, we are simultaneously building both democracy and civil society and the state."[2] The problem is that in Kazakhstan, as in many postcommunist societies, the society is weak and fragmented after many years of being repressed by a strong state. In contrast to postcommunist European countries, however, Central Asia's authoritarian states have constrained rather than enabled the development of civic activism.

The formation of civil society may be conceptualized as a "civilizing process" whereby individuals become citizens, civil relations develop between members of society, and within society the germ of public spiritedness is born.[3] The primary components of this civilizing process are the state, the individual, and society. A prerequisite of such development is the balanced, equal development and mutual equality of freedoms and obligations of all three of the elements that constitute civil society—the individual, the society, and the state. As in any modern state, however, individuals and social organizations are far from equal with the state. Moreover, certain groups in society—usually business organizations, the wealthy, and informal organizations with close ties to government officials—have much greater influence on state policies than their less well connected counterparts.

Western-style individualism, and Western models of civil society, are frequently criticized by state officials as alien to the Central Asian experience. Granted, merely copying and transferring to Kazakhstan social institutions and practices that have proven successful in other contexts is culturally insensitive and likely to be ineffective. Even the more democratic postcommunist countries choose not to adopt Western democratic practices if they are culturally suspect. For example, Lithuania considered and rejected the concept of trial by jury, deeming it unsuitable for Lithuanian society. As a member of a 2008 UNDP delegation to Vilnius, one of the authors was informed by the chairman of the Lithuanian Supreme Court that finding a truly independent pool of jurors in such a tiny country would be very difficult: "We in Lithuania cannot find so many independent jurors. The population of Lithuania is only two million, so to find jurors who are not godfathers or other relatives to each other will be very difficult."[4]

The wholesale application of Western institutions and practices in radically different social and cultural contexts is seldom a recipe for success. Central Asian leaders contend, and academic studies confirm, that exporting democracy, and particularly exporting specific forms of civil society, does not work.[5] Quite often such institutions and practices perform poorly, yielding results contrary to what might be anticipated. Kyrgyzstan is an example of a country frequently lauded in the West for its activist civil society, yet from the perspective of Central Asians Kyrgyzstan's politics are chaotic and unstable and do not contribute to the well-being of its people. Moreover, what appears to be grassroots political activism in Kyrgyzstan is in reality the overt manifestation of elite competition.[6] This example fully relates to the attempts to build civil society in Kazakhstan—to build it based on the patterns of the Western developed countries may be misguided. Kazakhstan can undoubtedly learn much from Western theories and practices of civil society, but the official position is that the country should shape and adapt these imports to suit its distinctly Central Asian society.

In the Kazakh context, a healthy civil society may help in bridging differences among the multiethnic population of this diverse country. Only about 60 percent of the population is ethnic Kazakh, with an additional 25 percent Russian and the remainder consisting of Ukrainians, Uzbeks, Tatars, Uighurs, Germans, Poles, and other nationalities. In addition, there are nearly five hundred thousand *oralmany,* Kazakh ethnic immigrants, who have returned to Kazakhstan from neighboring countries after an absence of seventy years in some cases. These *oralmany* often have difficulty fully integrating into Kazakh society due to cultural, educational, and linguistic differences.[7] As a new state, Kazakhstan is confronted with the difficult task of building a national identity that restores Kazakh pride in its heritage while accommodating the political, cultural, and spiritual needs of its diverse population.

Kazakhstan's government has sought to revive ethnic Kazakh traditions but has focused on developing a civic consciousness that emphasizes tolerance and respect for the country's ethnic and religious diversity. This inclusive approach stands in contrast to exclusivist programs advocated by postcommunist nationalists, including Yugoslavia's Slobodan Milosevic, Russia's Vladimir Zhirinovski, or the Kaczynski brothers in Poland. Since independence Kazakhstan's schools have sought to inculcate among all students the values of patriotism, responsibility, service, and obligation to society. Socialization of youth through education resembles Soviet practice, stressing unity, love of motherland, and the inevitability of a bright future. Collective interests predominate, while individualist values and critical facilities receive far less emphasis in the curriculum.[8]

The fundamental position of the state is that civil society development should not copy Western patterns wholesale but should utilize the best world experiences and practices, taking into account the character and specific features of Kazakhstan. One characteristic of Kazakhstan's politics is the virtual absence of political pluralism, which relates to a fear of competition degenerating into political instability, as it has in neighboring Kyrgyzstan. For example, the 2011 violence in Zhanaozen was portrayed by the government as instigated by émigré opposition forces aligned with a handful of domestic malcontents. Although official accounts repeatedly stressed the fair and transparent legal process applied to striking oil workers, Human Rights Watch reported that the government's actions grossly undermined workers' freedom of association and collective bargaining rights.[9]

Genuine pluralism is also absent from Kazakhstan's politics, as evidenced by the country's failure to conduct free and fair elections. Competition for seats in Kazakhstan's parliament (Majilis) is severely constrained; in the January 2012 elections two progovernment parties managed to surmount the 7 percent threshold to win seats alongside the propresidential Nur Otan (Shining Fatherland) Party. Although a marginal improvement over the 100 percent victory of Nur Otan in the 2007 elections, the dominance of the presidential party and its use of administrative resources, together with the charismatic appeal of President Nazarbayev, have created a situation where an Arab Spring or massive political protests similar to those in Moscow in late 2011 appear unlikely.[10]

In the Soviet era there was no possibility for the realization of civil initiatives. Social organizations such as clans and kinship networks did not disappear, but many functioned in an underground or semilegal status unique to Central Asian cultures.[11] In the perestroika period certain informal social organizations formed; indeed, Kazakhstan witnessed one of the earliest examples of mass protests when Kazakhs took to the streets in 1986 to protest the appointment of Gennadi Kolbin, an ethnic Russian, as first secretary of the republic's Communist Party.[12] Notwithstanding this early activism, Kazakhstan's *neformaly* (informal groups) were far fewer in number and influence than were those in the Baltic republics, Ukraine, or Russia. The presence of informal communication mechanisms and attempts to coordinate joint actions not under the control of the authorities hinted at the possibility of a revival of civil society. These efforts likewise suggested the preservation of civil ideals and values, albeit at a modest level.

Further development of civil society in Kazakhstan is constrained by the widespread practice of patron-client relations. These hierarchical ties promote dependence and inequality, privileging the wealthy and politically well-connected. During the Soviet period placement in the Communist Party *nomenklatura* was the key to influence and power; today the elite derive their favorable positions from wealth accumulated in the business sector, from ties to the propresidential Nur Otan Party, or through familial connections. These elite networks do engage in competition, but it is a form of competition generally conducted in secret and one that does not provide avenues for average citizens to participate in the usual give-and-take of politics. One can argue, therefore, that this type of political interaction is inimical to the growth of a healthy civil society.

Genuine, democratic political discussions require the existence of modern communications methods that facilitate the free circulation of information on public issues and administrative processes. Productive interaction of citizens representing various and competing group interests cannot take place without access to good information; logically, a healthy civil society needs a mass media not overly constrained by the state. Kazakhstan's mass media are somewhat freer than those in Uzbekistan or Turkmenistan, but information presented by television and radio is routinely shaped to the state's advantage. There are some opposition newspapers, but many have faced harassment and tax and administrative penalties from the authorities for critical reporting.[13] The Internet is an alternative source of information that can be utilized by civil society groups, but the government in 2009 placed blogs, social networking, and chat rooms under media legislation, legalizing state censorship of the web.

The official perspective of Kazakhstan's government is that relations between the state and civil society need not and should not be solely confrontational, as was the case in Eastern Europe prior to the collapse of communism. Cooperative relations between state and society are deemed necessary in order to preserve stability and promote national development. As in many parts of Asia, the concept of a "loyal opposition" on the British parliamentary model is deemed too risky in a transitional setting, opening the country to forces of fragmentation. This concern is especially acute during a period of globalization, when countries find their sovereignty infringed upon by forces beyond their control. To assess the relationship between civil society and the government from the perspective of nongovernmental organizations, we conducted a series of workshops designed to explore the contributions of civil society to public policy problems facing Kazakhstan and the various forms of NGO-state interaction.

Globalization and Civil Society Assistance Projects

In recent years there have been a large number of studies devoted to global civil society, as international nongovernmental organizations have promoted causes ranging from human rights to environmental protection to health issues.[14] International organizations such as Greenpeace, Women for Women, the Soros Foundation, and Human Rights Watch provide financing and political support for their domestic counterparts. Such assistance may strengthen civil society, but it also may generate a backlash among authoritarian rulers who fear erosion of their ability to exercise sovereign authority within their borders. Countries that have constrained the activities of international NGOs include Uzbekistan, Turkmenistan, Russia, and Egypt. Kazakhstan and Kyrgyzstan have generally welcomed international NGOs, but even here there is resistance to the wholesale imposition of foreign values and practices. In addition, a number of academic studies have questioned the impact of foreign NGOs in developing civil society.[15]

The authors, through funding provided by the U.S. Department of State's Bureau of Democracy, Human Rights, and Labor, conducted a series of civil society–building workshops in Kazakhstan over a period of three years, from 2006 through 2009. The workshops were a joint effort of the University of Louisville's Center for Asian Democracy and Civic Peace, an Astana-based nongovernmental organization. The following insights about

Kazakhstan's civil society and its interaction with the state were derived from the project.

First, we found that women play a large role in leadership of NGOs in Kazakhstan, confirming the hypothesis that civil society development must incorporate a major role for women. Kazakhstan stands out as a moderate Muslim country in which women are educated at levels equal to or even greater than men. Legally, women are treated as equals with men, although they tend to be underrepresented in the higher reaches of politics, business, and education. For example, in 2008 women made up 10 percent of the national Majilis and 17 percent of the regional *maslikhats,* and four of sixteen national-level ministers were women. The government enacted a plan (Strategy of Gender Equality 2006–2016) that is phasing in a quota system for women in the top levels of government. According to this plan, by 2016 women are supposed to constitute no less than 30 percent of all members of the national and regional legislatures and 30 percent of all personnel in the higher levels of administration.

Second, participants in the workshops stressed the importance of changing the psychology of average citizens and officials, in order to shift the political culture away from the *kollektiv* mentality of the communist era and toward a more personal sense of responsibility for governance. Few young people in Kazakhstan have internalized a concept of active citizenship. Given the opportunities in Kazakhstan for making money, many are more concerned with establishing a career or building a business than they are with participating in politics. However, in recent years mutual assistance organizations—many of them religious in orientation—have become more widespread in Central Asia, especially where local governments are unable or unwilling to provide basic services.[16]

Those young people who do participate in politics are often the less sophisticated, more traditional rural youth who are mobilized by the powerful propresidential party Nur Otan. Participants frequently commented on the traditional deference to elders and to authority in general, which tends to mute criticism of political figures. Many participants suggested that education, particularly through the university system, was key to enhancing democratic activism. This could be accomplished through a series of short courses or workshops in universities on various aspects of civic culture. In addition, some participants suggested that developing the links between universities and NGOs would prove valuable in developing civil society.

In discussions with officials and NGO leaders knowledgeable on human rights it became clear that neither officials nor average citizens have adequate information on their constitutional rights regarding political participation, which makes enforcement problematic. There still exists a paternalistic strain in the political culture, reinforced by the president's efforts to concentrate power in his office. In contrast to Russia, where there is growing anti-Americanism and a backlash against foreign support for NGOs, most Kazakh officials tolerate or even welcome Western links, as long as such assistance is not directly political (and some officials have interpreted this provision of the law broadly in order to constrain the operations of foreign organizations).

The workshops also illustrated the difficulty of developing the concept of a "loyal opposition" in the post-Soviet Central Asian context. Government officials often view any form of criticism of the government, or any organized opposition, whether in the form of political parties, interest groups, or mass protest movements, as disloyal challenges to state legitimacy. Political apathy is widespread, and government harassment of opposition figures generates little response among the public.

Several factors have combined to frustrate the emergence of the concept of a loyal opposition and the normal give-and-take of a fully democratic society. First is the obvious influence of President Nursultan Nazarbayev, who consistently promotes unity and stability and tends to reflect a Soviet-style view critical of formal political opposition. Second is the overwhelming dominance in the national Majilis and the regional *maslikhats* of a single propresidential party, Nur Otan. As in Russia, the progovernment party centralizes power in the hands of the executive and limits the potential for independent political action. The weakness of Kazakhstan's parliamentary institutions, and the flawed nature of the electoral process, makes an independent civil society even more important in democratic construction.

Third, the extraordinary economic performance of recent years and the consequent social and political stability has dampened demands for democratic participation, in a form of authoritarian social contract. Most Kazakhs want a stable environment in which to improve their material well-being and credit Nazarbayev with their country's relatively favorable position in Central Asia. Virtually all Kazakhs, even the most democratically minded, viewed the "color revolutions" in Kyrgyzstan, Ukraine, and Georgia as destabilizing these countries and doing more harm than good.

Fourth, Kazakhstan's mass media is dominated by a few major political and business interests and does not report objectively on political issues of interest to nongovernmental organizations. As in Russia, stories may be commissioned by the wealthy and powerful, political battles may play out in the media, and the media tend to promote the business or personal interests of the owners or government officials. Kazakhstan does not have a freedom of information law, and investigative journalists may be arrested and imprisoned if they report critically on government activities. The presidential family controls many of the country's media outlets, ensuring favorable press for the government. Reducing state control of the mass media and ensuring freedom of the press will be a critical step in strengthening NGOs and legislatures.

However, NGOs can in part substitute for a fully independent mass media. For example, during the 2005 presidential elections several NGOs acted as independent election monitors, calculating that the true vote for Nazarbayev was closer to 60–65 percent than the officially reported 91 percent. NGOs had estimated that the true size of the opposition vote would be about 40 percent, were free and fair elections held. In 2011 NGOs criticized the government for enacting a law placing new restrictions on religious associations. However, genuinely independent NGOs have limited financial support and frequently experience harassment or restrictions from the government.

Despite the authoritarian elements of the superpresidential political system, Kazakh political culture is considerably more complex than many Western observers have acknowledged. There are historical elements derived from the nomadic tradition that, when combined with the educational achievements of the Soviet era and the rapid economic growth of the postcommunist period, give Kazakhstan an advantage over its Central Asian neighbors. There is an increasingly affluent, well-educated middle class, concentrated in the larger cities. Kazakhstan also has a diverse society and a culture of religious and ethnic tolerance that bodes well for democratic development. This tolerance has been nurtured and promoted by the government as part of its soft-power campaign to strengthen ties with the West and stands in marked contrast to ethnic tensions in other post-Soviet Central Asian states.[17] But civil society remains constrained by the authoritarian nature of the system.

Globalization has opened up what was a closed political system, bringing both positive and negative influences to Kazakh society. Together with new economic, religious, and organizational freedoms have come problems of organized crime, poverty, narcotics, and the threat of terrorism. New states face a challenge of providing stability and security for the population and providing other public goods. From the perspective of the Kazakh state, nongovernmental organizations can improve the efficiency of state institutions, but only if they are closely monitored by authorities.

Evolving State-Society Relations

Immediately following the collapse of the Soviet system the newly established constitutional and legal system of Kazakhstan was focused on limiting the influence of political parties and public organizations on state affairs. The new state sought to disestablish the political monopoly of the Communist Party, limit the role of public organizations in the bodies of the state power, and constrain the role of labor unions in the economic sphere. As market reforms were implemented new policy issues and new public organizations emerged. During the first decade of independence relations between state institutions and nongovernmental organizations were often confrontational. However, even under those conditions some nongovernmental organizations managed to establish constructive cooperation with republican and regional authorities.

Legal limitations were an obstacle to a more effective cooperation. Political developments such as the constitutional reform of 2007 opened a new stage in the process of establishing a legal basis for the interaction of the state and NGOs.[18] Legally, NGOs, according to Kazakh law, are considered "noncommercial organizations" and must be registered with the authorities. However, in recent years the government has lowered the registration fee, and registered NGOs are exempt from paying taxes. In addition, the Law on Normative Legal Acts (1998) requires legislators to accept input from NGOs in the formulation of legislation.[19] In reality, such input is usually a formality. From the state perspective, the purpose is to co-opt NGOs as advisory bodies in the policy formulation process and to use them to supplement the policy implementation side when the state proves unwilling or unable.

In contrast to Anglo-American pluralist democracies, where civil society is understood as a sector almost completely independent of the state, self-sufficient and autonomous, the idea in Kazakhstan is quite different. Since civil society is extremely weak, the state assumes the role of supporter and nurturer, if not creator. Few Western governments would deem it necessary to adopt a lengthy plan for the advancement of civil society, as in Kazakhstan's *Conception of the Development of Civil Society in the Republic of Kazakhstan 2006–2011,* enacted by a decree of President Nazarbayev. The conception, which was designed to accelerate the development of civil society, called for the government to work out a plan for the implementation of various measures designed to strengthen Kazakhstan's civil society.[20] This idea of the state directing, supporting, and controlling civil society is alien to Western notions of how state and society interact.

The process of forming civil society in Kazakhstan has only just started. In any political system, civil society is in constant evolution. Weak civil societies may become stronger and more assertive; strong, independent civil societies may erode over time.[21] Conditions in Kazakhstan are more favorable for the development of civil society than under the Soviet regime—the process of moving from a dialogue between civil society and the government to building forms of partnership between the two is taking place, according to the regime. What is less likely under Kazakhstan's strong state model, with a relatively quiescent population, is a confrontational relationship between state and society.

Many of Kazakhstan's social problems are rooted in the backwardness of civil society and in the inability of state institutions to cooperate with social organizations. In Kazakh society there is still a deeply rooted belief that all depends on state power. The Soviet legacy and indigenous cultural tendencies have left the majority of Kazakhstan's citizens with low levels of political efficacy, though with relatively high levels of political awareness. Civic activism independent of government direction or support remains an alien concept, and state officials seem to prefer this state of affairs. Hence NGOs acquire special importance as channels for addressing public problems and for expressing public opinion in ways that are not threatening to the state. NGOs have the ability to reflect the specific interests of small social groups that may otherwise be neglected by the state. An important aspect of NGOs' activity is to address the urgent needs of citizens in acquiring social services that cannot be fully provided for by state structures.

At present nongovernmental organizations take an active part in solving a range of social problems. Dialogue and partnership between NGOs and power structures are established not only at the level of central ministries but also at the regional and local levels—with local representative (*maslikhat*) and executive (*akim*) authorities. However, there is a strong urban bias to Kazakhstan's civil society—the majority of NGOs operate in Almaty, Astana, and other big cities. In Almaty, for example, the Council of NGOs operates under the city administration, participating in discussions and helping solve significant social problems. In rural areas the authorities generally operate without any input from civil society organizations.

An important dimension of the maturity of Kazakhstan's NGOs is the formation and activity of umbrella associations that bring together broad categories of social organizations—societies of invalids, religious associations, women's organizations, youth movements, public associations involved in the fight against corruption, and others. Examples of the major umbrella organizations include the Civil Alliance of Kazakhstan (under Executive Director Alina Khamatdinova), and the Almaty Confederation of Nongovernmental Organizations Eriptes (led by Leila Akhmetova). The major function of these organizations is to unify the country's diverse NGOs, providing a more effective forum for them to engage with government. The strategy is largely one of partnership and cooperation with the state, rather than confrontation. On occasion, these NGOs may promote greater democratic accountability, as in Civil Alliance's monitoring of the January 2012 elections.[22]

Many NGOs carry out scientific and practical studies and conduct research on the country's political and social problems. NGO educational activities seek to improve the electoral culture among youth, fight corruption, enhance access to information, promote environmental protection, encourage the development of small and medium enterprises in the rural areas, and provide support to *oralmany* (ethnic Kazakh emigrants). The results of NGO research and their policy recommendations can help state agencies to understand the complexities of social problems; they generate alternative visions and look for new approaches to intractable problems. NGOs are often more flexible, creative, and mobile than the state bureaucracy in addressing policy issues. An additional benefit of civic participation is in the socialization of citizens; the activities of NGOs open up opportunities for personal self-expression and for realizing the creative potential of scientists and lay people.

From the regime's perspective, major problems for civil society at this stage of development include reforming legal provisions for NGO activities and addressing the issue of financing by the state and private sector and through international grants. A presidential decree amending legislation on the "state social order" that went into effect in January 2012 mandated that partnership councils be established to allow for NGO participation in and implementation of legislation. NGOs are expected to assist the state in dealing with social problems that are very difficult or unduly expensive. In return, the state will render financial and political support for NGO activities, aiding the development of NGOs for the purpose of minimizing state participation in certain social spheres.[23]

Civil Society and Kazakhstan's International Position

Kazakhstan's claims to regional leadership in central Asia and its efforts to be accepted by the Western community of states open the country to outside influences in support of civil society. One example of this external dynamic is Kazakhstan's chairmanship of the Organization for Security and Cooperation in Europe (OSCE) in 2010 and the subsequent OSCE summit in Astana.

As with all OSCE member states, Kazakhstan is bound by the various provisions of OSCE agreements, including the "basket three" commitments to human rights. In lobbying to chair the organization and host the summit, Kazakhstan opened its record to critical publicity from more democratic states.[24] In addition, the summit gave representatives of civil society an opportunity to express their positions. One of the authors was a delegate to the OSCE summit and participated in the review conference prior to the summit, where representatives of NGOs expressed their opinions and gave their proposals and recommendations. The review conference gave NGOs the chance to meet with representatives of the media and other governments and to establish contacts with NGOs from other parts of Central Asia and Europe.

Then–Secretary of State Hillary Clinton, who headed the U.S. delegation, met representatives of civil society organizations at Eurasian National University just prior to the summit. In her remarks to the group, Secretary Clinton observed,

> My very first stop was to come and meet with you [representatives of civil society], because strong democracies, thriving economies, and stable societies cannot be built by governments alone. There must be a partnership between governments and vibrant institutions and free societies that work together to solve the problems that we face in the 21st century. Thirty-five years ago, when

> the leaders of North America, Europe and the Soviet Union came together to sign the Helsinki Final Act, they committed themselves to a core set of human values, including the fundamental freedoms of expression, association, peaceful assembly, thought, and religion. These values are as fresh as they were 35 years ago, and they are absolutely critical to the building of sustainable societies and nations that are committed to creating a better set of opportunities for all of their citizens.[25]

Secretary Clinton went on to commend various human rights, democracy, and women's groups for their efforts to promote peaceful change and praised Kazakhstan's government for being more responsive to civil society than any other regime in Central Asia.

Former Kazakh foreign minister and chairman of the OSCE Kanat Saudabayev acknowledged at a summit press conference and in his statement to the summit opening that his country was seeking to work with civil society, stressing how important it was to normalize relations between the Islamic world and the West, to increase tolerance, and to achieve an effective dialogue between civilizations. "In the human dimension Kazakhstan has done all it can to foster constructive co-operation with civil society and has ensured the broadest possible involvement of non-governmental organizations in the Organization's activities and the many events in the run-up to and within the framework of the Summit," he stated. By organizing a conference for civil society groups just prior to the summit, Saudabayev argued, his country had more than fulfilled its promises in the human rights sphere.[26]

Assertions notwithstanding, Western democracies view Kazakhstan's record on democratic governance and civil society as marginal at best. From the perspective of Western democratic nations, Kazakhstan's government, while far more tolerant of civil society than authorities in Uzbekistan or Turkmenistan, routinely uses a variety of administrative measures to limit freedom of speech and the media. Journalists often engage in self-censorship, or they may find themselves subject to criminal libel suits. Freedom of association is guaranteed by the constitution, but Kazakh officials often harass groups or individuals who push the boundaries of what is politically acceptable.[27] Kazakh officials counter that the government accepts and even encourages civic activism, though it must be channelled and closely monitored to ensure social stability. Given the country's ethnic and religious diversity and the potential for fragmentation, achieving consensus is more critical for the ruling elite than preserving pluralism.

Civil Society and Democratic Development

Civil society in a modern polity is inextricably linked to the rule of law, since law delineates the proper spheres of autonomy and responsibility for the individual, social groups, economic organizations, and the state. Civil society, in its relationship to the state, can resort to various tactics and strategies, from strict confrontation to pragmatic partnership. However, in all cases the goal is to make the state as responsive to its citizens as possible, attentive to their interests. The more developed civil society becomes the more successful it is at keeping the state accountable to the citizenry. Genuine civil society embodies the concept of popular sovereignty rather than state sovereignty.

Hegel's key contribution to the concept of civil society is that it is a sphere of activity separate from the state, and from the individual, that becomes manifest in the modern world. But Hegel held civil society to include the economy, as did Marx and Engels. It was only with Gramsci that civil society would come to be differentiated from the market as well as the individual and the state. Only a strong civil society, according to Gramsci, could challenge the hegemony of the bourgeoisie. As Mary Caldor has argued, common to the evolving definitions of civil society throughout the nineteenth and early twentieth centuries was the notion of a rule of law protecting the individual within a defined territorial state. It was only with the Latin American and East European intellectual movements of the late twentieth century that the idea of civil society *against* the state emerged.[28]

Postcommunist transitional countries, after years of repression under Marxist-Leninist political systems, in general tended to eschew political ideologies. These governments either adopted purely pragmatic approaches to policy or mobilized nationalist sentiments to build social consensus. Civil society played virtually no role in the transition from communism, with the possible exceptions of Poland, Hungary, and Czechoslovakia. Regime change may be achieved through the efforts of civil society, as in the case of many of the Arab Spring countries, but civil society by itself cannot build a democratic order. In turn, democratic institutions often remain hollow shells without civil society's contribution toward deepening democracy.

One measure of political maturity is the level of self-government—the degree to which political institutions, occasionally at the national but more often at the local or regional level, make the most efficient use of people's talents and abilities. The modern democratic state does not simply dictate but rather delegates significant powers to those levels closest to the population. This may be done formally through a federal system, as in Canada, or more informally through a decentralized unitary system, as in Britain. Enhancing local self-government improves governance and increases trust among the population. To this end Kazakhstan, while rejecting a federal form of government as potentially destabilizing, has publicly touted its efforts to improve local self-government and encourage cooperation between local authorities and civil society organizations. In a state as geographically large as Kazakhstan, an overly centralized government apparatus has difficulty tailoring policies to specific local needs.

But local government in Kazakhstan is not very responsive to public opinion, nor is the civil service more generally, as Charman and Assangaziyev argue in chapter 6. Local and regional *akims* are appointed by the center, and neither they nor the *maslikhats* operate transparently or have any tradition that would lead them to cooperate with civil society organizations. At the local level participation is restricted to the ritual of voting, particularly in the rural areas. The central government's efforts at improving governance include pressuring local officials to engage in cooperative relations with civil society organizations to improve service delivery in such areas as health, education, housing, environmental protection, and cultural activities.[29] However, as in most postcommunist systems, the bureaucracies are notoriously unresponsive to the public, and local officials seldom advocate for their constituents.

A more responsive government requires an independent mass media and a free flow of information to generate trust in government, increase transparency, and expose corruption. Yet in Kazakhstan, as in other Central Asian countries, the flow of information still resembles that of the Soviet period—most originates at the governmental level and flows downward, rather than the reverse. Information is controlled and managed vertically, with the ruling elite using television, radio, and most newspapers to inform the population of government decisions and social activities. The idea of an independent, critical journalism is only now beginning to be understood, as the country opens up to the forces of globalization.

The shift from a managed mass media to one that is truly open, critical, and able to conduct a democratic dialogue between the political elites and the mass public will occur slowly and is not possible without the existence of fundamental individual rights and freedoms. The right to freely exchange information, together with the right of association, is critical to a dynamic civil society. As Jürgen Habermas has argued, social consensus can be achieved only through reasoned argumentation and mutual respect, which requires the freedom of individuals and groups to dispute and debate public issues.[30] Democracy provides the ideal context for such debates. However, independent mass media in open systems do not guarantee good governance or a better society. Competition for audiences and profits leads the media in democracies to cater to popular demand for entertainment, sensationalism, and superficial treatment of important issues.

In keeping with the professed goal of developing a modern economy and society, the government has invested in web technology. According to Kazakhstan's E-Government portal there were 2,466 mass-media outlets in 2006; of these about 10 percent were television and radio, with the remainder print media.[31] Roughly two-thirds of the media outlets are Russian-language, and about one-third are available in the Kazakh language. While the government claims that Kazakhstan's mass media operate freely, the major broadcast media are owned by either the state or members of the president's family and are heavily censored. Reporters without Borders ranked Kazakhstan 160 out of 179 countries in its Press Freedom Index for 2013, just ahead of Uzbekistan, but behind Tajikistan and Belarus.[32] Freedom House evaluated Kazakhstan's press in 2012 as "not free," scoring it slightly worse than the press in Tajikistan and Russia (but considerably better than in Turkmenistan).[33] The absence of a genuinely free press constrains the development of civil society and of democracy.

A mature democracy requires strong political institutions, including competitive political parties, in addition to societal pluralism. Indeed, strong political institutions are the key to channeling civic activism into productive channels. As Sheri Berman has observed, "If a country's political institutions are capable of channeling and redressing grievances, then associationism will probably buttress political stability and democracy by placing its resources and beneficial effects in the service of the status quo," but if "political institutions are weak and/or the existing political regime is perceived to be ineffectual and illegitimate, then civil society activity may become an alternative to politics for dissatisfied citizens, increasingly absorbing their energies and satisfying their basic needs."[34]

A basic weakness of post-Soviet political systems has been their inability to develop cohesive, organized political parties that command the allegiance of a substantial segment of the population. The patterns consist of hegemonic propresidential parties (Nur Otan in Kazakhstan or United Russia in the Russian Federation), personalistic parties, or oppositional parties that are unable to advocate clear alternative platforms. Nur Otan's monopoly of seats in the national Majilis following the 2007 elections was recognized by the government as an institutional weakness; hence the directive for the 2012 parliamentary elections that the second-place party would receive a share of the seats even if it could not surmount the 7 percent threshold. Parties are vital to an effective democratic process since they are the chief institutions that contest offices and aggregate specific interests voiced by individuals and civil society organizations, but real party competition cannot be created via government decrees. Monopolistic or hegemonic parties have little incentive to pay attention to the demands of civil society, leading to apathy and alienation, a situation that was present both in Eastern Europe in the 1980s and in the authoritarian Arab states in 2011.

Kazakhstan's government needs to accommodate the increasingly diverse interests of a growing middle class, the result of the country's dynamic economic growth since independence. President Nazarbayev remarked on his country's progress in a 2011 speech: in 1994, he noted, per capita GDP was just over U.S.$700; by January 2011 it had increased more than twelve times, exceeding U.S.$9,000. This record has not been approached by comparably dynamic economies over the same period—South Korea's GDP per capita increased threefold in a comparable twenty-year period following independence, Malaysia's economy doubled, Singapore's increased fourfold, Hungary's increased a respectable 500 percent, and Poland's increased by four times.[35] An affluent, educated middle class acquires the "action resources" that allow people to govern their lives. People who become empowered through economic development gradually develop an empowering culture of democratic values and demand more democratic government.[36] This process may not be linear, but the general insights of modernization theory have held up remarkably well in various contexts, and we might expect similar developments in Central Asia.

In the United States, religious associations constitute a large proportion of the most active civil society organizations. The post-Soviet states, including Kazakhstan, have seen a renaissance of religious traditions, which are in turn related to a growing nationalism and rediscovery of history. Kazakhstan's government consistently advocates religious tolerance and interconfessional dialogue, hosting meetings of the Congress of World Religions to display its commitment to religious diversity. The constitution guarantees freedom of religion and mandates a secular state. The U.S. State Department's 2010 report on religious freedom found no instances of discrimination against traditional religious groups (Muslim, Russian Orthodox, Jewish, Protestant, and Catholic) as long as they were legally registered, though some fringe groups, such as Jehovah's Witnesses and Hare Krishnas, and excessively zealous missionaries may face harassment from the authorities.[37] One of the government's major concerns is religious extremism and its potential threat to national security. The 2005 Extremism Law and National Security Amendments and a 2011 Law on Religious Activity and Religious Associations sought to eradicate unregistered religious activity in an effort to combat religious extremism. These laws give local officials considerable discretion in deciding which religious groups are acceptable and which can be disallowed, leading to intrusive police measures against nontraditional religions and suspected extremists.[38]

Democracy necessarily involves a tension between defense of an individual's rights and liberties (the liberal perspective) and the good of the larger society (the communitarian approach). Political culture in the United States reflects the liberal perspective of Locke; Kazakhstan's political belief system, as reflected in the government's position on civil society and the approach used by most civil society groups in working with the state, remains closer to the communitarian ideals of Rousseau. Both outlooks are majoritarian and essentially democratic, in theory if not in practice, but the American perspective frequently leads to a neglect or frustration of the common good, while in Kazakhstan preserving social order often trumps individual liberties.

From the perspective of the Kazakh state, the purpose of politics is to guide the people toward greater political maturity—it is a paternalistic state. Civil society's role is to be a pliant supporter of government policies, rather than a critic or watchdog. Effective governance means that the wise leader does not simply react to pressures from civil society but shapes and educates public opinion. In Rousseau's terms, the sovereign reflects the general will and on occasion may need to override particularistic interests for the broader good. Sovereign authority plays a critical role in ensuring the liberty and equality of all citizens in the polity through the social contract.[39] Kazakhstani officials claim a strong state is needed to establish the conditions for economic prosperity, protect the private sphere, and deliver effective and responsive governance. Civil society can play a vital role in this vision by articulating specific interests, providing services in areas where the state is unable or unwilling to assume responsibility, and monitoring the operations of national and local governments.

Civil society in Kazakhstan is still in its infancy (or at best, adolescence), and NGOs tend to embrace the role assigned them by the government. Still, high levels of education and political knowledge, a growing middle class, the relative openness of the country, rapid economic development, widespread access to the Internet, extensive international educational exchange programs, and the government's determination to build a reputation for regional leadership all provide a favorable environment for the continued development of civil society. While the state severely constrains the activities of civil society organizations, regime goals of being accepted by the Western democratic community create exogenous pressures that over time may strengthen civil society. The civil society organization leaders who participated in our workshops clearly demonstrated both political acumen in dealing with the state and commitment to their causes, giving us reason for optimism.

Achieving a balance between a dynamic (albeit socially responsible) market economy, a strong and yet law-based state, and an energetic civil society is not easy, particularly in the post-totalitarian moment. Kazakhstan has succeeded admirably in the economic arena, and its political system, while not yet democratic, is less repressive and more stable than those of many of its Central Asian neighbors. Civil society is the least developed of the three spheres. The major obstacles to a more effective civil society, as we have seen, are government controls over media, a low level of political activism (especially in the rural areas), and the tendency of state officials to ignore or discount the potential contributions of civic activists.

The prospects for civil society development in Kazakhstan, however, are better than those in other Central Asian countries, with the possible exception of Kyrgyzstan. Much, of course, depends on the next generation of leadership. If the post-Nazarbayev government can maintain the country's solid economic performance and social stability while relaxing political controls and strengthening representative institutions, Kazakhstan's civil society could well flourish.

Notes

1. See Charles E. Ziegler, "Civil Society, Political Stability, and State Power in Central Asia: Cooperation and Contestation," *Democratization* 17, no. 5 (October 2010): 795–825. One major protest occurred in the western town of Zhanaozen during celebrations in December 2011 marking the twentieth anniversary of Kazakhstan's independence. Striking oil workers from the OzenMunayGaz firm used the occasion to express their grievances against the company and local officials by rioting in the main square. Reportedly, sixteen demonstrators were killed by riot police. Nazarbayev blamed the incident on organized criminal elements influenced from outside the country; the president fired the leaders of OzenMunayGaz, the governor (*akim*) of Mangistau oblast, and his son-in-law Timur Kulibayev, head of the Samruk-Kazyna National Welfare Fund.

2. "Nazarbayev postavil zadachi Kazakhstanskim NPO: Itogi i obrashenie Grazhdanskogo foruma," *Kazakhstanskaya pravda,* no. 295 (October 16, 2003), http://www.centrasia.ru/newsA.php?st=1066278360.

3. On the role of the state in a civilizing process, see Norbert Elias, *State Formation and Civilization: The Civilizing Process,* vol. 2 (London: Basil Blackwell, 1984).

4. Personal communication to Ruslan Kazkenov, Vilnius, Lithuania, July 2008.

5. See Zoltan Barany and Robert G. Moser, eds., *Is Democracy Exportable?* (Cambridge: Cambridge University Press, 2009), especially the chapter by Adam B. Seligman, "Democracy, Civil Society, and the Problem of Tolerance."

6. Scott Radnitz, *Weapons of the Wealthy: Predatory Regimes and Elite-Led Protests in Central Asia* (Ithaca, NY: Cornell University Press, 2010).

7. UNDP-Kazakhstan, *Status of Oralmans in Kazakhstan* (Almaty, 2006), http://www.undp.kz/library_of_publications/files/6838-29587.pdf.

8. Jazira Asanova, "Teaching the Canon? Nation-Building and Post-Soviet Kazakhstan's Literature Textbooks," *Compare: A Journal of Comparative and International Education* 37, no. 3 (2007): 325–43.

9. Human Rights Watch, *Striking Oil, Striking Workers: Violations of Labor Rights in Kazakhstan's Oil Sector* (2012), http://www.hrw.org/sites/default/files/reports/kazakhstan0912ForUpload_0.pdf.

10. Ak Zhol and the Communist Party each managed to secure just over 7 percent of the vote in the 2012 elections, while Nur Otan received 81 percent. Joanna Lillis, "Kazakhstan: Genuine Pluralism Remains Elusive as Observers Slam Election," EurasiaNet, January 16, 2012, http://www.eurasianet.org/node/64845. See also Yermukhamet Yertsybayev, presidential advisor for political affairs, interview, December 2011, Interfax-Kazakhstan, http://www.interfax.kz/?lang=eng&int_id=13&category=exclusive&news_id=61.

11. Edward Schatz, *Modern Clan Politics: The Power of "Blood" in Kazakhstan and Beyond* (Seattle: University of Washington Press, 2004).

12. Human Rights Watch, *Conflict in the Soviet Union: The Untold Story of the Clashes in Kazakhstan* (Washington, D.C., October 1990).

13. Freedom House rated Kazakhstan's press as "not free" in *Freedom of the Press 2012*, http://www.freedomhouse.org/report/freedom-press/2012/kazakhstan.

14. Margaret E. Keck and Katheryn Sikkink, *Activists beyond Borders: Advocacy Networks in International Politics* (Ithaca, NY: Cornell University Press, 1998).

15. Pauline Jones Luong and Erika Weinthal, "The NGO Paradox: Democratic Goals and Non-democratic Outcomes in Kazakhstan," *Europe-Asia Studies* 51, no. 7 (1999): 1267–84.

16. Eric McGlinchey, *Chaos, Violence, Dynasty: Politics and Islam in Central Asia* (Pittsburgh: University of Pittsburgh Press, 2011); Alisher Khamidov, "Central Asia: Citizens Learning to Take the Initiative," EurasiaNet, May 23, 2012, http://www.eurasianet.org/node/65449.

17. Kazakhstan's embassy in Washington, D.C., for example, regularly releases stories about the country's commitment to the rule of law, political development, religious tolerance, and human rights.

18. S. F. Udartsev, "Konstitutsionnaya reforma 2007 g. v Kazakhstane v kontekste evolutsii formy gosudarstva," Democratic Party Adilet, http://dp-adilet.kz/ru/719.html, accessed January 24, 2012.

19. Asian Development Bank, "Overview of NGOs/Civil Society: Kazakhstan," December 2007, http://www.adb.org/Documents/Reports/Civil-Society-Briefs/KAZ/CSB-KAZ.pdf.

20. "Kontsepsiia razvitiia grazhdanskogo obshchestva v Respublike Kazakhstan na 2006–2011 gody," website of the president of Kazakhstan, http://www.akorda.kz/ru/kazakhstan/non-governmental_organizations/conception_for_developing_civil_society_in_the_republic, accessed January 8, 2012.

21. Robert Putnam's argument in *Bowling Alone: The Collapse and Revival of American Community* (New York: Simon and Schuster, 2000) was that America's civil society peaked in terms of activism in the 1940s–1960s but then began a period of long-term decline.

22. Kazinform, December 8, 2011, http://www.inform.kz/eng/article/2424818.

23. "O vnesenii izmenii i dopolnenii v nekotorye zakonodatel'nye akty Respubliki Kazakhstana po voprosam gosudarstvennogo sotsial'nogo zakaza," http://www.kazpravda.kz/_pdf/jan12/050112law.pdf, accessed January 9, 2012.

24. See Charles E. Ziegler, "Security, Sovereignty, and Democracy: The EU, the OSCE, and Central Asia," in *Competing for Influence: The EU and Russia in Post-Soviet Eurasia,* ed. Roger E. Kanet and Maria Raquel Freire (Dordrecht: Republic of Letters Publishing, 2012).

25. Hillary Rodham Clinton, "Remarks: Town Hall on Empowering Civil Society for Central Asia's Future," November 30, 2010, U.S. Department of State, http://www.state.gov/secretary/rm/2010/11/152169.htm.

26. Statement by Mr. Kanat Saudabayev, Astana, December 1, 2010, http://www.osce.org/cio/73861; Statement by Mr. Kanat Saudabayev, Vienna, November 15, 2010, http://www.kazakhstanlive.com/Documents/Speech%20Saudabayev%201511.pdf.

27. U.S. State Department, *2010 Human Rights Report: Kazakhstan,* April 8, 2011, http://www.state.gov/g/drl/rls/hrrpt/2010/sca/154481.htm#.

28. Mary Kaldor, "The Idea of Global Civil Society," *International Affairs* (London) 79, no. 3 (2003): 583–93.

29. Shahjahan H. Bhuiyan, "Decentralization and Local Governance in Kazakhstan," *International Journal of Public Administration* 33 (2010): 658–72.

30. Jürgen Habermas, *Structural Transformation of the Public Sphere* (Cambridge, MA: MIT Press, 1989).

31. E-Gov, Electronic Government of the Republic of Kazakhstan, http://e.gov.kz/wps/portal/Content?contentPath=/web%20content/citizenry/culture/cul_media/mass_med/article/787&lang=en, accessed January 24, 2012.

32. Reporters without Borders, *Press Freedom Index 2013,* http://en.rsf.org/press-freedom-index-2013,1054.html.

33. Freedom House, *Freedom of the Press 2012,* global rankings, http://www.freedomhouse.org/report-types/freedom-press.

34. Sheri Berman, "Civil Society and Political Institutionalization," *American Behavioral Scientist* 40, no. 5 (March/April 1997): 562–74.

35. Nursultan Nazarbayev, Address to the People of Kazakhstan, January 28, 2011, http://www.akorda.kz/en/speeches/addresses_of_the_president_of_kazakhstan/r.

36. Christian Welzel and Ronald Inglehart, "The Role of Ordinary People in Democratization," *Journal of Democracy* 19, no. 1 (January 2008): 126–40.

37. U.S. State Department, *International Religious Freedom Report—Kazakhstan,* July–December 2010, http://www.state.gov/documents/organization/171755.pdf.

38. Taylor J. Turner, "Freedom under Control: Registration of Religious Organizations in Kazakhstan," *Columbia Journal of East European Law* 2, no. 1 (2008): 272–311; Joanna Lillis, "Kazakhstan: Religious Law Restricting Faith in Name of Tackling Extremism?," EurasiaNet, November 12, 2012, http://www.eurasianet.org/node/66167.

39. Jean-Jacques Rousseau, *The Social Contract; and the First and Second Discourses* (New Haven, CT: Yale University Press, 2002).

8

In Good Times and Hard Times

Civil Society Roles in Kyrgyzstan Today

Charles Buxton

Models of Civil Society Analysis

The aim of this chapter is to discuss civil society development in Kyrgyzstan from the point of view of a capacity-building practitioner who has lived for over ten years in the country's capital, Bishkek, and has worked across the Central Asia region. The article takes as a base the definition of civil society used by the author in his work for INTRAC with partners in the region: "Civil society refers to associations that exist outside of the state or market, which maintain a degree of autonomy and independence, and have the potential to provide alternative views, policies and actions to those promoted by the state and market."[1] Like other development agencies, INTRAC has had to grapple with the external context that has such an influence on civil society (CS) activity. Here we begin with the most frequently used model in our region—the "3-sector" diagram, with its three circles identifying civil society as a sector alongside the state and market. Defining the contours and weight of the CS "circle" has been a big part of the effort to gain official recognition for it, and early studies of civil society in the transition countries of Eastern Europe and the former Soviet Union put great store on counting the number of nongovernmental organizations (NGOs) or donor funds spent on CS programs. Another image constantly in our mind is that of civil society as a "space" or "arena" for dialogue between different actors, official and unofficial, modernizing or traditional.

In the 1990s, when this story begins, prescriptive ideas abounded as to what NGOs should be or do. However, this chapter is more empirical than prescriptive in approach. It poses the issue of CS development in a different way, at least for the author, using a recent description of "five main functions of civil society."[2] The thinking behind this formulation is that while CS can play an important role in democracy and development, experience from around the world suggests that no single theory of what it is or does has proven to be correct. It may be more accurate to conclude that CS has many different functions (or roles) and that particular actors carry out whichever are appropriate to them and their context. The chapter tries to assess which roles Kyrgyzstan's civil society has developed over the last twenty years.

The first section provides a short description of nongovernmental organization development from 1991 to 2005, with a focus on NGO-government relations. The next section looks at CS activity in the period between two revolutions, in 2005 and 2010, and considers some of the reasons for the second of these events.[3] The final section reviews CS development in Kyrgyzstan to date against the "five functions" or "roles" identified by INTRAC in its global analysis.

The chapter was begun soon after the tragic events of April–June 2010 in Kyrgyzstan, events that gained the country a mention in the international headlines but for reasons that were highly distressing. The killing of ninety people on the main square in Bishkek and later some four hundred others in the country's second city, Osh, have cast a dark cloud over political developments in this still very young country. The loss of life of so many ordinary people, Kyrgyz and Uzbek, plus the injuries, arrest, and persecution suffered by so many others continues to traumatize society up till today. My own analysis of these events combines the impressions of a foreigner living in Bishkek and the professional viewpoint of someone working with CS and international development across the region.[4]

NGO-Government Relations in Kyrgyzstan, 1991–2005

In the 1990s Kyrgyzstan was often described as an "island of democracy in Central Asia" because of its liberal political atmosphere and openness with regard to NGOs. This was a time when NGOs "sprouted like mushrooms" (another common phrase) across the region, most of them supported by international funding and capacity building. Civil society became aware of itself as a "sector." The dominant ideology among international donors and local NGOs was neoliberal, in the sense that they saw civil society as an independent force countervailing the previously dominant state.

Many of the attempts to periodize the advance of the CS sector in Central Asia take its relations with government as a major factor.[5] Thus, if 1991–1995 was a period of initial setup of NGOs, the decade 1995–2005 saw not just a widening of project activities and a gradual process of organizational strengthening but also the development of links with the state sector (relations with the new private sector have lagged significantly behind). In Kyrgyzstan, President Askar Akaev officially recognized the role of civil society in development and in 2001 created a Public Council on NGO Affairs within the President's Office to serve as a permanent committee for coordinating government-NGO interactions.

There are several examples from the mid-1990s in which NGOs successfully lobbied for a variety of interests with government. Women's NGOs were among the first to do this. For example, it was largely thanks to their activities that the Ayalzat national program for women's advancement was adopted in 1996 and that gender analyses were conducted with regard to the new Family Code, Labor Code, and laws on the mass media and public service. Another example of substantial NGO input was in the drawing-up of Kyrgyzstan's overall development plan for the period through the year 2010, the so-called the Comprehensive Development Framework, and the National Strategy of Poverty Reduction, 2003–2005, when wide consultations were held and NGOs came up with numerous recommendations.[6]

This is not to idealize the situation. There were many who questioned the level of seriousness of government commitments to democracy and partnership with civil society. For example, they noted that only a small number of NGOs had real access to government—usually these were organizations based in the capital, Bishkek, or the oblast (provincial) centers and whose leaders had close personal contacts with state officials. It is widely agreed that successes in consultation were not carried through into the implementation and monitoring phases of state programs. There were a number of reasons for this—including a lack of political will, the complications of the programs themselves, and a lack of technical assistance and resources. Some local experts questioned from the start whether the Western model of civil society was necessarily appropriate for Central Asia due to the region's historical and cultural differences from Europe or the United States. We shouldn't forget that the 1990s were a time when many people in Kyrgyzstan, as in other Central Asia countries, were seeking out their pre-Soviet roots—that is, looking another direction altogether.

Another side of CS-government relations in Kyrgyzstan should not go without mention. The shooting of several protestors by government forces in Aksy in 2002 led to large-scale protests at the community level in the south and eventually a national mobilization of civil society organizations (CSOs) on issues such as press freedom and the right to demonstrate.[7] After the Aksy events many NGOs began to take an increasingly antigovernment line. Thus in 2003–2004 NGOs initiated a Civic Forum to campaign against President Akaev's referendum proposals for a mixed presidential-parliamentary system, and they campaigned energetically against corruption and dynastic tendencies emerging within his regime. Civil society organizations, whether urban-based NGOs or more traditional rural associations, certainly played a role in the lead-up to the March 24, 2005, revolution when Askar Akaev was ousted and fled the country, although this was more indirect than is sometimes assumed.

For those working in international development projects, the situation at the local level is often as important as the national situation. Kyrgyzstan's decision at the end of the 1990s to experiment with local government decentralization undoubtedly gave support to grassroots development programs. Local government bodies welcomed the input of NGOs and community groups in dealing with social and economic problems like repair of water supply systems or school buildings, health promotion campaigns, and projects to boost agricultural production—particularly when this involved external donor funding or access to training for local officials. In return the state was able to offer NGOs office space at reduced or no rent; and when cooperation prospered, local officials could even be persuaded to hold open hearings on budget issues or to set up public councils like the national one referred to above.

In recent years, many service-oriented NGOs have put significant time and effort into lobbying for a new law on social contracting. The proposals developed owe a lot to recent reforms carried out in Russia and Kazakhstan (based in turn on Western experience). Thus, in neighboring Kazakhstan the adoption of a Law on State Social Orders has led to substantial state financing for the civil society sector, enabling NGOs for the first time to carry out socially important work without relying solely on foreign funding. In 2009 the idea of state contracting was formally approved by the parliament in Kyrgyzstan and a few pilot projects have begun, for example, for organizations working with children with disabilities. Unfortunately, severe budgetary deficits have held back the expansion of the program, despite some financial support from donors like the European Union.

There are already a number of detailed accounts of the March 2005 "Tulip Revolution" in Kyrgyzstan.[8] For the author of this chapter, this is best viewed in terms of the two-year period from 2005 to 2007 because of the large number of events with a dramatic character and revolutionary potential that took place at that time. The high point in this process came in November 2006 during six days of mass demonstrations in Bishkek that were almost completely without violence. While thousands camped out in yurts on the main square, the new government headed by President Kurmanbek Bakiyev and the opposition were locked in dialogue over a new constitution. On November 8 a hastily assembled constitutional assembly proclaimed a new parliamentary system of government. The crowds went home celebrating. But within three months Bakiyev reneged on the deal, tore up the new constitution, and pushed his own version through the old parliament.[9]

Kyrgyzstan's CSOs between Two Revolutions (2005 and 2010)

A country cannot experience two revolutions (or even two "coups," as some call them) without a large degree of ensuing political and institutional fragmentation. However, using the advantage of hindsight, it is worth trying to move beyond partisan positions adopted during this period and see some overall cases of advance or degeneration within the CS sector in Kyrgyzstan.

The post-Akaev period started with a sense of euphoria. The new leaders, Bakiyev and Kulov, operated in "tandem" and created a sense of national unity; while the former was a southerner from Jalalabad oblast, the latter hailed from the north. In the presidential election held in July 2005, the "tandem" triumphed: Bakiyev was elected as president and Kulov became prime minister. Many of the most influential NGO leaders participated in the Constitutional Council set up by the new government, building on their work in 2003–2004 and actively developing amendments and alternatives to the existing constitution. Much of this work was done by experts in "smoke-filled committee rooms." But they had a political movement behind them—as seen above with regard to the November 2006 demonstrations that resulted in the adoption of a new constitution.

By contrast, the public discussion around the new Country Development Strategy (2006–2010) was much less active than for the previous plan. This document reflects some ideas from the political movement that brought President Bakiyev to power. However, the consultation process was limited and involved getting NGO feedback only after the document had been drafted by experts. The real discussion about development policy took place in a completely different way—through a major CS-led campaign to oppose new loans from the World Bank. This campaign took place in 2006–2007 and posed the question about what had been achieved through ten years of work by international development programs. The radicals argued that the results were inadequate, referring to poverty levels around 50 percent and increasing levels of government indebtedness to international financial institutions. The campaign led to the government's withdrawal from a new World Bank credit facility, the Highly Indebted Poor Countries (HIPC) program.[10]

The success of the prodemocracy forces in pushing through a new constitution in November 2006 seemed to have been undone when Bakiyev's version was foisted on parliament at the end of that year, enhancing the powers of the presidency. But this was not entirely the case. There were two areas in which civil society and political forces had made significant gains. First, the new proportional representation system gave Kyrgyzstan's minority parties the chance for more seats in parliament. Second, the new system included compulsory quotas for women, youth, and national minority deputies within the party lists. The case for women's quotas had been led by NGOs and the other quotas were added later. Women made up 30 percent of the new parliament, and a new Alliance for Women's Legislative Initiatives brought together deputies and CS activists in an attempt to balance Bakiyev's economic-growth-oriented strategy with attention to the much-neglected social sector.

A major mobilization took place throughout Kyrgyzstan during 2005–2007. Rather separate from Western-funded CS, some of the groups that successfully lobbied their cause were public-sector trade unions, coal miners, market stall–holders, and railway workers. A wave of land occupations around Bishkek was led by informal groups of migrants from rural areas. Demonstrations, occupations of government buildings, and blockades of main roads were among the tactics used by protestors around the country, week in, week out.[11] The Bakiyev government negotiated with the protestors on a case-by-case basis, according to the level of pressure exerted and the links between the protestors and people within the government. By contrast, consultative groups set up by the previous president for especially vulnerable groups (for example, pensioners and people with disabilities) were severely disrupted by the revolutionary events of 2005. It took a few years for these groups to find their place again in the government agenda, but they had done so by 2009–2010 (when many such mechanisms fell apart again).

A national NGO forum in summer 2007 exposed deep divisions between radicals and reformers in the CS sector, divisions that have scarcely healed since then. The radicals organized themselves into a "people's parliament" that met every couple of months until April 2010. Donors were increasingly disinclined to support overt political action, especially when radical leaders might quite easily criticize donor policy or the weakness of support given by Western agencies to democratic changes.[12] Their support to the CS sector had in any case declined significantly by this time. Funding was available to NGOs working within government programs or in tightly defined watchdog roles on particular themes. The previous sector-wide support for NGO resource centers, joint training programs, and institutional development had largely ended. A study of the sector conducted in 2006 concluded that out of the several thousand officially registered NGOs in Kyrgyzstan, only five hundred were active and sustainable.[13] The sector was therefore not only split politically but weakened as to its combined resources.

Unfortunately, the struggle waged by political and CS actors between 2005 and 2010 did not produce the results people had hoped for. And so Kyrgyzstan found itself experiencing a second revolution. The following are among the most important factors that led to these events.

1. *The failure of the Bakiyev regime to introduce the democratic changes promised in 2005.* The leaders of the 2010 revolution argued that it was President Bakiyev's refusal to implement promises to introduce a parliamentary system that led them to break with his government. Within nine months of their victory in March 2005, the unity of the revolutionary forces was seriously weakened after a bitter argument on this issue between the speaker of parliament, Omurbek Tekebaev, and Bakiyev. These two figures were responsible for a steady deterioration in the political atmosphere lasting until April 2010, with Felix Kulov and a fourth figure, Almazbek Atambaev, playing

a kind of middle role at several stages in the developing conflict. The relations between the main leaders included elements of north-south competition, personal antagonism, and according to the local press, financial interests too—reflecting the fact that most political figures in Central Asia since 1991 are also businessmen, and political power has been widely used as a way of making a fortune or protecting ill-gotten gains. The differences between the political programs promoted by various parties were, by contrast, much less visible.

2. *The increasingly corrupt, family-based, and criminal nature of the Bakiyev regime.* In April 2007 a mass demonstration took place in Bishkek after Kulov, recently sacked from his position as prime minister, openly called for the overthrow of the regime. On this occasion President Bakiyev was able to defend himself, but the stage was now set for a desperate struggle. Bakiyev was already heavily reliant on his large and influential family and the business and political clans linked closely to it. One of his brothers commanded the security forces, while his son was given increasingly tasty slices of the financial pie, including from 2009 the position of director of Kyrgyzstan's national development fund (through which all the main foreign funding was expected to flow). The murders of opposition journalist Gennady Pavlyuk and of wavering government officials Medet Sadyrkulov and Sergey Slepchenko took place at this time and nobody was brought to justice for them. This robbed the regime of whatever was left of its good reputation.
3. *Bakiyev's poor handling of Parliament.* The new parliamentary system adopted in November 2007 had some plus sides—for example, a new proportional representation system that strengthened the position of political parties and potentially reduced the influence of clan-based leaders. Bakiyev's new "party of power," Ak Zhol, gained 70 percent of the vote, and the Social Democratic Party and the Communist Party also won seats (see table 8.1 for more details). However, other opposition parties were excluded by a dubious use of thresholds at the provincial and city levels. And in 2009 Bakiyev reduced the power of Parliament, building up the presidential apparatus and weakening his base of support among the political elite.
4. *Deepening economic crisis in 2008–2010.* Bakiyev's decision in late 2009 to sell off the main power companies and simultaneously raise

electricity tariffs by two or three times showed he had lost touch with the people. This issue gave the opposition a chance to get the mass support that it had never enjoyed for its political program. In a public opinion survey carried out in early 2010, almost one-third of respondents said that their standard of living had "seriously deteriorated" in the previous year—with the main reasons being the increase in food prices, becoming unemployed, and energy tariff rises. Another 20 percent said their standard of living had gone down, though not so much, and 11 percent said they were living on the brink of penury.[14] All this led to a steadily increasing level of street protests during January–April 2010, including a major mobilization of the population in the remote mountain regions of Naryn and Talas as well as in Bishkek. As in 2005, political activism started in the remote and rural areas and came to the capital for the showdown.

5. *Unwillingness on both sides to compromise.* Few factions were interested in negotiations or stopping the slide into violence. In retrospect, we can see that the holding of two separate *kurultais* (traditional assemblies led by *aksakals*—community elders) in March 2010 (the state-sponsored meeting and the opposition-sponsored "people's" *kurultai*) represented the failure to come together to prevent an upsurge in violence. The failure of conciliation through this traditional mechanism led straight to the street clashes and (rather surprisingly, as in 2005) the overthrow of state power. All this gives much food for thought. Civil society activists and organizations took up a variety of positions in these events, but if the essence of a progressive CS sector is to solve problems in a "civil" or peaceful way, perhaps we all share some blame for not being active enough, not realizing that so many people could die in the ensuing conflicts.

Civil Society Responses to the April and June 2010 Events

An Extraordinary CS Forum was held on April 17, 2010, in Bishkek, attended by some two hundred people, including emissaries from the interim government. The forum made every effort to hear all points of view and to contribute to a stabilization of the situation in the country. At least two proposals were made as to how the new government could hold out the hand of compromise and achieve a wider legitimacy. There was

The Events of April and June 2010 in Kyrgyzstan

April 6–7. A gradual, step-by-step escalation of actions moved from Naryn, where the first large-scale meetings protesting the rise in electricity tariffs took place in early 2010, through the organization of the people's *kurultai* in March, to a sudden explosion in the provincial center of Talas on April 6 involving the sacking of public buildings and severe beating of the country's internal affairs minister. Later that evening, almost all the opposition's leaders were arrested at their homes in Bishkek. Hence the planned demonstration in the capital on April 7 took place largely without political direction. Columns assembled at different points in the city in the morning. One of them marched to the Ministry of Internal Affairs and demanded unsuccessfully the release of their leaders but managed to break into a police station and seize the arms stored there. The group headed for the central square, where a six-hour battle ensued, during which police or special services marksmen killed ninety people, shooting from the roof of the White House and other buildings. Some demonstrators were armed with guns; others used trucks to ram the iron gates of the White House compound. In early evening, the White House was occupied. Widespread looting took place that night around the city. In the ensuing days, the houses of members of Bakiyev's family and of other government figures around Bishkek were attacked and ransacked. In the suburb of Maevka and the provincial center of Tokmak, businesses and homes owned by members of national minorities were attacked and more loss of life and property

severe criticism of the sacking of not just political appointees from the previous regimes but administrative staff (for example, rank-and-file employees in Parliament and the Constitutional Court) and of the first round of appointments by the interim government, based on party allegiance rather than experience or professional level. Concern was expressed about conflicts already emerging between top leaders. Speakers noted the threat of continuing violence in both the south and Bishkek itself, where political mobilization (meetings, pickets, motorcades) was increasingly visible and criminal groups had begun openly threatening civil servants at different levels. To help local CSOs to react constructively, the forum called for citizens'/people's control committees to be set up in every oblast. A hotline took place. The law-and-order agencies staged an unofficial strike and were hardly seen for a month. An interim government was announced and citizens' militias gradually helped to restore order in the streets.

June 9–15. President Bakiyev had fled to his family base just outside Jalalabad. During April and May tension escalated in the south as supporters of the previous and new governments held demonstrations and counter-demonstrations, often involving the occupation of government buildings. It seems clear that key figures in the interim government requested that the leaders of the Uzbek community (which forms a majority in many parts of Osh and Jalalabad oblasts) help evict Bakiyev. However, this action led to an immediate backlash from the Kyrgyz community. On June 9–12 skirmishes took place in Osh city and adjoining areas, in response to a real or imagined threat of mass action by Uzbeks for greater autonomy and national rights in the south. There were also rumors about rapes carried out by youths from one community on girls from the other. Some four hundred people died in the escalating riots, ten times this figure were wounded, and many more lost their homes, burned down by gangs from the opposing communities while the army stood by or aided the Kyrgyz side. NGO and community leaders in Osh and Jalalabad had warned the authorities about rising tension a month before the conflict. They were among the first to respond to the situation, helping the wounded and passing food to families across the ethnic barricades. Then the violence subsided just as suddenly as it had broken out.

was set up for citizens' enquiries about missing people, lost property, and so on, and a central website was established to help with coordination.

The forum demonstrated, even at this early stage, a major contrast between civil society's reaction in March 2005 and in April 2010. In 2005 there had been widespread celebrations for several months. In 2010 the violence of the events and number of victims on both sides made this impossible. After the conflict in the south, the national self-image of Kyrgyzstan citizens (of whatever ethnic or national group) took a severe battering. Many people who saw themselves as good neighbors and internationalists found it impossible to accept that this could have happened without the other side or some "third force" being responsible. In 2005 a positive consequence of the revolution was a tangible improvement in press freedom and political comment. By contrast, the trauma of 2010 had a negative effect. Almost without exception, the true nature of the Osh events was covered up in the local press. It was left to a few brave human rights groups within the country to attempt to defend the Uzbek community. Foreign agencies that intervened or made unpopular statements were widely reviled.

Conflict-Prevention Activities by CSOs during Summer 2010

Civil society organizations were immediately in action, supporting victims and preventing further violence, after the April events. In the north they protested against the violence committed by police and in attacks on minority communities afterward. In the south NGO leaders warned that the standoff between pro-Bakiyev and anti-Bakiyev forces could quickly lead to intercommunal violence. During and after the riots of June, close-knit groups of experienced NGOs in Jalalabad did their best to coordinate the emergency response. Women's and youth organizations played a big role in relief efforts, working closely with UN and humanitarian agencies, the city and oblast authorities, and the Ministry of Emergencies. In Osh NGOs formed a coordination council on June 24, and on July 15 Osh and Jalalabad came together to establish a new "regional humanitarian forum."

During the summer of 2010 U.S.- and European-funded human rights and democracy NGOs gave substantial input regarding the revision of the constitution, the new electoral commission, and discussions in the government and independent media about the political situation in the country. Many of their suggestions became law (for example, through the referendum held that summer), and much of their advice became government policy. Some experts from the CS sector were absorbed into the new regime, whether in Parliament or the presidential administration.

At the same time a smaller number of CS leaders found themselves in the opposition on two main issues: first, the legitimacy of the new government and its "revolutionary" (nontransparent, party- or clan-based) way of making appointments and decisions; second, the issue of human rights for political opponents and the Uzbek community. Thus the first court case regarding the disturbances in the south was brought against a longtime human rights activist and leader of the Uzbek community in Jalalabad. Meanwhile, the new government had purged a large number of former judges. No policemen or ethnic Kyrgyz were brought to justice for the events of April and June. A national commission was set up to look at the April events, but only at the political aspects. Meanwhile, criminal cases launched against figures from the Bakiyev administration held responsible for the April carnage, from ministers down to rank-and-file policemen and soldiers, opened, only to be suspended after disturbances in court.

Development agencies and NGOs threw themselves into the humanitarian aid effort in Osh and Jalalabad. Indeed, this enabled them to do a lot of good without necessarily trying to find a common position on highly contentious political issues. As the April Civil Forum had showed, many activists were ready to try to discuss these issues sensitively and openly. But the conflict in June significantly soured the atmosphere and made it harder for NGOs to unite their constituencies. Suddenly a huge amount of foreign funding became available for conflict-prevention efforts. Many CSOs opened new projects on this theme. At the same time, many began to reconsider their strategies, priorities, and relations with government, given that the political and economic crisis was likely to last several years.

Central Asia's First Fully Open Parliamentary Elections

The peaceful manner in which the referendum and elections were conducted in 2010 was a relief. The referendum made Roza Otunbayeva the region's first woman president, and her patient, practical approach reassured both the international agencies and the local population. The center-left was represented by the Social Democratic and Ata Meken Parties. A major positive factor from the point of view of political stability was the participation of Bakiyev supporters in the political process in the new parties Ata-Jurt and Respublika—both to the right on the political spectrum. A negative factor was the rising tide of Kyrgyz nationalism, visible long before April 2010 and now being fanned by all and sundry. The complex nature of political party development in Kyrgyzstan is shown by table 8.1.

One of the major contradictions in "postrevolutionary" Kyrgyzstan is between democracy development as instanced in the electoral results shown in table 8.1, on the one hand, and economic slump on the other. In 2010 GDP fell by 1.4 percent at a time when all four of the country's neighbors in Central Asia achieved significant growth.[15] Prices rose for many basic products, and political instability discouraged new investment from outside. The renationalization of companies owned or controlled by the Bakiyev family appeared to many to represent a new carving up of

Table 8.1. Results of the Last Three Parliamentary Elections in Kyrgyzstan

Date of election	Type of voting system	Number of seats in Parliament	Results: parties that won seats, number of seats, percentage of those who voted
February 2005	Parliament reduced from two chambers to one. Voting system: first past the post	75 (previously 105 in two chambers)	Alga (pro-presidential party), 17 seats. Several other pro-Akaev politicians (including from Democratic Party of Women, Adilet) were elected. Akaev's son and daughter also won seats. The opposition parties (Party of Communists of Kyrgyzstan, Ata Meken, Asaba) gained only 6 seats between them.
November 2007	Proportional representation with quotas for women, national minorities, youth	91	Ak-Zhol (new "party of power" formed a month before the elections), 71 seats (48 percent of the vote). Social Democratic Party of Kyrgyzstan, 11 seats (5.25 percent). Party of Communists of Kyrgyzstan, 9 seats (5.05 percent). Ata Meken won sufficient votes overall but was disqualified for failing to meet the threshold in Osh.
October 2010	Proportional representation with quotas for women, national minorities	120	Ata Jurt (new party largely representing supporters of ex-president Bakiyev), 28 seats. Social Democratic Party of Kyrgyzstan (led by Otunbayeva and Atambaev), 26 seats. Ar-Namys (led by Kulov), 25 seats. Respublika (new party led by Babanov), 23 seats. Ata Meken (led by Tekebaev), 18 seats. None of these parties achieved 10 percent of the vote.

Note: The reduction in parliamentary chambers and seats in 2005 was designed by President Akaev to consolidate the country's political elite and streamline decision making. But the reduction in seats (with their lucrative corruption opportunities) caused major infighting within the elite, including Akaev's own supporters, and alongside increasing popular opposition to the regime brought about the president's downfall. In both 2005 and 2007, the influence of the current "party of power" was significant, whereby the regime used its so-called administrative resources to maximize its vote (or to organize simple vote rigging). In autumn 2010, the north-south split and the absence of an effective party of power after Kyrgyzstan's second revolution led to a "hung" result, in which neither the interim government nor its opponents received a real vote of confidence.

resources by the political elite rather than a serious program of state-led economic development. The loss of millions of dollars through financial machinations by Bakiyev's son and others meant that government coffers were empty. The rise in poverty indicators in 2010 was very serious indeed: 33.7 percent of the population were in poverty (31.7 percent in 2009) and 5.3 percent in extreme poverty (3.1 percent in 2009).[16] For local and international NGOs involved in sustainable livelihood programs, good work on the ground was being undone by events at the national level.

In Good Times and Hard Times: An Analysis of Civil Society Roles in Kyrgyzstan, 1991–2011

How can we assess CS development in the medium or long term? Are things getting better or worse? What is the impact of CS development programs? How can civil society best withstand the shock of political change or economic depression? These questions are obviously of great interest to those working in the development sector. One of the most substantial efforts to chart the course of CS development in former Soviet states is USAID's Sustainability Index for civil society. This marks the sector on seven criteria, bringing them together in an overall score between 1 and 7 (1 is high and 7 is low). For example, Kyrgyzstan's scores on the seven indicators in 2010 were as follows: legal environment, 4.0; organizational capacity, 4.3; financial viability, 5.3; advocacy, 3.3; service provision, 4.0; infrastructure, 3.7; and public image, 4.1. In the USAID report, these scores are accompanied by a short analysis. These were consolidated in the overall score of 4.1.

Table 8.2 shows Kyrgyzstan's overall scores in 2001–2010.[17] Hardly any change is visible. On the one hand, this probably reflects the reality of slow consolidation in the sector. On the other hand, the variations between the scores awarded for individual indicators and overall totals in each year give no sense of the roller-coaster ride experienced by CSOs in this decade. The

Table 8.2. USAID Sustainability Index Scores for Central Asia and Kyrgyzstan, 2001–2010

Sustainabiity index	2001	2002	2003	2004	2005	2006	2007	2008	2009	2010
Kyrgyzstan	4.3	4.0	4.1	4.2	4.1	4.1	4.1	4.1	4.1	4.1
Central Asia average	4.8	4.6	4.6	4.8	4.8	4.9	4.8	4.9	4.9	4.8

highest scorer in Central Asia, by a small margin, is Kazakhstan, which began the decade with the same score as Kyrgyzstan (4.3) and ended with 4.0. Kazakhstan and Kyrgyzstan get higher scores than the region as a whole, but the table gives scant recognition to the efforts made.

How can we get a more interesting or informative picture of civil society's main functions? In the final part of this chapter I present INTRAC's model of civil society's five main functions or roles and see how they have developed during the last twenty years in Kyrgyzstan, including during and after Kyrgyzstan's most recent revolution. As the authors of this analysis note, the proliferation of CS support programs around the world over this period has not been accompanied by the "crispness of purpose we previously enjoyed," and while NGOs have been funded by the aid industry, "there is actually less support for CS itself as a broader force in society." There is a need to look in more detail at countries as they move away from aid dependence and to examine the variety and special contributions of CSOs, social movements, indigenous, networking, and campaigning groups, and so on.[18] Short examples or references from INTRAC's own work as civil society developers or "capacity-builders" in Central Asia are given for each of the five roles.

Role 1: CS Helps Generate the Social Basis for Democracy

In the 1990s, a multitude of democratization programs, including funding for new political parties and electoral reforms creating a multiparty system, were rolled out in Central Asia. At the same time, market reforms aimed to create and support a new class of private sector entrepreneurs—that is, a new middle class. CS programs were seen as a necessary complement to these reforms. In theory, civil participation extends democracy to the grass roots, representing and protecting a multitude of often-minority interests. Democracy is about more than periodic acts of political authorization through voting—its strength derives from a citizenry that participates regularly and continually, in an open and egalitarian public sphere.

In INTRAC's work the 1990s are often referred to as the time when NGO setup and the first stages of organizational development took pride of place. Many of the new organizations were urban and led by professionals who had been educated and often had reached quite high positions in the Soviet period. By the end of the decade, international donors could see the pluses and minuses of this work a bit more clearly. For example,

INTRAC's Five Main Roles of Civil Society

1. Helps generate the social basis for democracy
2. Promotes political accountability
3. Produces social trust, reciprocity, and networks
4. Creates and promotes "alternatives" through collective action
5. Supports the rights of citizens and the concept of citizenship

some NGOs were not reaching out into the wider community as much as had been hoped.[19] The donors began to support a variety of informal associations at the village level. Many local experts argued that the roots of democracy could be found in Kyrgyz nomadic society. A debate began about whether programs working for local social and economic development should collaborate with the newer, registered NGOs or with more traditional groups.

INTRAC's program in Central Asia focused on community development in rural areas, starting with an analysis of traditional forms of mutual help and the new imported methodologies and then in the mid-2000s working with a network of over twenty NGOs that were supporting self-help groups engaged in a wide variety of economic, social-psychological, cultural, and political activities. Indeed, the groups drew on rich traditions of collective activity, but they had to cope with an entirely new political and economic system—in which rural communities were struggling to survive.

In retrospect, we can see that it is hard to develop a social base for democracy, however serious and long-term the CS efforts may be, if there are serious problems in developing a satisfactory political or economic base for democracy. In Kyrgyzstan (as in other countries in the region) political elites "captured" governmental power quite early in the process and it proved difficult to dislodge them. Thus the Akaev family was overthrown, only for the Bakiyev family to begin establishing another dynasty.

On the economic front (closely interwoven with political power), a hasty and often criminal process of privatization produced a private sector without legitimacy in the eyes of the population. The poorer the country becomes, the less chance there is to develop a broadly based middle class, which, in the eyes of many Western development agencies, is the main social base for civil society.

In civil society theory, the experience of negotiating between different interests at a local level will "scale up" to the national level, affecting the political culture positively. This will happen as a normal part of associational civic life. However, it would be hard to claim that in Kyrgyzstan the many positive examples of social partnership at the local level (NGOs and local government cooperating on repairing roads, opening youth clubs, and supporting small farmers and women's groups) have translated substantially to the development of a healthy political culture at the higher levels. Indeed, the events of 2010 (as in 2005) have evoked considerable discussion in the local media about the failure of the country's leadership and political class.

On the other hand, table 8.1 shows that a measure of political pluralism has developed in Kyrgyzstan; indeed, the constitution and electoral code have been changed several times in the course of the last twenty years, with this aim being loudly proclaimed. The cynics will say that the real aim was to restrict, not extend, democracy. This may indeed be true, but we can still see some real battles.

Role 2: CS Promotes Political Accountability

A more ambitious aim entertained by some donors was to develop NGOs that could operate as watchdogs with regard to political parties and processes; that is, they could counterbalance elite control of the state system. From the early 1990s, special programs were developed around Central Asia to build NGO expertise in specialist fields such as election monitoring, budget monitoring, corruption monitoring, and so on. While most funding went to new groups, sometimes support was given to associations of lawyers, journalists, or accountants dating from the Soviet period. From the 2000s, increasing attention was given to developing the advocacy and lobbying skills of NGOs generally. Efforts were made to begin this process at community level by enhancing local government accountability and developing intersectoral relationships. However, the watchdog role took more time to develop and a lot depended on the readiness of the authorities to respond positively.

By the early 2000s, Kyrgyzstan had a number of confident and experienced NGOs whose leaders were ready to demand accountability from their government and international donors alike. In the middle of this decade, CS coalitions formed to force the authorities to conduct fair elections, to clean up behind international companies, as at the gold mine Kumtor, and as noted above, to oppose new loans from the World Bank. Whether taking the fight to the government, big business, or international agencies, most CS leaders were inclined toward a reform strategy, while a few opted for more radical opposition.

The fall of Akaev showed how the critique of "authoritarian" post-Soviet regimes (dominant among external analysts over the previous fifteen years) had somewhat obscured their underlying weakness and limited room for maneuver. Indeed, the economies of countries like Kyrgyzstan and Tajikistan are extremely weak, and geopolitical rivalry in the region (for example, between the United States and Russia, or the West and the Muslim world) can easily destabilize them. After 2005, the phrase "fragile state" was used increasingly frequently to describe Kyrgyzstan, and most external donors downgraded or abandoned their previous support for the political opposition.

Political accountability is thus less popular with donors in Central Asia than it used to be.[20] And some "accountability" projects involving CSOs in the region appear to be designed more to help international agencies ensure proper use of their development aid (now channeled through government) than to significantly build civil society in the receiving country.

Role 3: CS Produces Social Trust, Reciprocity, and Networks

From the mid-1990s, many donors gave support to traditional, nonformal, and unregistered associations through community initiatives linked to education, health, and local economic development programs. These groups tried, with varying degrees of success, to counter the widespread disillusion and disorientation following the breakup of the USSR. The phrase "social capital" was used to refer to the type of environment in which transactions can take place without fear that they will not be honored. Trust, it was argued, is crucial to the working of the market, that is, the relations between buyers and sellers, employees and employers. Collective public (or CS) action is often carried out through horizontally structured organizations "that are more or less mutual, cooperative, symmetrical, and trusting."[21] In both the political and economic spheres in Central Asia of the 1990s, there was very little trust or social capital to be seen. It had to be re-created through the formation of new links between people and organizations (for example, self-help groups, mosques, residents' associations). And once again, local experts pointed to the traditions of mutual help, especially in rural communities.[22]

As stated above, the development of civil society in the former Soviet states has taken place alongside that of "wild capitalism." Economies that crashed to 50 percent of their previous volume in 1991–1995 stayed at this low level for a decade and more. A few individuals took advantage of managerial skills, networks, or insider knowledge from the Soviet period to build new business empires; the majority experienced impoverishment. During the 1990s this process was less violent in Central Asia than, for example, in Russia. But in the power vacuum that occurred after the fall of Akaev in 2005, as the new government struggled to get hold of the situation, mafia elements were able to achieve a kind of breakthrough resulting in a succession of murders and property disputes directly involving the political elite. In all this we can see setbacks for the creation of trust between citizens.

Unity within the civil society sector has suffered too. CSOs in Kyrgyzstan have been split since the first major opposition actions against Akaev in 2003–2005. Akaev gave people a sense of freedom; then, as the external situation worsened (with the wars in Afghanistan and Iraq and the failure of neoliberal reforms), he began to backtrack and to strengthen his own position, relying on family and clan networks. It was natural for CS groups to oppose this. However, the political divisions that ensued have impeded the development of a unified sector with generally accepted lobbying positions and representative bodies. For those involved in NGO capacity building, the problems also include power issues within organizations and the varying level of confidence, management, and negotiation skills of staff and leaders.[23]

Role 4: CS Creates and Promotes "Alternatives" through Collective Action

In reality, during the 1990s a ready-made alternative to the previous communist system was imported—political pluralism and the market economy—and people came together to set up and register Western-style NGOs.[24] According to most civil society theory, however, new ideas, activities, institutions, and socioeconomic solutions arise "naturally" through citizens' interaction—whether at the communal, national, or international level. Perhaps the best way to see this complex process is as an arena of different competing ideas and practices. In a time of turbulent change, many different alternatives are likely to be posed by citizens' groups. In Central Asia of the 1990s, some people joined the new NGOs, while others tried to mobilize against the negative effects of economic collapse and increasing inequality—for example, by organizing strikes and protests against late wages, cuts in pensions, and so on.

Political movements in Central Asia were much weaker than in Russia and some of the other former Soviet republics. In the literature on transition, the explanation usually given is that Central Asia was not "ready" for independence. While this phrase jars somewhat, certainly there had been less of a conscious and organized independence movement than in some of the other Soviet republics. This had an effect on the level and type of CS activity post-1991.

Are there any alternatives to the dominant neoliberalism? In April 2010 radical speakers in Bishkek's main square called for the execution of the Bakiyev brothers and expropriation of the wealth of the new bourgeoisie. However, as in 2005 there was a quick fallout between revolutionary and reformist elements in the new transitional government. While in opposition, the leaders of the new government had consistently opposed Bakiyev's sell-off of strategic economic assets such as the energy companies. However, potential foreign investors in Kyrgyzstan will undoubtedly push for the sale of these assets to private companies. Bakiyev's fatal attempts to sell off Bishkek's main power station and the Northern Energy company shows how narrow the space for maneuver is in Kyrgyzstan.[25]

All this means that Gramsci's definition of civil society as constituting an "arena in which hegemonic ideas concerning the organization of social and economic life are both established and contested" has continuing resonance in Kyrgyzstan.[26] And the ideas that propel collective action in civil society may not necessarily be liberal or "civil." For development CSOs, one of the lessons is that it is hard to make transformative social change without strong and progressive political movements to articulate these messages in government and the international arena.

The search for alternatives continues in different sectors within CS in Kyrgyzstan. The efforts of the ecological movement deserve a separate article, as does the women's movement. Officially, the country is "for ecology" and "for women's rights." But the opposing forces are so great that it is often difficult to determine which opinion is "mainstream" and which is "alternative." Therefore environmental and women's groups are constantly forced to lobby for new policy, to write "alternative reports," and so on.

Role 5: CS Supports the Rights of Citizens and the Concept of Citizenship

Finally, I must mention briefly another contested concept—that of citizenship. By this I mean the roles and responsibilities of citizens and the state vis-à-vis each other. This concept was quite well developed in the Soviet period—within a secular, modernizing, federalist, socialist frame. One of the main differences post-1991 is that the countries of Central Asia are now separate and independent nation-states. Another is the new market economy and pluralist political setup. Within this new frame, the role of CS is to represent and negotiate multiple civic interests with the state. In return, citizens and CSOs will accept the legitimacy of the state.

To enable CS to carry out its role, externally funded programs have from the early 1990s supported civic education (at both secondary and higher levels) in Kyrgyzstan. CSOs have been encouraged to use a rights-based approach in their work, appealing to universal rights as defined by a range of international agreements or agencies. Within the region, promoters of the new concept of citizenship included secular nationalists (for example, the presidents of the five countries) very interested in developing and promoting new national ideologies. Obvious opponents include radical Islamists who reject secularism and in some cases promote a religious entity (caliphate) without national borders.

The notion of citizenship takes on increasing importance when the role of CS comes under attack. Perhaps there was a time in the 1990s when the global movement for CS led people to believe the "third sector" could solve all a country's problems. This was overly ambitious, a fallacy. Many became disillusioned because of the failure of weak and under-resourced (or sometimes even corrupt) CSOs to do what was expected of them. This has led many to focus on citizenship instead of or alongside civil society. As a concept, citizenship has two advantages: (1) it poses the issue of individual responsibility (what you can do as an individual, a citizen); and (2) it does not divide people or organizations into sectors (a government official and a businessman are no less citizens than are NGO staff or supporters).

Working in a Post-conflict Situation—NGOs in Southern Kyrgyzstan, 2010–2011

In autumn 2010 I made several visits to NGO partners and international agencies in Osh and Jalalabad, exploring the situation soon after the tragic events and bringing together ideas for civil society capacity building with a priority on peace building and reconstruction. One of the first conclusions was about the worrying decrease in NGO activity outside Bishkek. In Jalal-abad, CS partners calculated that out of three hundred NGOs registered in the oblast, only fifteen were active in early to mid-2010. In Osh, too, there had been a marked decreased in CS activity since 2005; out of just under fourteen hundred NGOs registered, only thirty-two were active at the start of 2010, seventeen of them based in the city. This demonstrated dramatically the reduced levels of external donor support and the urgent need for NGOs to find alternatives to it.

Nonetheless, local NGOs were able not only to organize emergency aid to the population in the summer and autumn of 2010 but to play a gradually increasing role liaising with government. In Osh, INTRAC's partners were active in lobbying both the town hall and the interim government, meeting representatives of the Presidential Apparatus twice a month, and using its Internet site to disseminate information. They made increasing use of "cluster" meetings called by the UN agencies, bidding actively to take part in humanitarian aid and reconstruction programs. Local human rights NGOs played an invaluable role helping people to sort out problems with documents, welfare payments, housing, compensation for destroyed businesses, and so on.

Many international agencies and staff were new to the area, and there were some misdirected efforts in the rush to provide essential aid to victims of the violence. Meanwhile, local government was not trusted by the Uzbek community because of its inability or reluctance to defend their members. A spate of land seizures by ethnic Kyrgyz from outlying districts, occupying land belonging to Uzbek farmers in areas around Osh city, threatened new explosions. The capacity needs assessment identified new needs like conflict prevention and mediation skills, social-psychological counseling, better understanding of humanitarian aid standards, and so on.

CSOs themselves did not come through the conflict unscathed. Political or ethnic divisions emerged in some; in others, key staff began leaving the country or found jobs with higher salaries in international NGOs. On the other hand, some positive processes could be seen from early in the recovery process. These included the participation of young people as new civil society recruits in volunteer efforts and reconstruction projects; renewed efforts to influence local government and demand better and fairer services; closer NGO networking (for example, in the new Regional

Humanitarian Forum); and citizens' journalism (for example, community bulletins featuring positive reconstruction stories and news flashes on mobile phones giving accurate, nonsensational information to counter the effects of gossip and scaremongering).

As noted above, local self-government and decentralization have been key donor strategies in Kyrgyzstan since 2000 and have provided many opportunities for state-NGO collaboration on the ground. From the mid-2000s the system faced another challenge—the constant changes in key personnel due to political upheavals—and the pace of decentralization began to falter. At the present time there are huge challenges at the national level, such as making the new parliamentary system work properly or reforming the judiciary—which may demand prior attention. Nonetheless, in late 2011 the government reaffirmed its commitment to decentralization and local budgets.[27] And Roza Otunbayeva, the new president, actively promoted consultative committees at all levels in government.

In August 2010 the mayor of Osh, a Kyrgyz nationalist and former Bakiyev ally, managed to thwart all efforts by the Bishkek authorities to remove him. In 2011 nationalists took key positions in Jalalabad. INTRAC launched a project with local NGO partners in the two oblasts to "reduce the potential for conflict by improving the accountability and responsiveness of government in ensuring basic rights and services for marginalized and vulnerable sections of the community."[28] The project brought together CS and government representatives, training them in research skills and supporting a number of mini research studies. These were chosen by the participants themselves and included some very sensitive topics, for example, an assessment of the government's post-June 2010 reconstruction program, a study on state support to those wounded in the violence, and a study on compensation to businesses that suffered.

Despite the violent conflict in the south, our experience demonstrated that it is still possible to bring together ethnically diverse groups of men and women, and representatives from civil society and local government, to work together productively. As might be expected, almost all the participants reported that their life had changed completely since "the war" in June 2010. However, research studies chosen by participants (working in groups) showed that they were prepared to tackle complex and sensitive issues. For the training team, the challenge was to ensure that the research themes were realistic and a professional approach was employed. Government workers were under competing pressures from presidential and local elections and their participation was more problematic, but the project succeeded in boosting civil society links with key local government experts and had mixed success linking into new consultative mechanisms established by the president in the wake of the 2010 events.

Notes

1. INTRAC, International NGO Training and Research Centre, a registered charity based in the UK, working to support civil society in international development (www.intrac.org). INTRAC has been working in Central Asia since 1995.

2. See John Beauclerk et al., *Civil Society in Action: Global Case Studies in a Practice-Based Framework* (Oxford: INTRAC, 2011).

3. The author's book, Charles Buxton, *The Struggle for Civil Society in Central Asia: Crisis and Transformation* (Sterling, VA: Kumarian Press, 2011), contains an extended analysis of the lead-up to and main events of the March 2005 "Tulip" Revolution.

4. The chapter draws on analyses made for INTRAC and the European donor consortium ACT-Development during 2010–2011, as well as media and NGO sources and interviews on the ground.

5. See INTRAC's NGO mapping studies in the five countries in the early 2000s, reviewed in Janice Giffen et al., *The Development of Civil Society in Central Asia* (Oxford: INTRAC, 2005). See also Elmira Shishkaraeva et al., *Obzor istorii stanovleniya i razvitya sektora nepravitelstvennykh organizatsii v Kyrgyzstane* (Bishkek: ACSSC/AKDN/Soros Foundation Kyrgyzstan, 2006).

6. Giffen et al., *Development of Civil Society in Central Asia,* 163–66.

7. The Aksy demonstrators were protesting boundary changes that ceded parcels of land in the eastern Tien Shan Mountains to China.

8. For example, see Aleksandr Knyazev, *Gosudarstvenny Perevorot: 24 marta 2005 goda v Kirgizii* (Bishkek: Public Fund Institute of National Strategy, 2007); or Sally Cummings, introduction to special issue on the Kyrgyzstan Revolution, *Central Asia Survey* 27, no. 7 (September–December 2008): 223–29.

9. See Buxton, *Struggle for Civil Society in Central Asia,* chapter 4.

10. For a description of the anti-HIPC campaign, see Charles Buxton, "Central Asia NGO Networks and Global Civil Society," *Central Asia Survey* 28, no. 1 (March 2009): 43–58.

11. See chart and case studies in Buxton, *Struggle for Civil Society in Central Asia,* 88–95.

12. See a case study by Asiya Sasykbaeva from NGO Centre Interbilim in John Beauclerk et al., *Civil Society in Action,* 23–26.

13. Erkina Ubysheva, *Portret NPO Kyrgyzstana: Mneniya i realnost* (Bishkek: ACSSC, Soros Foundation, Allavida, 2006).

14. *Delo No,* October 2, 2010, 10.

15. Kyrgyzstan, 1.4 percent; Tajikistan, 6 percent; Kazakhstan, 7 percent; Uzbekistan, 8.5 percent; Turkmenistan, 9.2 percent. Wikipedia/IMF.

16. *Times of Central Asia,* October 2011.

17. For more details, see USAID, Where We Work, last updated May 29, 2012, http://www.usaid.gov/locations/europe_eurasia/dem_gov/ngoindex/.

18. Beauclerk et al., *Civil Society in Action,* 3–19.

19. Anne Garbutt, "Civil Society Strengthening in Central Asia," in *Changing Expectations? The Concept and Practice of Civil Society in International Development,* ed. B. Pratt (Oxford: INTRAC, 2003).

20. See a case study of the NGO Centre Interbilim in Beauclerk et al., *Civil Society in Action,* 23–26.

21. See Robert Putnam, *Making Democracy Work: Civic Traditions in Modern Italy* (Princeton, NJ: Princeton University Press, 1994).

22. See Lucy Earle et al., *Community Development in Kazakhstan, Kyrgyzstan and Uzbekistan,* Occasional Papers Series no. 40 (Oxford: INTRAC, 2004).

23. See Kazbek Abraliev and Charles Buxton, *Leadership in Transition: Developing Civil Society Leaders in Kyrgyzstan,* Praxis Paper 19 (Oxford: INTRAC, 2007), 17–30.

24. The alternative to Soviet state socialism came either directly from Western agencies (donors, INGOs) or indirectly through the perestroika ideological filter in Eastern Europe and Russia.

25. On the one hand, it was hard to see how a penniless government like Bakiyev's could refit and manage these enterprises effectively; on the other, the people were asked to carry an unacceptable burden. The planned tripling of tariffs on central heating and electricity was clearly linked to this disastrous privatization. (Northern Electric was sold for U.S.$3 million when critics said it was worth U.S.$20 million.)

26. Quoted in Anthony J. Bebbington et al., eds., *Can NGOs Make a Difference? The Challenge of Development Alternatives* (London: Zed Books, 2008).

27. See INTRAC study on decentralization and donor programs, 2000–2010, for Soros Foundation Kyrgyzstan / Swiss Development Cooperation, posted on www.intrac.org.

28. This project was funded by the British Embassy, Astana, under the Foreign and Commonwealth Office's Conflict Pool.

9

Civil Society in Chains

The Dynamics of Sociopolitical Relations in Turkmenistan

Charles J. Sullivan

Democracy, broadly defined, is best characterized as a type of governing system in which a "substantial" portion of a population partakes in both the "exercise" and "contestation" of power according to a set of formal democratic institutions.[1] In referring to such institutions, a view commonly accepted among scholars in the political science discipline today is that in order for democracy to flourish, the state must encourage the development of a civil society. Bearing this in mind, Central Asia stands out as one of the most autocratic regions in the world, in which formal democratic institutions exist only on paper. What then can be said about the current state of civil society in countries such as Turkmenistan, where authoritarianism reigns supreme?

Nearly twenty years have passed since the Soviet Union disintegrated into fifteen newly independent states. Since the collapse of the USSR, instead of embracing liberal economic and political reforms, the Turkmen government continues to exercise strict control over the country's social, political, and economic spheres. Consequently, this chapter posits that in spite of the death of the country's first post-Soviet leader, Saparmurat Niyazov, Turkmenistan under the stewardship of President Gurbanguly Berdymuhammedov remains very much an isolated country governed by a stable authoritarian ruling regime, making it exceedingly difficult for civil society to flourish.

Overall, the purpose of this chapter is to offer an assessment of the extent to which the political space in Turkmenistan could potentially experience democratization in the near future, mainly by analyzing the current state of civil society development in Turkmenistan. That said, to know the nature of the ruling regime in Ashgabat is to understand the current state of civil society development in Turkmenistan. In brief, upon analyzing the manner in which the Turkmen government regulates the activities of civil society groups within its borders, this chapter argues that instead of making progress toward liberalization, Turkmenistan has regrettably undergone what is referred to as "authoritarian entrenchment" on account of a series of factors concerning the nature of the country's economy, certain negative aspects related to Soviet rule, and the contemporary governing style of the ruling Turkmen elite. As a result, civil society in Turkmenistan remains extremely weak. Finally, this chapter concludes with a discussion on whether economic modernization is likely to help foster the development of a more independently oriented civil society in Turkmenistan over time, followed by a recommendation on how the democratically oriented countries of the world can help spur the evolution of Turkmen civil society from its current "cooperative" state to a more "contestative" type. Hence, although the chances that Turkmenistan will experience democratization in the near future are rather bleak, this chapter nonetheless contends that the international community can help foster civil society development by adhering to a strategic approach. In making such an argument, a supplementary aim of this chapter is to advance academic discussion on the political situation in Turkmenistan, a country about which not very much is known, and in doing so offer some tentative, not definitive, conclusions.

State-Sponsored Civil Society

On December 21, 2006, "President-for-Life" Saparmurat Niyazov of Turkmenistan unexpectedly passed away. Niyazov, who had ruled over Turkmenistan since independence in the wake of the Soviet collapse, was soon succeeded by Gurbanguly Berdymuhammedov, a former minister in the Turkmen government. Looking back on the late Turkmen leader's legacy, Niyazov was often depicted in the Western media as an "erratic" figure, infamously known for renaming the days of the week and months of the year, instituting obscure holidays, closing down most hospitals outside of Ashgabat for no apparent reason, authoring the *Rukhnama* ("Book of the

Soul") and making it required educational reading, building grandiose monuments in the capital city, and assuming the heralded title of Turkmenbashi. The late Niyazov also deserves to be remembered for fostering a personality cult, repressing ordinary citizens' civil liberties and political rights, and driving the country into international isolation by effectively sealing Turkmenistan's borders. In the end, the political legacy of the first Turkmen president can thus be aptly summarized as that of a neo-Stalinist leader who governed over a former Soviet republic as if it was his own possession.[2]

Niyazov's legacy, for the most part, however, proved to be short-lived. For shortly after assuming office, Turkmenbashi's successor, President Berdymuhammedov, began implementing a series of reforms. Specifically, Berdymuhammedov oversaw the restoration of secondary education and university curriculums to ten and five to six years, respectively, issued calls for increased access to the Internet, vowed to reopen many of the hospitals that Niyazov had closed, and reversed the former president's decree on the Turkmen government not recognizing university degrees received from abroad.[3] Furthermore, Berdymuhammedov sought to do away with the Turkmenbashi cult by reinstating the old Turkmen calendar, removing Niyazov's portraits from government and public buildings and his profile from television broadcasts, redenominating the national currency so that Niyazov now appears on only a single banknote, and dismantling the Arch of Neutrality (which once boasted a life-size golden figure of Niyazov that rotated atop the memorial so that it always faced toward the sun).[4]

At first glance, it seems as if Berdymuhammedov may be following in the footsteps of the former first secretary of the Communist Party of the Soviet Union Nikita Khrushchev in carrying out his own "de-Niyazovization" campaign.[5] Despite initially optimistic signs, however, this chapter posits that over the course of the past several years no significant economic or political reforms have been implemented by the Turkmen government. Furthermore, corruption remains endemic throughout society, and the government's stance on human rights remains a serious concern.[6] Moreover, the reforms undertaken by Berdymuhammedov have not borne much fruit to date, for neither has the degree of Internet freedom provided to Turkmen citizens improved nor has the government streamlined the process for students who seek to attend foreign universities.[7] Hence, aside from the issuance of platitudes about the necessity for reform and the dismantling of the Turkmenbashi cult, not much has actually happened since the transition from Niyazov to Berdymuhammedov in early 2007. To this day, Turkmenistan resides securely within the grip of a highly authoritarian ruling regime. As a consequence, civil society in Turkmenistan remains weak.

Yet what is civil society? According to the Centre for Civil Society at the London School of Economics, civil society "refers to the arena of uncoerced collective action around shared interests, purposes and values." The center notes as well that although civil society's "institutional forms are distinct from those of the state, family and market . . . in practice, the boundaries between state, civil society, family and market are often complex, blurred and negotiated," thus making it somewhat ambiguous in nature.[8] For sake of clarity, then, borrowing from Larry Diamond and Robert Putnam, this chapter conceptualizes civil society as an "autonomous" realm in which citizens operate through "organizations" (such as various types of "cultural associations," "educational" institutes and universities, interest groups, media outlets, "civic" associations, and "commercial networks") so as to collectively realize shared interests.[9] Such a conceptualization endorses the general view that the guiding purpose of civil society is to limit the power of the state by pressuring the government to adhere to existing formal democratic institutions. Diamond further argues that, aside from limiting the power of the state, civil society groups instill "democratic values" within society, provide a venue for disempowered groups to voice their concerns, narrow social "cleavages" by encouraging people to join voluntary associations, and serve as a check against the misappropriation of power by monitoring and publicizing governmental "abuses" of authority.[10]

Recently, however, such a definitional standard has come under review in the political science discipline (particularly in the Eurasian studies division) because it appears as if an altogether different type of civil society predominates in Central Asia. In discussing how to conceptualize civil society in Central Asia, Charles Ziegler contends that "neither the Tocqueville/Putnam concept of associational life, fostering civic responsibility in a democratic polity, nor the Kuron/Michnik idea of civil society as providing a protected sphere which resists the tyrannical (communist) state, adequately captures post-Soviet politics." Instead, Ziegler argues on behalf of conceptualizing civil society in Central Asia as a variant of the type defined above, in which "the state exercises partial control over associational life, managing or co-opting some groups, and attempting to marginalize others." Thus, mainly as a consequence of the governing style of ruling elites coupled with the "political culture" of the region in general, Ziegler posits that a more "cooperative" civil society flourishes in parts of Central Asia today.[11]

In general, this chapter does not dispute the argument advanced by Ziegler. However, it is important to note (as Ziegler does) that the guiding purpose of the vast majority of civil society groups in Central Asia today is not to limit the power of the state over society but instead to work alongside the state in delivering social services to the general population.[12] In Turkmenistan, it is only this "cooperative" variant of civil society that is authorized to operate.

So how does the Turkmen government regulate civil society today? Overall, the ruling regime primarily utilizes two strategies in its dealings with civil society groups: registration and repression. In doing so, the regime allows only the "cooperative" type of civil society to flourish.

Today in Turkmenistan, the law of the land stipulates that all civil society groups must comply with the 2003 Law of Turkmenistan on Public Associations. Article 17 of this law reads,

> Public organizations regardless of their type are registered by the Ministry of Justice of Turkmenistan in accordance with the procedure established by the Saparmurat Turkmenbashi Civil Code of Turkmenistan and other legislation of Turkmenistan.
>
> Public associations must be included in the Single State Register of Legal Entities in accordance with the procedure established by the legislation of Turkmenistan.
>
> An unregistered public association is not allowed to conduct activities. A person who conducts activities on behalf of an unregistered public association is liable under the legislation of Turkmenistan.[13]

Upon reading this law, it is rather obvious that only those groups that the ruling Turkmen elite believe do not pose a threat to their hold on political power are granted registration rights. All of the rest, unfortunately, risk the wrath of the state if they try to operate independently. Hence, the only version of civil society permitted in Turkmenistan is the "state-sponsored" variety.[14]

Bearing this in mind, it is important to highlight that some civil society groups receive registration authorization from the Turkmen government and are permitted to operate within Turkmenistan today. To serve as an example, Victoria Clement's enlightening study on civil society in Turkmenistan reveals that organizations such as Keik Okara (which provides citizens with a number of services, such as foreign-language instruction, access to the Internet, and information pertaining to HIV/AIDS, to name but a few of its services) have received registration authorization from the Turkmen government. Turan Mugallym, dedicated primarily to educational development in the rural countryside and to teaching English to government employees, is another civil society organization currently in operation. Yet why do these particular civil society groups receive registration authorization from the Turkmen government? Simply put, organizations such as Keik Okara and Turan Mugallym (which Clement refers to as GONGOs, or "government-organized nongovernmental organizations") receive registration authorization because the ruling Turkmen elite believe that such groups can provide certain social services, be it either to government employees or to the general population. Moreover, these groups do not seek to challenge the authority of the ruling regime, nor could they, since such organizations are wholly dependent on the government for registration authorization.[15]

What about civil society groups that are denied registration authorization? What happens to these organizations? In brief, on account of their governing style, the ruling Turkmen elite see to it that such groups are essentially driven underground through a mixture of intimidation and violence. To date, a great deal of evidence collected by international nongovernmental organizations reveals that the Turkmen government under Berdymuhammedov's stewardship continues to repress civil society groups and human rights activists. Accordingly, Amnesty International maintains that the Turkmen government silences civil society groups by refusing to release activists such as Mukhametkuli Aymuradov from prison; barring the family members of oppositionists such as Khudayberdy Orazoz (currently in exile) from leaving Turkmenistan; and threatening activists with arbitrary arrest, prison sentences, and/or confinement to psychiatric wards for lengthy periods. To this day, the Turkmen government also refuses to disclose the whereabouts of (to name but a few) Boris Shikhmuradov (a former minister of foreign affairs who received a life sentence for his role in the alleged 2002 failed coup attempt to oust Niyazov) and Ovezgeldy Atayev (the former speaker of Parliament, who was deposed shortly after Niyazov's death). Additionally, the Turkmen government has shown no inclination to investigate the deaths of activists who perished while in custody, such as Ogulsapar Muradova (who worked for the Turkmenistan Helsinki Foundation and served as a correspondent for Radio Free Europe/Radio Liberty, was arrested in 2006, and inexplicably died while in custody) or permit human rights organizations such as the Turkmen Initiative for Human Rights (chaired by Farid Tukhbatullin, who was initially imprisoned by the Turkmen government for his work on human rights issues but eventually released in 2004, only to be forced to emigrate to Austria, where he now resides and has as of late received "credible threats against his life") to freely operate within the country.[16] In fact, Crude Accountability declares that no "independent" nongovernmental organization has received registration authorization from the Ministry of Justice since Berdymuhammedov assumed office in mid-February 2007.[17]

Finally, in case some still remain of the opinion that the new Turkmen president is actually a reformer deep down inside, it is worth mentioning that on September 30, 2010, Berdymuhammedov called on members of the Ministry of State Security to "be uncompromising warriors against those who slander our democratic, legal, secular state and try to destroy the unity and cohesion of our society."[18] Simply put, these are not words that a leader committed to reform would issue to a governmental agency capable of silencing civil society by resorting to illegal means. Sadly, civil society thus remains powerless, since neither Berdymuhammedov nor the ruling Turkmen elite wish to permit such organizations to flourish. Yet in order to understand why the Turkmen president, along with the ruling Turkmen elite, continues to restrict civil society development, it is crucial to comprehend the nature of this ruling regime.

Understanding Authoritarianism

Political scientists have yet to agree on a definition of authoritarianism. Part of the reason that no such definition exists is because authoritarianism is a new subfield in the comparative politics field of the political science discipline. That said, if democracy is best characterized as a type of governing system in which a "substantial" portion of a population partakes in both the "exercise" and "contestation" of power according to a set of formal democratic institutions (such as the holding of "free and fair" elections at regular intervals; the enshrinement of a set of civil liberties and political rights; the "division" of political power along institutional lines; respect for the supremacy of the "rule of law"; and the authorization of civil society groups and parties to engage in sociopolitical activities without interference for the purposes of "scrutinizing" government policies and "channeling" participation into the political system), then it is helpful to conceptualize authoritarianism as its mirror image.[19] Accordingly, authoritarianism can be characterized as a type of system in which power is "exercised" and "contested," but only by a small portion of a population and according to an altogether different set of institutions. In such systems ruling elites hold fraudulent elections; retain the services of a secret police, which monitors the population and infringes on people's civil liberties and political rights; govern through a "ruling party," which helps guard against "elite defection" and works to ensure that power does not "divide" along institutional lines; establish "patronage" networks, which subvert the rule of law; and utilize both "legal" and extralegal tools to disrupt, "suppress," and/or "co-opt" oppositionists.[20]

Bearing such a definition in mind, it is accurate to characterize Turkmenistan as a country governed by a regime that is highly authoritarian in nature. In 2011 Freedom House awarded Turkmenistan an ignominious score of 7 out of 7 (thereby making Turkmenistan one of the top nine most undemocratic countries in the world), due to the government's lack of respect for citizens' political rights and civil liberties.[21] In 2010 the Polity IV Project also bestowed on Turkmenistan an extremely unfavorable rating of –9, classifying the country's government as an "autocracy."[22] In 2009 *Parade Magazine* ranked Gurbanguly Berdymuhammedov as the ninth "worst dictator" in the world, coming in just ahead of (recently deceased) Muammar al-Qaddafi.[23] Finally, in 2011 Human Rights Watch issued a scathing report on Turkmenistan, citing the government's lack of toleration for freely operating civil society groups, control over media outlets, and unwillingness to allow any international nongovernmental organizations (INGOs) entry to ensure the humane treatment of political prisoners being held in detention facilities.[24] Needless to say, despite the death of Niyazov, Turkmenistan under Berdymuhammedov remains very much a country governed by a highly authoritarian ruling regime. Yet how stable is this regime? Overall, in order to comprehend the extent to which the ruling regime in Turkmenistan exists as a stable governing entity, it is necessary to further classify the regime in terms of its institutional framework and assess the various factors that help to ensure its continuity. Regretfully, this chapter argues that Turkmenistan will likely remain a country governed by a stable authoritarian ruling regime due to the nature of its economy, certain negative aspects related to Soviet rule, and the governing style of the ruling Turkmen elite.

Categorizing Authoritarianism

One of the most interesting debates in the political science discipline today concerns how scholars should classify governing systems. On this point, Diamond argues that although many ruling regimes today claim to be democratic in nature, few of them can actually be counted among the ranks of consolidated liberal democracies. That said, scholars have yet to develop a coherent "regime classification" framework that encompasses all types of political systems. In response, Diamond contends that scholars should recognize at least six different types of regimes: (1) "liberal democracies," which "extend freedom, fairness, transparency, accountability, and the rule of law from the electoral process into all other major aspects of governance and interest articulation, competition, and representation"; (2) "electoral democracies," in which power is contested at regular intervals via the holding of "free and fair" elections to decide which societal actors govern; (3) "ambiguous regimes," which serve as a "residual" group; (4) "competitive authoritarian" systems, in which democratic institutions are not well respected by ruling elites, while opposition groups are unable to attain power because of an unfair political system favoring those in power; (5) "hegemonic electoral authoritarian" systems, in which a "ruling party" remains in power indefinitely as a result of underdeveloped democratic institutions; and (6) "politically closed authoritarian" systems, in which formal democratic institutions do not exist.[25]

It thus seems that several "regime types" fit within the authoritarian framework, beginning with "competitive authoritarian regimes," followed by "hegemonic electoral authoritarian" systems, and concluding with regimes that can be characterized as being "politically closed," "totalitarian," and/or "sultanistic" in nature. To begin, Steven Levitsky and Lucan Way define "competitive authoritarianism" as a type of "hybrid" in which "formal democratic institutions are widely viewed as the principal means of obtaining and exercising political authority" but "incumbents violate those rules so often and to such an extent . . . that the regime fails to meet conventional minimum standards for democracy." In other words, in such systems elections are not wholly fraudulent nor are they free of state interference. Likewise, although legislatures do not provide rubber stamps, they do not serve as an institutional check against the abuse of power either. Finally, although the media are not completely controlled by the government in such a setting, journalists are occasionally victimized by agents of the state.[26]

At the other extreme lies "totalitarianism," defined as a type of "sociopolitical system . . . characterized by an all-embracing despotic interference of the state in all manifestations of the life of the social organism and the life of individuals."[27] In discussing this Juan Linz claims that totalitarian regimes possess (1) a "center of power" in which authority is wielded by "an individual and his collaborators or a small group that is not accountable to any large constituency and cannot be dislodged from power by institutionalized, peaceful means"; (2) an all-encompassing "ideology" that essentially dominates social life; and (3) a "single mass party" along with "mass organizations," which work to mobilize people to partake in realizing "utopian" goals as well as ensure control over society. Linz also notes that some totalitarian regimes use "terror" to atomize citizens and purge ruling elites on occasion.[28]

Finally, Linz defines a "sultanistic regime" (or "personal rulership") as a unique type in which all political power is vested in a single person. Under such a regime, everyone who holds ranking government posts owes their political fortunes to the head of state. The ruler is also not hindered by any laws or institutions; instead, he makes the laws and institutions as he sees fit and relies on a secret police to maintain power. In terms of governing style, the ruler treats the country over which he presides as his very own possession.[29] Linz explains, "He and his collaborators, with his consent, take appropriate public funds freely, establish profit-oriented monopolies, and demand gifts and payoffs from businesses for which no public accounting is given. . . . The economy is subject to considerable governmental interference but not for the purposes of planning but of extracting resources."[30]

Where does Turkmenistan reside within this classification framework? Obviously, based on the aforementioned assessments of a variety of INGOs, it would be wrong to classify Turkmenistan as a "competitive authoritarian regime," mainly because of the absence of any real formal democratic institutions. As an example, in 1992 Niyazov allegedly garnered 99.5 percent of the popular vote in the country's first-ever presidential election. In

1994, 99.9 percent of all voters supposedly supported extending Niyazov's presidential tenure. Finally, in 1999 the Halk Maslahaty (People's Council) declared Niyazov the "president-for-life."[31] Furthermore, after Niyazov's death, the speaker of Parliament, Ovezgeldy Atayev (who was supposed to assume the presidency, according to constitutional statute), was imprisoned, while the Halk Maslahaty hastily convened to revise the Turkmen Constitution so that Berdymuhammedov could assume the presidency.[32] That said, although Turkmenistan under Niyazov did resemble a "personal rulership," it would be imprudent to classify the ruling regime in Turkmenistan as such at present because not enough research has been conducted on the political dynamics of the Turkmen government under Berdymuhammedov. Simultaneously, in spite of the government's despotic nature, classifying it as "totalitarian" without a detailed analysis of the nature of sociopolitical relations in Turkmenistan would be misguided. Hence, taking into consideration all of the aforementioned definitions, coupled with Diamond's own evaluation of Turkmenistan as a "politically closed authoritarian" system, this chapter gauges that the nature of the ruling regime in Turkmenistan is best characterized as residing somewhere between "hegemonic electoral authoritarianism" and "totalitarianism."[33] Bearing this in mind, this chapter seeks to assess the durability of the ruling regime by means of analyzing the structure of the economy, certain historical institutions, and the governing style of the ruling Turkmen elite. Such an analysis will in turn provide some insight into whether the current state of civil society development in Turkmenistan is likely to undergo a change anytime soon.

Authoritarianism in Ashgabat

How can we account for regime continuity in Turkmenistan? Overall, instead of making any progress toward liberalization, Turkmenistan has undergone what has been referred to elsewhere as "authoritarian entrenchment," a term that seemingly implies that the ruling regime remains firmly in power because of a supportive structural foundation.[34] Bearing this in mind, this chapter posits that Turkmenistan will likely remain a stable country governed by an authoritarian ruling regime well into the foreseeable future on account of a set of structural and contingent factors. The first factor is the nature of the country's economy, with its emphasis on significant natural gas reserves along with how the ruling Turkmen elite manage the economy.

Are countries with natural resource–based economies prone to authoritarianism? Generally speaking, some quantitative studies point to an unfortunate but evidentiary "yes." For example, Michael Ross argues that the majority of such countries are governed by authoritarian regimes, citing a significant statistical relationship between "oil and mineral wealth" and authoritarian rule. Consequently, Ross comes out in support of the "resource curse" thesis, further positing that three "causal mechanisms" work to ensure the continuation of authoritarian rule: a "rentier effect"; a "repression effect"; and a "modernization effect." With respect to the "rentier effect," Ross argues that governments that accumulate revenues from the sale of natural resources strive to ensure the continuation of authoritarianism by means of keeping taxes low, using revenues derived from the sale of natural resources to establish "patronage" networks, and relying on natural resource–based revenues to "inhibit" the development of interest groups. Additionally, Ross argues that authoritarian governments utilize such revenues to suppress prodemocracy movements, thus alluding to the "repression effect." Finally, with respect to the "modernization effect," many countries with natural resource–based economies remain underdeveloped, largely on account of the government's unwillingness to allocate resources for industrial development. Hence, Ross argues that the lopsided nature of a resource-based economy can serve to undermine economic diversification and thereby prevent the rise of a host of actors capable of pressuring the state into realizing various interests. Taken together, under such systems, ordinary citizens are not afforded the opportunity to participate in policy making, thereby paving the way for authoritarian rule to endure.[35]

At this time, it remains unknown as to how much natural gas Turkmenistan possesses, with the *BP Statistical Review of World Energy* maintaining that the country possesses up to 100 Tcf of natural gas reserves and the Turkmen government boasting in excess of 700 Tcf. Moreover, it has recently been estimated that the country's South Yolotan–Osman gas field holds up to 140–500 Tcf of gas, making it one of the world's largest known fields.[36] What is less clear, however, is how the Turkmen government allocates the revenues derived from the sale of its natural gas reserves. In general, the Turkmen government exhibits many characteristics of a "rentier state," exacting rents from the export of its resources and providing inexpensive utilities to the population in return for citizen passivity. Unsurprisingly, the cost of diesel fuel in Turkmenistan is extremely cheap.[37] As well, Pauline Jones Luong and Erika Weinthal claim that Turkmenistan "embodies the classic model of the rentier state," since the ruling regime "has employed substantial mineral rents to fill its capital city, Ashgabat, with gold-plated statues and four-star hotels while its largely rural population receives free gas, water, and salt but is deprived of basic education and healthcare."[38] Additionally, evidence exists in support of a "modernization effect" owing to the country's lopsided economic development. After all, Turkmenistan's economy, for the most part, consists of subsistence agriculture functioning alongside its lucrative oil and natural gas industries.[39] Judging by the fact that Turkmenistan has been free from the rule of the Communist Party of the Soviet Union for more than a generation, it is safe to assume that those in power in Ashgabat are (to put it mildly) not preoccupied with modernizing the economy. Finally, on observing the country's ignominious Freedom House and Polity IV Project rankings, it is posited here that a substantial portion of the proceeds from gas sales is most likely directed toward financing the Ministry of National Security (formerly known as the Committee on National Security), which serves as the guardian of the ruling regime and is tasked with repressing citizens and social groups deemed to be a threat. Theoretically speaking, since Eva Bellin argues that "the robustness of the coercive apparatus is directly linked to maintenance of fiscal health," it seems that any authoritarian regime would have to keep its secret police force well financed in order to remain securely in power.[40] Altogether, the country's abundance of natural gas reserves, coupled with the way the ruling Turkmen elite manage the economy along with the proceeds from gas sales, likely plays a significant role in enhancing the durability of the ruling regime.

The second factor that contributes to the buttressing of the authoritarian ruling regime in Turkmenistan deals with the various negative experiences associated with the era of Soviet rule, with particular reference to the manner in which the Communist Party restricted civil society development. Interestingly, some scholars, such as S. Frederick Starr, contend that certain "legacies of Soviet rule" (such as exceptionally high literacy and education rates, "traditional" Central Asian institutions like *mahallas* and *waqfs*, and the USSR's "imperial" ruling style, which permitted local actors to acquire "self-initiative" and engage in "self-management") have helped foster a breeding ground from which civil society organizations can emerge.[41] Yet in spite of these legacies, other negative aspects of Soviet rule (namely the fact that the Communist Party sought to do away with all autonomous social groups that sought to contest its claim to power) severely hindered civil society development in Central Asia.[42] In a historical sense, an independently oriented civil society was never afforded the opportunity to flourish in Soviet times. Instead, the Soviet state sought to regulate the dissemination of knowledge, owing mainly to the totalitarian nature of the Stalinist regime of the 1930s and 1940s and the unwillingness of the party throughout the post-Stalinist era to tolerate opposing viewpoints. Geoffrey Hosking reveals how the party restricted civil society development during the Soviet era: "The state monopoly of information and mass communications, backed by a vigilant security police, made any serious intellectual or cultural life impossible. The conflict of diverse viewpoints and the assimilation of uncomfortable facts, both prerequisites for the formation of public opinion and the conduct of serious politics, were altogether precluded."[43]

Additionally, it is important to recall that over approximately thirty years' time, the party forced a large, multiethnic, preindustrial society to endure revolution, civil war, collectivization, industrialization, the Terror, and the Great Patriotic War (1941–1945), resulting in the deaths of countless millions, the shattering of traditional institutions, and the decimation of family units. Thereafter, over the course of the next forty years, civil society activists and dissidents were incarcerated, exiled, or forced to emigrate as a consequence of speaking out. In short, civil society ceased to exist throughout much of the Soviet era (with the exception of the early half of Khrushchev's tenure during his de-Stalinization campaign) because the party simply did not tolerate dissent.[44] To be certain, civil society experienced a revitalization in the 1980s under the banner of former general secretary Mikhail Gorbachev's glasnost campaign, during which a debate concerning the Soviet past swept across newspapers, scholarly journals, and television screens. Still, it is noteworthy that glasnost would never have been possible without Gorbachev's active encouragement of the Soviet intelligentsia to provide substance to what he referred to as the "blank pages" of Soviet history.[45] This chapter argues that this negative legacy of the Soviet era has imprinted a lasting handicap on the development of civil society in Central Asia because, in spite of their exceptionally high literacy and education rates, former Soviet citizens were never afforded the opportunity to participate in an independently oriented civil society.

The third and final factor that contributes to the buttressing of authoritarian rule in Turkmenistan today deals with the governing style of the ruling elites, with specific reference to both the nature of the relationship between the Turkmen president and other ruling elites and the foreign policy agenda that has been endorsed by the Turkmen government since the mid-1990s. On the first point, aside from oppositionists and civil society activists, members of the Turkmen government are also regularly victimized by the ruling regime through purging campaigns initiated by the sitting head of state. This Soviet-style tactic, which Stalin perfected in the 1930s and which I refer to as "deck shuffling," is occasionally instituted by the Turkmen president to guard against the formation of an "alternative power base."[46] Looking back, opposition estimates reveal that Niyazov purged as many as fifty-eight deputy prime ministers during his rule. Not to be outdone by his predecessor, Berdymuhammedov utilized this tactic in 2007 by removing Chief of the Presidential Guard Akmurat Rejepov, Transportation Minister Orazberdy Khudoiberdiyev, and Ashgabat mayor Orazmyrat Esenov. Upon assuming the presidency, Berdymuhammedov also sacked Interior Minister Akmamed Rahmanov, along with National Security Minister Geldymuhammed Ashirmuhammedov. Several months later, the new Turkmen president once again purged the sitting interior minister (Hojamyrat Annagurbanov), along with two other deputy interior ministers.[47] Hence, in contrast to the prevailing political instability in Central Asian countries such as Kyrgyzstan, where "revolution" has gripped the capital city twice in the span of five years (mainly because of elite infighting), politics in Ashgabat remains quite predictable (and consequently stable) to this day on account of the Turkmen president's periodic purging of the ruling elite.[48]

With respect to the governing style of the ruling Turkmen elite, part of the reason that authoritarian rule reigns supreme in Turkmenistan is because the Turkmen government has no foreign enemies that constitute an existential threat. For several years after gaining independence, Niyazov proclaimed his country's neutrality in international affairs. To this day, Turkmenistan retains its neutral status. In doing so, I have argued elsewhere that "by adhering to positive neutrality, the Turkmen government seeks to ensure that no state will contest its sovereignty, violate its territorial integrity, or meddle in its domestic affairs." That said, it is also worth mentioning that Turkmenistan has succeeded in maintaining "working relations" with the United States and Russia, thereby lessening the chances of the ruling regime being toppled on account of a falling out of favor with either Washington or Moscow.[49]

Although Turkmenistan currently faces a host of problems, such as inflation, rising wealth inequalities, widespread corruption, and a high unemployment level, this chapter contends that authoritarian rule in Ashgabat remains quite stable (mainly on account of the aforementioned three factors working in tandem), thus allowing for the ruling Turkmen elite to dictate the terms on which civil society groups can participate in social affairs.[50]

Of course, it is possible that the ruling regime in Turkmenistan could collapse, either through a combination of elite infighting and popular protests or by armed intervention. An abundance of natural gas reserves coupled with a prior history of restricting civil society development and domination by a ruling elite wedded to neutrality thus cannot guarantee the continuation of authoritarian rule in Turkmenistan indefinitely. That being the case, this chapter posits that the aforementioned structural and contingent factors serve to buttress the ruling regime's hold on political power, thereby rendering it unlikely that Turkmenistan will break free from authoritarianism anytime soon.

Modernization and Democratization?

Overall, it seems unlikely that Berdymuhammedov and the ruling Turkmen elite will institute a radical change in sociopolitical relations vis-à-vis civil society anytime soon. Yet can economic modernization help bring about the right set of conditions for an independent civil society to flourish? To date, some scholars seem to think that economic development assists in laying the foundations for democracy to emerge over time. Ronald Inglehart maintains that "economic development, cultural change, and political change go together in coherent and even, to some extent, predictable patterns." He contends that people in societies undergoing economic modernization are more likely to embrace a set of "cultural values" that help facilitate development because the primary goal of a society undergoing economic modernization is to experience growth so that people can meet their "survival needs" and overcome "scarcity" conditions. In doing so, "traditional" systems come to be replaced by "modern" ones capable of overcoming scarcity and ensuring order by means of utilizing technological advancements and relying on a "centralized bureaucratic" state apparatus. Once a society's basic needs have been fulfilled, however, certain social groups begin to reorganize their priorities, eschewing economic growth and survival in favor of "environmental" concerns and "well-being," thus sparking a "cultural shift" that is "conducive" to democratic governance.[51] On a related note (and seemingly in support of this argument), Carles Boix and Susan Stokes's results (which challenge Przeworski and Limongi's findings in their acclaimed study on modernization theory) lend credence to "endogenous democratization."[52]

Other scholars remain unconvinced that economic modernization leads to democracy. To the contrary, Samuel Huntington contends that economic modernization initiates an alteration in a given society's structural shape. Accordingly, Huntington argues that this development coincides with greater popular demands for participation in the political system. Yet only those systems equipped with "effective institutions" capable of managing "increased political participation" will experience "political development."[53] On another note, Bruce Bueno de Mesquita and George Downs caution that we should not expect certain countries that have experienced "significant economic growth" over the past few years to transform into democracies soon, mainly because the ruling elites in these countries have uncovered how to maintain control over their respective political systems. Hence, Bueno de Mesquita and Downs are of the opinion that since ruling elites in certain countries are able to limit the "availability" of "coordination goods" in society (such as by restricting civil liberties and political rights but also by controlling media outlets and repressing civil society groups), such regimes are able to remain in power while their economies prosper.[54] Finally, in discussing "democracy promotion," Thomas Carothers contends that proponents need to realize that ruling elites at the helm of authoritarian regimes are most of all interested in self-preservation and will thus stymie the implementation of reforms if they believe that such policies may ultimately weaken their hold on power. That being the case, Carothers argues that "sequentialists" (who emphasize working with authoritarian ruling elites in enhancing "state capacity" and the "rule of law") are "misguided" in their thinking because such political figures are not interested in restructuring their systems to the extent that doing so would undermine their abilities to govern.[55]

So, can economic modernization help bring about the right set of conditions for civil society groups to freely operate in Turkmenistan? At present, despite the possibility that the ruling Turkmen elite could ultimately decide to begin modernizing the economy, the likelihood of such an occurrence appears rather dim at the moment for several reasons. First, much of Turkmenistan's economy remains under state control, while the ruling regime has not indicated that it intends to engage in privatization anytime soon. In fact, "more than half" of the country's workforce is employed in the agricultural sector, which happens to remain under the de facto control of the government. Land also cannot be sold or exchanged, so many people are forced to lease from the government and pay high taxes.[56] This is significant because the absence of private property hinders civil society development, in that people will be disinclined to participate in such activities if the government regulates much of their economic livelihoods. On this point, Starr proclaims that "civil society is possible only when large numbers of citizens possess some form of private property and when their right to that property is protected by law."[57] Moreover, Starr seemingly argues that private property is a necessary precondition for civil society because the owning of property ushers in a new social mind-set, particularly in regard to the nature of sociopolitical relations: "Until large numbers of people throughout the region have gained a modicum of private property, it is unlikely that they will look to themselves and to one another to meet the needs of society, rather than to the government."[58]

Second, although Berdymuhammedov has recently sought to revitalize a variety of Niyazov-era pipeline projects and aspires to transport Turkmen natural gas reserves westward across the Caspian Sea and southward into South Asia, it appears as if Turkmenistan will continue to pump the bulk of its gas reserves to China and Russia for the time being. This is because the ruling Turkmen elite have not yet established an attractive business climate for foreign investors. As a result, since the government has not undertaken any "meaningful economic reforms" (such as "respecting property rights," "simplifying the bureaucracy," and "enforcing the rule of law") to improve the investment climate, foreign businesses are not expected to begin lining up to invest in Turkmenistan anytime soon.[59] That being the case, operating in tandem with the absence of private property, the largely unattractive business climate in Turkmenistan also stymies the growth of commercially oriented civil society groups. Consequently, this state of affairs further contributes to the underdeveloped nature of Turkmen civil society.

Third, it is important to note that economic modernization is unlikely to take place since the ruling Turkmen elite are cognizant as well as fearful of its long-term "political consequences." On this point, borrowing from

Huntington, if "one-party systems" are best defined as "the product of the efforts of a political elite to organize and to legitimate rule by one social force over another in a bifurcated society," then economic modernization will serve to empower the "excluded social force" with time. After all, as a society reaps the benefits that technology offers and people become more educated, it also becomes easier for citizens to engage in collective action against the state.[60] Hence, although the ruling Turkmen elite could potentially prove themselves adept at managing the sociopolitical effects of modernization in the short term, the fate of authoritarian rule in the long term would nonetheless ultimately grow more uncertain if they began initiating reforms. As such, it remains unlikely that a civil society will soon flourish, particularly on account of the predispositions of the current leadership in addition to the aforementioned structural conditions.

The Significance of Foreign Assistance

This chapter has thus far argued that, instead of experiencing democratization, Turkmenistan remains firmly "entrenched" in authoritarianism. Consequently, civil society remains very underdeveloped. Furthermore, although modernization theory has recently experienced somewhat of a revitalization in academia, this chapter argues that economic modernization will in all likelihood not lead to the development of a robust Turkmen civil society, at least in the short-term future, mainly because the ruling Turkmen elite seek to retain their hold on political power. That said, the issue of whether the West should foster civil society development in countries like Turkmenistan merits discussion. Overall, Charles Ziegler has already noted that the governing style of ruling elites, coupled with the "political culture" of the region in general, has led to the development of an alternative brand of "cooperative" civil society in Central Asia, which differs significantly from the more "contestative" brand prevalent in Europe that helped usher in the 1989 revolutions and the collapse of communism.[61] Although this chapter agrees with such an insightful observation, it is important to note as well that without significant outside backing, civil society groups interested in promoting causes such as respect for human rights and increased government accountability will not be able to flourish in a harsh political environment. Hence, authoritarianism will continue to reign supreme in countries like Turkmenistan, especially if democratically oriented countries choose to look the other way and not vociferously protest when such regimes forcefully repress civil society groups. Thus, although the prospects for economic modernization leading to civil society development in Turkmenistan appear rather dim at the moment, it is still possible that an independent civil society could emerge over time. The essential point worth emphasizing again, however, is that such a civil society would only (possibly) arise in Turkmenistan with foreign assistance.

In time, perhaps the world will bear witness to the ruling Turkmen elite lessening its grip over civil society activities with the integration of Turkmenistan into the global economy, thereby allowing for the country's "cooperative" civil society to evolve into a more "contestative" European-style civil society. Yet this chapter argues that such an occurrence is likely to come to pass only when democratically oriented countries choose to make fostering civil society development in countries like Turkmenistan a priority and begin pressing the Turkmen government to embark on implementing meaningful reforms. In terms of strategy, since it is arguably unrealistic to expect the ruling Turkmen elite to experiment with the political system, this chapter posits that it would be best for democratically oriented countries to start by stressing to the ruling Turkmen elite the benefits of gradually reforming the economy. On this point, in drawing on Olga Avdeyeva's work, democratically oriented countries could plausibly make use of a set of strategies such as "coercion," "persuasion," and "acculturation" to try to induce a change in the behavior of the Turkmen government. Still, it bears noting that there is no guarantee that any sustained effort in terms of promoting civil society development in Turkmenistan will yield positive results. That said, Ashgabat could prove to be susceptible to outside pressure, if not by means of "persuasion" alone then perhaps via "coercion" (which, according to Avdeyeva, entails utilizing "material rewards and punishments"), "acculturation" (which, Avdeyeva argues, is "driven by cognitive pressures to adopt socially legitimated beliefs, ideas, and behaviors"), or some combination thereof.[62]

In summary, this chapter argues that in order for civil society to subsist in a harsh political environment like Turkmenistan, such groups in all likelihood require the support of an influential outside state actor (or a community of states working in tandem) along with a host of INGOs to champion their cause on the world stage and bring added pressure onto the ruling regime that restricts them. To be certain, the championing of a more vibrant and independent civil society may not necessarily force the Turkmen government's hand in terms of initiating a change in its ways. But at this point in time, it seems even more unlikely that civil society in Turkmenistan will come to flourish on its own.

This chapter argues that in light of the predispositions of the current leadership, coupled with certain structural conditions, civil society in Turkmenistan will remain in an underdeveloped state for the foreseeable future. Yet in spite of this bleak forecast, it is important to note that although the constraints on civil society in Turkmenistan are powerful, they are not necessarily absolute. To the contrary, they can be loosened over time, but only if the ruling Turkmen elite somehow come to appreciate the long-term benefits of engaging in meaningful reform. Such a perspective, in turn, has the greatest chance of achieving predominance among the ruling Turkmen elite with active encouragement from the international community. Only one question thus calls out for an answer at this time: in considering the challenges and opportunities facing modern Central Asia today, do the democratically oriented countries of the world view fostering civil society development in countries like Turkmenistan as a worthy or futile cause?

Notes

1. For more on this definition, see Robert A. Dahl, *Polyarchy: Participation and Opposition* (New Haven, CT: Yale University Press, 1971), 1–8. Accordingly, Dahl defines polyarchies as "regimes that have been substantially popularized and liberalized, that is, highly inclusive and extensively open to public contestation" (8).

2. For a discussion on the origins of the Turkmenbashi cult, see Michael Denison, "The Art of the Impossible: Political Symbolism and the Creation of National Identity and Collective Memory in Post-Soviet Turkmenistan," *Europe-Asia Studies* 61, no. 7 (2009): 1167–87. See also Mark Steyn, "One-Man Stan," *Atlantic Monthly*, March 2007, http://www.theatlantic.com/doc/200703/steyn-niyazov; Freedom House, "Country Report: Turkmenistan," in *Nations in Transit 2008*, http://www.freedomhouse.org/report/nations-transit/2008/turkmenistan; Paul Theroux, "Letter from Turkmenistan: The Golden Man: Saparmurat Niyazov's Reign of Insanity," *New Yorker*, May 28, 2007, 55–65.

3. Chemen Durdiyeva, "Berdimukhammedov Embarks on Significant Educational Reforms," Central Asia–Caucasus Institute Analyst, June 27, 2007, pp. 3–5, http://www.cacianalyst.org/publications/analytical-articles/item/11435-analytical-articles-caci-analyst-2007-6-27-art-11435.html; Joshua Kucera, "New Turkmen President Tones Down Despotism," *San Francisco Chronicle*, August 28, 2007, http://www.sfgate.com/cgi-bin/article.cgi?f=/c/a/2007/08/28/MNPNR5FMB.DTL&type=printable.

4. "Turkmen TV Dropped the Logo of the Golden Profile of the Late President," *Kommersant,* July 9, 2007, p. 6, http://enews.ferghana.ru/article.php?id=2028; Bruce Pannier, "Turkmenistan: April Returns to Ashgabat," Radio Free Europe/Radio Liberty, April 25, 2008, http://www.rferl.org/content/article/1109635.html; David Stern, "A Turkmen Dismantles Reminders of Old Rulers," *New York Times,* May 5, 2008, http://www.nytimes.com/2008/05/05/world/asia/05turkmen.html; Farangis Najibullah, "Turkmenistan Redenominates Currency, Further Dismantles Personality Cult," Radio Free Europe/Radio Liberty, January 2, 2009, http://www.rferl.org/content/Turkmenistan_Redenominates_Currency_Further_Dismantles_Niyazov_Personality_Cult/1365812.html.

5. With respect to the term "de-Niyazovization," see Sebastien Peyrouse, "Berdymukhammedov's Turkmenistan: A Modest Shift in Domestic and Social Politics," *Journal of Central Asian Studies* 19, no. 1 (2010): 79.

6. With respect to corruption, Transparency International awarded Turkmenistan a score of 1.6 for the year 2011, ranking the country at 177 (tied with Sudan and Uzbekistan) out of a total of 182. See Transparency International, Corruption Perceptions Index 2011, http://cpi.transparency.org/cpi2011/results/.

7. Human Rights Watch, "Turkmenistan," in *World Report 2011,* http://www.hrw.org/world-report-2011/turkmenistan.

8. See London School of Economics, Centre for Civil Society, http://www.lse.ac.uk/CCS/home.aspx, accessed October 11, 2012. LSE's Centre for Civil Society has been closed. To view the definition in its entirety, see Victoria Clement, "Creating Space for Civil Society in Turkmenistan," working paper, National Council for Eurasian and East European Research, 2009, http://www.ucis.pitt.edu/nceeer/2009_824-02h_Clement.pdf.

9. Larry Diamond, "Toward Democratic Consolidation," *Journal of Democracy* 5, no. 3 (1994): 4–17; Robert D. Putnam, *Making Democracy Work* (Princeton, NJ: Princeton University Press, 1993). Diamond defines civil society as "the realm of organized social life that is voluntary, self-generating, (largely) self-supporting, autonomous from the state, and bound by a legal order or set of shared rules" (5).

10. Diamond, "Toward Democratic Consolidation," 7–11; Samuel P. Huntington, "Will Countries Become More Democratic?" *Political Science Quarterly* 99 (Summer 1984): 204; Seymour M. Lipset, *Political Man* (Baltimore: Johns Hopkins University Press, 1981), 52. Diamond also argues that civil society groups help "recruit" leaders, "disseminate" information, and "strengthen" democratic institutions. In doing so, civil society helps legitimize the state (9–11).

11. Charles E. Ziegler, "Civil Society, Political Stability, and State Power in Central Asia: Cooperation and Contestation," *Democratization* 17, no. 5 (2010): 795–825.

12. Ibid., 815–16. Ziegler's research on civil society development in Central Asia focuses mainly on Kazakhstan.

13. United Nations High Commissioner for Refugees, Law of Turkmenistan on

Public Associations, October 21, 2003, http://www.unhcr.org/refworld/country,,NATLEGBOD,LEGISLATION,TKM,4562d8cf2,44a3c5584,0.html. See also Law of Turkmenistan on Public Associations, October 21, 2003, http://www.unhcr.org/refworld/pdfid/44a3c5584.pdf.

14. For a discussion on how Turkmen citizens perceive the 2003 Law of Turkmenistan on Public Associations, see Clement, "Creating Space for Civil Society in Turkmenistan," 5.

15. Ibid. See also Victoria Clement, "Grassroots Educational Initiatives in Turkmenistan," in *Globalization on the Margins: Education and Postsocialist Transformations in Central Asia,* ed. I. Silova (Charlotte, NC: Information Age Publishing, 2010), 354–62.

16. Amnesty International, "Individuals Continue to Be at Risk of Violations in Turkmenistan," December 12, 2009, http://www.amnesty.org/en/library/asset/EUR61/001/2009/en/d17a0647-f8ef-11dd-92e7-c59f81373cf2/eur610012009en.pdf. With respect to Farid Tukhbatullin receiving "credible threats against his life," see Crude Accountability, "Reform in Turkmenistan—A Convenient Façade: An Analysis of President Berdymukhammedov's First Four Years in Power," 2011, p. 13, http://crudeaccountability.org/wp-content/uploads/2012/04/201104-ReformInTurkmenistan.pdf . Crude Accountability describes itself as "a consensus-driven organization that is committed to environmental and social justice and to the protection of the Caspian Sea." See the Crude Accountability website, http://crudeaccountability.org/mission/staff-board/.

17. Crude Accountability, "Reform in Turkmenistan," 15.

18. Ibid., 12.

19. In wording my definition of democracy, I drew on the following: Dahl, *Polyarchy;* Charles E. Lindblom, *Politics and Markets: The World's Political-Economic Systems* (New York: Basic Books, 1977); David Beetham, "Freedom as the Foundation," *Journal of Democracy* 15, no. 4 (2004): 61–75; Guillermo O'Donnell, "Why the Rule of Law Matters," *Journal of Democracy* 15, no. 4 (2004): 32–46; Diamond, "Toward Democratic Consolidation"; and Samuel P. Huntington, *Political Order in Changing Societies* (New Haven, CT: Yale University Press, 1968).

20. In wording my definition of authoritarianism, I drew on the following: Juan J. Linz, *Totalitarian and Authoritarian Regimes* (Boulder, CO: Lynne Rienner, 2000); Jason Brownlee, *Authoritarianism in an Age of Democratization* (New York: Cambridge University Press, 2007); Lucan Way, "Authoritarian State Building and the Sources of Regime Competitiveness in the Fourth Wave: The Cases of Belarus, Moldova, Russia, and Ukraine," *World Politics* 57, no. 2 (2005): 231–61; Eva Bellin, "The Robustness of Authoritarianism in the Middle East: Exceptionalism in Comparative Perspective," *Comparative Politics* 36, no. 2 (2004): 139–57; and Steven Levitsky and Lucan Way, "The Rise of Competitive Authoritarianism," *Journal of Democracy* 13, no. 2 (2002): 51–65.

21. Freedom House, "Country Report: Turkmenistan," in *Nations in Transit 2011,* http://www.freedomhouse.org/template.cfm?page=22&year=2011&coun

try=8153; Freedom House, "Combined Average Ratings—Independent Countries," in *Nations in Transit 2011*, http://www.freedomhouse.org/sites/default/files/inline_images/CombinedAverageRatings%28IndependentCountries%29FIW2011.pdf. Freedom House scores are measured in terms of a seven-point scale for "political rights" and "civil liberties," with low and high scores indicating positive and negative trends, respectively.

22. Monty G. Marshall and Keith Jaggers, "Polity IV Country Report 2010: Turkmenistan," Polity IV Country Reports, Center for Systemic Peace, June 1, 2011, http://www.systemicpeace.org/polity/Turkmenistan2010.pdf.

23. "The World's 10 Worst Dictators," *Parade Magazine*, March 22, 2009, http://www.parade.com/dictators/2009/the-worlds-10-worst-dictators.html?index=9.

24. Human Rights Watch, "Turkmenistan."

25. Larry Diamond, "Thinking about Hybrid Regimes," *Journal of Democracy* 13, no. 2 (2002): 21–35. Diamond stresses that this classification framework is "illustrative" and not "definitive" in nature, since "most regimes are 'mixed' to one degree or another" in that they possess democratic and nondemocratic features (28, 33). Diamond defines "liberal democracy" in his note 18.

26. Levitsky and Way, "Rise of Competitive Authoritarianism."

27. Michael Geyer and Sheila Fitzpatrick, "After Totalitarianism: Stalinism and Nazism Compared," in *Beyond Totalitarianism: Stalinism and Nazism Compared*, ed. M. Geyer and S. Fitzpatrick (New York: Cambridge University Press, 2009), 12. This definition can be found in I. T. Frolov and A. V. Ado, eds. *Filosofskii slovar* [Philosophical Dictionary], 6th ed., revised and expanded (Moscow: Izdatel'stvo politicheskoi literatury, 1991) (in Russian).

28. Linz, *Totalitarian and Authoritarian Regimes*, 65–142.

29. Ibid., 151–53.

30. Ibid., 152.

31. Steyn, "One-Man Stan."

32. Stephen J. Blank, *Turkmenistan and Central Asia after Niyazov* (Carlisle, PA: Strategic Studies Institute, 2007), 21–22, http://www.strategicstudiesinstitute.army.mil/pdffiles/pub791.pdf.

33. Diamond, "Thinking about Hybrid Regimes," 30. Diamond labels Turkmenistan as the only "politically closed" postcommunist authoritarian regime. He labels the other Central Asian countries "hegemonic electoral authoritarian" regimes.

34. With respect to "authoritarian entrenchment," see Levitsky and Way, "Rise of Competitive Authoritarianism," 60. However, this term is not actually defined in the article.

35. Michael L. Ross, "Does Oil Hinder Democracy?" *World Politics* 53, no. 3 (2001): 325–61.

36. Peter C. Glover, "Turkmenistan Joins the National Gas Elite: The South Yolotan-Osman Gas Field Is One of the World's Largest," *Energy Tribune*, December 8, 2008, http://www.energytribune.com/articles.cfm/1046/

Turkmenistan-Joins-the-Natural-Gas-Elite-The-South-Yolotan-Osman-Gas-Field-is-one-of-the-Worlds-Largest.

37. Paul Bradbury, "Oil and Gasoline Prices in Countries of the Former Soviet Union," Suite 101.com, February 13, 2011, http://suite101.com/article/oil-and-gasoline-prices-in-countries-of-the-former-soviet-union-a346878 (site discontinued). For more on the cost of utilities and gasoline in Turkmenistan, see Theroux, "Letter from Turkmenistan," 60.

38. Pauline Jones Luong and Erika Weinthal, *Oil Is Not a Curse: Ownership Structure and Institutions in Soviet Successor States* (New York: Cambridge University Press, 2006), 80.

39. "Turkmenistan Economy," Economy Watch, June 30, 2010, http://www.economywatch.com/world_economy/turkmenistan/.

40. Bellin, "Robustness of Authoritarianism in the Middle East," 144; see also Charles J. Sullivan, "Halk, Watan, Berdymuhammedov! Political Transition and Regime Continuity in Turkmenistan," *Journal of Central Asian Studies*, forthcoming. Incidentally, Theroux argues that revenues derived from natural gas exports in 2006 amounted to around $3 billion ("Letter from Turkmenistan," 59). Overall, it is worth reemphasizing that there is no direct evidence showing that a substantial portion of the proceeds from gas sales is allotted toward financing the Ministry of National Security. That said, quoting Freedom House, "The Ministry of National Security (MNB) has the responsibilities held by the Committee for State Security during the Soviet period—namely, to ensure that the regime remains in power through tight control of society and by discouraging dissent." Furthermore, alongside the MNB, Freedom House singles out the Ministry of Internal Affairs and the "Presidential Guard" as agencies tasked with similar stately responsibilities. Members of such agencies, Freedom House argues, "receive favorable treatment relative to the rest of the population, such as higher salaries and privileged accommodation." See Freedom House, "Country Report Turkmenistan," 2008.

41. S. Frederick Starr, "Civil Society in Central Asia," in *Civil Society in Central Asia*, ed. M. H. Ruffin and D. Waugh (Seattle: University of Washington Press, 1999), 31–32. In Starr's defense, his chapter was written not too long after the collapse of the Soviet Union. In addition, Starr's argument remains valid, for he acknowledges in this same work that the Soviet regime "suppressed" civil society in Central Asia (31–32).

42. For a discussion as to why the Bolsheviks, from the beginning of communist rule, refused to share political power, see Z, "To the Stalin Mausoleum," *Daedalus* 119, no. 1 (Winter 1990): 295–344.

43. Geoffrey Hosking, *The Awakening of the Soviet Union* (Cambridge, MA: Harvard University Press, 1990), 35.

44. With respect to the Soviet Union's handling of dissidents, see Joshua Rubenstein, *Soviet Dissidents: Their Struggle for Human Rights* (Boston: Beacon Press, 1980); and Ludmilla Alexeyeva, *Soviet Dissent: Contemporary Movements for National, Religious, and Human Rights*, trans. Carol Pearce and John Glad

(Middletown, CT: Wesleyan University Press, 1985). With respect to Khrushchev's de-Stalinization campaign, see William Taubman, *Khrushchev: The Man and His Era* (New York: W. W. Norton, 2003).

45. Alec Nove, *Glasnost in Action: Cultural Renaissance in Russia* (Cambridge, MA: Unwin Hyman, 1990). I also recommend William Taubman and Jane Taubman, *Moscow Spring* (New York: Simon and Schuster, 1989).

46. Sullivan, "Halk, Watan, Berdymuhammedov!"

47. Freedom House, "Country Report: Turkmenistan," in *Nations in Transit Report 2006*, http://www.freedomhouse.org/report/nations-transit/2006/turkmenistan. Freedom House calculations here are derived from estimates provided by the exiled oppositionist Republican Party of Turkmenistan; Aisha Berdyeva, "Turkmenistan: President Pardons with One Hand, Purges with the Other," *Eurasia Insight*, August 23, 2007, http://www.eurasianet.org/departments/insight/articles/eav082307.shtml; "Turkmen President Dismisses Two Senior Officials," *International Herald Tribune*, May 22, 2007. See also "Turkmen President Sacks Two Senior Officials," *People's Daily* Online, May 23, 2007, http://english.peopledaily.com.cn/200705/23/eng20070523_376967.html; Sullivan, "Halk, Watan, Berdymuhammedov!"; "Turkmen Police Reforms Insufficient," Institute for War and Peace Reporting, November 8, 2007, http://iwpr.net/report-news/turkmen-police-reforms-insufficient. According to the institute, Berdymuhammedov's campaign to "shake up" the Interior Ministry was (allegedly) in response to charges of corruption in the police forces. That said, the institute is of the opinion that only removing high-level officials from their posts will not serve to change the "culture" of the Interior Ministry. One could thus reasonably presume that Berdymuhammedov initiated this latest "deck shuffling" campaign not to combat corruption but to replace ranking Niyazov-era officials with a new group of subordinates loyal to the new Turkmen president.

48. For a nuanced discussion on the causes of political instability in Kyrgyzstan, see Eric McGlinchey, *Chaos, Violence, Dynasty: Politics and Islam in Central Asia* (Pittsburgh, PA: University of Pittsburgh Press, 2011).

49. Sullivan, "Halk, Watan, Berdymuhammedov!" See also Luca Anceschi, *Turkmenistan's Foreign Policy: Positive Neutrality and the Consolidation of the Turkmen Regime* (London: Taylor & Francis, 2008).

50. Stefan Mitas, "Turkmenistan's Economic Bubble," *Bloomberg Business Week*, February 10, 2009, http://www.businessweek.com/globalbiz/content/feb2009/gb20090210_156547.htm.

51. Ronald Inglehart, *Modernization and Post-modernization: Cultural, Economic, and Political Change in 43 Societies* (Princeton, NJ: Princeton University Press, 1997), quote on 5.

52. Carles Boix and Susan C. Stokes, "Endogenous Democratization," *World Politics* 55, no. 4 (2003): 517–49.

53. Huntington, *Political Order in Changing Societies*. See also Samuel P. Hun-

tington, "Political Development and Political Decay," *World Politics* 17, no. 3 (April 1965): 386–430.

54. Bruce Bueno de Mesquita and George W. Downs, "Development and Democracy," *Foreign Affairs* (September/October 2005): 77–86.

55. Thomas Carothers, "The Sequencing Fallacy," *Journal of Democracy* 18, no. 1 (2007): 12–27.

56. Myrat Nurgeldi, "Turkmen Farmers Caught between Collectivization, Privatization," Radio Free Europe/Radio Liberty, March 27, 2010, http://www.rferl.org/content/Turkmen_Farmers_Caught_Between_Collectivization_Privatization/1995317.html.

57. Starr, "Civil Society in Central Asia," 32.

58. Ibid.

59. Charles J. Sullivan, "Pipeline Politics in the Post-Soviet Space: The View from Ashgabat," *Journal of Energy and Development* 34 (April/May 2011): 121–28.

60. Samuel P. Huntington, "Social and Institutional Dynamics of One-Party Systems," in *Authoritarian Politics in Modern Society: The Dynamics of Established One-Party Systems*, ed. S. Huntington and C. Moore (New York: Basic Books, 1970), 11, 17–19.

61. Ziegler, "Civil Society, Political Stability, and State Power," 795–96.

62. Olga Avdeyeva, "When Do States Comply with International Treaties? Policies on Violence against Women in Post-communist Countries," *International Studies Quarterly* 51 (2007): 877–900.

10

Bridging the Divide between Neoliberal and Communal Civil Society in Tajikistan

Sabine Freizer

As others have written in this volume, civil society is a highly debated term, and it is being translated in different ways and forms throughout Central Asia. Among all the countries examined here, Tajikistan is undoubtedly the furthest from the states of Western Europe where the concept had its origins in eighteenth-century modern thought. It lived through a vicious civil war that started in May 1992 and ended after the signature of the General Agreement on the Establishment of Peace and National Accord in June 1997. Since then peace and stability have gradually been secured, but many problems remain.

With the lowest per capita GDP among the former Soviet countries, Tajikistan is the poorest country in Europe and Central Asia. The global economic crisis hit the country hard, with the annual rate of economic growth plummeting to just 3.9 percent at the height of the crisis in 2009, when it had been close to 10 percent in 2002 and 2003 (by 2011 it had recovered somewhat to almost 7 percent).[1] Infrastructure collapse, energy shortages, and plummeting access to quality medical and educational services threaten future growth. Corruption, weak rule of law enforcement, lack of competitive elections, and poor access to diversified sources of information sustain an increasingly centralized and autocratic presidential regime. Poverty, inequality, unemployment, and social exclusion risk becoming a source of future conflict.[2] In this environment, what forms of civil society can take hold and help society protect its interests?

Previous studies of civil society in Tajikistan have tended to describe it as divided and weak.[3] Some have gone so far as to claim that "the civil society discourse is not a useful discourse through which to examine present day Tajikistan."[4] A decade ago the main criticism of studies of civil society in Tajikistan was that they were overly focused on nongovernmental organizations (NGOs), which were of peripheral importance in the country, and did not sufficiently pay attention to "local partners who matter" in a civil society that "is predicated on the social fabric as it exists and is evolving."[5]

Since then, and especially since a 2005 special issue of *Central Asian Survey* on civil society in Central Asia and the Caucasus, studies of civil society in Tajikistan have taken a much wider definition of civil society and sought to analyze its character, activities, and effectiveness. In 2004 I argued that Tajik civil society was deeply divided between communal and neoliberal forms, with the latter best represented by NGOs and the former by traditional community groups.[6] This division appeared to be hindering civil society from exerting influence on political, economic, or social change. Yet in the aforementioned *Central Asian Survey* special issue I revised this conclusion, finding that, based on two case studies of civil society organizations, one NGO and one group of community organizations, there was room to conclude that the civil society dichotomy was not as wide as originally assumed and Tajik civil society was worthy of international support.[7] This chapter is largely based on my 2005 article but updated to further my arguments and findings based on newer writings on civil society in Tajikistan and some country-level developments.

Rival Concepts of Civil Society

As described in the introduction of this book, civil society can be divided into different ideal types, which reflect how the concept has been the reinvented during the past twenty years in different geographic regions of the globe.[8] In the former communist states of Eastern Europe and western parts of the Soviet Union, civil society was largely understood to fit within a neoliberal definition, first represented primarily by activist associations and later by nongovernmental organizations. In mainly non-European contexts, especially in countries with Muslim majorities, civil society was conceptualized as being more communal, made up of a myriad of groups above the family unit, including at the level of the extended family, neighborhood, or village, and bringing people together because of common interests, beliefs, sense of identity, or religious persuasion.[9]

Over the past five years observers of civil society in Central Asia have tended to agree that both of these types of civil society are evident in postwar Tajikistan.[10] This is not surprising, as the country is not only a postcommunist but also a non-Western Muslim-majority society. Tajikistan's current-day political, economic, and social environment is comparable to a certain degree to the east central European one of the 1980s and to the Muslim world's in the 1990s. In the following section I will thus take these two civil society "ideal types" as a starting point to demonstrate that communal civil society has a long history in the country, while neoliberal civil society is mostly being created from scratch.

Neoliberal Definitions of Civil Society

In Tajikistan, as in other parts of East and Central Europe, neoliberal forms of civil society began to appear in the late 1980s. The political openness that accompanied glasnost offered public space for the creation of new organizations that focused on environmental protection, the promotion of Tajik language and culture, women's issues, religious revival, and so on. They attracted mainly the urban middle classes—scientists, professors, teachers, and students—and bypassed many rural communities. Some of these civil society activists were dissidents and strongly believed in the need for fundamental change.[11] Activists in Rastokhez, which was founded under the inspiration of Popular Front parties in other republics of the Soviet Union and developed a nationwide political program, may be considered to be part of this group.[12] But overall the new civil society organizations defended local concerns and interests and cooperated with state structures. One such group was Ehyoi Khojand, founded in September 1989 by city intellectuals who successfully organized a referendum in 1990 to return the original name of Khojand to what was then called the city of Leninabad (Sughd region).[13]

During and immediately after the Tajik civil war, a shift occurred in the composition of neoliberal civil society as many of these urban-based movements disappeared and local NGOs were founded. Glasnost-era activists joined political parties, such as the Democratic Party of Tajikistan, chose to leave public life, or were displaced or killed by the conflict. Meanwhile NGOs appeared to meet the large-scale humanitarian and social needs of war-ravaged populations. The number of NGOs increased dramatically. The International Center for Not-for-Profit Law (ICNL) estimated that a total of twenty-seven hundred civil society organizations (CSOs) were registered as noncommercial organizations (NCOs) in Tajikistan in 2006, compared with thirty-three groups in 1993. But since then the number of registered groups has stagnated around two thousand as new legislation in 2009 forced all previously legal not-for-profits to reregister and some procedures have become much more difficult to complete.[14] Several prominent NGOs have been either shut down or threatened with closure in the past few years—as was the case in October 2012 when the human rights group Amparo was closed, allegedly for operating without a proper license.[15]

NGO development has mainly been an urban phenomenon, with large swaths of rural territory remaining largely untouched. The NGOs were fundamentally different from the early glasnost-era organizations because they were less advocacy based, and so they became heavily engaged in service delivery. Initially the first NGO leaders organized out of a narrow spirit of self-help. As one NGO director explained, in 1993 "we understood that the country was not going to do anything to help its citizens, so we had to unite to protect . . . our friends, our colleagues, to create new spheres of activity."[16] International development agencies provided the essential funding, skills development, and access to broader NGO networks to sustain the sector's development.

Communal Definitions of Civil Society

In the theoretical discourse, a second definition of civil society, which I prefer to term "communal," has gained currency over the past decade. Communal civil society is less focused on formal structures and organizations but more on the host of informal group activities and meeting places that connect individuals, build trust, encourage reciprocity, and facilitate exchange of views on matters of public concern. Communal civil society most often involves traditional networks of solidarity, based on primordial communities of kinship and patronage bound by a set territory in the local community, the site of face-to-face encounters. Based on this definition, civil society is mainly concerned with ensuring that all members of the group have the necessary means for survival. It organizes to offer services, community infrastructure, and other essentials. In this context *civility* signifies providing the basic material and economic conditions to people to ensure that they can function in the group. It does not, however, focus on the promotion of equality of political and social rights.

It can be argued that communal civil society has existed in Tajikistan for centuries, resisting full state capture during the Soviet era.[17] Still today trust and solidarity networks are primarily built around kinship ties. Through kinship ties (the *avlod*), individuals express and defend their common interests, providing mutual aid and support.[18] Communal civil society based on kinship traditionally has been strengthened by links based on proximity. In the pre-Soviet era *mahallas* developed in urban areas as relatively independent associations of citizens. They brought people living in the same territory together on a voluntary basis. *Mahallas* were self-governing, and members gathered regularly to exchange information, settle community problems, provide support for life-cycle rituals, and define public opinion. They were not religious organizations and had no function in proselytizing, but *mahalla* committees often met in neighborhood mosques and teahouses (*chaihana*).[19] To regulate personal and family problems inhabitants turned to councils of elders (*shura aksakal*). They helped organize traditional feasts and gatherings (*maraka*) to celebrate births, marriages, and funerals. In Soviet Tajikistan the traditions of community voluntary action (*hashar*) and community giving to help those in need (*sadaqa*) were largely maintained in rural areas. *Mahallas* were reincarnated in the kolkhoz, where they organized some service provision and local infrastructure maintenance and resolved community disputes.[20] At times communal civil society worked with or behind the state, but rarely in Tajikistan's history did it openly oppose the state.[21]

In the late 1980s and early 1990s political entrepreneurs—regional postcommunist leaders and traditional Sufi leaders of popular Islam—successfully mobilized rural communities around religion and regional identity (*localism*) through traditional solidarity structures of communal civil society. In a period of mounting political and economic instability these elites appealed to citizens' local-level grievances and search for identity. Thus, as of 1990 Islamists, many linked to the Islamic Renaissance Party, successfully mobilized traditional groups using kin- and territory-based networks, especially in the Vaksh and Karategin Valleys.[22] They acted through the large number of informal mosques, *chaihana*, and madrassas that had been constructed in rural areas in the 1980s through *hashar* and the tacit or open support of kolkhoz leaders.

During the Tajik civil war, communal civil society played a significant yet ambiguous role. On one hand *mahallas'* status increased as international humanitarian aid agencies often distributed aid through them. On the other hand, warlords, field commanders, and other militarized groups undermined traditional community leaders' position in society. Villagers asked them for assistance and protection, rather than turning to the *mahalla* or *aksakal.* To build trust within local communities, warlords carried out many functions of communal civil society, organizing *maraka, sadaqa,* and village improvement projects.[23]

This continued for more than a decade after the war, when in some communities, especially in the Karategin Valley, warlords continued to wield much power to impose their worldview. In 2002 one interviewee described how warlords could, for example, ban dancing at weddings or female attendance in school beyond the ninth grade.[24] Almost a decade later, these warlords continue to exert pressure and are being joined by younger insurgents, some with contacts to global Salafi-inspired jihadists.[25] These groups are far from civil and at times impose their strict interpretations of Islam on their communities through communal structures.

International Cooperation with Civil Society

When international development agencies began to operate in Tajikistan during and immediately after the civil war, their civil society development effort was premised on a neoliberal understanding of civil society. International donors were more eager to strengthen new NGOs than to build the capacities of communal initiatives. They were weary of partnering with communal groups, considering that such groups reinforced nationalist tendencies and corrupted structures and promoted inequality—and were thus part of the causes of the Tajik conflict, rather than its resolution. Several authors at the time were critical of international donors' preference for dealing with NGO staff over indigenous community leaders.[26]

Nevertheless, by 2002 a change was taking place, as international organizations became enamored with the concept of "community development." The United Nations, World Bank, USAID, and Aga Khan Foundation (AKF) began to look for new ways to collaborate with Tajikistan's often isolated, poor, and desperately needy rural communities.[27] Here, where no local NGOs functioned, they had few alternatives but to work with communal civil society or local government. The UNDP/UNOPS Reconstruction, Rehabilitation, and Development Program became actively involved in supporting the latter through *jamoat* development committees. The Aga Khan Foundation chose to cooperate with the former, as will be described further below.[28]

However, the international reorientation toward communal civil society is not without its critics. As Charles Buxton pointed out in 2009, international donors' "discovery" of communal civil society was quickly followed by Central Asian governments' counterattack and their attempts to enlist and co-opt civil society actors in the creation of new national ideologies.[29] Failing to deliver on earlier promises of democratic transition, increasingly authoritarian governments sought legitimacy by reference to the development of civil society, based on the embrace of supposedly traditional values and eastern "communal rights" (as opposed to individual rights). Western and international donors' endorsement of communal civil society fed into authoritarian governments' aspirations to amalgamate state and society into one. Central Asian leaders' embrace of communal civil society (for example, *mahallas*) was also an attempt to transform them into state agents. While village organizations might prove convenient partners and appear more rooted in the community than their NGO counterparts, Suda Masaru cautions that "the new politics of civil society can be hijacked to justify the continuation of the arbitrary control of administrators who are not accountable to citizens."[30] In the conclusion of her comprehensive article on community development in Central Asia, Lucy Earle warns that the uncritical promotion of traditional community groups by donors "can have negative development consequences, particularly for women and marginalized groups. . . . Donors are shying away from addressing the underlying structures of power."[31]

Did donor agencies find the right civil society partners in Tajikistan? Did neoliberal or communal civil society play a more effective role over the past decade? To respond to this question I will consider two case studies, observed in depth in 2002–2004, including a Tajik NGO that fits into the neoliberal conceptualization of civil society and several Tajik village organizations that belong to communal civil society. Based on this I will test the hypothesis offered in the introduction that neoliberal and communal forms of civil society in postwar Tajikistan are increasingly close and able to cooperate.

Postwar Neoliberal Civil Society: The Case of the NGO Ghamkhori

One of the largest, most sustainable NGOs to develop in postwar Tajikistan was Ghamkhori (Assistance), based in the southern town of Kurgan Tuppe. Created in 1997, the initiative was inspired by the liberal motto "it's better to teach how to fish than to give fish." From the onset Ghamkhori's mission was to break the war-affected populations' dependence on external aid. Ghamkhori started its activities in heavily destroyed rural areas, targeting returning refugees and displaced persons as well as those who had never fled. According to the organization's statute, Ghamkhori's goal was to improve the socioeconomic existence of the population by increasing levels of popular knowledge in the fields of health and women's and children's rights protection. It was first registered in May 1999 and reregistered in September 2007 as a public organization.

Ghamkhori represents a pure example of a Western-driven initiative, as the impetus to create and register the NGO did not come from a group of Tajiks but from an international consultant and researcher completing a Ph.D. on Tajikistan.[32] She brought the official founders of the organization together. None of them had been significantly involved in prewar civil society organizations or appeared driven by a clear mission that had developed through wartime activism. Ghamkhori's leadership and core staff were composed of middle-class professionals, in many cases ethnic or national minorities, whose status was being challenged in the postwar era. They included Uzbeks and Russians as well as Tajiks from various regional backgrounds. From 1997 to 1999 the organization had twelve staff and by 2000 it had forty. The leadership of the NGO made a concerted attempt to ensure that staff would not be selected based on friendship or family ties. People were hired after a lengthy interview process, based on their professional skills and ability to be communicative, innovative, and critical.

Even though most of those who worked for Ghamkhori acknowledged that they were initially drawn to Ghamkhori because it offered them a good salary, rather than for ideological reasons, they claimed that their engagement in the NGO had a transformative effect. Staff described undergoing a significant mentality change since joining Ghamkhori—which made them more aware of women's roles and rights and the importance of community action. The director of the organization, Bahodur, admitted that, in 1997, "I did not think that women have any rights. Only after I started working here did I start to understand that women's rights are not optional but something that must be exercised."[33] Several of the women staff members gained new confidence and decided to further their education and public engagement. Asked whether they may one day return to a job in the state sector, many explained that they preferred to work in an NGO like Ghamkhori because it allowed them more independence and was based on team effort. One member explained, "It's different working here. It is work which is close to a person's soul, where no one dictates what you should do. You work as you wish to, in a way that makes you proud of your effort."[34]

Ghamkhori was committed to promoting the liberal notion that citizens should take responsibility for their individual welfare, encouraging local communities to take on new responsibilities under conditions of declining state provision of public goods. The NGO filled in gaps where the Soviet system of social services allocation had collapsed. It also addressed serious new health and social problems that were the consequence of the conflict and postcommunist transition. For example, the population of southern Tajikistan was confronted with a rapid spread of infectious disease as access to clean drinking water plummeted. To tackle these and similar problems, Ghamkhori organized interactive courses on hygiene, reproductive health services, and alternative medicine. Dissemination of this information was necessary because, according to Bahodur, "people did not know how to survive or to protect themselves" after the disintegration of the Soviet-era social safety net.[35] The organization sought to change individuals' basic expectation that health care and disease prevention are the business of the government to a general acceptance that they are first and foremost a personal responsibility.

Ghamkhori's second aim was to improve women's and children's rights protection. Women were identified as Ghamkhori's main target group because of the decrease in their status since the early 1990s. Ghamkhori considered that it would be successful in its work "when after our lessons a woman's psychological vision of being a slave is broken. She understands that she has rights and that she can also express her opinions. She realizes that men and women are equal."[36]

Ghamkhori's programs

Unlike many NGOs, Ghamkhori has concentrated its efforts on carrying out one main program since 1997, entitled the Khatlon Social Mobilization

Project (KSMP). Teams of four teachers (for boys, girls, men, and women) and a midwife weekly visited communities for six to eight months, providing educational sessions in hygiene, reproductive health, family relations, and rights, as well as basic medical services and training. KSMP also provided rural teachers and midwives with interactive teaching and consultation skills. The goal of the project was to "mobilize and empower communities as a whole, and women in particular, to improve their own lives."[37] Since 2005 the project has also explicitly aimed at HIV/AIDS information and prevention.

Though the project sought to initiate a debate on citizens' rights and responsibilities, it began by addressing less controversial health concerns. In choosing this approach the organization focused on building trust, taking into account local mentalities and beliefs. Their positions as professionals and teachers provided Ghamkhori staff with respect in villages. However, as one staff member explained, they were accepted among villagers because they "knew the psychology of people in rural areas. . . . If you don't know life in rural areas—you can't work here."[38] Once trust between Ghamkhori staff and village beneficiaries solidified, greater emphasis was put on social questions, and it was found that such questions were in many ways of greater interest to the villagers.

To ensure the sustainability of the KSMP, Ghamkhori began in 1999 to support the strengthening of communal civil society organizations through *mahalla* committees. Ghamkhori found that in a majority of villages citizens were passive, waiting for government authorities to take steps to improve community life, organize garbage collection, clean irrigation channels, and repair schools and clinics. However, this work was not being carried out. As Olivier Roy has demonstrated, previously the kolkhoz was largely responsible for local self-governance, but once the kolkhoz disintegrated few village-level structures existed to formally represent grassroots interests.[39] Village-level committees could help fill this gap in local self-governance, but those that existed after the war tended to be inactive. Ghamkhori staff thus encouraged communities to reactivate their *mahalla* committees, getting them to meet regularly to identify development priorities and organize voluntary community work.[40]

Through this effort, Ghamkhori facilitators aimed to strengthen traditional means of community organizing, but in doing so they did not want to legitimize some of the more discriminatory and patriarchal forms of local decision making. The NGO recommended that *mahalla* leadership be elected rather than appointed by *jamoat* leaders. It also sought to guarantee female and minority participation in the *mahalla* committees. Initially this posed difficulties, but gradually the NGO convinced all sides. Ghamkhori requested that half of the members of village *mahalla* committee be women, selected among informal women leaders who could help to solve conflict situations connected with the infringement of women's rights. As one of Ghamkhori's main donors at the time noted, "A key strategy to promote greater representation and influence of marginalized groups, such as women and ethnic groups, is providing formal representation for these groups within a legitimate decision-making structure such as the *mahalla* committee."[41] Ultimately, through its community development program Ghamkhori hoped to contribute to the institutionalization of village-level participatory decision making—including all community members.

In May 2000 Ghamkhori set up a women's center in Kurgan Tuppe to provide medical, psychological, and legal assistance to women, which continued to function in 2012.[42] Ghamkhori identified the need for such a center when through KWHP women came forward with accounts of psychological and physical trauma.[43] For many women it was the first time they had spoken publicly about these issues. Women had nowhere to go to for support. They did not trust governmental institutions, the militia, lawyers, medical professionals, or the judiciary, having often found them to be unresponsive. The center offered free legal assistance (including through an emergency hotline) and representation; the largest percentage of cases concerned divorcees. The center's lawyers succeeded in increasing awareness and in making judicial authorities more sensitive to the protection of women's rights. In 2001 the center's lawyers won 6 cases, while in the first ten months of 2004, 18 cases were won and 4 were taken to the Tajikistan supreme court. Nearly ten years later, from January to June 2011, the lawyers won 175 cases.[44] In its strategy to diminish violence against women, Ghamkhori also tried to change government policies and practices—encouraging the government to more readily react against violations of women's rights—which culminated in the passage of legislation against domestic violence in December 2012.[45] At the center, Ghamkhori aimed to create a place where all women, regardless of background, would feel welcome. Women who visited the center explained, "Here we are all equal. You don't divide us into rich and poor, or rural and urban, educated or illiterate, Uzbek or Tajik. From you we feel that we are all simply women and we have even learned to change our attitudes to ourselves."[46]

Ghamkhori did not meet the full expectations of neoliberal civil society, in which civil society is described as well placed to check "potential abuses of power" or to "counterbalance the state."[47] Through its community development programs, Ghamkhori nevertheless strengthened the institutional base for citizen political action, nurtured informed grassroots participation, and contributed to the development of an inclusive political culture and the peaceful resolution of local conflicts. It also crucially increased the institutional base for female participation in public life by facilitating greater women's representation in communal decision-making structures and the protection of women's rights through its legal work. In a country where women had few legal rights vis-à-vis their spouses (or mothers-in-law) fifteen years ago, Ghamkhori has had a significant effect on increasing awareness of women's rights among the legal and medical community to reduce physical, psychological, and economic affronts against women.

Ghamkhori's Linkages and Funding

Ghamkhori's relationships with local communities significantly contributed to its success. Unlike most NGOs that first attempt to cement their position in cities and then branch out, Ghamkhori started its activities in the rural districts, establishing its women's center in Kurgan Tuppe four years later. All Ghamkhori staff resided in local communities, and several were active in schools and *mahallas* independently of the NGO. Past studies of NGOs have warned that when organizations are too deeply embedded in the communities in which they operate they risk being co-opted by local elites.[48] Yet Ghamkhori understood local power structures and appeared able to draw on this authority without being co-opted by it. The NGO found that explaining its work to local religious leaders, collective farm presidents, *mahalla* heads, and other informal community leaders—often getting their authorization to start a new activity—facilitated its tasks.

Ghamkhori initially faced challenges establishing its legitimacy with government, but over time it was accepted as an ally. The NGO sought authorization from state officials to start activities and kept them informed of progress. Gradually the state began to "see the potential for NGOs to broaden the development services under an overall guiding hand from government" and to understand that "the government may benefit from the resulting public gratitude and approval."[49] This was especially the case among regional-level (oblast) governmental authorities. When the NGO interacted with government officials it was to request authorization, offer them information, or provide training, rather than to lobby for specific interests. Ghamkhori also worked with religious authorities to develop approaches in accordance with the Koran to address some of the sensitive issues it was raising.

Ghamkhori's ties with NGOs based in other parts of Tajikistan and abroad were its weakest link. Its relations with international NGOs were almost entirely those of a funding recipient. Ghamkhori was largely dependent on international donor support to carry out its projects. From 1997 to 2012 it received funding from the European Union (TACIS LIEN), ACT-Central Asia, CARE, Caritas, the International Organization for Migration, Oxfam Novib, the Swiss Agency for Development and Cooperation, UNIFEM and UNDP. Ghamkhori did not collect any membership dues or receive financial support from the government. In this Ghamkhori was no different from the vast majority of Tajik NGOs.

According to the neoliberal conceptualization of civil society, external funding can strengthen local NGOs. Yet Ghamkhori found that partnership with international donors challenged its mission, programs, and sense of self-worth. In January 2002 Ghamkhori signed a grant agreement with one international NGO for $38,636. While earlier cooperation with the international NGO had been excellent, disagreements between the donor and grantee concerning project implementation methodologies soon surfaced. Six months into the project, Ghamkhori's leadership stated, "We thought that the more projects we have, the better. But when we started working with [the international NGO] it really weakened our organization; we are weaker now then we were a year ago."[50] In September 2002 Ghamkhori chose to pull out. In doing so Ghamkhori expressed a readiness to "just say no" to funding opportunities that conflicted with its mission; it put its own priorities ahead of the donor's.

Ghamkhori's funding arrangement with another international donor with which it has cooperated since 1997 was more effective. Partly this was because the relationship was not solely project based. The donor was also interested in process and measured success in terms of Ghamkhori's organizational development more than its quantitative project outputs. It agreed to cover not only costs directly related to project implementation but also office rent and other overhead expenditures. As a well-established church-based organization it shared many of Ghamkhori's values and goals. It considered its partnership with Ghamkhori to be a multiyear commitment rather than short-term support. Ghamkhori's experience demonstrates the importance for local NGOs of choosing their donors strategically and having the strength to turn away from them if they feel that their mission is being compromised.[51]

Postwar Communal Civil Society: MSDSP Village Organizations

While Ghamkhori can best be described as belonging to neoliberal civil society, village organizations (VO) supported by the Mountain Societies Development and Support Program (MSDSP) of the Aga Khan Foundation fit more closely within a communal definition. MSDSP initiated its village organization development program in the Gorno-Badakhshan autonomous oblast in 1998, extending it to the Karategin Valley in 2000, where this case study was carried out.[52] MSDSP's commitment to developing village organizations was based on the assumption that "rural economic development is best catalyzed and sustained through village level institutions that are autonomous and transparent, and that contribute to democratic norms of behavior and to the growth of civil society."[53]

Rather than being based on new or transplanted models of civil society organizations, the village organizations supported by MSDSP were founded in traditional forms of community organizing and based on preexisting organizational structures. The VO leadership and members interviewed explained that they considered the VO to be a continuation of past forms of village mobilization—within the *mahalla, chaihana,* or *shura aksakal*—that enabled them to continue with their Soviet-era activism. "Everything that we are doing now [through the VO] existed before, but was not as well documented," explained Davlatjon Hokimov, the VO head of Kalai-Surh.[54] For the head of the Khuja Ainee VO it was necessary to create a village organization structure, because after Tajik independence, "we could no longer get anything as a kolkhoz, so we had to change."[55] The VO leadership and members depicted their villages as extremely cohesive and active under the Soviet system, but they explained that community passivity set in with war and independence as resources dried up. When the VOs were (re)invented with MSDSP assistance they were based on preexisting structures and sought to revive traditions of self-help, volunteerism, and mutual aid.

Those who led the Karategin Valley village organizations were deeply embedded in their communities and had distinguished themselves previously by their skills and activism. In the VOs leadership was shared between the president, deputy, bookkeeper, and head of the women's group. All were elected to their positions in village-wide elections attended by at least 80 percent of local families. Among the six VOs surveyed, two of the VO heads had served previously as the *mahalla rais* within the kolkhoz; in the other cases they had been active in the *mahalla* but in a subordinate position. Thus there was a continuation in community leadership. The four new leaders were from a young generation and tended to be former kolkhoz technicians, teachers, and medical professionals held in high esteem for their professional qualifications, even though their economic position had decreased substantially since independence. Family ties often bound members of the VO leadership: in two instances out of six the head of the women's group was the wife of the VO president. None of them were members of any political parties.

The VO leaders seemed primarily motivated by community pressures, a sense of duty, and the desire to maintain the respect of their peers rather than the opportunity to amass personal gains.[56] The positions were unpaid. Yet the leaders also appeared to live well. It was unclear whether they were elected to VO positions because the community felt that they had the appropriate professional capacities or because they fit within a class of what Roy calls "rural notables," who had controlled much of Soviet-era village life and were sufficiently well placed in wider patronage networks to be able to bring resources into the community.[57]

Village Organization Activities

The leaders of the VOs shared a commitment to restoring to their local communities the material, physical, and economic conditions they had in the prewar period. Currently access to food and employment are major problems in the Karategin Valley. With the financial and material support of MSDSP, VOs distributed vegetable seeds, tree seedlings, chickens, and goats. Several VOs carried out microcredit programs for women, based on a revolving fund, to promote small income-generation activities. To rehabilitate destroyed road, water, and electricity links, MSDSP offered VOs funds and materials. They encouraged the VOs to contribute the needed physical labor for community infrastructure development and maintenance through *hashar*.

Significantly, the VO leaders were not only technical managers who implemented MSDSP-funded projects; they also played a broader role in the community, similar to that of traditional *aksakal* and *mahalla* leaders. VO presidents helped maintain community cohesion and resolve local conflicts. The VO leadership was often called upon to mediate in family crises and disputes between neighbors. When faced with problems, many citizens preferred to approach the VO president or his staff in the first instance and only as a last resort to turn to higher-level authorities, the police, or the courts. Though not considered a religious authority, the VO president often took part in religious activities and discussions; the deputy VO president was in several instances the village mullah. People approached them when planning marriages or funerals, to ask for assistance with organization and sometimes with raising funds.

The VO structure aimed to reduce opportunities for private gain by VO leaders and ensure that leaders would be accountable to the entire village through the organization of regular village meetings. MSDSP insisted that the leadership of the VO not be authorized to execute decisions without consulting the village organization as a whole. As stated in the VO charter, "It is this holding of leaders accountable that is the essence of a participatory organization, where the leaders know that they are accountable not to outsiders but to insiders."[58] The VOs organized monthly VO meetings, when local needs and the means to satisfy them were discussed. This strengthened the institutionalization of village-level structures and promoted participatory and deliberative decision making. At the monthly general gatherings 80 percent of households were required to be present for a decision to be agreed upon. Yet women rarely took part in the VO meetings; they met separately.

As the literature on communal civil society predicts, the VOs promoted community solidarity, self-help, and trust while seeking to ensure that all members of the group had the necessary means for survival. At the same time, the VOs did not openly engage in advocacy or serve as a controlling mechanism over the state. They did not have a real, positive effect on the local economy. In its own assessment of its work in 2008 AKF/MSDSP found that, compared to 2003,

- While average household income in program areas had increased by 75 percent, the gap between rich and poor had widened, and a large percentage of the population remained poor and able to satisfy only basic needs;

- Income had shifted toward cash and nonagricultural sources. Remittances, salaries, and pensions represented the main sources of cash income for households, making them vulnerable to external influences such as the global economic crisis as well as policy changes that affected migrant workers;
- There had been decreases in crop self-sufficiency (i.e., the percentage of households able to grow enough staple crops to meet their minimum daily caloric requirements) and crop productivity (potato and wheat), particularly in the Gorno-Badakhshan autonomous oblast and Khatlon.

These findings on the limited effect of VOs on economic well-being encouraged MSDSP to shift its focus to strengthen local public, private, and civil society partners to take over implementation of activities it previously ran, to establish some twenty-five hundred community-based saving groups to provide access to basic financial services to their members, and to focus more on market development through strengthening the capacities of local service providers.[59] Assessing the impact of these new program activities is unfortunately beyond the scope of this chapter.

VO Linkages and Funding

The Karategin Valley VOs were deeply embedded in the communities in which they were located but largely isolated from groups in other parts of the country or abroad. The Karategin Valley VOs had few or no contacts with Tajik neoliberal civil society organizations or any NGOs other than MSDSP. Nevertheless, the VOs fit within Tajikistan's dense system of social networks based on kin and regional/village origin. Thus it is likely that some VO leaders were in contact with prominent or powerful persons from the Karategin Valley who moved to the capital, Dushanbe. All six VO presidents interviewed claimed that they had never had contacts with local field commanders. They also had few ties with higher-level echelons of government. Semiofficial links existed between the VO and the *jamoat* (the lowest level of government), as VO leaders generally contacted the *jamoat* to obtain authorization to start new projects. The VO leadership was closely linked with local religious authorities, and many VO meetings were held in village mosques or *chaihana*. Yet none of the VO staff interviewed claimed to have links with more politicized Islamic groups—the Islamic Renaissance Party, Hizb ut-Tahrir, or others.

Securing linkages between the VOs and the community's youth and women was a challenging task. In three out of the six Karategin VOs observed, women and men held separate monthly meetings. Inevitably women discussed "women's problems" or the projects that benefited them directly, such as microcredit for women. Less frequently they talked about community issues, such as infrastructure development or social service provision. The extent to which women's views fed into broader VO decision making was ambiguous. Youth under eighteen were not allowed to participate in VO meetings, and little was done to include them in decision-making processes.

The main linkages that the VOs had were with MSDSP staff. In addition to funding, MSDSP provided them with material support, training, and moral guidance. MSDSP's staff in the district offices was originally from the Karategin Valley and included former governmental officials, scientists, technical experts, field commanders, and other community leaders. Thus they tended to be highly respected in the VOs with which they worked, not only because they represented a large donor organization but also because they had a status that predated their engagement with MSDSP. Like Ghamkhori's staff, they were deeply embedded in local communities.

Though village-level organizations had existed for centuries, their reactivation and transformation into VOs were largely dependent on the availability of foreign funding. Before independence, through villagers' voluntary contribution of funds, materials, and labor and support from the kolkhoz, the village-level organizations financed the construction and maintenance of community social and physical infrastructure. When these resources disappeared during and after the civil war many village-level organizations became dormant. VOs were often set up in reaction to this. According to one VO president, "Because many people were poor in the village, we saw the creation of the VO as a way to get assistance from MSDSP."[60] Without the availability of foreign funding communities had little incentive to self-organize, for as another VO president explained, "We did not organize before because there were no funds. Where there is no money you don't feel like doing anything, even talking."[61]

The Karategin Valley VOs were heavily dependent on international donor funding, especially from their main donor, MSDSP. There was no guarantee that the VOs would survive once MSDSP funding ended. This was a problem that MSDSP was conscious of, and as one staff member explained, "One of the key capabilities we want to judge ourselves on is the capacity and ability of the village organizations to access resources from other parties. We want them to go out to other people and get resources."[62] Even though the Karategin Valley VOs could no longer depend on voluntary contributions, they continued to collect membership fees and to organize community work activities based *hashar.* Membership fees tended to range between twenty diram and one somoni per person (one dollar equals three somoni). The poorest contributed in kind.

Heavy reliance on MSDSP risked making the VOs' initiatives donor driven. MSDSP claimed that it supported the development of VOs to "build the capacity of the community to analyze village resources, plan together as a group, access resources, implement planned activities, [and] assess the success of implemented activities."[63] This implied that VOs should determine community needs and how to meet them. Nevertheless, as one VO head explained, "When we have a VO meeting people decide what they want. But MSDSP and other IOs [international organizations] have their own criteria, which it was necessary to meet."[64] The projects that the VO proposed tended to be ones that they knew MSDSP was interested in. These focused on food production, physical infrastructure development, and income generation. Yet VO leaders interviewed talked about how there was a need for social infrastructure development, medical projects, information dissemination, and educational, sports, and social activities. These were not funded by MSDSP, and the VOs thus did not work on them. Thus even though MSDSP was conscious that "VOs should be careful that they do not become just the 'delivery mechanism' for other agencies; that they do not turn themselves into 'clients,'" this was exactly what VOs tended to do in practice.[65]

Opportunities for Bridging between Communal and Neoliberal Civil Society

Based on contemporary theoretical literature on civil society we could expect significant differences in the missions, projects, linkages, and structures of communal and neoliberal civil society organization in Tajikistan. Yet, on the contrary, we find many commonalities between Ghamkhori and the VO cases. The two groups frequently responded similarly to the constraints and opportunities they faced in the Tajik postwar, postcommunist context.

The local community was the main source of inspiration and strength for Ghamkhori, like the VOs; both focused their assistance on small geographic communities. The literature argues that communal, rather than neoliberal, civil society seeks to build relations within society, to facilitate the development of community expressions of solidarity. Yet we find that our case study NGO shared the same mission to connect individuals, build trust, encourage mutual aid, and facilitate public participation in decision making on issues of community concern. Ghamkhori was not absorbed by state-society issues but rather by society-society problems.

Ghamkhori and the VOs were trusted in the communities in which they operated, and the norms and values they expressed emerged out of a deep understanding of local experiences. Yet here there was a significant difference between neoliberal and communal civil society. Ghamkhori's staff was expressively driven by a vision of how society should behave to ensure its own survival based on the concept of self-help. It also promoted universal values of women's rights protection, which were often at odds with indigenous concepts of women's roles in society. Ghamkhori and its staff thus aimed to transform community values. Yet, working at the community level, Ghamkhori did so gradually, presenting its ideals in ways that would be accepted in more traditional and isolated environments. The VOs did not in the same manner seek to change community behavior or value structures.

Charismatic and dedicated leadership proved essential to both types of organization, yet while Ghamkhori relied on professional staff, the VOs' leaders tended to emerge from preexisting, kin-based social networks. Both groups recruited middle-aged, educated, experienced persons. They provided employment to those whose positions in state structures either had disappeared or were now barely remunerated but who continued to be respected in local communities. Contrary to Roy's argument, in Ghamkhori's case NGO recruitment did not "foster a privileged class of employees who stand apart from the local populace."[66] As the literature on communal civil society predicts, the VOs' leadership was largely based on existing social networks; positions were given to those who already had moral status and authority in the prewar period, based on their skills, activism, or family ties.

A more significant variation between these case studies concerned the opportunities communal and neoliberal groups gave to new social actors, especially women, to take on leadership roles. Ghamkhori provided an opportunity for women and minorities to become politically engaged, nurturing a new cadre of civic leaders, while the VOs neither limited nor promoted women's access to decision making, tending to maintain existing power relations.

Though both Ghamkhori and the VOs showed a willingness to adopt participatory decision-making structures, in practice they were run by a centralized leadership. Thus their decision making was dependent on the fairness, experience, knowledge, and contacts of their leaders. Ghamkhori tried to establish a board as an oversight body to hold the NGO leadership accountable. Yet the NGO found it difficult to mobilize enthusiastic volunteers to participate. The NGO director ultimately made most decisions. As he admitted, "To some outsiders it may seem as though I am the dictator who decides everything here."[67] Through weekly staff meetings and decentralization of program management, he attempted to encourage decision making by others, but it took several years before was he able to break the staff's social and cultural reliance on vertical decision making. According to an outside assessor, eventually Ghamkhori's supervision and monitoring systems would become one of the NGO's major accomplishments.[68]

The VOs organized monthly village meetings at which decisions were supposed to be made on the basis of discussion and consensus. But it is questionable to what extent these gatherings were a means by which leaders were held accountable and decision making was shared.[69] As the VOs were linked to clan and family structures, the pressure to first satisfy family, then community needs remained. This is the negative effect that can occur when, "at the social level, clan networks have become increasingly active in the villages, and have largely usurped both the interest-aggregation role of parties, and the role of the state in distributing resources, jobs and social benefits."[70] It appears overly optimistic to state that village-level meetings and elections held VO leaders fully in check, ensuring that they did not employ the VO to their economic and administrative advantage, to promote individual interests.

Social service provision, rather than advocacy, was the main activity carried out by Ghamkhori and the VOs. Authors have warned of the negative impact of taking welfare provision out of the state's sphere of responsibility and putting it in the hands of civil society. Ina Zharkevich argues that "in many cases it further diminishes the capacity of the state and undermines its legitimacy in the eyes of people through the creation of a parallel service delivery mechanism."[71] But in Tajikistan, a 2003 referendum had already ended free and universal provision of medical and educational services. Due to the absence of sufficient resources, competition, access to information, and interest aggregation, medical and educational services were rapidly becoming the privilege of the few. Both types of civil society organizations studied strengthened citizens' coping mechanisms based on mutual aid. They helped fill crucial gaps in state social provision. They provided services to disenfranchised groups—mountain villagers in the case of the VOs and women in Ghamkhori's case. Ghamkhori assisted mainly with social infrastructure, while the VOs developed and maintained physical infrastructure. But they could not have a real effect on local economies.

Ghamkhori and the VOs both strengthened the basis for citizens' potential action by empowering local citizens to participate in public life through the institutionalization of village-level decision making. In Tajikistan, where most local executives are appointed, citizens acting within the VOs and the *mahallas* elected their leadership rather than acquiescing to their appointment by the *jamoat*. Regular VO and *mahalla* meetings were accompanied by public debates on the prioritization of needs and ways to address them. The public, formalized, and participatory nature of village meetings helped increase transparency and interest aggregation. Due to their involvement in decision making and project implementation, community members felt a greater sense of ownership, responsibility, and pride.

Compared with communal civil society, neoliberal civil society in these two cases was more successful in "improving political accountability," which Zharkevich, in a study for INTRAC, defines broadly as ranging "from creating an effective legal environment to establishing the channels of communication between society and the state." As she also notes, it is unclear whether communal forms of civil society have the capacity to improve political accountability above the self-government or district levels.[72] But Ghamkhori successfully promoted local-level democracy by emphasising women's full participation in decision making, the dissemination of information, and the provision of legal representation to the disenfranchised. This was most evident when the women's center successfully convinced women to address their grievances to the courts and assisted them in winning cases, thus helping pave the way for the passage of legislation against domestic violence in December 2012. An extensive 2007 study of civil society organizations in Tajikistan commissioned by the Aga Khan Foundation also concludes that "it has come to be understood in Tajik society generally that without the democratization of gender attitudes, Tajikistan cannot become a democratic society and NGOs have the leading role in the implementation of gender equality. . . . A special area of Tajik CSO activity, the gender question, and one which also relates closely to CSO activity on rehabilitation (medical, psychological) is the prevention of violence against women."[73]

Neither Ghamkhori nor the VOs succeeded in fully avoiding the state or in opposing it. The two groups did not hope for any form of governmental financial assistance, but to a certain degree both groups accommodated local government by providing it with information and seeking authorization to carry out activities. Overall the two cases were more engaged in "gap filling" and "selective collaboration" between local communities and the state than in censuring or rolling back government in political or economic spheres.[74] It may be argued that Ghamkhori in particular contributed to improving relations between the state and citizens—restoring some of citizens' trust in state institutions' effectiveness and honesty. This conforms to recent findings that civil society organizations in Central Asia have been most successful when their initiatives have been implemented within the existing legal framework and in coordination with authorities, rather than in confrontation with the political regime.[75]

Ghamkhori and the VOs were both primarily funded by international nongovernmental organizations. In an extremely poor economic environment, where local resources are usually depleted to meet basic needs, neither group could envision becoming self-sustainable. Though much has been written about NGOs' negative tendency of overrelying on international funds for their survival, in these cases the VOs were as reliant on external aid as Ghamkhori was. The VOs succeeded in collecting some of their own funds from membership fees and volunteer contributions, but this did not significantly affect their sustainability. Neither group obtained funding from the government. Due to their dependency on external donors, whose money was primarily provided on a project basis, the VOs, like Ghamkhori, were forced into short-term projects that may not have met what they perceived as their primary needs. Both groups struggled with the challenge of dual accountability: to the donors and to the community. Only Ghamkhori was self-sufficient and familiar enough with donor relations to pull out of a funding arrangement when it felt that it was becoming more accountable to the donor than to its beneficiaries. The VOs did not do so and instead on several occasions were obliged to put aside projects requested by the community—mainly to provide social infrastructure—which MSDSP did not consider to be priorities. Both Ghamkhori and the VOs found that their missions and values were less likely to be compromised when the funders they cooperated with shared their values and missions and were engaged in a regular dialogue with them over project objectives and strategies.

The cases of Ghamkhori and the Aga Khan Foundation–supported VOs suggest that neoliberal and communal forms of civil society in Tajikistan have, over the past decade, increasingly begun to resemble each other. In key aspects related to their types of leadership and dedication to full participation of women the two groups studied differed. Yet in their missions, programs, linkages with local communities, and funding they have a great deal in common. Clear missions, dedicated and respected leadership, ability to build trust within communities, and understanding of donor and civil society–governmental relations are essential for success regardless of whether a group fits a more neoliberal or a communal conceptualization of civil society. An NGO like Ghamkhori increasingly understands the importance of cooperating with rural grassroots associations, closing the gap between communal and neoliberal civil society. Thanks to these links it is able to address grassroots-level needs and avoid becoming elitist, donor-driven, and ineffectual. In a comprehensive 2010 study of civil society in Tajikistan, Zharkevich argues that "further research is necessary to understand to what extent traditional and religious forms of civil society, which possess substantial leverage in the countryside, can work in alliance with secular modern institutions, what kind of values they promote and what role they can play in the state building process."[76]

While not denying the need for more current field-based research, the two cases described in this chapter suggest that communal-neoliberal civil society alliances are possible and can support state building by improving political accountability and transparency. Yusufbekov Yusuff, Babajanov Rustam, and Kuntuvdiy Natalya, in their study for the AKF, also find that "some of the more advanced NGOs have begun to understand the need for association for the solution of regional problems."[77] Buxton, based on a 2002–2004 INTRAC mapping exercise, also argues that "national-level associations are vital for any attempt to influence policy in the NGO's own country." He calls for "deeper embedding of NGOs in their societies," or "indigenization."[78]

The ongoing bridging between neoliberal and communal forms of civil society should also not ignore the role of global civil society, as it is linked to external organizations' (mainly nongovernmental or intergovernmental organizations) increased interest in cooperating with both neoliberal and communal civil society.[79] Western donors and civil society activists have been introducing many neoliberal values to communal forms of civil society. They have been less keen on challenging existing power structures and inequalities, especially as the VO case demonstrates with regard to women's positions in society. At the same time, the most effective NGOs, like Ghamkhori, have remained embedded in and committed to local communities. As we have seen, by providing mainly financial assistance, international donors risk negatively affecting local civil society groups' definition of priorities and needs and ultimately undermining their popular credibility. For international intervention to strengthen local groups, the partnership should be based on common values and agreement about long-term objectives. In addition it should be multidimensional: not only financially based but also politically oriented.

The two cases studied in this chapter have had only limited success in opposing the state or policies devised by international organizations. For this to occur, we can nevertheless assume that international supporters of civil society should take one step further and not only help neoliberal and communal Tajik civil society groups to bridge gaps between each other but also extend their ties to global civil society. The civil society campaign in neighboring Kyrgyzstan against the country joining the World Bank's Highly Indebted Poor Countries (HIPC) program in 2006–2007 is a recent example of the "strength of a campaign making use of well-worked out arguments developed at the international level."[80] It is when these links between Tajik civil society groups and their counterparts around the world are secured that Tajik civil society—communal and neoliberal, or a bridging of the two—is most likely to become stronger, as political actors and politics return to Tajikistan's civil society debate.

Notes

I would like to thank the persons at Ghamkhori and MSDSP who assisted me in my fieldwork, as well as Dr. Kamol Abdullaev, who has been instrumental in helping me understand political developments in Tajikistan. An earlier version of this essay was published as "Neo-liberal and Communal Civil Society in Tajikistan: Merging or Dividing in the Post War Period?" in *Central Asian Survey* 24, no. 3 (September 2005): 225–43. Used by permission.

1. World Bank, *Tajikistan Country Brief 2011,* http://web.worldbank.org/WBSITE/EXTERNAL/COUNTRIES/ECAEXT/TAJIKISTANEXTN/0,,contentMDK:20630697~menuPK:287255~pagePK:141137~piPK:141127~theSitePK:258744,00.html#econ.

2. For a discussion of the fragility of Tajikistan's statehood, see International Crisis Group, *Tajikistan: On the Road to Failure,* Asia Report No 162, February 12, 2009; and Ina Zharkevich, *The Role of Civil Society in Promoting Political Accountability in Fragile States: The Case of Tajikistan* (Oxford: INTRAC, 2010).

3. Jude Howell and Jenny Pearce, *Civil Society and Development: A Critical Exploration* (Boulder, CO: Lynne Rienner, 2002).

4. Shirin Akiner, "Prospects for Civil Society in Tajikistan," in *Civil Society in the Muslim World: Contemporary Perspectives,* ed. A. Sajoo (London: I. B. Tauris, 2002), 185.

5. Ibid.; Olivier Roy, "Soviet Legacies and Western Aid Imperatives in the New Central Asia," in Sajoo, *Civil Society in the Muslim World,* 144.

6. Sabine Freizer, "Central Asian Fragmented Civil Society: Communal and Neoliberal Forms in Tajikistan and Uzbekistan," in *Exploring Civil Society: Political and Cultural Contexts,* ed. M. Glasius, D. Lewis, and H. Seckinelgin (London: Routledge, 2004), 130–40.

7. Sabine Freizer, "Neo-liberal and Communal Civil Society in Tajikistan: Merging or Dividing in the Post War Period?," *Central Asian Survey* 24, no. 3 (September 2005): 225–43.

8. Much of the current debate on civil society in Central Asia also occurs in other regions, especially in the Muslim world and in the past few years in the Middle East. For one compilation on civil society in different contexts, see, Glasius, Lewis, and Seckinelgin, *Exploring Civil Society.* The Global Civil Society yearbooks (2001–2011) serve as a useful record of the different types of civil society (and their critics) worldwide. For more information see, Global Governance, London School of Economics, http://www.lse.ac.uk/globalGovernance/publications/Home.aspx (the website continues to function as of June 2014 even if the Center for Global Governance at the London School of Economics has closed).

9. Scholars from the Islamic world were frequently at the forefront of the reconceptualization of civil society outside Europe. See, for example, Mustapha Kamel Al-Sayyid, "The Concept of Civil Society and the Arab World," in *Political Liberalization and Democratization in the Arab World,* ed. Rex Brynen, Bahgat Korany, and Paul Noble (London: Lynne Rienner, 1995); Abdou Filali-Ansary, "State, Society and Creed: Reflections on the Maghreb," in Sajoo, *Civil Society in the Muslim World;* Hasan Hanafi, "Alternative Conceptions of Civil Society: A Reflective Islamic Approach," in *Alternative Conceptions of Civil Society,* ed. Simon

Chambers and Will Kymlicka (Princeton, NJ: Princeton University Press, 2002); Masoud Kamali, *Revolutionary Iran, Civil Society, and State in the Modernization Process* (Aldershot, UK: Ashgate, 1998); and Sajoo, *Civil Society in the Muslim World: Contemporary Perspectives.*

10. See, for example, Zharkevich, *Role of Civil Society.* A similar dichotomy is evident in Uzbekistan, according to Suda Masaru in "The Politics of Civil Society, Mahalla and NGOs: Uzbekistan," in *Reconstruction and Interaction of Slavic Eurasia with Its Neighbouring Worlds,* ed. Ieda Osa-mu and Uyama Tomohiko, Slavic Eurasian Studies, no. 10 (Sapporo: Slavic Research Centre, 2006), 335–36.

11. On this period, see Muriel Atkin, "Thwarted Democratization in Tajikistan," in *Conflict, Cleavage and Change in Central Asia and the Caucasus,* ed. K. Dawisha and B. Parrott (Cambridge: Cambridge University Press, 1997); Aziz Niyazi, "The Year of Tumult: Tajikistan after February 1990," in *State, Religion and Society in Central Asia: A Post-Soviet Critique,* ed. V. Naumkin (Reading, UK: Ithaca Press, 1993).

12. Tatiana Abdushukurova, program director, Open Society Institute of Tajikistan, interview by author, Dushanbe, May 2002.

13. Jumaboy Niyazov, head of the Humanitarian Council, interview by author, Khojand, August 2002. He remembered how at that time "the situation called for the creation of such associations and gatherings to support perestroika, to fight against the communist *nomenklatura.* People created assemblies to support the idea of perestroika."

14. International Center for Not-for-Profit Law, NGO Law Monitor: Tajikistan, last updated December 12, 2012, http://www.icnl.org/research/monitor/tajikistan.html.

15. The European Union delegation in Tajikistan issued a statement on the matter on November 1, 2012, "Local EU Statement on Closure of the Association of Young Lawyers 'Amparo,'" news release, http://eeas.europa.eu/delegations/tajikistan/documents/press_corner/2012/local_eu_statement_-_closure_of_ngo_amparo_en.pdf.

16. Yuri Skochilov, head, Youth Eco Center, interview by author, Dushanbe, May 2002 .

17. For more on the Soviet-era social organizations that provided a range of activities and services to benefit workers, youth, women, intellectuals, artists, and so on, see, Deniz Kandiyoti, "Post-Soviet Institutional Design and Rural Livelihoods in Uzbekistan," mimeographed paper, London, 2004; and Mark Waite, "The Role of the Voluntary Sector in Supporting Living Standards in Central Asia," in *Household Welfare in Central Asia,* ed. Jane Falkingham et al. (Houndmills, UK: Macmillan, 1997).

18. Kamol Abdullaev, "Current Local Government Policy Situation in Tajikistan," mimeographed paper, Dushanbe, 2002.

19. Because the term *mahalla* exists in other parts of the Muslim world and is used in Arabic, Turkish, Persian, and Urdu, it is often perceived as an Islamic insti-

tution. But a *mahalla* is not a religious body; instead it defines the neighborhood or an administrative subdivision of local government.

20. It is remarkable that the *mahalla,* which in pre-Soviet times was traditionally strong in urban areas (which are now generally part of Uzbekistan), remained within the Tajik lexicon and during the Soviet period gained informal meaning in rural areas as part of the collective farm (kolkhoz). In 1985 legislation was passed defining official functions for the *mahalla* and beginning its transformation into a structure of local self-government. However, unlike in neighboring Uzbekistan, in Tajikistan the legal status of the *mahalla* was not further formalized in the 1990s. For more on *mahallas* (in Uzbekistan), see Daniel Stevens, "NGO-Mahalla Partnerships: Exploring the Potential for State-Society Synergy in Tajikistan," *Central Asian Survey* 24, no. 3 (September 2005): 281–96; Marianne Kamp, "Between Women and the State: Mahalla Committees and Social Welfare in Uzbekistan," in *The Transformation of Central Asia: States and Societies from Soviet Rule to Independence,* ed. Pauline Jones Luong (Ithaca, NY: Cornell University Press, 2004), 29–58; and Masaru, "Politics of Civil Society, Mahalla and NGOs."

21. Historians debate whether *mahallas* and similar communal structures were captured by the state or rather survived bureaucratic manipulation, in fact changing the nature of Soviet institutions. The latter is Olivier Roy's main argument. Olivier Roy, *New Central Asia: The Creation of Nations* (New York: New York University Press, 2000); and Roy, "Soviet Legacies and Western Aid Imperatives." Opponents include Pauline Jones Luong, in her introduction to Luong, *Transformation of Central Asia.*

22. Muriel Atkin, "The Politics of Polarization in Tajikistan," in *Central Asia: Its Strategic Importance and Future Prospects,* ed. Hafez Malik (New York: St. Martin's Press, 1994); Olivier Roy, "Kolkhoz and Civil Society in the Independent States of Central Asia," in *Civil Society in Central Asia,* ed. Holt Ruffin, Daniel Waugh, and Frederick Starr (Seattle: University of Washington Press, 1999), 112–13; Roy, "Soviet Legacies and Western Aid Imperatives."

23. For more recent descriptions of Tajik "social organization" and their resistance to the Soviet system and civil war, see Anna Matveeva, *The Perils of Emerging Statehood: Civil War and State Reconstruction in Tajikistan; An Analytical Narrative on State Making,* Crisis States Working Papers, series 2, no. 46, March 2009, 8–1. See also Zharkevich, *Role of Civil Society,* 20–24; and Yusufbekov Yusuff, Babajanov Rustam, and Kuntuvdiy Natalya, *Civil Society Development in Tajikistan* (Dushanbe: Aga Khan Development Network, 2007), 17–20. They prefer to call these "traditional institutions of civil society and religious/spiritual life."

24. Twenty-year-old female informant, interview by author, Shulmak, Tajikistan, July 30, 2002.

25. International Crisis Group, *Tajikistan: The Changing Insurgent Threats,* Asia Report no. 205, May 24, 2011.

26. Howell and Peace, *Civil Society and Development,* 196–201; Roy, "Soviet Legacies and Western Aid Imperatives"; Akiner, "Prospects for Civil Society in Tajikistan."

27. In 2001 Counterpart Consortium undertook a "Community Outreach Program" to increase the capacities of grassroots initiatives, while Mercy Corps International began implementing the "Peaceful Communities Initiative" in the Ferghana Valley. USAID initiated a three-year, $22 million Central Asia Community Action Investment Project to fund community groups to carry out infrastructure development and maintenance activities in 2002. The World Bank began an extensive study on community-driven development in Central Asia and cofounded the Central Asian Community Empowerment Network.

28. Matveeva, *Perils of Emerging Statehood*, 49.

29. Charles Buxton, "NGO Networks in Central Asia and Global Civil Society: Potentials and Limitations," *Central Asian Survey* 28, no. 1 (2009): 45–46.

30. Masaru, "Politics of Civil Society, Mahalla and NGOs," 368.

31. Lucy Earle, "Community Development, 'Tradition' and the Civil Society Strengthening Agenda in Central Asia," *Central Asian Survey* 24, no. 3 (2005): 257–58.

32. Colette Harris, author of *Control and Subversion: Gender Relations in Tajikistan* (London: Pluto Press, 2004).

33. Bahodur Toshmatov and Mikhail Fedorov, Ghamkhori director and deputy director, interview by author, Kurgan Tuppe, Tajikistan, June 14, 2002.

34. Hoorshed Bojev, Ghamkhori project supervisor, interview by author, Kurgan Tuppe, Tajikistan, June 1, 2002.

35. Bahodur Toshmatov, Ghamkhori director, interview by author, Kurgan Tuppe, Tajikistan, June 11, 2002.

36. Ibid.

37. Ghamkhori information leaflet, 2004, Dushanbe.

38. Dilorom Markhamova, Ghamkhori project supervisor, interview by author, Kurgan Tuppe, Tajikistan, May 30, 2002.

39. Roy, "Soviet Legacies and Western Aid Imperatives," 131–45. According to the Tajik constitution, the lowest level of governmental authority is the *jamoat,* made up of five to fifteen villages.

40. The *mahalla* committees also had a conflict resolution aim, as in mixed ethnic villages where unified structures could be set up they helped nurture community cohesion, tolerance, and trust.

41. Chris Buckley, Tajikistan director, Act Central Asia, email communication, May 21, 2003.

42. The crisis center's main donor until 2008 was the Swiss Agency for Development and Cooperation in Tajikistan, but other organizations, including Act Central Asia, have also provided funds.

43. Malika Sobirionova, Ghamkhori project supervisor, interview by author, Kurgan Tuppe, Tajikistan, June 9, 2002. KWHP stands for Khation Women's Health Project.

44. Ghamkhori website, ghamkhori.tj/eng/content/view/32/49/, accessed December 2012.

45. "Tajik Parliament Approves Law Against Domestic Violence," Radio Free Europe/Radio Liberty, January 3, 2013.

46. Ghamkhori, Kurgan Tuppe Women's Center, *Final Report to the Swiss Agency for Development and Cooperation in Tajikistan* (Kurgan Tuppe, 2001).

47. Larry Diamond, Marc Plattner, Yun-han Chu, and Hung-mao Tien, eds., *Consolidating the Third Wave Democracies* (Baltimore: John Hopkins University Press, 1997), xxxi; and Ernest Gellner, *Conditions of Liberty: Civil Society and Its Rivals* (New York: Penguin, 1994), 5.

48. Jonathan Goodhand and Peter Chamberlain, "Dancing with the Prince: NGOs' Survival Strategies in the Afghan Conflict," in *Social Reconstruction in Times of Transition: From Conflict to Peace in a Changing World,* ed. Deborah Eade, Oxfam Working Paper (Oxford: Oxfam, 2000), 91, 98; Roy, "Soviet Legacies and Western Aid Imperatives," 142.

49. David Lewis, *The Management of Non-governmental Development Organizations: An Introduction* (London: Routledge, 2001).

50. Toshmatov and Fedorov, interview.

51. For a detailed assessment of Ghamkhori's activities, see Barbara Parker, assessment report, September 2005, ghamkhori.tj/download/Barbara%20 Parker%20eng.pdf.

52. In 2002, when most of this research was carried out, MSDSP was supporting four hundred village organizations in Gorno-Badakhshan and seventy-two in the Karategin Valley. In 2012 it claims to have aided over fourteen hundred village organizations and to have facilitated the creation of close to one hundred VO unions, benefitting over 140,000 people, of which over 40 percent are women. This information is available on the Aga Khan Development Network site, www.akdn.org/publications/2012_tajikistan_overview.pdf, accessed December 2012.

53. Aga Kahn Development Network, AKF Activities in Tajikistan, 2002, http://www.akdn.org/akf/tajikrep_02.pdf.

54. Davlatjon Hokimov, VO head, interview with by author, Kalai-sur, Tajikistan, June 29, 2002.

55. Saifullo Gazoev, VO head, interview by author, Khuja Ainee, June 23, 2002.

56. When asked what satisfaction he receives from his position as VO *rais,* one VO head responded, "Who wants to take all this responsibility? Who wants to write all these things down? For no money? I think about my responsibilities all the time, they worry me, its stressful." When queried about whether or not he is proud of his work, the same *rais* answered, "I am not proud. But of course I am proud if my work can bring benefit to the community. Then people say good things about you, and of course you feel proud." Hokimov, interview

57. Roy, "Soviet Legacies and Western Aid Imperatives," 93.

58. MSDSP, VO charter, Khorog, 2001.

59. Aga Kahn Development Network, Rural Development in Tajikistan, www.akdn.org/rural_development/tajikistan.asp, accessed December 2012.

60. Pavlatmurod Piramavdov, VO deputy head, interview by author, Karashahr, Tajikistan, June 26, 2002.

61. Dilovarsho Eshanov, VO head, interview by author, Loyova, Tajikistan, June 22, 2002.

62. Mark Whitton, interview by author, July 13, 2002. In 2002, out of six VOs visited, only one actively lobbied other international organizations for funding.

63. MSDSP, *Five Year Strategy, 2002–2006* (Khorog, 2002), 17.

64. Alimordhon Rakhimov, VO head, interview by author, Shulmak, Tajikistan, June 30, 2002.

65. MSDSP, VO charter.

66. Roy, "Soviet Legacies and Western Aid Imperatives," 143.

67. Bahodur Toshmatov, Ghamkhori director, interview by author, Kurgan Tuppe, Tajikistan, June 14, 2002.

68. Parker assessment report.

69. In two of the Karategin Valley VOs it seemed evident that the head of the VO had benefited disproportionately from MSDSP's aid: one constructed a drinking-water line to his personal property, while another placed a chicken incubator meant for the community in his garage.

70. Kathleen Collins, "Clans, Pacts and Politics in Central Asia," *Journal of Democracy* 13, no. 1 (2002): 148.

71. Zharkevich, *Role of Civil Society,* 6.

72. Ibid., 7. Zharkevich concludes her much broader study of civil society organizations in Tajikistan by saying,

> CSOs in Tajikistan have increasingly engaged in dialogue with authorities and state institutions at different levels, trying to influence the norms and practices of the legal system, as well as to monitor and improve the delivery of the social services provided by the state. These were successful provided that civil society worked within the existing legal framework, [and] did not overtly oppose the political system but rather tried to change existing legislation and norms within the state institutions. Tajikistan shows that CSOs are likely to have a durable and sustainable contribution to the social life of the country and improvement of political accountability once their initiatives are implemented in coordination with authorities or aimed at dialogue with the existing legal system rather than confrontation. (43)

While this conclusion seems to be in line with my own findings based on my study of two cases, I do not feel competent to endorse it fully without more of my own research.

73. Yusuff, Rustam, and Natalya, *Civil Society Development in Tajikistan,* 51.

74. David Lewis, "Civil Society in Non-Western Contexts: Reflections on the "Usefulness" of a Concept," Civil Society Working Paper 13, Centre for Civil Society, London, 2001, 150.

75. Zharkevich, *Role of Civil Society.*

76. Ibid., 7.

77. Yusuff, Rustam, and Natalya, *Civil Society Development in Tajikistan,* 58.
78. Buxton, "NGO Networks in Central Asia," 47, 55.
79. Mary Kaldor, *Global Civil Society: An Answer to War* (Cambridge: Polity, 2003).
80. Buxton, "NGO Networks in Central Asia," 55.

Part 5

The International Context

11

State, Civil Society Actors, and Political Instabilities in Post-Soviet Kyrgyzstan

The Changing International Context

Graeme P. Herd and Maxim Ryabkov

The introduction has highlighted various conceptions of civil society, demonstrating the important differences in the ways civil society is conceived and actualized. Civil society is a highly contested concept, and its role and significance are far from being understood. Indeed, can one apply the concept of civil society, with its origin in the West, to the Central Asian postcolonial, post-Soviet, authoritarian states? This chapter addresses the following questions: Does civil society have a place in the current regional security architecture, given the rapidly changing international context? If so, what might that place be?

This chapter outlines several critical factors that are likely to leave Kyrgyz civil society in its current place as mediator of international incentives to Kyrgyz political elites. The significance of this role has dramatically diminished over the last ten years, as the Western-driven reform agenda in the country has more or less failed and the interest and the influence of Western donors is falling, leaving more space either for the more customary Russian and Kazakh presences or for the new Chinese and Turkish ones. With this change, and especially if Afghanistan fades from the agenda after 2014, we expect civil society will conform to new incentives and roles.

A Survey of Regional Security Macrodynamics

Kyrgyzstan's reputation as the most "pluralist" or liberal political society in Central Asia accounts for the large volume of democracy and civil society assistance provided by the United States and Europe over the past two decades. Following the terrorist attacks of September 11, 2001, Kyrgyzstan assumed a new role as transit hub for NATO forces in Afghanistan, with troops and materiel funneled through the airport at Manas, just outside Bishkek. These two frequently conflicting roles—as democracy aid recipient and forward military base—shape Kyrgyzstan's complex position at the vortex of Central Asia's security dynamic.

With the withdrawal of the International Security Assistance Force (ISAF) and U.S. troops from Afghanistan in 2014, the role and function of the United States as an economic donor, security provider, and strategic counterweight to Russia have been significantly diminished. As the National Committee for American Foreign Policy has predicted, "Central Asia must compete for attention with the dozens of other regions and issues confronting U.S. policymakers."[1] The high-water mark of U.S. influence in the region following 9/11 has now passed. Central Asia will become of secondary military-strategic significance to the United States, though the Northern Distribution Network will facilitate not just a reduction but also a transformation of the U.S. presence, and the meaning attributed to that presence, in the region.

For the European Union ISAF states this is true, only more so. After twenty years of EU engagement with the region, including in 2007 the elaboration of an EU strategy ("the neighbors of neighbors"), we can conclude that the EU has, in fact, few real interests in Central Asia beyond hydrocarbon imports. As of 2010 (the last year for which complete data are available), Kazakhstan was the twentieth-largest trading partner of the EU and represented 1.1 percent of its foreign trade, while no other Central Asian state was among the first fifty trading partners (Uzbekistan represented 0.1 percent of EU foreign trade and the other three Central Asian republics are invisible).[2] The financial crisis of 2008 has led to a freezing of EU investments in Central Asia, and, when there has been time for EU leaders to think strategically, the Arab Spring, Libyan operation Unified Protector, and now the Syrian crisis are of primary concern—the southern vector is as much, if not more, of a contemporary priority as eastern engagement. Indeed, even as EU diplomatic missions have been opened through Central

Asia and a human rights dialogue maintained, there is little evidence that the EU has had a normative impact or influence in the region. The consolidation of "competitive authoritarian" and "neo-patrimonial" regime types that strive to exercise stricter control over the activities of opposition parties and civil society institutions, rather than transition to and then consolidate as market-democratic states, testifies to this.

The alternative external influences—Russia and China—share common norms and have at least compatible, if not shared, interests. For example, Russia and China share normative solidarity when it comes to the importance of upholding sovereignty and territorial integrity and the declared noninterference in domestic affairs, which is in practice a resistance to political reform based on a Western agenda for Central Asia rather than actual noninterference.[3] The most powerful regional actors and institutions in Eurasia—the Russian Federation–dominated Central Security Treaty Organization (CSTO) and the China-dominated Shanghai Cooperation Organization (SCO)—socialize and institutionalize a common set of assumptions and norms and cast their normative shadows across Central Asia. The events of 9/11 and the U.S. response—to kill or capture terrorists—were understood to legitimize preexisting antiradical Islamist narratives in Eurasia and beyond. In addition, Eurasian power-elite understandings of the nature of color revolutions in Serbia, Georgia, Ukraine, and Kyrgyzstan—Western security services in collusion with NGOs ("CIA-Soros") attempting to implement a postmodern coup d'état—reinforced a shared commitment to oppose the "export" of such revolutions by the West and legitimized the subversion of independent civil society activists in the name of tackling foreign subversion (a good example is Russia's "foreign agent" law, which presupposes that "structures financed from abroad"—for example, Human Rights Watch and Transparency International—are "serving foreign interests," in the words of President Putin). More recently, the Arab Spring and Chinese and Russian opposition to humanitarian intervention in Syria provide a contemporary normative bond, as does a shared preference for virtual domestic politics—China fakes communism while Russia fakes democracy.

Kyrgyzstan: The Challenge of Fragile States and Regional Crises

The Kyrgyz crisis of 2010 shares and exemplifies many of the challenges, obstacles, and dilemmas generated by complex emergencies. It embodies the nature of wars among peoples rather than between states, conflict generated by state failure rather than interstate rivalry, and catastrophes whose second- and third-order cascading transborder and international effects can be worse than those of the first order and in which few strategic blueprints exist to provide post-conflict-management roadmaps, let alone "security solutions." In short, it captures one type of strategic threat identified by the EU Security Strategy of 2003, U.S. National Security Strategy of 2002, 2006, and 2010, and the Russian National Security Strategy of 2010—regional crisis and fragile states.

On June 10, 2010, in the southern Kyrgyz city of Osh, violence erupted, spreading to Jalalabad two days later, with reports of armed gangs, interethnic violence, rape, and stampedes at border crossings into Uzbekistan. Between four hundred and five hundred people were reportedly killed and over two thousand wounded, with four hundred thousand (8 percent of the Kyrgyz population) displaced—three hundred thousand internally and one hundred thousand as refugees into Uzbekistan's neighboring Andijan province. China, India, Turkey, South Korea, Germany, and Russia, among others, airlifted their foreign nationals out of the area of conflict to Bishkek and beyond.

What were the causes of such violence and what are the likely implications? A report by the OSCE minorities high commissioner noted "attempts at ethnic cleansing" by Kyrgyz against Uzbek minorities in the south, as the provisional government was unable to provide order or security for the population.[4] Latent interethnic animosity can be understood as the trigger for the civil conflict in the south and as the means through which violence was instrumentalized by the Kurmanbek Bakiyev clan leaders, behind-the-scenes power brokers, former advisors and security service loyalists, and organized crime figures, to serve other ends.[5] Bakiyev's successors, however well intentioned, had great difficulty coping with the violence.

Although ethnic Uzbeks constitute only a fraction of the total population, they form a majority in some southern provinces. These communities had historically coexisted and cooperated with other ethnic groups, ethnic intermarriage was high, Osh and Jalalabad residents identified themselves more by city residence than ethnicity, and many were bi- or trilingual (Kyrgyz-, Uzbek-, and Russian-speaking). Nevertheless, ethno-nationalist tendencies under the Bakiyev regime resulted in a gradual "Kyrgyzisation" of local government functions (school directors, hospital administrators, local government officers), while Uzbeks dominated economic structures.

In addition to social stratification, the global financial crisis resulted in a reduction in remittance money and workers returning to the region from Russia, placing greater pressures on infrastructure and provisions.

Violence created a power vacuum, and this served two ends. First, from an official perspective, it provided the means through which the Bakiyev clan could reassert its control over the extremely lucrative drug trade flows in the south. Osh and Jalalabad are major drug transit hubs where heroin is repackaged before being exported by plane, train, or land. The large and heterogeneous Bakiyev clan ("eight brothers and the eight brothers each with eight sons") was heavily implicated in drug trafficking. President Bakiyev himself disbanded the relatively successful Drug Control Agency (partly funded by the UN and U.S.) in October 2009, placing drug policing under the Interior Ministry. The U.S. State Department characterized this move as a "significant blow to regional counternarcotics efforts."[6]

Second, violence served a political objective—namely to demonstrate that the interim government was not in control of the situation and would have to postpone or cancel a planned referendum on June 27 to adopt a new constitution underpinning a parliamentary rather than presidential republic.

The political weakness of the interim government should not be overlooked, particularly its inability to exert authority over the Interior Ministry and army garrisons in the south, which human rights observers and Roza Otunbayeva have accused of being complicit in attacks, robberies, and violence: "We have been left with a demoralized police force, stuffed with Bakiyev personnel. . . . We have security forces, many of whom joined one side in this conflict in the south."[7] The interim government consists of an alliance of three formerly opposition parties and its authority is commensurate with its ability to take a united stance. Unfortunately, the glue that holds this alliance together is opposition to the ousted Bakiyev regime, particularly the former president himself and his immediate family members, rather than a clear vision of Kyrgyzstan's future political order.

Within this context, the constitutional referendum planned for June 27, 2010, went ahead. The referendum was monitored by a total of 189 international observers representing more than thirty countries and eighteen international organizations (for example, CSTO, CIS, OSCE, SCO, ODHIR), plus thirty accredited foreign media outlets. More than 90 percent voted "yes," and around eight percent voted against it. Some 2.7 million people were eligible to vote, and turnout was nearly 70 percent.[8]

Roza Otunbayeva reportedly invited the CSTO to intervene with peacekeepers on June 12, when the violence was at its height, but then retracted this invitation, sparking serious debates as to the likelihood of intervention by an external force—perhaps a UN-mandated peacekeeping mission and/or third party mediators that would form a political buffer zone. The practical usefulness of such an intervention appears nil, in retrospect. In reality the crisis quickly resulted in the victory of the Kyrgyz side, subsequent repression and expropriation of the defeated Uzbeks, distortion of the humanitarian assistance, and prevention of any meaningful external conflict mediation.

Additionally, the institutions that potentially would conduct the operation had neither the will nor the capacity to commit sufficient resources. Military-political debates centered on the realization that getting an intervention force into Kyrgyzstan would be easier than getting it out. The complex emergency looked set to represent a quagmire and credibility trap that would be expensive, prolonged, and more than likely bloody. In a "war among the peoples" (no borders or uniforms), intervention forces run the risk of being caught in the crossfire and disowned if the provisional government falls, and so perceived of as an occupying force, one that would be caught up in internal power struggles.

For Russia a dilemma presented itself. Russian intervention under the cover of the CSTO risked failure; though the CSTO had never yet undertaken a collective security operation, failure to intervene brought into question the CSTO's purpose and capability (in terms of resources, equipment, and political will to enact collective security responsibilities through peacekeeping missions). Was the CSTO a Potemkin-like structure, designed to support imperial illusions ("sphere of privileged interest") but unable to withstand realities ("sphere of reluctance")? As Dmitri Trenin notes, "The most the CSTO proved capable of was a meeting of the Secretaries of the Security Councils of the organization's member states. That is a good thing, but it is clearly not enough."[9] The real dilemma facing Russian interests can be restated: too much violence had a potential to return Bakiyev to power or, worse, the potential for extraregional spillover; too little unrest and interethnic clashes would fail to delegitimize the emergence of democratic political movement in Central Asia, in particular the Otunbayeva government and its determination to hold a referendum on a parliamentary form of government.

What light does the Kyrgyz case study and the issue of intervention shed on the operation of collective security in Central Asia? The Kyrgyz crisis highlights serious flaws in collective security self-regulation only in the context of violations of state sovereignty and territorial integrity by other states in the state-centric international system. First, the state itself—as exemplified by the president, his family, and immediate patronage networks—can pose a clear threat to security. Political elites not espousing extreme ideologies but successfully plundering their societies, appear as more prominent sources of insecurity than Hizb ut-Tahrir, for example. Second, nonstate actors involved in intrastate conflict with spillover potential to other states and societies within the potential collective security regime, whether they are terrorist groups, organized criminals, political extremists, or a combination thereof, are not addressed by the CSTO charter. This is all the more surprising as containment of the potential consequences of such intrastate conflict cannot be guaranteed even within the collective security regime—that is, from Vancouver to Vladivostok.

Third, what Western observers may perceive as pluralism and civic activism can in the Kyrgyz context be described more accurately as the manifestation of clan and ethnic animosities, as the events of 2010 demonstrated. Russian and Chinese leaders are well aware that social upheavals in Kyrgyzstan and elsewhere in Central Asia undermine stability. The perceived threat of imminent regional chaos and instability, more than any philosophical opposition to democracy, explains Moscow's and Beijing's fear of color revolutions and their efforts to develop institutional mechanisms for collective security and cooperation.

China, the SCO, and Central Asian Stability

In 2012 China celebrated the twentieth anniversary of diplomatic relations with the five Central Asian republics. In 1994, in the context of a tour of Central Asia, Chinese premier Li Peng highlighted four principles that were both compatible with the "One China" policy and flexible enough to govern and regulate China–Central Asia relations: peaceful coexistence and good neighborly relations, promotion of mutually beneficial cooperation, noninterference in domestic affairs, and respect for each other's independence and sovereignty.[10]

Analysts of this relationship argue that China does not have a clear-cut formal grand strategy for Central Asia but rather the sum is the product of a series of disparate goals and parts.[11] Clearly, though, China's core interest in "stability maintenance" provides a unifying logic that gives structure and sense to China's interactions with Central Asia. "Domestic" or "internal" threats to Chinese statehood are diverse and range from managing corruption, pollution and chronic water shortage, social discord, huge wealth disparities, and massive internal migration flows to meeting the expectations of an expanding urban middle class. Internal "stability maintenance" is dependent on continued economic growth through the import of strategic resources (metals, minerals, and energy), support for an official strategic narrative based on the notion of "peace development," and using good multilateral relations with Central Asia as a hedge against future potential containment efforts.

Established on June 15, 2001, in Shanghai, the SCO is an intergovernmental organization consisting of China, Kazakhstan, Kyrgyzstan, Russia, Tajikistan, and Uzbekistan. India, Iran, Mongolia, and Pakistan have observer status, while Belarus and Sri Lanka are dialogue partners.[12] The SCO provides China with a diplomatic bridgehead, a multipurpose forum to achieve its interests in Central Asia (and increasingly beyond), and can be understood as a mechanism "of multivector diplomacy and rhetoric" that allows China to "implement the 'soft embrace' of Central Asia in a non-confrontational context."[13] It provides a forum for elite interaction, particularly at the executive level—head of state, foreign and defense ministers and intelligence services—that helps forge normative solidarity and common-threat perception, not least over the constructively ambiguous so-called three evils: ethnic separatism, religious extremism, and international terrorism. It also allows elites to prevent potential foreign and security policy developments in Central Asia that would run in directions detrimental to their interests.

For China, the ability to manage transnational politics in order to contain spillovers that could exacerbate the "Xinjiang problem" is paramount. The Xinjiang problem—Xinjiang Uighur Autonomous Region—most recently highlighted by a spike in violence in 2008 and 2009, has been attributed to a number of causes, ranging from ethnic-based social exclusion and relative economic deprivation grievances to the area's political and economic geography as a border region and Chinese government policies.[14] As terrorism and separatism are viewed in China as primarily being motivated through material inequalities and deprivation rather than ideological impulses, economic growth and development of Xinjiang through greater trade with Central Asia will both help balance China's internal development and reduce "splitist" tendencies, in particular notable among indigenous populations in Xinjiang, Tibet, and to a lesser extent Gangsu and Inner Mongolia.[15]

In terms of the economic relationship, Central Asia also represents a sixty-million-strong market for Chinese products, a location to export its capital, production, and labor. China's economic presence in and significance for Central Asia has rapidly grown. In 1992 total annual trade turnover between China and Central Asia stood at $459 million. By 2002 the figure had increased more than five times and stood at $2.2 billion. By 2007 this had reached $19.6 billion, an eightfold increase, and the following year, 2008, it was $30 billion. In 2010 Chinese trade with Central Asia exceeded that of Russia.[16] China has increased its own efforts to provide strategic loans to Central Asia, most notably at the June 2012 SCO Summit.[17] Although China has promoted multilateral economic cooperation among SCO member states, the bulk of its trade, credits, and investments have been conducted bilaterally.

Good political relations in Central Asia help legitimize the official narrative of responsible regional power and "peaceful rise" (*heping jueqi*) by demonstrating that it is in the Chinese interest and demonstrating its commitment to regional security through multilateral bodies. At the same time, good multilateralism in Central Asia secures China's strategic rear by facilitating Eurasian land-transit routes through to the energy-rich Middle East and so represents a latent Chinese hedging potential to be used against the future possibility of Great Power balancing of China. Thus China has stressed that the SCO operates not *against* the U.S./West but *without* it and can be understood to represent a platform for wider cooperation with non-Western actors.[18]

The passivity of the SCO's response to social upheaval in Kyrgyzstan can be attributed to three factors: "First, upholding the unqualified norms of sovereignty and territorial integrity are key features of both Russian and Chinese diplomatic discourse. Second, China was sensitive to the nature of the conflict in Kyrgyzstan in relation to both potential and actual internal unrest in China and the SCO's own well established 'three evils' security concept: terrorism, extremism, and separatism. Third, the contingency that evolved in Kyrgyzstan was not one that was practiced at SCO military exercises."[19] In addition, this type of crisis is not addressed by the intergovernmental CSTO or OSCE, as the very members of these intergovernmental organizations are the incumbent elites who are parties to international conventions and whose state policy and actions contributed to the conflict.

The Kyrgyz crisis, located in a divided civil society, suggests that Afghanistan in South Asia and China in East Asia could have had their sovereignty and territorial integrity violated had this complex emergency spiraled out of control. In a sense the collective-security thinking in China, Russia, and Eurasia is touchingly nostalgic for a lost era of interstate warfare, absolute sovereignty and centralized elite-decision-making structures. It unconsciously betrays an almost Brezhnevian sympathy for strategic stagnation and status quo in an era when it is increasingly recognized that structural and systemic root causes of instability tend to be ever more nonstate based and solutions lie in human security and development agendas that are targeted at individuals, societies, and regions. In addition, the 2010 crisis has shown the limited ability and even readiness of international actors to use the civil society structures in Kyrgyzstan.

Regime Type and the International Context

In Russia, Central Asia, and China, superpresidential, oligarchic, and bureaucratic hybrid political systems prove virtual, resilient, and durable.[20] In the case of Central Asia, at least, regime types have been characterized as both competitive authoritarian and neopatrimonial. "Competitive authoritarian" regime types systematically create an "uneven playing field" by enforcing unequal access to state resources and institutions, such as the legal system and media. Incumbents act as judge and jury, relying on de facto, informal proxy, and patronage means of control to fuse together state and ruling party interests and to set and change the rules of the game as appropriate to the needs of elite and power continuity. In the process, a self-reinforcing dynamic is set in motion: the more efficient and effective competitive authoritarian "hyper-incumbencies" become, the less the need to resort to significant fraud or repression, the more opposition parties are co-opted (or collapse), and the greater the international legitimacy of the system. "Neopatrimonialism" can be defined as the institutionalization of two systems or logics, one based on personal loyalties, informal dependencies, and patron-client patrimonial rule and the other on constitutional rules of formal subordination and authority set by rational, legal state institutions and bureaucracies. Paradoxically, from the resultant systematic uncertainty and insecurity this fusion generates, a self-reinforcing and sustaining dynamic allows for various system types—"sultanistic," "oligarchic," "bureaucratic," and "soft"—to self-reproduce and so sustain themselves.[21]

Competitive authoritarian and neopatrimonial regime types may be considered two sides of the same coin in that both support and flourish in conditions of poorly institutionalized state structures and policy-making processes, compounded by a weakly defined understanding of national interest, historical animosities, and a tendency of states to define themselves in opposition to their neighbors. The nature of these regimes makes them susceptible to external manipulation, not least as elites favor immediate and short-term bargains that privilege their own need for power continuity over the longer-term interests of state independence. Perhaps more importantly, Central Asian elites share a common perspective on state power and state-society relations with their larger authoritarian neighbors that reinforces their ability to resist Western-inspired civil society norms and projects.

Civil Society and International Security

The role of civil society in Kyrgyzstan has to be seen in light of its failure to become a liberal democracy, indeed an emergence of a hybrid, distinctly post-Soviet regime normatively akin to Putin's Russia. Western efforts are currently directed at maintaining relations with the state, rather than the civil society. Despite the ritual condemnation of nationalism, international partners have generally accepted that Kyrgyzstan will not be an island of democracy and will remain, for a while at least, a typical post-Soviet oligarchic ethnocratic state, if arguably closer to the brink of dysfunctionality than Uzbekistan or even Tajikistan.

Central Asian civil society groups have always faced the danger of donor dependency, and as Westerners are losing interest, civil society is also likely to become less distinctly urban and liberal and more part of the local political scene. This shift follows the changing political economy, which makes civil society groups more dependent on their ability to manipulate the state as lobbyists for international partners rather than actors with their own agenda. Practically all Western initiatives are promoted with the help of local counterparts, organizations or individuals that basically constitute the official civil society—NGOs, academia, political observers and analysts, journalists, entrepreneurs, lawyers, and civil society activists. These implementing partners mediate in the creation of incentives for governmental counterparts to cooperate with the donors—in exchange for study visits, equipment, and funding.

The perception of nontraditional security threats in Central Asia and in particular Kyrgyzstan is conceptually linked to what may be called "uncivil" society, the poor and dissatisfied part of society that is prone to accepting extremist and violent ideas.[22] Linked to ethnic and religious identities and endowed with a penchant for criminality, this partly imagined "uncivil" society is neither the authoritarian state nor the middle-class urban liberal opposition—neither the police nor the human rights NGO. On the contrary, "civil society" is usually defined, for the operational purposes of international assistance, as public-good promoting, liberal, and, as a result, eligible for international sponsorship NGOs.

This essentially normative definition of "civil society" differs sharply from the classical concept of civil society as a collection of parochial interests, variably endowed with a capacity for collective action. More important, the political realities are such that public-good-promoting NGOs are not the only entities that characterize associational life, which can be sectarian, radically right-wing, and profit motivated. Notice, for example, how Robert Putnam, in *Making Democracy Work*, measures the potential of civil society in medieval Italy by the number of public notaries and the demonstration of social capital in North Italy in the nineteenth century by the activity of clandestine communist and religious groups.[23]

We shall not rehearse the general theoretical arguments in detail here, as they are addressed in the introduction to this volume and elsewhere.[24] Our focus is on the political institutional implications of imposing the NGO-based definition of civil society on the state–international community–society relations in Central Asia. One of the implicit dangers here is that the normative civil/uncivil distinction is determined by the identification of security threats on the basis of authoritarian elite interests, which are conflated with those of the state and society. Ethnic political movements, and religious groups with or even without explicit political messages, are classified as nontraditional, extremist, and not promoting the unity of the people.

Civil or Uncivil Society?

The distinction between "civil" (NGO-based) and "uncivil" society is key to the international securitization of socioeconomic underdevelopment.

Such a distinction has to be understood as part of a more general discourse that considers civil society to be, by definition, neoliberal and therefore young, urban, progressive, and middle-class and therefore a force for pluralism, liberalization, respect for human rights, basic freedoms, and democratization. This conflation reflects a need by Western donors to have ideologically similar implementing partners able to counter and balance an authoritarian state. As civil society has become a normative rather than descriptive term, a definition of an ideological position and organizational form, the Hizb ut-Tahrir or an ethnic separatist movement, or even a business community, cannot be civil society. This, however, leaves them unclassified: What are they? If neither state nor family, does it therefore follow that they must be civil society in the descriptive sense of the term?

The border constructed between the civil and uncivil society poorly reflects the realities on the ground. In July 2010 an ethnic Uzbek human rights activist, Azimzhan Askarov, was arrested and later sentenced to life by the Kyrgyz state on dubious charges and through a flawed process. He was for the Kyrgyz state an ethnic Uzbek politician and his fate was part of the repressions against ethnic Uzbeks after June 2010, supported by the long-term framing of the minority as disloyal and prone to religious extremism. The convenient definition of legitimate civil society as ethnically blind cannot, however, accommodate very plausible situations in which political mobilization turns ethnic and someone is an ethnic activist and a liberal politician at the same time. The lost nuance is crucial for any politics of inclusion that would be sufficient for resolving the problem of domestically generated "security threats" in Kyrgyzstan, ethnic conflict in particular.[25]

The production of security threats involves various social groups and formal state institutions, where the opposition of "civil" and "uncivil" society is lost. The Tulip Revolution of 2005 is an interesting example of that. The revolution itself was initially presented in the Western media and expert circles as an expression of a "vibrant" civil society. Despite the initial perception of the collapse of President Akaev's rule as a grassroots rebellion for democracy, more credible later accounts characterized the event as elite driven, with (liberal) civil society organizations playing a marginal role. The bulk of mobilization was the action of "uncivil" society, and especially political and business elites able to tap the allegiances and incentives at the community level. The winning coalition thus straddled the presumed ideological and social divisions, with urban liberals playing second fiddle at best.[26] The subsequent developments—the presidency of Kurmanbek Bakiyev in 2005–2010—only confirm this assessment, showing how easily liberal-minded activists and NGOs could be marginalized.

It is probably fair to say that business, local community, often ethnic nationalist political activists, and perhaps at times religious groupings jointly define as civil society that which eventually matters in explaining the political dynamics in Kyrgyzstan and which limits the autonomy of the state. The events of April and June 2010 demonstrate this even further, confirming the following conclusion by Scott Radnitz: "Antiregime mobilization in this context can transpire as a defensive response by actors lacking other means to secure their interests—protecting power and property, in the case of independent elites; defending those elites' interests, for the masses."[27] In other words, the not-for-public-good civil society, encompassing moneyed interests and embracing illiberal communitarian ideas, constitutes the key engine of political change, embracing multiple roles and functions: it provides the effective, if not particularly salutary, limit on the autonomy of the state (including the security apparatus); it captures and accommodates this state and provides the mechanisms for political change.[28]

The urban liberal NGOs, and especially those that are genuinely committed to the cause of political pluralism and democratization, are dependent on an ideologically hostile local environment to simultaneously give them a compelling raison d'être and provide their Western international donors a need to address. In this sense, such urban liberal NGOs constitute an "alternative" civil society actively competing within itself for access to international contacts and resources.

Looking to the aftermath of the 2005 revolution, we witnessed a growing threat of ethnic conflict. Ethnic clashes were portrayed after June 2010 as resulting from ethnic nationalism, be it Kyrgyz or Uzbek. According to this understanding, the conflict itself could best be characterized as a result of a state policy of ethnic exclusion, with the 2010 escalation flowing from the collapse of an inherently unsustainable balance of ethnic politics that had, like a house of cards, been established by the Bakiyev regime. However, the politics of exclusion concerned not only an ethnic minority, but also a minority within the elite. First and foremost, a patronage network distributed rent-generating positions, state jobs, and control over businesses according to one's proximity to the ruling elite, and only secondly by ethnicity. In this circumstance, the urban middle classes continued to be privileged, through their ability to draw on international aid.

Of greatest importance for this current discussion, the conflict presents another example of the political ambiguities associated with the positioning of civil society as a liberal check on the authoritarian state and one that supposes exclusive ethno-nationalist attitudes toward ethnic issues—the hallmark of illiberal "uncivil" society. In 2010, as the Kyrgyz-Uzbek conflict escalated and became the key, even defining, issue in domestic politics, urban civil society was split by the degree to which it was ready to support the majority of the Kyrgyz in blaming the Uzbeks and the extent to which it was prepared to remain muted in criticism of Kyrgyz behavior. Combinations of liberal and nationalist discourses, at times rather nuanced, emerged to satisfy psychological and political needs.

Moreover, this dependence on external support places NGOs in competition with the state. While the nonprofit implementing partners that constituted civil society were failing to promote policy reform in Kyrgyzstan, the Kyrgyz state successfully obtained subsidies, first with a fast transition to the "market economy," albeit without rule of law, and then by tapping the resources of security-motivated aid after 9/11.

It is difficult to quantify the dependency of the Kyrgyz state on various forms of aid. Kyrgyzstan receives funds through very many multilateral and bilateral channels, in money and in kind. Considerable military assistance is given in exchange for geopolitical favors and arguably makes aid conditionality less effective.[29] More important, we see now that Western funding is overshadowed by that from countries not sharing the West's human rights and other reform agendas: China, Russia, India, and Turkey. The post–June 2010 developments showed a sort of beneficiary conditionality—donors, notably Westerners, had to comply with certain conditions to have the right to provide humanitarian aid or implement their projects. The controversy over the Osh city development ended in July 2012 when the city's mayor, Melis Myrzakmatov, announced that houses would be demolished, and the international community's decision not to contradict him in order to preserve good relations appeared to suggest that a mayor of a city in southern Kyrgyzstan could call the bluff of the international community.

The reassertion of the state and of the incumbent political elites was not the explicit purpose of international engagements. Yet in many ways it was helped by the concept of the "weak" state, and also by the treatment of ministries, parliaments, and political parties as if they were fragile communities in need of help.[30] Post-9/11 engagements, both military and civil, had an urgency about them that justified being less cautious about the impact on civil society. It is characteristic how the OSCE brushed aside the criticism of its police reform program by human rights organizations in Kyrgyzstan and continued to provide various forms of equipment and training to the Kyrgyz police, while the Bakiyev regime was rapidly becoming a serious danger to the country and even to itself. This favoring of the state reflected a mutual dependency in a geopolitical game, in which the Kyrgyz state was able to secure the role of a gatekeeper for foreign subsidies. Tapping into global institutional resources, it managed to survive in its largely Soviet format, despite an incongruity between these institutional forms and the economic base that was insufficient to support them. The economic basis for state autonomy (relative, of course) came from international donors.

Clan or Community?

It is also interesting how, in the context of development aid, "civil society" is kept distinct from "community." The latter is the passive beneficiary, the former the active mediator or implementer. The difference is real, but its reality reflects the degree of professionalization of activism, and therefore its dependence on external funding and political support. In this frame, "community" is considered inherently good, but in need of assistance. Neglected are the hierarchical, parochial, exploitative relations within actual communities, and this neglect is reinforced by the conceptual and institutional separation of community and civil society.[31] Separate (in discourse, but not in reality) from community is "clans," which as a term captures the negative aspects of informal politics.[32] This distinction between communities and "clans" is also burdened with normative and emotional associations, whereas the empirical phenomena these words purport to refer to are certainly mixed.

Implications for International Security

The case of the Tulip Revolution, as well as the less understood case of Kyrgyz-Uzbek conflict, demonstrate how security threats emerge from an interface of the state and various social interest groups. Bakiyev's regime was a serious security threat, as it continued to destroy the capacity for Kyrgyzstan to govern itself.[33] The aftermath of the Tulip Revolution represents not only the shattered hopes and dreams of urban revolutionaries and activists in civil society but also the further criminalization of Kyrgyz economic life and the erosion of legitimacy of both national and international institutions. This renders the roles of civil society—whether liberal or illiberal—intertwined with that of the state.[34]

According to this interpretation, the sharp organizational distinction between liberal civil society and its uncivil and illiberal "double" is a function of the international dependence of civil society, of a competition for external support in which civil society often loses out to the state—the state needs support to counter illiberal civil society, and support for this end reduces funding for liberal civil society. This distinction and dynamic are greatly facilitated if not wholly created by the politics of international aid. The other side of this coin is the identification, manufacture, and production of internationally important security threats at the interface between state institutions and societal groups, notably "communities." In this context, civil societies are the source of hostilities and instabilities, not their panacea, raising the specter of "war among the peoples," as multiethnic states fail and violently implode, and so reinforcing aid and donor support for states. In the case of Kyrgyzstan, if it holds true that its geopolitical relevance is generated by Afghanistan's future evolution and because of a rivalry and interdependence with Russia and China, then liberal civil society has little chance to flourish, even as an implementing partner.

The combination of geopolitical changes and the domestic situation in Kyrgyzstan places the country on the periphery of world politics. Its liberal civil society does not have the capacity to play a role of its own and should not count on external actors to privilege it over security-oriented cooperation with the state. This chapter has highlighted the marginal role that formal civil society played at pivotal moments in the continuous Kyrgyz crisis and how much donor dependence shapes civil society's existence. The Bishkek-based middle class will remain employed, as individuals and organizations, by Western and perhaps increasingly non-Western donors. However, they do not constitute an active agent of sociopolitical change, able to credibly monitor the government's actions and provide a consultation space for societal interests. Kyrgyz civil society is belowdecks in the Kyrgyz ship of state, unable to influence the direction or speed of travel. If this analysis is correct, the future of Kyrgyz civil society is likely to depend critically on a combination of shifting external influences and local politicking, where liberal and illiberal components are freely mixed.

Notes

1. NCAFP, "Central Asia: Strategic Context Twenty Years after Independence," *American Foreign Policy Interests* 33 (2011): 141.

2. Eurostat, *External and Intra-EU Trade: A Statistical Yearbook, Data 1958–2010* (Luxembourg: Publications Office of the European Union, 2011), 31, http://epp.eurostat.ec.europa.eu/cache/ITY_OFFPUB/KS-GI-11-001/EN/KS-GI-11-001-EN.PDF.

3. Graeme P. Herd, "Colourful Revolutions and the CIS: 'Manufactured' versus 'Managed' Democracy?" *Problems of Post-Communism* 52, no. 2 (March/April 2005): 3–17.

4. "OSCE Says Attempted Ethnic Cleansing Underway in Kyrgyzstan," *Deutsche Presse-Agentur* (Vienna), June 15, 2010.

5. Neil Melvin, *Promoting a Stable and Multiethnic Kyrgyzstan: Overcoming the Causes and Legacies of Violence,* Central Eurasia Project, Occasional Papers Series No. 3 (New York: Open Society Foundations, March 2011).

6. Peter Leonard, "Heroin Trade a Backdrop to Kyrgyz Violence," Associated Press Worldstream, Jalal-Abad, Kyrgyzstan, June 24, 2010, http://abcnews.go.com/International/wireStory?id=11000057&page=1.

7. Dmitry Solovyov, "4 Die in Raid by Kyrgyz Security Forces; Rights Groups Say Soldiers Beat Villagers," *Gazette Montreal,* June 22, 2010; "Kyrgyz Police Officers, Soldiers Accused of Marauding in Kyrgyz Southern City," June 24, 2010, 24kg.org (Bishkek), http://www.24kg.org/osh/77390-v-gorode-oshe-kyrgyzstan-nekotorye-milicionery-i.html; "UN Agencies Fear Escalation in Kyrgyz 'Ethnic Tinderbox,'" Agence France-Presse, June 15, 2010, http://www.expatica.com/ch/news/swiss-news/un-agencies-fear-escalation-in-kyrgyz-ethnic-tinderbox-_76787.html.

8. Simon Shuster, "Kyrgyzstan Endorses New Constitution; New Constitution Strips Power from the President and Gives More Authority to Parliament," *Globe and Mail* Online, June 28, 2010, http://www.theglobeandmail.com/news/world/asia-pacific/kyrgyzstan-endorses-new-constitution/article1621116/.

9. Dmitri Trenin, "The Kyrgyz Bell," op-ed, June 29, 2010, Carnegie Moscow Center, http://www.carnegie.ru/publications/?fa=41126.

10. James MacHaffie, "China's Role in Central Asia: Security Implications for Russia and the United States," *Comparative Strategy* 29 (2010): 857.

11. Raffaello Pantucci and Alexandros Petersen, "China's Inadvertent Empire," *National Interest,* November–December 2012, 30–39; Robert E. Bedeski and Niklas Swanström, eds., *Eurasia's Ascent in Energy and Geopolitics; Rivalry or Partnership for China, Russia and Central Asia?* (London: Routledge, 2012); Huasheng

Zhao, "Central Asia in China's Diplomacy," in *Central Asia: Views from Washington, Moscow and Beijing,* ed. Eugene Rumer, Dmitriĭ Trenin, and Huasheng Zhao (Armonk, NY: M. E. Sharpe, 2007), 137–208; Guangcheng Xing, "China and Central Asia," in *Central Asian Security: The New International Context,* ed. Roy Allison and Lena Johnson (London: Royal Institute for International Affairs, 2001), 152–70.

12. Joseph S. Cheng, "The Shanghai Cooperation Organization: China's Initiative in Regional Institutional Building," *Journal of Contemporary Asia* 41, no. 4 (November 2011): 632–56.

13. Stanislav Zhukov and Olga Reznikova, *Tsentral'naia Aziia i Kitai: Ekonomicheskoi vzaimodeistvie v usloviakh globalizatsii* (Moscow: IMEMO RAN, 2009), as cited in Simon Pirani, review of *China's Energy Geopolitics: The Shanghai Cooperation Organization and Central Asia,* by T. N. Marketos, *Central Asian Survey* 30, no. 1 (March 2011): 173.

14. Justin V. Hastings, "Charting the Course of Uyghur Unrest," *China Quarterly* 208 (December 2011): 893–912; Chris Hann, "Smith in Beijing, Stalin in Urumchi: Ethnicity, Political Economy and Violence in Xinjiang," *Focaal: Journal of Global and Historical Anthropology* 60 (2011): 108–23; Michael E. Clarke, *Xinjiang and China's Rise in Central Asia, 1949–2009: A History* (London: Routledge, 2011).

15. Graeme P. Herd, Rouben Azizian, and Yu Yixuan, "Perspectives from the U.S., Russia and China on Countering Ideological Support for Terrorism," in *The United States, Russia, and China: Confronting Global Terrorism and Security Challenges in the Twenty First Century,* ed. Paul J. Bolt, Su Changhe, and Sharyl Cross (Westport, CT: Praeger Greenwood, 2008), 89–103.

16. Cholpon Orozobekova, "Beijing's Stealthy Expansion in Central Asia," Radio Free Europe/Radio Liberty, January 12, 2011; Cholpon Orozobekova, "China Quietly Expands Footprint into Central Asia," *New York Times,* January 2, 2011; James Brooke, "China Displaces Russia in Central Asia," *VA News,* November 6, 2010; James MacHaffie, "China's Role in Central Asia: Security Implications for Russia and the United States," *Comparative Strategy* 29 (2010): 859.

17. Stanislav Pritchin, "SCO at Central Asian Crossroads: Political Demand for Region Is Rapidly Growing" (in Russian), *Nezavisimaya Gazeta* (Moscow), website June 18, 2012.

18. David Kerr, "Central Asian and Russian Perspectives on China's Strategic Emergence," *International Affairs* 86, no. 1 (2010): 127–52.

19. Kushtarbek Shamshidov, Pál Dunay, Graeme P. Herd, and Maxim Ryabkov, *The 4th GCSP-OSCE Academy-NUPI-NESA-GCMC Seminar, "Central Asia 2011,"* Geneva Papers, Conference Series no. 24 (Geneva: GCSP, February 2012), 31, http://www.gcsp.ch/Resources-Publications/Publications/GCSP-Publications/Geneva-Papers/Conference-Series.

20. See, for example, Vadim Kononenko and Arkady Moshes, *Russia as a Network State: What Works in Russia When State Institutions Do Not?* (London: Pal-

grave, 2011); Richard Sakwa, *The Crisis of Russian Democracy: The Dual State, Factionalism and the Medvedev Succession* (Cambridge: Cambridge University Press, 2011).

21. Susan Stewart et al., eds., *Presidents, Oligarchs and Bureaucrats: Forms of Rule in the Post-Soviet Space* (Burlington, VT: Ashgate, 2012), 52–53; Eric McGlinchey, *Chaos, Violence, Dynasty: Politics and Islam in Central Asia* (Pittsburgh: University of Pittsburgh Press, 2011); Charles Buxton, *The Struggle for Civil Society in Central Asia: Crisis and Transformation* (Sterling, VA: Kumarian Press, 2011); Scott Radnitz, *Weapons of the Wealthy: Predatory Regimes and Elite-Led Protests in Central Asia* (Ithaca, NY: Cornell University Press, 2010).

22. See Andrey Kazantsev's discussion in chapter 1, this volume. See also Buxton, *Struggle for Civil Society in Central Asia.* For an excellent earlier though now dated survey, see M. H. Ruffin and Daniel C. Waugh, *Civil Society in Central Asia* (Seattle: University of Washington Press, 1999).

23. Robert Putnam, *Making Democracy Work* (Princeton, NJ: Princeton University Press, 1994).

24. The literature contains a lot of criticism of excessive expectations of "civil society," defined as liberal, internationally oriented groups, with references to both recent and historical experience. Thomas Carothers, "Civil Society," *Foreign Policy,* no. 117 (1999–2000): 18–24; David Rieff, "A False Dawn of Civil Society?" *Nation,* February 4, 1999, http://www.thenation.com/article/false-dawn-civil-society; Sheri Berman, "Civil Society and the Collapse of the Weimar Republic," *World Politics* 49, no. 3 (April 1997): 401–29. A recent paper argues that the NGO-focused concept of civil society does not reflect the way civil society functions in all countries, the counterexample in that case being Scandinavia. Lars Tragardh, "Rethinking the Nordic Welfare State through a Neo-Hegelian Theory of State and Civil Society," *Journal of Political Ideologies* 15, no. 3 (October 2010): 227–39.

25. Cf. Sheri Berman's conclusion about Egyptian civil society, which is, in her view, an institution of religious rather than secular opposition: "The Egyptian case teaches us that at least in certain contexts, the civil society skeptics may have a clearer vision than the boosters. The growth of civil society should not be considered an undisputed good, but a politically neutral multiplier—neither inherently 'good' nor 'bad,' but dependent for its effects on the wider political environment and the values of those who control it." Sheri Berman, "Islamism, Revolution, and Civil Society," *Perspectives on Politics* 1, no. 2 (June 2003): 257–72.

26. See Radnitz, *Weapons of the Wealthy.* His case study of an early stage in the collapse of the Akaev rule—the Aksy events—also demonstrated in detail the role of an "uncivil" community mobilized through patronage networks: Scott Radnitz, "Networks, Localism, and Mobilization in Aksy, Kyrgyzstan," *Central Asian Survey* 24, no. 4 (December 2005): 405–24.

27. Radnitz, *Weapons of the Wealthy,* 196.

28. See Berman, "Islamism, Revolution, and Civil Society."

29. Lora Lumpe, *U.S. Military Aid to Central Asia, 1999–2009: Security Pri-*

orities Trump Human Rights and Diplomacy, Central Eurasia Project Occasional Paper Series No. 1 (New York: Open Society Project, October 2010).

30. See the argument of the "weak" state for the Tajik context in John Heathershaw, "Tajikistan amidst Globalization: State Failure or State Transformation?" *Central Asian Survey* 30, no. 1 (2011): 147–68.

31. Cristine Bichsel, "In Search of Harmony: Repairing Infrastructure and Social Relations in the Ferghana Valley," *Central Asian Survey* 24, no. 1 (2005): 53–66.

32. Kathleen Collins, *Clan Politics and Regime Transition in Central Asia* (Princeton, NJ: Princeton University Press, 2006). The vision of "clan" as the impediment to reform reflects this denial of legitimacy to private interest, awarding its expressions the status of a premodern institution. Much of what Collins sees as "clan" relations appears to be the mundane conflict of private interests, perfectly compatible with a liberal view of human nature as essentially egoistic but also in need of social capital for pursuit of its interests.

33. The escalation of the Kyrgyz-Uzbek conflict in 2010, following up on the political marginalization of minorities, is a prime example of a nontraditional threat.

34. Another case of the political ambiguities associated with the positioning of civil society as a liberal check on the authoritarian state and illiberal "uncivil" society is the attitude of civil society groups toward ethnic issues. In 2010, as the Kyrgyz-Uzbek conflict escalated and became the key matter of domestic politics, urban civil society had also split in the degree to which it was ready to go along with the majority of the Kyrgyz in blaming the Uzbeks or at least to silence possible criticism of the Kyrgyz.

Conclusion

Charles E. Ziegler

In this volume we have examined various facets of civil society and state-society relations in Central Asia to better understand the diverse societal actors and their relationship to the authoritarian governments of the region. We found that while there are autonomous spaces where social organizations can function free from state interference, these vary considerably. Central Asian authoritarianism comes in different shapes, from soft paternalism to chaotic clan rule to virtual totalitarianism. Similarly, there is wide variation in the level and nature of civic activism among the five Central Asian states. Uzbekistan and Turkmenistan are closest to the totalitarian end of the spectrum, leaving little space for social activism and quashing those organizations that fail to toe the party line. Kazakhstan tolerates civic activism but seeks to co-opt and channel participation toward regime-endorsed goals. Kyrgyzstan's state is weak and ineffective; in this environment domestic and internationally funded nongovernmental organizations (NGOs) operate freely but lack the political influence of powerful regional and clan structures. Tajikistan's low level of economic development and strong traditional structures constrain civic activism, but even here communal and neoliberal organizations play a role in providing much-needed services.

Most of the authors here agree that a cooperative relationship between government and non-governmental organizations is not necessarily inimical to civil society, a position that contrasts with Western-oriented approaches to civil society that emphasize state-opposing behavior. Obviously, Central Asian states suffer from low levels of political quality, defined as having competent and efficient political institutions, a rule of law, and low levels of corruption. If political quality is related to a vibrant civil society, then Central Asia does indeed score low on both.[1] But that does not mean that a functioning civil society is absent in the region; more accurately, it takes quite different forms from those in Western democracies and appears to be developing at differential rates.

The institutional legacies of communism have an impact on civil society, but the variations among the post-Soviet states, and more broadly among the former Eastern European countries, indicate that history is not destiny. In Central Asia the totalitarian communist experience left these societies with low levels of trust and notably uncivil organizations in the form of criminal, clan, terrorist, or religious extremist groups and a general disregard for democratic political institutions and the rule of law among elites and the populace at large.

The authors differ, however, on whether traditional clan structures are conducive to the development of negative, rather than positive, social capital. Andrey Kazantsev stresses that, as in Sheri Berman's study of Weimar Germany, the absence of effective institutions can allow strong networks of extremists to hijack the state toward ends harmful to democracy. It privileges bonding over bridging capital and promises disruption of society if not controlled by a strong center. So in a way this is self-fulfilling: a repressive state encourages (inadvertently) social fragmentation and bonding, then represses the pluralist tendencies rather than channeling them through functioning institutions. Central Asia's political institutions, as in many authoritarian settings, may be superficially democratic, but their parliaments, parties, and courts do not provide for genuine accountability or responsiveness.

Other contributors focus more on the positive elements of traditional social structures in Central Asian civil society. Dilshod Achilov finds in moderate Islam an important contribution to cooperative forms of civil society. Kazakhstan's government has pursued inclusionist policies to control civil society, encourage moderate Islam, and marginalize extremism—to strictly monitor any contestational forms of religious activity. Much of the middle class and officialdom in this highly secular society is, together with the president, suspicious of Islam and the potential for radicalism among the youth. But Nazarbayev's inclusionist policy has allowed the limited development of Islamic economic and social activities, most notably in the area of financial services and educational institutions, thus dampening the potential for religious radicalism. Political Islam, however, is viewed as a threat to stability and the incumbent regime and is severely constrained, with the regime prohibiting religious parties and forcing registration of all religious communities.

In Tajikistan, Sabine Freizer finds civil society developing, albeit slowly, out of a mix of neoliberal and communal nongovernmental organizations. The balance may be more toward the latter in Central Asia, more toward the former in Western societies, but the point is that both sectors meet the civil society definition of being separate from the state and the family. In line with previous research, she finds that international assistance may undermine the work of both neoliberal and communal NGOs by requiring these groups to follow a Western agenda more in line with donors' priorities than with local needs. Village organizations can address social needs without challenging cultural norms; in Tajikistan they helped organize community work in the aftermath of that country's civil war. But neoliberal NGOs seek to change value structures (to "universal" values) and in so doing often come into conflict with traditional values and behavior. Remarkably, Freizer finds that neoliberal and communal forms of NGOs are increasingly coming to resemble each other in Tajikistan.

The new Central Asian states were faced at independence with weak national identities. Islam has the potential to serve as framework for national unity, as Reuel Hanks argues, but this role has not been realized. While Islam at first glance may provide the glue for new nations, it can also lead to deep divisions between fundamentalist believers and more secular elements in society, as in Egypt, Turkey, and Pakistan. Islamic religious organizations perform important social functions at the local level, but centralizing government elites are suspicious of local activity that evades their control system. For this reason the Uzbek government has absorbed the *mahalla* committees into thc state apparatus. Furthermore, many Central Asians remain ignorant of the major tenets of Islam, a continuing legacy of Soviet efforts to undermine various forms of religion. Young people with only a vague grasp of Islam are easily radicalized, contributing to the region's negative social capital.

The resurgence of Islam throughout Central Asia following the collapse of communism has been especially pronounced in Uzbekistan and Tajikistan, but it has affected even the more secular Kazakh and Kyrgyz societies. The search for a new identity distinct from communist atheism and Western liberalism has led Central Asians to return to their religious roots, whether real or constructed. From a secular perspective, there are disturbing trends—more women are wearing the veil, for example, and bride kidnappings are on the rise in certain parts of Central Asia. Whether Islam will remain a moderate source of national identity or polarize society between fundamentalists and secularists remains to be seen, but there is the perception that religious radicalization is a threat. With NATO and the United States scaling back their military forces in Afghanistan, many Central Asians fear their countries may come under the influence of resurgent "Wahhabi" extremists.

In Central Asia identity is also closely tied to ethnicity. All the new states contained substantial numbers of nontitular minorities at independence, and dramatic population shifts have occurred over the past two decades as minorities have emigrated, titular ethnics have immigrated, and millions of migrant workers have sought employment abroad. Minority rights have become an important issue in this context, and Marlene Laruelle gives us a better sense of the complexity of social organizing among minority groups. Even in tolerant Kazakhstan, which promotes a "civic" notion of citizenship and celebrates the multiethnic character of the country, national social activism must be confined to the nonpolitical. Minority groups are an important part of civil society, but they are monitored and directed by the state toward official goals, both domestic and international. From the perspective of the state, this controlled strategy creates positive social capital, though in Putnam's terms such organizations develop ties that bond rather than bridge.

Civil society organizations can help keep government accountable to citizens, a key component of both democracy and effective governance. Central Asian officials generally maintain an elitist, Soviet-style perspective that dismisses ideas of democratic accountability. Ken Charman and Rakhymzhan Assangaziyev find Kazakhstan's efforts at making civil service more responsive to the public indicative of a desire for improved governance and stability within an authoritarian framework. But since the government is reluctant fully to engage civil society organizations, which could address policy issues where the state is unwilling or incapable, the potential for better governance is not fully realized. There is still very much a top-down, paternalistic approach to society, even in the more liberal countries of Central Asia.

Kazakhstan is much better governed than the other four Central Asian countries, but state effectiveness could likely be improved with more inclusive participation of civil society in service provision. Charman and Assangaziyev point to the bureaucratic attitudes of civil servants who, in the classic style of James Scott's high-modern authoritarianism, are convinced that only they know what is best for the population.[2] Overtly political organizations are seen as more threatening by the state, which explains the assertions by many civil society organizations (CSOs) that they are not engaged in politics, only social service provision. But the Central Asian states, like their Soviet predecessor, regard most social activism as political and therefore a potential challenge to state authority.

In utilizing a comparative perspective toward one specific area of service provision—health care—Erica Johnson finds that health and social welfare NGOs in Central Asia have not developed antagonistic relations with the state, as has occurred in the Middle East and Central America. Rather, health delivery organizations are dependent on and work together with the state, reinforcing rather than challenging its legitimacy. Remarkably, support from international donors has resulted not in CSOs aligning against the state but in depoliticized health care service providers readily cooperating with authoritarian regimes. Under these conditions, health care NGOs are unlikely to become agents for political change.

Central Asia still suffers—probably more than any other former Soviet states—from the old Soviet mentality of people relying on the state to do things for them and the state grudgingly allowing, at best, "nonpolitical" participation through controlled or highly regulated groups that concentrate on the implementation side of policy. There is some gradual movement toward a stronger, more active society and some consulting with NGOs before legislation is passed (especially in Kazakhstan and Kyrgyzstan, and among younger people), but, disturbingly, the trend may be toward antistate and potentially violent participation through radical religious organizations. The strong presidential nature and centralization of these states leave few access points for civil society organizations.

Moreover, all the Central Asian regimes deliberately seek to maintain intrusive controls over NGOs. Uzbekistan and Turkmenistan are particularly active in erecting barriers to CSO formation and operation; Kazakhstan, which formerly provided a more welcoming environment for civil society, has also tightened the screws on religious and labor organizations in recent years. Terrorism, though real and increasing, provides officials with a convenient pretext for restricting NGO activity, since criticism of the government can be framed as disloyalty toward the state. Central Asian leaders appear to have learned from Russia's example, where mass protests in 2011 and 2012 against flawed elections were met with harsh repression and intimidation against activists. Kazakhstan and Tajikistan, along with Russia, both received downgrades in their Freedom House civil society measures in 2012; Turkmenistan and Uzbekistan were already at the bottom of the scale on indicators for protection of civil society.[3]

Kyrgyzstan presents cause for limited optimism. Civil society made clear progress in the wake of Kurmanbek Bakiyev's ouster, as Charles Buxton demonstrates, though civic activity remains heavily dependent on external support, while poverty and corruption constrain social organizing. Freedom House's 2013 report noted that among Central Asian states only Kyrgyzstan, with a civil society rating of 4.75, did not actively limit independent political, social, or religious activity. Buxton discerns some hopeful signs in terms of the response of NGOs and the new government following the violent events of June 2010. However, the media are divided along ethnic lines, and the judicial system appears to be politicized in favor of ethnic Kyrgyz. The potential for civil society to engage in bridging and thus heal the scars of ethnic violence is not apparent.

Charles Sullivan's chapter details how the Turkmen government—one of the most repressive regimes in the world—constrains civil society. Virtually a totalitarian system, Turkmenistan is isolated by design and has very little contact with democratizing forces from the Western world. Sullivan stresses elements of continuity between the Niyazov and Berdymuhammedov regimes—expectations of a reform process following Niyazov's death in 2006 have not been realized. Turkmenistan, like Kazakhstan, is a hydrocarbon-rich rentier state, and like other major oil and gas exporters experiences high levels of corruption, authoritarian governance, and weak civil societies.[4] In Turkmenistan, a large state economic sector and a weak private economy work against civil society formation, as in Uzbekistan. While Sullivan emphasizes the need for external pressure on Ashgabat to permit civil society activity, the regime has effectively shielded Turkmen society from most foreign influences, making such a strategy problematic.

Central Asians generally prefer a strong state, not a weak one on the Western liberal model. Weak states are associated with Tajikistan's civil war or Kyrgyzstan's chaos and are not appealing to the populations. Many people—especially the older generation—tend to accept state paternalism and therefore are unlikely to engage in active, self-motivated behavior, which is at the root of successful civil society. This may change as a new generation replaces those who came of age during Soviet times, but the process will be gradual.

Civil society in authoritarian states does exist, but its key features differ markedly from civil society in liberal states. First, to be successful civil society needs to avoid confrontation with authorities (this is not a recommendation, but merely an observation). Dedicated civil society activists can find niches in "nonpolitical" service provision, such as environmental, health, women's, and children's issues, but if civil society goals or methods conflict with official preferences they may be repressed. All civil societies employ a mix of cooperation and contestation in relations with the state; the balance in Central Asia's authoritarian context is clearly oriented toward cooperation.

Second, human rights issues, ethnic questions, and religious activities are especially problematic since it is very difficult to depoliticize these issues. Unsanctioned protest movements are especially threatening to these regimes, whose leaders see in the color revolutions and Arab Spring uprisings challenges to their grip on power.

Religious activism is particularly sensitive in Central Asia, where authoritarian leaders fear its potential to mobilize opposition. Islamic traditions, norms, and networks are reemerging, and they are finding eager adherents among disaffected youth. Since much of this activity has been driven underground by repressive state policies, it is unclear whether resurgent Islam constitutes a force for positive or negative social capital. However, social activism in Central Asia appears to have more in common with religious-influenced movements in the Middle East than with the secular oppositions of the color revolutions.

The Central Asian states are small, landlocked, and surrounded by larger powers determined to exploit their natural wealth or to shape the Eurasian security environment to their own advantage. Democratic influences from the United States or the European Union are countered by the authoritarian practices of Russia and China, and the entire region is susceptible to destabilizing influences from nonstate actors in the form of terrorists, religious extremists, drug dealers, and refugees. Yet the Central Asian states have become adept at playing the larger powers off against each other, maximizing their ability to maneuver. Regimes may vocalize support for civil society in order to maintain links to the Western world, as Ruslan Kazkenov and Charles Ziegler find in the case of Kazakhstan. Kyrgyzstan and Tajikistan have also played this game. The "multivectored" foreign policies pursued to a certain extent by all these regimes (with the exception of isolationist Turkmenistan) confer greater leverage against their powerful neighbors and maximize their sovereignty.

International efforts at building civil society do provide valuable assistance to fledgling NGOs in Central Asia, as Charles Buxton has found during years of work on the ground in Kyrgyzstan. Though constrained by limited resources, civil society organizations played a vital role in restoring stability in the wake of Kyrgyzstan's ethnic violence. But the tenuous success of civil society assistance depends on a volatile combination of domestic politics and broader geopolitical change, as Graeme Herd and Maxim Ryabkov argue in their contribution. As the U.S. and NATO regional footprint fades after 2014, international support for democratic forces and civil society may diminish.

Central Asia appears poised for change. The leaders of two key states—Uzbekistan and Kazakhstan—are aging, and the absence of viable institutional arrangements or designated successors suggests their transitions will be difficult. Tajikistan and Turkmenistan likewise have no provision for orderly political succession. Kyrgyzstan may be doing marginally better politically, but deep social divisions and ethnic tensions compound the country's problems. All Central Asia's states are corrupt, all but one are poor, and most are poorly governed.

With the dramatic transformation of the Middle East and North Africa, Central Asia has emerged as one of the more uniformly repressive regions of the world. Can civil society become a force for political change in Central Asia as it has in northern Africa? Parallels do exist, but the evidence suggests that progress toward greater democratic participation and civil activism in the region is not likely in the near future. One consistent theme stressed by all the contributors to this volume is the complexity and diversity of the five Central Asian states in terms of their civil societies, economies, and polities. While not denying the possibility of democratic diffusion, we should in the short term expect highly individual variations on an authoritarian pattern rather than broad regional trends toward democratic development.

Notes

1. Stefanie Bailer, Thilo Bodenstein, and V. Finn Heinrich, "Explaining the Strength of Civil Society: Evidence from Cross-Sectional Data," *International Political Science Review* 34, no. 3 (2012): 289–309.

2. James C. Scott, *Seeing Like a State: How Certain Schemes to Improve the Human Condition Have Failed* (New Haven, CT: Yale University Press, 1998).

3. Freedom House, *Nations in Transit 2013,* http://www.freedomhouse.org/sites/default/files/NIT%202013%20Booklet%20-%20Report%20Findings.pdf.

4. One of the best of the many recent works on rentier states is Michael L. Ross, *The Oil Curse: How Petroleum Wealth Shapes the Development of Nations* (Princeton, NJ: Princeton University Press, 2012).

Acknowledgments

The generous support of the U.S. Department of State and the Center for Asian Democracy at the University of Louisville is gratefully acknowledged, as is the assistance of Adam Meier, the State Department's acting division chief of the Office of Citizen Exchanges. The concept for this volume originated in a project on civil society in Kazakhstan, funded by the State Department and carried out under the auspices of the Center for Asian Democracy at the University of Louisville. The project was directed by Charles Ziegler, Ruslan Kazkenov, and Kazbek Kazkenov from 2006 to 2008. Two workshops on civil society were held in the capital Astana in 2007 and 2008, and seven regional workshops were conducted in Karaganda, Atyrau, Ust-Kamenogorsk, Shymkent, Ural'sk, and Aktau.

I am also extremely grateful to Dr. Blair Ruble, former director of the Kennan Institute at the Wilson Center; the Kennan Institute's Joe Dresen; and Bill Pomeranz. In addition to the contributors to this volume, I thank Bruce Parrott, Eric McGlinchey, Vadim Ni, and Regine Spector for valuable contributions. Jason Abbott, director of the Center for Asian Democracy at the University of Louisville, kindly provided funding to complete the manuscript. In addition, Stephen Wrinn's editorial support and encouragement have been invaluable throughout the review and publication process.

Finally, this book is dedicated to Janna and Alan.

Contributors

Dilshod Achilov is assistant professor of political science at East Tennessee State University.

Rakhymzhan Assangaziyev is director, Kazakhstan Program, World Bank, Astana, Kazakhstan.

Charles Buxton is program manager in Central Asia for INTRAC, based in Bishkek, Kyrgyzstan.

Ken Charman is professor of economics and management at Kazakh-British Technical University in Almaty and visiting fellow, Royal Institution of Great Britain.

Sabine Freizer is senior fellow with the Atlantic Council and former director of the Europe Program for the International Crisis Group.

Reuel R. Hanks is professor of geography at Oklahoma State University and editor of the *Journal of Central Asian Studies.*

Graeme P. Herd is professor, associate dean, and director, School of Government, Plymouth University, United Kingdom.

Erica Johnson is lecturer and director of masters studies in the Global Studies Department, University of North Carolina at Chapel Hill.

Andrey A. Kazantsev is director of the Analytical Center, Moscow State Institute of International Relations, and scientific advisor to the Russian Council on Foreign Relations.

Ruslan Kazkenov is director of the Kazakhstan NGO Civil Peace and head of the UN HCR Office, Astana, Kazakhstan.

Marlene Laruelle is senior research fellow with the Central Asia and Caucasus Institute and Silk Road Studies Program, Johns Hopkins University.

Maxim Ryabkov is an international development consultant based in Köln, Germany.

Charles J. Sullivan is assistant professor of political science and international relations, Nazarbayev University, Astana, Kazakhstan.

Charles E. Ziegler is professor of political science and Distinguished University Scholar, University of Louisville.

Index

Page numbers that appear in *italics* refer to tables.

Asia in the New Millennium

Series Editor: Shiping Hua, University of Louisville

Asia in the New Millennium is a series of books offering new interpretations of an important geopolitical region. The series examines the challenges and opportunities of Asia from the perspectives of politics, economics, and cultural-historical traditions, highlighting the impact of Asian developments on the world. Of particular interest are books on the history and prospect of the democratization process in Asia. The series also includes policy-oriented works that can be used as teaching materials at the undergraduate and graduate levels. Innovative manuscript proposals at any stage are welcome.

Advisory Board

Books in the Series

The Future of China-Russia Relations
Edited by James Bellacqua

Contemporary Chinese Political Thought: Debates and Perspectives
Edited by Fred Dallmayr and Zhao Tingyang

The Mind of Empire: China's History and Modern Foreign Relations
Christopher A. Ford

State Violence in East Asia
Edited by N. Ganesan and Sung Chull Kim

Challenges to Chinese Foreign Policy: Diplomacy, Globalization, and the Next World Power
Edited by Yufan Hao, C. X. George Wei, and Lowell Dittmer

Korean Democracy in Transition: A Rational Blueprint for Developing Societies
HeeMin Kim

Modern Chinese Legal Reform: New Perspectives
Edited by Xiaobing Li and Qiang Fang

Growing Democracy in Japan: The Parliamentary Cabinet System since 1868
Brian Woodall

Inside China's Grand Strategy: The Perspective from the People's Republic
Ye Zicheng, Edited and Translated by Steven I. Levine and Guoli Liu

Civil Society and Politics in Central Asia
Edited by Charles E. Ziegler

www.ingramcontent.com/pod-product-compliance
Lightning Source LLC
LaVergne TN
LVHW050147080826
844660LV00002B/104